The Ambivalence of Scarcity and Other Essays

Studies in Violence, Mimesis, and Culture

SERIES EDITOR

William A. Johnsen

The Studies in Violence, Mimesis, and Culture Series examines issues related to the nexus of violence and religion in the genesis and maintenance of culture. It furthers the agenda of the Colloquium on Violence and Religion, an international association that draws inspiration from René Girard's mimetic hypothesis on the relationship between violence and religion, elaborated in a stunning series of books he has written over the last forty years. Readers interested in this area of research can also look to the association's journal, *Contagion: Journal of Violence, Mimesis, and Culture.*

The Ambivalence of Scarcity and Other Essays

Paul Dumouchel

Michigan State University Press · *East Lansing*

♾ The paper used in this publication meets the minimum requirements of ANSI/NISO
Z39.48-1992 (R 1997) (Permanence of Paper).

 Michigan State University Press
East Lansing, Michigan 48823-5245

Printed and bound in the United States of America.

20 19 18 17 16 15 14   1 2 3 4 5 6 7 8 9 10

LIBRARY OF CONGRESS CONTROL NUMBER: 2013957626
ISBN: 978-1-61186-132-7 (pbk.)
ISBN: 978-1-60917-417-0 (ebook: PDF)
ISBN: 978-1-62895-000-7 (ebook: ePub)
ISBN: 978-1-62896-000-6 (ebook: Mobi/prc)

Book design and composition by Charlie Sharp, Sharp Des!gns, Lansing, Michigan
Cover design by David Drummond, Salamander Design, www.salamanderhill.com
Cover painting is a detail from *Les huîtres* by Jean-Marie Pirot Arcabas © 2013 Artists
Rights Society (ARS), New York / ADAGP, Paris, and is used with permission.

**g green
press
INITIATIVE** Michigan State University Press is a member of the Green Press Initiative
and is committed to developing and encouraging ecologically responsible
publishing practices. For more information about the Green Press Initiative and the use of
recycled paper in book publishing, please visit *www.greenpressinitiative.org*.

Visit Michigan State University Press at *www.msupress.org*

Contents

Acknowledgments

"The Ambivalence of Scarcity" originally published as "L'ambivalence de la rareté" in *L'Enfer des choses* (Paris: Seuil, 1979); "Indifference and Envy: The Anthropological Analysis of Modern Economy" originally published in *Contagion* 10 (2013):149–160; "A Mimetic Reading of Helmut Schoeck's Theory of Envy" originally published in *Passions in Economy, Politics and the Media,* ed. W. Palaver and P. Steinmair-Pösel (Wien: Lit Verlag, 2005), 103–122.

"Mimetism and Autonomy" originally published as "Mimétisme et autonomie" in *L'auto-organisation de la physique au politique*, ed. P. Dumouchel and J.-P. Dupuy (Paris: Seuil, 1983), 353–364. "Violence and Nonviolence" originally published as "Violence et Non-Violence" in *Esprit* 60 (1981): 153–165. "Differences and Paradoxes: Reflections on Love and Violence in Girard's Work" originally published as "Différences et paradoxes: réflexions sur l'amour et la violence dans l'œuvre de Girard" in *René Girard et le problème du mal*, ed. M. Deguy and J.-P. Dupuy (Paris: Grasset, 1982), 215–223. "Mimetic Theory: Concepts and Models" originally published as "La teoria mimetica: concetti e modelli" in *Studi Perugini* 10 (2000): 71–88. "De la *méconnaissance*" originally published in *Lebenswelt aesthetics and*

philosophy of experience 1 (2011): 97–111, http://riviste.unimi.it/index.php/
Lebenswelt/issue/view/214/showToc.

"Hobbes: The Sovereignty Race" originally published as "Hobbes: La
course à la Souveraineté" in *Stanford French Review* 10 (1986): 153–176.
"Ijime" originally published in *Contagion* 6 (1999): 77–84. "From Scapegoat to God" originally published as "De chivo expiatorio a Dios" in
revista Anthropos 213 (2006): 88–98. "Violence and Indifference" originally
published as "Violence et indifference" in *Comprendre pour agir: violences,
victimes et vengeances*, ed. P. Dumouchel (Québec: Presses de l'Université
Laval, 2000), 207–225. "Mimetism and Genocides" originally published as
"Mimétisme et génocides" in *Cahier de L'Herne René Girard* (Paris: L'Herne,
2008), 247–254. "Inside Out: Political Violence in the Age of Globalization"
originally published in *Contagion* 15/16 (2009): 173–184, 271–281.

Introduction

The first essay, which gives this collection its title, is the English translation of my contribution to *L'enfer des choses: René Girard et la logique de l'économie*, which Jean-Pierre Dupuy and I published in 1979. "The Ambivalence of Scarcity" is an attempt to apply mimetic theory to modern economics and to economic phenomena, but also to explain why economic issues and economics as a discipline occupy such an important place in the modern world. The "ambivalence" in the title refers to the fact that in many social and economic discourses, both political and academic, scarcity plays, or can play, a double role. First, scarcity, in the form of want and deprivation, is viewed as a cause of violence and conflicts and as a problem to be solved. We spontaneously tend to see poor neighborhoods as dangerous neighborhoods and assume that high levels of poverty and unemployment lead to social unrest. However, want, lack, and needs are also considered as central, indispensable economic incentives that should be harnessed judiciously for economic growth. This constitutes the second opposite value of the ambivalence. Scarcity is viewed then both as a threat, as a danger to social order, and as one of its foundations, perhaps as its most important and solid basis, for it is scarcity, understood as an "incentive," that underpins economic growth, and economic growth is seen as our best defense against social unrest and disorder.

Furthermore, this ambivalence is not only explanatory, in the sense that we simply use scarcity to explain different and opposite social phenomena: economic growth, on the one hand, violence and social conflict, on the other. It is also has a moral dimension. We judge in a different way, more leniently, violence that we believe was caused by dire deprivation rather than by greed or the desire to satisfy an addiction. Simultaneously, we consider that even extreme hardships, if they are imposed to encourage economic activity or to ensure financial recovery, are justified in spite of the bitter pain and distress they may bring.

This muddle in our thinking is indicative of more than a mere intellectual confusion. It suggests something true about the way scarcity functions in our societies. Economists and others have, in fact, a simple way of disentangling the two contradictory values of scarcity: they do this by appealing to the real quantity of goods and resources available. If goods are so rare that the basic needs of large portions of the population cannot be satisfied, then, they argue, unrest and disorder are likely to ensue. If, however, goods are more plentiful, though not excessively abundant, agents will be motivated to work, to invest the necessary time and effort to better their situation. It is therefore the size of the set of goods and resources available that separates the good from the bad aspect of scarcity. However, given that, whatever its size, a limited set of goods and resources that is unable to satisfy the needs of all is nothing but the definition of scarcity itself, we must conclude that it is scarcity that divides scarcity from scarcity and that disconnects its positive from its negative value. The problem with this way of thinking is not only that it is circular and imprecise (for exactly what is the level of deprivation at which wants and needs act as incentives rather than as occasions of disorder is far from clear). Indeed, since economists recognize and claim that higher levels of production bring greater needs and more diverse desires, it follows that scarcity, and therefore levels of scarcity, cannot be identified with any definite amount of goods and resources. Neither extreme nor moderate scarcity can be associated with any real quantity of goods and resources; it is not possible to disentangle the two sides of the ambivalence. In consequence of this circular relationship between levels of production and the size and extent of needs and desires, it follows that scarcity, the "fact" that goods and resources are insufficient to satisfy the needs of all, should not simply be identified with the inevitable, real limits on goods and resources. Scarcity cannot be reduced to the "parsimony of nature."

What is scarcity then, and how should we understand its role and function? Interestingly enough, it is only at a certain point in time and in one particular social and cultural area that the "fact" that goods and resources are insufficient to satisfy the needs of every member of the community came to be seen as the fundamental issue around which the entire social organization was progressively made to revolve. Furthermore, this society later, paradoxically, reached general levels of abundance never before seen in the world. My claim is that this "fact"—namely, that goods and resources are insufficient to satisfy the needs of everyone, independent of whatever quantity of goods and resources are actually available—is *socially instituted* rather than "discovered," for this "fact" is a question of distribution, access, and responsibility, all of which are important issues in economics, but none of which is naturally given.

The central thesis of this essay, which makes it essentially Girardian, is that the means through which scarcity is instituted also protect us against our own violence. Scarcity is thus a means of protection against violence, and, like the sacred, it is a violent means of protection against violence. Scarcity came about through a transformation of the moral ecology of human relations. More precisely, scarcity was socially instituted by the progressive abandoning of traditional obligations of solidarity, obligations that constrained agents to shoulder duties to help and support specific individuals among those in need. As many anthropologists have noted, in principle, as long as such obligations are binding, no member of the group is in danger of dying of hunger unless all are. Of course, there must be many situations in which this ideal of solidarity has not actually been achieved. However, in such cases scarcity has not been the problem, but the failure of various individuals to fulfill their obligations. It is only when many individuals start to distance themselves from their reciprocal obligations of solidarity in general, when they become sufficiently detached from the duties those obligations entail, that scarcity, want, lack of resources can come to be seen as the problem. The more these obligations are abandoned, the more scarcity is viewed as the "real" cause of the difficulties so many agents face.

These duties to help are, however, also obligations of violence. They force agents to take part in the conflicts of others, of their brothers, sisters, uncles, aunts, cousins, lords, and vassals, conflicts that originally did not necessarily concern them in any way whatsoever. These obligations, which in normal times protect agents from violence, in times of crisis can easily fuel the conflagration. Because they burden individuals and groups with responsibilities to help and take revenge, they tend to spread violence and extend conflicts. Abandoning these obligations can prevent conflicts from extending to others. The strategy of protection against violence involved here is the inverse of what is at work in the sacred. The sacred is organized around rituals that seek to restore the troubled social order, prohibitions that forbid actions leading to conflicts and violence, and obligations that tie agents and groups to one another for their own protection while simultaneously providing an outlet of permissible violence that they can exert outside of the group.

Scarcity, on the contrary, has neither rituals nor obligations; each individual is simply sent back to his or her own "initiatives" and interests. It does not seek to protect agents from violence or hardship by making them reciprocally responsible, but to prevent the spread of violence by removing each person's incentive to participate in the conflicts of others. Instead of protecting agents from violence and prohibiting violence among them, scarcity, the abandoning of obligations of solidarity, reduces the contagious dimension of violence, which in traditional societies is reinforced by the obligations that draw agents into conflicts even when they were neither present at the triggering events nor concerned by them.

Scarcity is nonetheless like the sacred in that it protects us against our own violence violently, though that violence takes a different form. It is indirect rather than direct, and tends to be impersonal. Abandoning reciprocal obligations of solidarity is equivalent to abandoning others to whom we were previously attached by these obligations, allowing the evil, whatever it is, to befall them. Consequently, if one fails or loses in a conflict or is in need for whatever reason, one is unlikely to be helped by anyone because if those who have obligations fail to fulfill them, it is hardly to be expected that others who do not have any specific obligations will step forward, especially given that they are reticent to fulfill their own obligations of solidarity. Once abandoned by their group of solidarity, individuals simply fall through the net of reciprocal duties and obligations. They are left to fend for themselves alone. It follows that the victims of scarcity are in many cases not the victims of anyone in particular; often no one has threatened or attacked them. They are just in need, but no one will help them; mainly, they are the victims of everyone's indifference. Sometimes other agents may think that what happens to them is unfortunate, but each also rightly believes that he or she has no particular obligations toward them, rightly at least in terms of reciprocal obligations of solidarity, which are now being abandoned. Often these victims are best seen as "collateral damage" in conflicts of which others are the principals, the rivals. The others do not feel any particular hate or animosity toward those (indirect) victims of their conflict, just indifference. Finally, because scarcity, unlike the sacred, does not have any ritualized outlet that periodically purges the community of its violence, these anonymous victims of indifference tend to become the victims of everyone. They are held to be personally responsible for the evil that befalls them and therefore undeserving of the help that in any case we do not provide them. They can and actually do serve everyone as surrogate victims of our own violence. Therefore, the same violent process that protects us against violence also allows scarcity to appear, and thus produces its victims.

This transformation in the moral ecology of human relations structures our societies and determines the forms that violent conflicts take among us. It is important to insist on the fact that this is a *real transformation*. This change in the moral ecology of human relations does not primarily concern the way people think about or view their obligations toward one another; it mainly concerns the obligations that there are and the way in which they exist—that is to say, which obligations people have toward one another and among one another, which obligations they are held responsible for, which are they expected to discharge, and which they are allowed to ignore. What makes scarcity arise and become real in our social life does not depend on what people think but on what they do. It is in consequence of these changes in action that goods and resources in whatever quantity become insufficient to satisfy the needs of all. This abandoning of reciprocal obligations of solidarity also creates between social agents a form of "exteriority" that protects them from their own violence, not by reducing the number of conflicts among them but by curtailing conflict's ability to propagate and invade the whole community.

Because the changes in question are real, the economic discourse on want and scarcity is founded and justified to the extent that it corresponds to a real situation, even if it fails to describe it adequately. The problems it raises are real and need to be addressed. The same applies to the moral issue of social justice. In a world where scarcity constitutes the basic arrangement, such a question cannot be avoided. It is thus both scarcity and the knowledge that bears on it that are socially instituted by the abandoning of reciprocal obligations of solidarity; both the reality of want and the economic, social, political, and moral discourses that try to deal with the challenges it raises are "made real," instituted, by this transformation in the moral ecology of human relations. Note, however, that it is not these discourses that "construct" the social reality of scarcity. Scarcity is instituted. It is not "socially constructed," at least not in the sense that peoples' beliefs concerning the "parsimony of nature" or the importance of economic activity "create" scarcity. What comes first here is action, not discourse or beliefs: innumerable acts of fulfilling or abandoning one's obligations. These actions do not mainly or essentially concern the "economic domain." They relate to the total range of human behavior. The subsequent arrival of scarcity on the social scene is in every sense an unintended, unforeseen consequence: the result of human actions, but not of human design. Scarcity does not come from people having certain beliefs concerning wealth and poverty; on the contrary, it is because scarcity has been instituted by the transformation of the moral ecology of human relations that people come to have the particular beliefs that they have about wealth and poverty.

This is why the economic and political discourses about scarcity are not simply "false." As long as scarcity continues to structure our social life not only are the problems with which they grapple real, but the solutions they offer can be efficient. These discourses are not false, but they are nonetheless incomplete. They fail to perceive their own social and moral relativity as well as the conditions that determine their possible veracity. They do not see that "economic rationality" is a particular case of mimetic behavior and that mimetic theory can specify the conditions under which agents will generally behave *as if* they were maximizing a utility function.

◆   ◆   ◆

Scarcity characterizes human relationships in the modern world. We live in a society where reciprocal obligations that attach specific persons to one another have all but disappeared, and, in the rare cases where they still exist, they have lost their compulsory dimension. Enforcement agencies, that is, the state, hold us to our universal obligations—for example, to refrain from trespassing on the property of others and from engaging in certain forms of discrimination—but obligations among individual agents, unless they are formally legalized in the form of a contract recognized by law, fall outside their jurisdiction. More important, such obligations, even within the context of the family, have lost the ability to police themselves. Coercing agents into discharging them now constitutes illegitimate violence. Physically punishing your children or sequestering your daughter to prevent her from marrying a member of an enemy clan or a different religion is a crime today. Not so long ago (and in some places and among certain communities this is still the case) such practices were considered normal forms of behavior corresponding to what a responsible parent should do.

Written over the last thirty-five years, the essays contained in this book explore various aspects of this transformation of the moral ecology of human relations understood as a dynamic mimetic process. Scarcity was not given once and for all, but was slowly established as traditional obligations of solidarity progressively lost their binding force. The process still continues today and is bringing about important transformations in the central institutions that scarcity made possible: the market and the modern state. The chapters have been grouped into three different parts: "On Economy and Economics," "On Mimetic Theory," and "On Violence and Politics in Modern Societies." This division, though not arbitrary, is somewhat misleading since most of the essays in each part also deal with the topics of one or both of the other parts.

All chapters in "On Economy and Economics" pursue a mimetic analysis of different aspects of modern economics and economic phenomena. "Indifference and Envy: Girard and the Anthropological Analysis of Modern Economy" revisits the substantivist-formalist debate in economic anthropology in light of the mimetic reading of modern economies. The next chapter, a criticism of Helmut Schoek's *Envy: A Theory of Social Behaviour*, also briefly addresses the question of social justice in a world where scarcity constitutes a means of protection against violence. This is a question to which I return in the conclusion. "*Homo mimeticus* as an Economic Agent," which ends this first part of the book, constitutes a quick foray into the issue of what mimetic theory could bring to economics.

Part 2, "On Mimetic Theory," focuses on two important issues: first, the historical morphogenetic dimension of mimetic theory and, second, the role

and place of *méconnaissance*, "misrecognition," in mimetic theory. Mimetic
theory is a morphogenetic theory: it explains the emergence of new social
and institutional forms that were not originally contained in the founding
mechanism. These unpredictable social arrangements arise as a result of the
encounter between the blind mechanism that puts an end to the collective
violence of the crisis and random events, random in the sense that they are
external to the mechanism itself. They range from ecological accidents to any
kind of local particularity. Scarcity is one example of a new social arrangement that proceeds from the founding mechanism, but so are sacred kingships and the domestication of animals. "Mimetism and Autonomy" deals
with this issue; it tries to show how the sacred understood as a closed social
system nonetheless leads to cultural and technological innovations. "Violence and Nonviolence," the next chapter, explores the relationship between
Girard's analysis of violence and nonviolent militancy, while "Differences
and Paradoxes: Reflections on Love and Violence in Girard's Work" provides a detailed analysis of the different meanings of the term "differences" in
Girard's work. Actually, both chapters also deal with the issue of misrecognition, though indirectly. "Violence and Nonviolence" criticizes the reading
of Girard's work that sees it as a foundation for nonviolent political activism. The criticism shows that this is based on a misunderstanding, and it
raises for the first time an issue that will become central in part 3: the place
of political action in mimetic theory. "Creation and Conversion in Girard"
also deals with the issue of cultural novelty, but this time in the context of
literary creation. It inevitably raises the question of *méconnaissance* and of
its "revelation," both of which, according to Girard, play fundamental roles
in the production of major literary works. "Mimetic Theory: Concepts and
Models" is about precisely what its title says: the fundamental concepts and
models of mimetic theory. My main argument is that the contribution of
mimetic theory should not be reduced to the substantial theses it puts forward and that the conceptual innovations it introduces are at least as important as its theses. The last chapter in this part, "'De la *méconnaissance*,'" is
about misrecognition and how we should understand the effect of Christian
Revelation. Girard argues, as we know, that Christian Revelation puts an end
to the misrecognition that is at the heart of the scapegoat mechanism and
in consequence renders it both inefficient as a means of protection against
violence and culturally barren. I submit that this claim should be understood

in the sense that Christian Revelation does not so much do away with misrecognition as displaces it. Sacrificial violence, violence against surrogate victims, does not disappear, but, as Girard argues, its ability to protect us against our own violence is transformed, in many ways reduced, and this transformation leads to the appearance of a culture that, paradoxically, functions fundamentally as a critique of culture.

Part 3, "On Violence and Politics in Modern Societies," is the most varied. The essays it assembles range from a mimetic reading of Hobbes's political philosophy to suicide attacks to an analysis of violence in Japanese high schools. This diversity reflects my own slow evolution in coming to terms with the issue of political violence. The first chapter, "The Ambivalence of Scarcity," focused on the transformation of the moral ecology of human relations that institutes scarcity as a means of protection against violence. It suggested that economics rather than politics plays the fundamental role in the management of violence in modern societies. Yet the significance of political violence in recent history and its sudden return to the stage of world politics after the end of the Cold War cried out for an explanation in terms of mimetic theory. Nonetheless, it was not clear how political violence in the modern world was related to the model put forward in "The Ambivalence of Scarcity." It is only in my *Le sacrifice inutile: Essai sur la violence politique* (2011) that things finally fell into place and the relationship between scarcity and the rise of the modern state as the holder of the monopoly of legitimate violence and simultaneously as the main perpetrator of political violence became clear to me.

The first essay in this part, "Hobbes: The Sovereignty Race," proposes a Girardian reading of Hobbes's theory of the social contract. It asks a question that Hobbes avoids and yet which should be central to his project: who should be the sovereign? The answer is that, given the premises of the contract, the only Sovereign rationally acceptable to all the participants in the Hobbesian social contract is the "enemy of all," suggesting that Hobbes's sovereign occupies the place of the scapegoat in Girard's theory. The next chapter analyses a phenomenon of bullying in Japanese high schools that is known by the name of *ijime*. I argue that *ijime*, which generally ends with the suicide of the bullied child, is akin to the scapegoat mechanism. Yet it neither proceeds from a real crisis that threatens the whole community with violence, nor is it an explicit ritual, like a sacrifice. It is similar to a ritual in that it manifests a form of regularity and is recurrent, but it is not explicitly codified or reserved for socially identifiable specialists. Like the scapegoat mechanism, it consists in a spontaneous act of mimetically unanimous violence against a unique victim, who, however, is not made sacred after his or her death. *Ijime* is a strange phenomenon that is, so to speak, halfway between a spontaneous mechanism and a codified ritual. "From Scapegoat to God" compares *ijime* with another similarly hybrid social phenomena: the collective assassination of rainmaking kings in the Sudan, which was beautifully analyzed by Simon Simonse in *Kings of Disaster*.[1] Like the victims of *ijime*, the collectively murdered kings are never made sacred after their death. While bullying in Japanese high schools is a social phenomenon, the collective murder of a rainmaking king is a political phenomenon, the final point of a conflict between different factions within the community. This chapter asks why these victims of collective violence are not made sacred.

Finally, the last four chapters of the book directly address the question of modern political violence which, like the hybrid phenomena described in the two previous chapters, fails to make its victims sacred and bring about lasting peace. "Violence and Indifference" is about how indifference both protects us against violence and engenders violence; it is about how indifference, understood not as a psychological disposition but as a social phenomenon, constitutes a central cultural and political expression of the transformation in the moral ecology of human relations that is responsible for the rise of scarcity. "Mimetism and Genocides" provides a mimetic and sacrificial analysis of genocides. "Suicide Attacks: Military and Social Aspects" provides a sacrificial reading of suicide attacks based on an analysis of the position of female suicide bombers within their community of origin and the reaction to their death. Finally, "Inside Out: Political Violence in the Age of Globalization" deals with the transformation of the anthropological space of hostility, its simplification, and the confusion that results concerning the distinction between legitimate and illegitimate violence, which today is the prerogative of the modern state rather than the sacred.

In the conclusion, "Ethics, Economics, and the State," I address the issue of social justice in a world where scarcity plays a fundamental role in protecting us against violence. I also try to analyze the deep relationship that exists between ethics, viewed as a particular way of understanding and practicing morality, and economics, the social institution of scarcity.

◆   ◆   ◆

Girard's approach disrupts the way we usually partition the world. This is not only because mimetic theory establishes continuities and relationships among domains that are not usually seen as related, like religion and literary criticism, or ballet and ritual sacrifice; it is also because Girard's view brings together distant domains as explanatory, rather than as a thesis that needs to be defended. That is to say, instead of simply claiming, for example, that there is a relationship between ritual sacrifice and Greek tragedy, Girard directly proceeds to illuminate the origin of sacrifice through readings of Greek tragedies. This difference of outlook is fundamental and has played a major role in the difficult reception of Girard's work within academia. Even if part of his work could easily fit under ordinary headings—for example, "Psychoanalysis and Ritual" or "Christianity and the Modern World"—Girard has never written articles with such trite titles.

One of the main reasons why is that Girard is not interested in theses concerning the relations among different disciplines, but in objects and in texts. It is in the process of interpreting texts, like the book of Job, or of discovering the various guises under which the same object, for example, sacrifice, or a theme, such as doubles, presents itself, that Girard takes advantage of what at first sight appear like distant correlations. He does not so much try to justify the resemblances that he highlights, but immediately takes them as significant and enlightening in relation to the object under scrutiny. Girard de facto challenges the separation among disciplines and existing domains of research. He does not simply propose that borders among domains of inquiry be relaxed; he transgresses them. Because of this he has often been accused of lacking rigor and overlooking important distinctions and differences among the objects that he brings together in his explanations.

The fact is that Girard has always been more attentive to similarities than to differences, or perhaps, to be more exact, that he thinks that similarities and differences are often two aspects of a single process. For example, in a conflict between individuals or groups, parties often insist all the more on the differences that separate them as the conflict itself renders them more and more alike. In this case, similarities accrue as a result of the adversaries' efforts to differentiate themselves from each other. The differences between them therefore cannot be taken at face value, independently of their conflictual relation and of its homogenizing consequence. A related phenomenon can be found in academic domains where always finer distinctions are made between related objects of inquiry so as to hide the similarities between them, making us unable to discover the process that is generating both differences and similarities. It is therefore not quite accurate to claim, as I did above, that Girard does not try to justify the resemblances he discovers between distant objects because, within the context of mimetic theory, they are justified. The difficulty is that the surprising assemblages that mimetic theory justifies are used in turn to justify mimetic theory.

This circularity is however an inescapable and normal aspect of the scientific enterprise. As both Norwood Hanson[2] and Thomas Kuhn[3] argued quite a while ago, and as many philosophers of science from Popper to Quine, from Putnam to Hacking, have repeated since, scientific theories inform the manner in which we observe the world; theoretical presuppositions carve up the objects we seek to explain. Objects of inquiry are not simply offered to a neutral gaze in their unbiased integrity; different outlooks lead to different partitions of the world that stage different objects to be explained.

It does not follow that these objects are mere illusions or that they do not exist. There are, of course theoretical artifacts. Just as a scientific instrument—for example, a microscope—can present us with false evidence appearing real, theories sometimes populate the world with nonexisting entities, like ether and phlogiston. However, what is involved here is different: all scientific objects are necessarily constructed out of theoretical presuppositions rather than simply found, like pebbles on a beach. They exist, are real, nonillusory to the extent that they pick out stable regularities and patterns that can enter into causal explanatory processes.

Some difficulties nonetheless do follow from this circularity, primarily because it usually remains unnoticed. All researchers are raised and educated within a particular scientific tradition whose partitioning of the world seems natural to them; other ways of dividing it appear artificial and unjustified. It is only when serious difficulties arise within the received view and in the presence of a plausible alternative explanation that some researchers, but not all, will begin to question the value of their inheritance. The difficulty in doing this is further compounded because, in this case, there seems to be no common ground to which the disputants, both the tenants of the old order and the advocates of the new paradigm, may appeal to decide the debate. For example, what sacrifice is in Girard's theory is quite different from what it is for many anthropologists. In consequence, not all the same objects will count as instances of sacrifice for both, or as institutions and practices that resemble or are "like" sacrifice. Nonetheless, there is enough overlap for the debate to take place and for all to feel that they are in some sense "talking about the same thing." How, then, are we to decide between them?

There are some generally received criteria, and Girard usually insists on two of them: explanatory power and simplicity. One approach should be preferred to another to the extent that it can account for a wider range of phenomena and that it is simpler. The problem is that simplicity is not really a "simple" criterion. It is neither easy nor simple to determine which of two theories is the simplest. And explanatory power is also hard to measure because people disagree about what they want from an explanation.

Yet it is possible to argue for the simplicity and explanatory power of an approach, not by trying to measure it from the outside, as we do when we compare it with a different theory, but by demonstrating it at work so to speak—that is to say, by making visible the explanatory power and simplicity of the theory by applying it to phenomena that are different from the ones that it was originally designed to explain. By doing this we confirm in action the theory's ability to account for a growing range of phenomena. This is what the essays collected in this volume try to do: to show the reach and unity (simplicity) of mimetic theory by putting it to work on philosophical texts, economics, and economic phenomena, as well as violence in modern societies, terrorism, and genocides. All these topics are closely related to one of the theory's central objectives—that is, explaining violence and its relation to cultural phenomena—but they are external to the original domain where it was applied by Girard—that is, ancient and traditional societies and, with respect to the modern world, literary creations rather than social phenomena, at least until his last book, *Battling to the End*.

This endeavor falls under the category of what Kuhn calls "normal science": efforts to extend and clarify a paradigm by addressing with it problems that are at first sight foreign to its domain—for example, bullying in Japanese high schools—and by inquiring into its conceptual structure. Though the different chapters of this book focus on these two aspects of normal science to different extents, they cannot be entirely separated. Conceptual analysis can hardly be carried out without reference to empirical issues, and empirical inquiries generally imply theoretical clarifications.

Many friends of mimetic theory often lament its limited reception within academia. This state of affairs is certainly not something we should rejoice in, nor is it, however, something that should surprise us excessively. The theory's slow and difficult reception within established disciplines bears witness to the significance of the change of outlook it implies. Remedying this state of affairs does not require us to make the theory more acceptable, or more in conformity with the canon of received scientific enquiry, but to use it to explain different objects and phenomena, for it will only impose itself by proving its usefulness to our understanding of the world, rather than its compliance with today's research expectations.

PART 1

On Economy
and Economics

The Ambivalence of Scarcity

Scarcity and Violence

Economists and thinkers in the liberal tradition, such as Hume, Locke, and Malthus, generally explain violence, vice, and misery by a single cause: scarcity. This idea is very frequent in modern economic and social thought. It can also be found in Marx; the way it is expressed is different, but the idea is the same. In *The German Ideology*, Marx and Engels say that the development of productive forces is a condition sine qua non for the end of the class struggle and advent of worldwide communism, for "without it *want* is merely made general, and with *destitution* the struggle for necessities and all the old filthy business would necessarily be reproduced."[1] Other more recent authors have formulated it in new ways. Advocates of the global village and postindustrial society, such as Marshall McLuhan, express the harmful influence of scarcity in more or less this way: we will never really be able to really communicate with one another until material objects have lost their hold over us.

No matter how it is formulated, it is easy to recognize the unity and simplicity of the underlying idea. Necessity suspends morals. People do not choose evil over good; they do not choose. Want holds us in its snare. Nature's parsimony condemns us to war. Scarcity forces people's desires to converge on the same objects and sets us against one another in necessary rivalry.

It is well known that all enlightened minds who have had faith in humanity's progress, especially in the concurrence of material and moral progress, have based their belief on this. They have believed in it so strongly that today there is no need to be enlightened to consider that the state of things, not people, is most to blame for violence and today's woes.

This idea was tailor-made to seduce economists. Those who had just discovered the causes of the wealth of nations and how to conquer misery could only rejoice in the inherently complementary nature of abundance and peace. This is why, since Montesquieu, they have always taught that "peace is the natural effect of trade."[2]

Yet there is another reason that has led economists and liberal thinkers to explain violence and evil in general by necessity and needs. In their theories, necessity and needs appear in the form of scarcity. The law of scarcity is the primary constraint of economic systems, the basic economic fact. Explaining violence by scarcity has quasi-mathematical obviousness, and demonstrating it is child's play.

In economic theory, scarcity is defined thus: goods and resources are available to people in limited quantities, which are insufficient to satisfy the needs and desires of all. Scarcity is thus a clear, simple and distinct idea: the quantity of goods and resources available, the limitation of resources, nature's parsimony. Linking this quantity with the dimension or scope of human needs reveals how scarcity constrains human activities. Since such needs are supposed to be very large, not to say infinite, they form an unreachable limit. Thus, the amount and the relation coincide: the quantity of goods and resources available is a direct expression of the constraint of scarcity.

It is now easy to see how scarcity can engender conflict. If goods and resources are insufficient to meet the legitimate needs of each individual, it is inevitable that violence will follow, either in the form of injustice or in the shape of open, physical violence intended to eliminate those who are in excess. Scarcity is a necessary cause of conflict. There is a veritable arithmetic of violence. Good intentions are powerless. Scarcity violates people and forces them to fight one another.

This is thus a rational explanation for violence. It avoids value judgments and has no need to postulate any form of violent instinct, which would be an obscure and uncertain crutch. Elementary deduction proves that scarcity is a cause of violence. Simultaneously, this explanation identifies economic activity as the best foundation for peace since it is a means of ensuring future abundance. Furthermore, it teaches us that economic activity, which is a "strategy for fighting against the scarcity that manifests itself through value phenomena,"[3] is also a strategy for fighting against violence.

Moreover, because economic activity attacks evil at its root, and focuses primarily on overcoming scarcity and establishing universal prosperity, it has the advantage of rationality over other means of eliminating violence. The struggle against scarcity does not employ violence against violence. It does not compromise with evil. On the contrary, it seeks to eradicate the cause. If violence has its roots in scarcity, then growth of economic activity, because it produces abundance, is the only guarantee of lasting peace, and the only way to provide a definitive solution to the problem of violence.

In his study on the genesis and triumph of economic ideology,[4] Louis Dumont very astutely points out that establishing economic activity as an independent domain of inquiry required a double emancipation, with respect to both politics and morals. However, what it seems Dumont does not see is both that these instances of emancipation are complementary and the primordial role played by the classical explanation of violence by necessity. When we translate the explanation into economists' language, it becomes: scarcity causes violence.

Dumont says that economic activity had to acquire moral worth of its own, and that the moral value in question was the public good. It is difficult to understand how this moral value could have been accepted in traditional society if it contradicted private moral values. Yet we know that this was the case. The establishment of this moral value in Mandeville's *The Fable of the Bees*,[5] which Dumont studied, amounts to nothing less than an apology for pride, envy, and desire, which are all vices strictly punished by traditional morals. It is difficult to grasp what the public good could be, or rather what moral value it could have, if its price was all those vices.

However, if we begin with politics, everything becomes clear. Dumont notes that in Marx we find politics absorbed into economic activity. This requires, as a preliminary step, the establishment of a political value specific to economic activity. Dumont does not say much about this political value. Yet it is the crux of the matter.

It suffices to remember that the fundamental point of any form of politics is domestic peace and external defense. If we also keep in mind that the domestic peace, order, and unity of a given political whole largely determine its ability to resist outside aggression, it is clear how economic activity has been able to acquire prodigious political power.

Indeed, traditional political thought has always held that order produces order and disorder engenders disorder. The political problem of order, societal cohesion, and domestic peace requires that all instances of disorder, disagreement, dissent, conflict, and rivalry be avoided, and that activities that can lead to such things be carefully regulated. In traditional terms, the essential political problem is to maintain order in every part of society so that the whole remains well-ordered, and to prevent any part of the social body from exploiting or destroying any other part. It is to ensure reciprocity of obligations.

With respect to domestic peace, the great advantage of economics over any form of political thought is its claim to be able to provide a solution without having to deal with the concrete conditions that delimit the problem. By linking disorder to scarcity, and violence to limited resources, economic thought makes economic growth, spread of trade, and entrepreneurial freedom the best foundations for peace. By making envy, desire, and pride the driving forces behind economic growth, economic activity transforms real rivalries and larval violence into means of achieving domestic peace. The causes of disorder become sources of order. If they promote growth, then we should leave free reign to pride, envy, and avarice, to the most brazen exploitation, and to oppression of the weak by the strong. Not only does the explanation of violence by scarcity break the links between private disorder and public disorder, but it transforms rivalries into means of attaining domestic peace. Dissent among individuals guarantees the harmony of the social body. Economic thought dissociates the individual consequences of actions from their social consequences, and indeed opposes them.

This dissociation also means that politicians no longer have to enforce the ancient, venerable laws, customs, and values that used to guarantee the morality of every citizen in order to ensure public order. It recognizes the social impotence of morality. Trade's efficiency in producing peace allows politics to do without morals. The political efficiency of economic activity demolishes traditional morals.

By consecrating the social impotence of traditional morals, the links between scarcity, vice, misery, and violence give economic activity its own moral value. Indeed, it is only to the extent that scarcity and limited resources were seen as the causes of the wrongs and violence that afflict humanity that wealth—in other words, the good offered by economic activity—could be construed as having moral value. Moreover, the reason there have been no obstacles to the growth of envy, desire, and avarice is because scarcity is the cause of violence, and limited resources are the origin of evil. Envy and desire become highly commendable because they are the forces driving economic activity, and economic activity will save us from poverty and conquer the scarcity and necessity that cause and create much greater evils, namely, violence and destruction, vice and misery. Economic activity becomes more moral than morals. It goes beyond old-fashioned do-good moral intentions. As Keynes pointed out in a frightening sentence: "For at least another hundred years we must pretend to ourselves and to everyone that fair is foul and foul is fair; for foul is useful and fair is not."[6]

However, economic activity may fight scarcity, but it does not eliminate it. Thus, the reason envy, desire, and avarice drive economic growth is because limited resources force everyone to serve self-interest. Trade often involves power relations simply because of scarcity, which engenders competing desires. The dubious feelings that are at the origin of economic activities do not prove that humans are evil because they are produced by the state of the world. Only economic growth can put an end to this.

In this, there is a double dialectic that closes economic activity to all objections from traditional morals and at the same time expels such morality from the category of socially effective strategies. The political role of economic activity, which is to guarantee order by eliminating the cause of violence, namely, scarcity, establishes economic activity's moral value and destroys the social effectiveness of traditional morality.

Thus, using scarcity to explain violence, vice, and misery has been indispensable for economic activity to gain its own political and moral value. Without it, the private vices of nascent individualism would have been perceived as pure causes of disorder. It is because wealth produces order that economic activity has been able to become a social ideal, absorb politics, and relegate morals to the no-man's-land of interior life. The explanation of violence by scarcity was necessary in order to understand the brutality of trade, and so as to avoid seeing economic competition as a cause of disorder.

Now, everyone knows that the division of scarce resources among rational self-interested individuals is what is supposed to establish economic activity, to establish the paradigm of *hominess oeconomici*, who make decisions according to their preferences and according to the problems of choice and decision that scarcity of resources creates in our world.[7] The liberal tradition's explanation of violence teaches us that this situation can have two outcomes. Economic order emerges out of the division of scarce resources among rational individuals interested in satisfying their needs and desires. Scarcity pushes people to work, incites them to trade. It is the original motivation for commerce, which brings peace. Yet from this same division of scarce resources among these same rational individuals come conflicts, war, destruction of already scarce resources, the vicious circle of violence and misery.

These two results of the original situation are both equally rational and necessary. If we imagine *homines oeconomici* not as egotistical monsters but as rational individuals seeking to promote their own self-interest, then it is impossible to determine which solution they will adopt. Economic violence and order are indistinguishable. They are both based on the same situation. The outcome of the original situation that is supposed to institute economic activities is undecidable: it can be violence just as easily as economic activity. The paradox of economic activity is that is it cannot be differentiated from violence.

The undecidability of the original situation of the division of scarce resources must be called the ambivalence of scarcity. Scarcity has two values: it is both a cause of violence and the foundation of economic activity. The ambivalence of scarcity is not marginal or secondary. It is not exterior to the logic of economic activity. On the contrary, it is one of the founding elements and resides at the heart of economic undertakings and theory.

It is a founding element because the ambivalence is that of the original situation that established economic activity. It is also a founding element because the indispensable institution of the moral and political value of economic activity is based on the ambivalence of scarcity.

Indeed, the reasoning that makes economic activity the best means of conquering violence is based on scarcity's two contradictory values. Constitution of the moral and political value of economic activity employs both the beneficial and the harmful aspects of scarcity simultaneously. The negative aspect is present because, if scarcity were not a cause of vice and violence, economic growth and trade would not guarantee peace: if there were no negative aspect, the public good could not be a moral value established at the cost of envy and pride. The positive aspect is present because scarcity is the foundation of order in the form of commerce and trade since the fundamental economic fact, namely, nature's parsimony, pushes people to invent arts and industries that bring prosperity.

Establishment of economic activity as a social ideal requires both the beneficial and the harmful aspects of scarcity. The reasoning that establishes the political and moral value of economic activity does not hold together unless scarcity appears as both a source of disorder and a foundation of order—in other words, unless scarcity is ambivalent.

Yet this foundation has to be hidden, and scarcity's active ambivalence in economic texts has to be invisible. The reason for this is simple. If both of scarcity's contradictory aspects are indispensable for establishing economic activity, the invisibility of the ambivalence is equally necessary or else the edifice will be undermined by uncertainty. Indeed, once the ambivalence of scarcity has been identified, economic activity's claim to ensure order seems vain. Its institution, based on the paradigm of *homines oeconomici* who all seek to promote their self-interest in a world where resources are limited, seems incomprehensible. The ambivalence of scarcity cannot be admitted without seeing that violence and economic activity are the same thing.

There seems to be only one way to meet the double imperative of the presence/absence of the ambivalence of scarcity. In order for both aspects of scarcity to operate without acknowledgment of the ambivalence of the concept, we only need to distinguish scarcity from itself. It suffices to separate scarcity from scarcity, and to assign violence to one and economic activity to the other. A principle other than violence and order has to be employed to differentiate the two sides of ambivalent scarcity if we want the arbitrary nature of the dissociation process to remain hidden. This principle can be nothing but the principle that underlies the concept itself: quantity.

Economists have always distinguished between scarcity and scarcity. This distinction explains why the ambivalence of scarcity has not been noticed more often. The real quantity of available goods and resources is the principle for this distinction. Scarcity separates scarcity from scarcity.

The liberal tradition claims that there is no paradoxical identity of the situation that establishes economic activity and the conditions that engender violence. The two situations are similar, but not identical. A difference that is both tiny and huge separates them. It is an extremely significant difference. A situation in which there is moderate or relative scarcity establishes economic activity. Extreme scarcity—in other words, necessity—engenders violence. Both situations truly are similar: the only difference is the quantity of goods and resources available. If the quantity is so small that all people's needs cannot be met, then violence will necessarily erupt. If there is more available, but still not enough to fulfill everyone's desires, then envy will be a useful spur to economic activity.

This mathematical, quantifiable difference demonstrates the simplicity and consistency of economic thought. Indeed, it is precisely the law of scarcity, the fundamental economic fact, that distinguishes violence from economic order and, once more, establishes that order. The passage from less to more, the growth of the real quantity of available goods and resources, untangles economic activity from violence. The law of scarcity institutes economic order.

The distinction between relative scarcity and extreme scarcity keeps the two faces of the ambivalence apart. It prevents any confusion between violence and economic activity, and thus makes it possible for beneficial scarcity and harmful scarcity to coexist in economic writings. It guarantees the political effectiveness of economic activity. Thanks to it, the economic solution to the problem of violence simply reproduces the establishment of economic order. Just as the passage from less to more, from extreme to relative scarcity, separates violence from economic activity, the passage from more to even more, from relative scarcity to abundance, distinguishes commercial competition from perfect peace and veritable communication.

Halfway between extreme scarcity and happy, peaceful abundance, relative scarcity seems to provide rational support for the ambiguity of economic activities and commercial relations, which are both rational and agonistic, and involve trade that brings both peace and power relations. The distinction between extreme scarcity and relative scarcity explains the proximity between violence and economic activity, and the absolute distance that separates them.

The following is what a famous introductory treatise on economic analysis says about scarcity. In a section devoted to the law of scarcity, Samuelson and Nordhaus write: "If an infinite amount of every good could be produced. . . . There would be no *economic goods*, i.e., no goods that are relatively *scarce*. And there would hardly be any need for a study of economics or for 'economizing.'" They quickly add: "Compared with developing nations or previous centuries, modern industrial societies seem very wealthy indeed. But higher production levels seem to bring in their train ever-higher consumption standards. . . . People feel that they want and 'need' indoor plumbing, central heating, refrigerators, education, movies, radios, television, books, autos, travel, sports and concerts, privacy and living space, chic clothes, clean air and water, safe factories, and so forth."[8] Prudent economists do not take positions on the nature or ground of such needs. They say that people *feel that they want and "need."* . . . If we were to ask Samuelson and Nordhaus about this, they would probably answer that economists do not have to ask this kind of question. They consider social facts to be like things, and the needs expressed by economic actors to be objective data that are true for them and about which no value judgments are to be made.[9]

Thus, if these needs are just as true and real as others, strange consequences follow. To say like Samuelson and Nordhaus that "higher production levels seem to bring in their train ever-higher consumption standards" is either to say something completely banal and insignificant or, with the addition of "people feel that they want and 'need,'" to say that there is a circular causal relationship between available goods and people's needs. Indeed, people work, exchange goods, and invent art and industry only to meet their needs, to reduce the gap between the size of their needs and the quantity of goods to which they have access. It is thus needs that determine production levels. However, if higher production levels make "people feel that they want and 'need,'" then it is the quantity of goods produced that directly determines the size of the needs. We thus find ourselves before a case of circular causality in which needs determine the quantity of goods necessary, and the quantity of goods produced determines the needs. In other words, higher levels of production lead to increased needs, and increased needs require even higher levels of production.

The reciprocal determination of production by needs and needs by level of production means that it is impossible to reduce the gap separating available goods and resources from desires. The quantity of goods and resources can increase infinitely, and since it directly controls the size of needs, the scarcity constraint remains unchanged. Scarcity is never reduced; it is perpetually renewed.

The circular causality mechanism that links production to needs invalidates the classical idea of scarcity as limited resources or as nature's parsimony. It makes it impossible to draw a distinction between extreme and moderate scarcity. Scarcity corresponds to no real quantity of available goods and resources. There is no arithmetic of violence. Peace does not follow from abundance, and war is not a consequence of poverty.

The distinction between extreme and relative scarcity is fictional and mythical because there is an unsolvable aporia of scarcity. Scarcity corresponds to no real quantity. The original situation is truly undecidable. Properly speaking, scarcity is ambivalent. It founds economic activity and engenders violence, and these two contradictory values are indispensable for accepting economic activity as a social ideal. The aporia of scarcity means the eternal proximity of violence. It means that the undecidability of the original situation is forever tied to economic activity, no matter how many goods and resources are available, no matter how much growth there is.

The aporia and ambivalence complement each other. The "aporetic" distinction between extreme scarcity and relative scarcity hides the ambivalence of scarcity. It makes it possible for both values of scarcity to coexist in economists' texts. It thereby establishes economic activity as a social ideal. There is no doubt that the opposite dynamic is also operating. The ambivalence obscures the aporia. The moral and political value that we give to economic activity prevents us from correctly assessing the reciprocal determination of needs by levels of production and levels of production by needs. The ambivalence of scarcity dissimulates the eternal vanity of growth that has now led humanity down a suicidal path with respect to its natural environment.

There is a well-known political discourse on economic activity. It very clearly describes the difficulties with and reason for growth and discusses inequality along with legitimate rights for all. It teaches us that too much inequality increases social tensions. The resulting upsurge of conflict can reduce economic activity and cause a drop in production. The reduction in growth increases the number of dissatisfied people, and thus conflict grows. Thus, the vicious circle of economic unbalance and social disorganization is set in motion. However, it also teaches us that too little inequality reduces economic motivation, and thus growth. Once again, poverty spreads and "all the old filthy business will necessarily be reproduced."

Political discourse on economic activity shows that reduction in growth (scarcity) engenders disorder and social disorganization, conflict and violence. It also teaches us about the ambivalence of inequality (scarcity), which is both an economic motivation and a source of violence, both a driving force behind growth and a cause of conflict, thus both an assurance of peace and a guarantee of latent disorder.

Political discourse on economic activity, inequality, and growth imitates and repeats in its own way economists' discourse on scarcity and violence. It once again links the ambivalence and aporia. The specific rate of growth suggested by politicians as a precarious solution for activating the positive virtues of inequality without mobilizing its conflict-causing consequences very closely resembles economists' moderate scarcity. Yet use of inequality as an economic motivation for growth is based on the ambivalence of scarcity because, in the end, the reason for the growth—in other words, an increase in the real quantity of available goods and resources—is to eliminate inequality.

Accepting economic activity as a social ideal requires giving economic activity its own political value. Today's political discourse on economics, growth, and inequality reiterates the political value of economic activity. Indeed, it is the embodiment of that value. It is proof that the ideal has been accepted and established. The fact that economists and politicians repeat the same things suggests a strange thesis, but we certainly cannot reject it a priori. Economic activity protects us from our own violence. It prevents our conflicts from destroying society. It prevents Western society from committing social suicide.

Economists, and especially researchers in the social sciences, have long taught us to distinguish economics from the concrete set of economic activities to which that science applies. We thus cannot accept a thesis that blurs the boundaries of such an elementary distinction. We cannot imprudently conclude that what is true in the science is also true in practice, and vice versa.

The ambivalence of scarcity gives economic activity its political value. It is what we have to look to in order to get to the bottom of the problem. Yet scarcity is both the basic economic fact and a central category in economic science. It is the foundation for the science and for concrete economic activities. There is no hasty, imprudent conclusion from the (theoretical) political role of the economy to the (practical) political role of economic activities for the precise reason that the thesis that we are proposing is an assertion about scarcity itself. Aporetic, ambivalent scarcity is efficient. It is what separates individual consequences of actions from their social consequences and puts our conflicts in service to economic order.

The point is thus not so much to criticize economics or to track the absurdities scattered throughout the texts of some of the early thinkers in the liberal tradition, but to understand in a new, deeper way the object that escapes both the science and the thinkers: scarcity. Our approach will be deeper and more novel because economics perceives neither the ambivalence nor the aporia of scarcity. Indeed, it seems that its entire field of application is determined by those two blind spots.

However, people will still object that political discourse on economic activity cannot be taken at face value. Indeed, political discourse on the economy is ideological, and, as everyone knows, ideology always means something different than what it says. Thus, even though political discourse on the economy clearly expresses the links uniting economic activity and violence, we have to suppose that the discourse, specifically because it says this, means something else. In other words, in the end, it means anything but what it says. With such methodological principles, one certainly does not run much of a risk of unsettling one's prejudices!

Nonetheless, it is precisely when we leave the closed field of ideology to which Dumont confines his study that the hypothesis of economic activity's prophylactic role with respect to violence becomes crucial. While it may be true that economic ideology had to acquire its own moral and political value, and emancipate itself from traditional values, it is just as certain that we cannot confine such emancipation to the more or less independent domain of values and ideas. Even if we suppose that ideology both acts on and is determined by social reality, we cannot limit economic activity's rise in standing to this ideal sphere.[10]

Indeed, economic activity's acquisition of moral and political value happened at the same time that all social relations and human activities were invaded by economic logic. The genesis and spread of the economic ideology occurred in parallel with the transformation of society into a market society. This social mutation means that economic activity must have truly, socially, acted like a moral and political system. This means that economic values have become standards that determine the actions of members of society and that the economic organization of society has been able to maintain order.[11] Today's political discourse on the economy is explicitly aware of this political and moral function of economic activity, even though it obscures its precise operation. We should not close our ears to this.

We should not reject out of hand the methodological principles that govern scientific research, but we should nonetheless challenge precepts that cannot be falsified. The maxim that requires that the meaning of an ideology be eternally other than its explicit content cannot be falsified. There is no reason to hold on to it.

Scarcity and Community

What is scarcity? It has been clear for some time now that we can no longer be satisfied with the classical definition of scarcity. Scarcity is limited means, restricted quantities of goods and resources, the parsimony of nature. The causal circularity that links needs to levels of production has dispelled this naturalist illusion of real quantity.

Yet in the end, to reject real quantity seems to be to refuse to see the pressure that hunger and real environmental constraints place on many communities. This pressure has been described in too many historical and ethnographical documents for us to be able to ignore it. If we reject the parsimony of nature as if it were a naturalist myth, are we not demonstrating ethnocentrism and admitting our ignorance as children born with silver spoons in our mouths, protected from famine and natural catastrophes by industrialization and the prodigious growth of productive forces that took place in the West?

We can deny neither environmental effects nor the pressure of hunger. We also cannot deny the diversity of ecological responses by archaic societies in their efforts to both adjust to their environments and adapt their environments to them. However, it is modern societies, the richest ones on the planet, that have convinced themselves that resources are scarce and that there are insufficient economic means. Using examples of extreme hunger, we can show that there is no primitive experience of scarcity.

In a remarkable book entitled *Stone Age Economics*,[12] Marshall Sahlins brings together the findings of many years of work and establishes a general theory of primitive, that is, archaic, economies. Sahlins analyzes an enormous quantity of data, while at the same time warning us about his own attempt to construct an ideal type, an abstract model of the economic organization of primitive societies based on data scattered among many societies that are different in numerous ways. The model that Sahlins describes exists nowhere but in his head. Nonetheless, what makes his approach interesting is specifically this provisional generalization. The societies that are the sources of the material he has chosen are similar in that they are primitive. In other words, they have no government, no strong central authority. No one has the monopoly of violence. Sahlins thus calls them acephalic societies—in other words, headless. If we were to criticize Sahlins, it would not be so much for generalizing, since stateless societies do indeed fall into a category, but for his insistence on speaking of a primitive economy, as if there were such a thing as an economy in primitive societies.

In fact, Sahlin's second warning specifically concerns the economy and economic activities: "Something more is involved than the simple point that economics is functionally related to the social and political arrangements of tribal societies. Economics is not distinguishable from these arrangements."[13] It is useful to insist on this point because we all spontaneously believe that, in the end, material conditions and productive forces determine the economy and thus the entire social structure. Primitive societies provide proof to the contrary. Truly embedded in social structure, primitive economies are oriented primarily toward the general function of that structure. Economic imperatives do not exist, or if they do, it is as basic givens of human nature; social organization is such that economic imperatives cannot appear.

It is thus the anthropologist's arbitrary action that isolates certain objects and practices that we can call economic. Structurally, there is no primitive economy. "What are in the conventional wisdom of economic science 'exogenous' or 'noneconomic' factors, such as kinship and politics, are in the tribal reality the very organization of the economic process."[14] The fact that "economic activities" are embedded in the social structure and bent toward noneconomic, political and ritual purposes largely explains the aberrant, deeply a-economic features of primitive economies.

We can approach primitive economies in two different ways to show how they differ from modern economies: either through what Marxists call the "mode of production"[15] or through exchange—in other words, what should be the market.

Sahlins says that the dominant productive institution in primitive societies is the basic family unit, the household. The basic family unit is often slightly "expanded" in comparison with our own because it generally includes, in addition to the father and mother, one or two married children with their spouses and children. This is the basic unit of the family or domestic mode of production.

Labor is divided mainly, but not uniquely, along gender lines. Often, the work performed by the husband and wife is sufficient to ensure the family's survival. Simple technology is used. Most tools can be employed independently by a single individual, and each household deploys a complete productive apparatus. People produce essentially to consume—in other words, in accordance with their own needs. Even objects produced for trade do not escape this rule because meeting producer-consumers' needs, not making a profit, is the reason for trade. Within each household, goods and services are pooled, which ensures that each has what he or she needs to survive and work. The producers own the means of production, if not officially, at least in that they produce for themselves and not for others.

Taken alone, family-based production appears dispersed and anarchic. It is segmented, and the segments are not complementary, but redundant. Each unit is organized to produce independently from all the others. Since production is oriented essentially toward consumption, the domestic mode of production in fact contains a veritable antiaccumulation mechanism.

There is another important feature of the domestic mode of production: underproduction. There is underproduction in relation to us, obviously, and especially underproduction in the strict sense, in relation to the society's own productive potential. Such underproduction can be seen in three ways. First, available resources are underused. Second, workers or the labor force are underemployed, which means that technological means are not fully utilized. Third, there is what Sahlins calls "Chayanov's Rule."

Chayanov's Rule says that the greater a household's capacity for work, the less each individual member will actually work. This means that those who can produce the most actually produce the least in relation to their capacities, and thus that part of the production- and work-capacity is unemployed. Chayanov's Rule also says that in the domestic mode of production, consumption is the purpose of production. Since the most powerful production units do not work at full steam, unlike weaker units, who tend toward full output, the level of consumption is apparently set by the weakest production units. In any case, it is not set by the strongest, but probably by traditional consumption standards that are independent of possible increases in levels of production. Chayanov's Rule means that the aporia of scarcity does not occur in primitive societies. There is no causal circularity linking production levels with consumption levels.

At the same time, if consumption levels are set by traditional norms, the level of production of primitive societies, though lower than the society's own capacity, is nonetheless adequate if it meets the norms. It is in this sense that Sahlins speaks of primitive societies as the first affluent societies.[16]

Another characteristic of the family-based mode of production allows us to discuss exchange: the economic insufficiency of some households. Segmented as it is, even though the production standard is much lower than the household's real economic capacity, the family-based mode of production involves the failure of a number of units of production—in other words, the inability of many households to meet their own needs. The rules of social solidarity that govern exchange then intervene to compensate for the failure. The wealthiest take care of the needs of the poorest.

Various rules of solidarity govern exchange within the community. Except in some special cases, outside the community the rules tend to be inverted, and exchange turns into extortion, theft, and violence, pure and simple. Sahlins speaks of reciprocity as a continuum, starting with the core family unit and diminishing as we get farther away. Social space looks like a series of concentric circles, in the center of which is the home and family unit. The next circle contains more distant kin, then there is the village, the tribe, and finally the outside, intertribal space.

In the center, exchanges are governed by what Sahlins calls "generalized reciprocity," which refers to pure solidarity, free gifts that require no return. In most cases, this also applies to exchanges among kin. "Balanced reciprocity" rules the village and tribe. This is what we usually call reciprocity: each gift requires an equivalent gift in return. Proportionally, as we move outward from the village to the tribe, the timeframe and conditions for the return gift are specified more strictly. Any failure in this area is a major misdemeanor.

In contrast, as we go from kin to household, such failures are tolerated, and then considered normal. We no longer keep accounts.

Outside the tribe reigns what Sahlins calls "negative reciprocity": various attempts to get something for nothing with impunity. This goes from transactions conducted to obtain an advantage or maximize one's gain at a trading partner's expense, to theft, violence, and raids. It is significant that the exchanges that correspond most closely to our criteria of trade—in other words, exchanges governed by self-interest—occur only outside the community. Even more significant, primitive peoples put them in the same category as violence.

The solidarity systems that govern exchanges within the community in accordance with the way the social space is organized are influenced by three factors that encourage greater solidarity. Status in the kinship hierarchy determines the extent of generalized reciprocity. As Sahlins says, "In primitive society social inequality is more the organization of economic equality. Often, in fact, high rank is only secured or sustained by o'ercrowing generosity: the material advantage is on the subordinate's side."[17] The same goes for wealth. It requires greater generosity: charity must be extended beyond natural social limits.

The last rule of exchange that maintains the group's cohesion concerns the special nature of subsistence goods, which counteracts through greater solidarity the atomization of the family based mode of production. Food is generally in a special category. It cannot be exchanged for anything other than food. In fact, it cannot be exchanged. Within the community, food is not exchanged; it is given. While sharing someone's meal sometimes supposes sharing one's own in turn, gifts of food are always presented as free offerings.

Food is also different from other goods in that the realm in which there is generalized reciprocity with respect to subsistence goods is larger than that for other goods. We give, without compensation, food to people with whom we exchange shell necklaces for pottery. We give food to those who need it, also for nothing in return. As Polanyi notes, in primitive societies, no one is in danger of dying of hunger unless everyone is.[18]

Once again, outside the community, the rules are reversed. Food is sometimes exchanged. Subsistence goods are weighed against jewelry and tools.

Similarly, if sharing and gifts of food signify friendship and a community of interest, refusal to share implies distrust, and refusing a gift is equivalent to declaring war.

One problem remains: the intrinsic solidarity of primitive exchange is worth nothing if there is nothing to exchange. As we said, underproduction is part of the structure of the family-based mode of production. If a number of families fail to meet their own needs, and if the households with the greatest productive potential tend not to deploy their full work capacity, we can wonder, given the weakness of its means, how the family-based mode of production manages to meet everyone's needs.

The answer lies in the community's social organization. The task of producing more in order to meet the requirements of the needy falls on the shoulders of their close relatives and those highest placed in the political hierarchy. The rules of solidarity that govern exchange also lead to greater production by some households. Logically, the increase in production should appear in the form of variations in Chayanov's Rule. While Sahlins remains prudent on this topic because there is insufficient data, it seems that this is indeed what happens.[19]

Thus, we have rapidly sketched the main features of primitive economies. Surprisingly, what we call "economic motives" play no role in them. The desire for profit and the constant will to promote one's self-interest do not seem to determine primitive people's economic behavior. Despite Adam Smith, they expect their daily bread to come more from their neighbors' generosity than from the latter's self-interest. Members of primitive societies reveal themselves to be very poor *homines oeconomici*. The conventions of social solidarity, not maximization of self-interest, are what determine increases in production.

The fact that the economy is embedded in social structures is what explains these strange results. Indeed, just as the reciprocity systems that govern exchanges change as we move to different locations in the circular social space, the center of which is the home and the periphery the tribe, so do all activities, economic or not. The atomization of the family-based mode of production also reflects the segmented social organization of kinship relations that structure the family, lineage, clan, and tribe. The determining role of kinship relations in increases in production confirms this impression.

The economy is thus in no way autonomous. It is an aspect of the goals and general function of the social organization. But what is this function, and what are these goals?

Sahlins provides a simple, unequivocal answer to this question. The primary feature of the social organization of primitive societies is absence of government, absence of strong central authority. He says that the absence of government is equivalent to the state of war described by Hobbes at the beginning of *Leviathan*.[20] In other words, it is equivalent to a state in which every individual can have legitimate recourse to violence at any time. It is a state of insecurity in which violence is always possible, if not always present. The absence of specialized political institutions with a monopoly over violence and able to enforce the law entails that the overall social organization has to have a pacifying role. Like other social relations, economic activities are organized so as to prevent and avoid conflict.

Based on what we already know, it is easy to grasp this pacifying function of social organization. The refusal to take advantage of a transaction and the insistence on balance in exchanges can be explained if we suppose a fear of offending and the constant danger that the slightest affront or vexation could turn into violence in a world where each has to render justice himself or herself. The same can be said about other rules and prohibitions that govern interactions among individuals. Simultaneously, we see that undivided solidarity becomes the norm as we get closer to the family unit, where it is most important to keep the peace. The solidarity and unity that reign inside the village with respect to food and the obligation to provide for those in need are clearly apt to reduce opportunities for conflict. Food is life itself, and in this sense it is too precious for disputes to be allowed to arise over it.

These ties of solidarity do not apply only in economic activities, but in all areas. Everything is designed to prevent rivalry, and when certain forms of rivalry are permitted or required, they are directed toward objects that are exterior to the community (feats in battle) or are structured so that they do not give rise to violent disputes: people are invited to rival each other in terms of generosity. Violence is driven toward the outside of the community and prevented from appearing inside it. Reciprocity's evolution toward the negative reciprocity of intertribal exchanges is proof of this.

It seems that we are very far from scarcity, and that this detour through primitive societies has not shown us what it is. Yet in fact we are at the heart of the matter. The widespread economic and social solidarity that is characteristic of primitive societies prohibits the social construction of scarcity—in other words, a set of goods and resources that is insufficient to meet the needs of all. Whatever the quantity of goods and resources available, nothing logically equivalent to scarcity will appear. This is because there is no privative/exclusive appropriation of goods and resources; social solidarity prohibits it. It is impossible to experience scarcity in primitive societies because in them it does not exist.

The demonstration is simple and rigorous. The social structures of primitive societies create obligations among people. They construct a space of solidarity in which people are required to help one another or, better, where each is responsible for the others. No one is abandoned to his or her fate. The community takes care of each of its members. This is true in economic activities and in all other areas. An affront to one member of the community is an affront to the entire community.

This solidarity is expressed in the economy in the form of unconditional sharing of subsistence goods. Those who do not manage to meet their own needs are taken care of by their relatives or those who are better off. Under such conditions, so long as the community exists, there are enough goods to meet everybody's needs. If the goods become insufficient, the very links that structure the community will disappear. In other words, the community will no longer exist. The conditions that make it possible to experience scarcity are never met. In primitive societies, the notion cannot be constructed. Scarcity can arise nowhere in the social space of primitive societies. No one is in danger of dying of hunger if all are not.

In the appendix to chapter 5 ("On the Sociology of Primitive Exchange") of *Stone Age Economics*, Sahlins provides us with a series of ethnological notes on wealth and reciprocity. From this information we can draw one certain conclusion: generally, when resources decrease, solidarity increases. In times of famine, the ties uniting the community tend to grow stronger. Each individual tries harder to fulfill his or her duties and obligations to relatives, the poor, and the gods. Reduction in the real quantity of goods and resources strengthens all social bonds, not only economic links, and, as Sahlins says, those bonds have a pacifying function. Primitive peoples place the danger that we call scarcity in the same category as violence.

Yet there must be times when resources are insufficient and obligations can no longer be kept. This is certain. Sahlins reports information from a study by Firth[21] on a prolonged famine suffered by the Tikopia. Initially, the solidarity of social ties tended to increase. Then, as the crisis grew longer and the famine grew worse, the social space changed. Solidarity became concentrated around the family unit, and practices distinctive of intertribal space started to penetrate into the village. Throughout the crisis, appearances were maintained, but people became hypocritical when the famine grew too severe. People hid food so that they would not have to share it and stole whenever possible. Nonetheless, within the home, undivided solidarity continued to be the rule.

If the famine had become even worse, the community might have been destroyed, and it certainly would have been obliterated by the violence that would have set people against one another long before hunger had killed them all. It is impossible to experience scarcity in primitive societies because the emergence of scarcity is equivalent to the destruction, pure and simple, of the community. The social space, which is entirely structured by solidarity obligations, contains no place where there could be a set of resources insufficient to meet the needs of all. When that does arise, it is equivalent to the collapse of the social space and destruction of the society. In primitive societies, experiencing scarcity equals experiencing violence. Such societies are right to put them in the same category.

From this rapid overview of primitive economies, we have already learned a few things about scarcity. Scarcity is defined neither by any quantity of goods and resources nor by parsimony of nature. Scarcity is constructed in the fabric of interpersonal relations. The structure of the social space does or does not make it possible for this object, namely, scarcity, to appear. However, it is a purely social object. Scarcity exists nowhere but in the network of intersubjective exchanges that creates it. Scarcity is a form of social organization, nothing else.

In primitive societies, the aporia of scarcity does not exist. When solidarity governs exchange, there is no circular causal mechanism between needs and levels of production. Finally, violence and scarcity are one and the same in primitive societies. The emergence of scarcity[22] leads to the destruction of the community, its death. This means either its physical death, in the form of extermination of its individual members, or ethnocide—in other words, the collapse of traditional social structures and disappearance of the culture.

While the second form of death is by far the most frequent, it should not make us forget the first, the real one, in which violence erupts in all its harshness. Indeed, there is no doubt that acculturation with the West today is the only thing that enables primitive societies to survive scarcity, to trade the first death for the second. Yet the physical destruction of the community is the only thing that makes it possible to grasp the dimension of the enigma that the modern world constitutes: a social organization based on scarcity!

Primitive peoples and the liberal tradition are in complete opposition. Make no mistake. The liberal tradition sees scarcity as a cause of violence. Primitive peoples see scarcity as violence. The difference is huge, and it is not simply a question of language. The economic order cannot survive knowledge that violence and scarcity are one and the same. In order for the economy to be established and maintained, scarcity has to have two values. The ambivalence of scarcity is its foundation. The concept of causality maintains the space between scarcity and violence indispensable to the economic system.

The Mimetic Crisis

The economic system is based on scarcity. Study of primitive societies teaches us that violence and scarcity are the same. How can the violent destruction of a community acquire a positive value? This is, in fact, the question that we have to answer if we want to understand the ambivalence of scarcity.

René Girard has done so in an important book entitled *Violence and the Sacred*.[23] Of course, his answer mainly concerns primitive societies, in other words, those in which, as we know, the ambivalence of scarcity does not occur. We will see below that only Girard's thought and what we have learned from it can explain the ambivalence of scarcity. This explanation very simply maps Girard's thought onto the economic phenomena of the modern world. In order to achieve this, we need only read Girard carefully. This is what we will do in the following pages.

The reason that primitive peoples assimilate scarcity with violent destruction of the community, collapse of the social space, is that, for them, it is inseparable from what Girard calls the mimetic or sacrificial crisis, the breakdown of cultural order and the spiral of vengeance and countervengeance that gradually encompasses the whole community. In order to understand scarcity, we can thus begin by looking at the mimetic crisis and its mechanisms, the course it takes and its resolution.

The basic hypothesis concerns mimetism, the deeply mimetic nature of desire. In Girard's theory, desire has no specific object. Strictly speaking, it has no object. Desire is not object-based, but mimetic. It is always imitation of another desire, a desire for the same object. It is always desire for what someone else desires. Girard says that "desire chooses its objects through the mediation of a model; it is the desire of and for the *other*. . . . The model designates the desirable while at the same time desiring it."[24]

Mimetic desire is an inexhaustible source of conflict. By desiring what the other desires, the subject transforms his or her model into a rival, a veritable obstacle that blocks the way, the way that was, in fact, pointed out to the subject by the model himself or herself. Simultaneously, since mimesis is universal, the subject's desire can also strengthen that of the model, fixing it on the object, which may have originally been nothing more than a passing fancy.

Properly speaking, mimetic desire creates obstacles. It makes desires converge on the same objects and makes people clash in violent reciprocity. It gathers them together around a single object only to bring each into opposition with all the others. Yet while mimesis is first, while it emerges before the object, and even, at the limit, creates the object, it is inseparable from the illusion that the object comes first. The subject does not perceive the automatic mechanism that projects his or her desire against that of his or her model. The subject always thinks he or she desires the object for its intrinsic qualities, or spontaneously. The rivalry itself reinforces this illusion. The adversaries are convinced that there are enormous differences between them: otherwise they would not be in conflict. They cannot imagine that the difference is rooted in sameness. The apparent and misleading primacy of the object persuades both rivals that each is the victim of the other. It is always the other who began, but in reality, there is no beginning, because mimetic desire is first and universal.

Resulting from mimetic desire, human conflicts are characterized, on the one hand, by the fact that it is impossible to assign them an origin, to discover *the* guilty party, and, on the other hand, by the fact that each opponent believes in the complete, unique responsibility of his or her adversary.

Left to itself, mimetic desire increases and intensifies. This is because, clearly, mimesis is contagious and spreads by imitation. If there is nothing to stop its progress, it grows little by little and branches further and further. It is impossible to limit it. We cannot suppose that it will stop on its own before it contaminates the whole community. However, as it spreads it also gets worse, and, whatever the outcome of individual rivalries, whether failure or success, it leads in a straight line to the same result.

The object receives its value from the Other. If the subject succeeds in obtaining the desired object, he or she will soon see the victory transform into failure. Indeed, since the object is no longer mediated by the model, it loses the value that made it so desirable. Success can only be disappointing. Under these conditions, the subject, unable to gain access to the mimetic truth of desire, will inevitably choose his or her models in accordance with their ability to create obstacles for him or her. Through a demented, but logical, shortcut, the subject, convinced that success conceals failure, will target a failure that alone can contain hidden success. Of course, the subject does not really target failure, but the Other's success, which he or she wants to seize. Only the Other's ability to be an obstacle can convince the subject that his or her fingers will close around something substantial. Mimetic desire is structurally condemned to failure. Whether it begins with failure or success, it always leads to failure.

After the model has been transformed into an obstacle, the metamorphosis of the obstacle into a model amplifies rivalry. From then on, the Other will be the focus of rivalry: the model/obstacle that must be both conquered and assimilated. The object that was originally at stake in the rivalry will gradually fade away and disappear completely. It will no longer be a question of fighting a rival for an object, but of slaughtering and destroying the Other. Mimetic rivalry culminates in violence, and violence reveals the eternal truth of rivalry, the nothingness of its object. The object does not come first; mimetism does.

Violence can arise in conflicts even before the object disappears. However, when it arises, it leads to the same result: derealization of the initial stake in the conflict. Adversaries are fascinated with each other, and the object fades away when the Other comes on stage.

The uncontrollable spread of mimesis, the exacerbation of conflict, and gradual contamination of the whole community by reciprocal violence constitute what Girard calls the mimetic or sacrificial crisis. Once violence has penetrated into the community, it will necessarily increase and continue spreading.

A question inevitably arises when mimetic desire is presented in this way, in its pure form, free of any foreign elements, in the simple, virtually mechanical flow of its effects. If violence is the end toward which mimetic desire ineluctably leads, if mimesis propagates by imitation and never stops growing, how is it that there is something other than violence and conflict? In other words, why is there not nothing? "If there are really such events as sacrificial crises, some sort of braking mechanism, an automatic control that goes into effect before everything is destroyed, must be built into them."[25]

"If desire is mimetic by nature, all consequent phenomena must necessarily tend toward reciprocity."[26] It is toward this reciprocity that we now have to turn if we want to understand the self-regulating mechanism that resolves the crisis. At the level of the object, all rivalry already involves some reciprocity, but mimetic rivalry also supposes reciprocity at the level of desire. Exacerbation of rivalry makes the reciprocity clearer. Once the object has disappeared, the rivals are nothing more than doubles animated by the same desire to destroy the Other. They are nothing more than carbon copies submerged in the same violent reciprocity.

Yet while exacerbation of conflict increases reciprocity, it also hides it more thoroughly. Violence turns the model into an antimodel. Each adversary does everything he or she can to be different from the other. This opposite, symmetrical thirst to differentiate themselves makes them even more similar. One combatant's action calls for the adversary to do something that is both identical and opposite to block the blow. Thus, paradoxically but logically, the effort they put into differentiating themselves makes the rivals resemble each other more and more.

The eternal return of the same haunts the adversaries and feeds their rivalry. People are incapable of acknowledging that their disputes are not motivated by differences. The more intense the rivalry becomes—in other words, the more the differences fade away and the rivals become doubles—the more intolerable the knowledge of their identity becomes. In the end, it is to avoid seeing that they are similar and that nothing separates them that people come into conflict.

Adversaries lose their difference, rivals become doubles: this is a real phenomenon, even though those involved will do anything to deny it. "As the crisis grows more acute, the community members are transformed into 'twins,' matching images of violence."[27] Since violence truly homogenizes people, since it makes them all identical and thus interchangeable, the crisis will come to a stage where each and any adversary can become the enemy of all, the repository of all the hatred accumulated in the community, the unique victim against whom the violence of all the others will be exercised, but which will simultaneously slake their desire for violence. Against this unique victim, the community will rediscover its unanimity minus one, which is the normal resolution and outcome of the sacrificial crisis.

Almost nothing would be required to transform the suspicions of one into the certainty of all. Thanks to mimesis, the belief will spread through the entire community in no time, each member persuaded by the fact that all the others are also persuaded. Girard says: "The firm conviction of the group is based on no other evidence than the unshakable unanimity of its own illogic."[28]

> the universal spread of "doubles," the complete effacement of differences, heightening antagonisms but also making them interchangeable, is the prerequisite for the establishment of violent unanimity. For order to be reborn, disorder must first triumph. . . . All the rancours scattered at random among the divergent individuals, all the differing antagonisms, now converge on an isolated and unique figure, the *surrogate victim*.[29]

The violent climax is followed by the most complete calm, and the rediscovered peace convinces yesterday's adversaries of the guilt of the scapegoat. The substitution of a surrogate victim for all the other members of the community requires the "universal spread of 'doubles,' the complete effacement of differences, heightening antagonisms but also making them interchangeable." The perfect identity of the doubles means that the choice of victim is purely arbitrary: no difference justifies it. Nonetheless, the victim will seem absolutely unique. A fantastic difference will be associated with the victim because of the violence that converged on him or her and, especially, because of the peace that follows his or her immolation.

In order to understand the substitution mechanism and the real transfer of the community's violence from all doubles onto a single surrogate victim, it is better to look at it from the point of view of the antagonists themselves. While the antagonists' reciprocity and the doubles' identity come back to haunt them, they obstinately reject those truths, and try to differentiate themselves, illogically, through the violence that makes them the same. Doubles never really possess knowledge about their identity; otherwise they would no longer be in conflict. That knowledge has to be defined as belonging to the outside observer. The knowledge belongs to those who are not involved in the dispute, are outside and foreign to the antagonists and therefore do not risk being contaminated by their violence.[30]

In one way or another, outside knowledge and inside knowledge have to coincide for the transfer to be real. For convergence onto the surrogate victim to operate as an effective means of purging doubles of their violence, their identity and reciprocity have to become obvious to the antagonists. At the same time, misapprehension has to remain so that the arbitrary nature of the choice of victim is not perceived.

The doubles are partially aware of the reciprocity linking them, but they reject this knowledge. As the violence increases, knowledge of the doubles' identity becomes more obvious and less tolerable, more irrefutable and less acceptable. Rejection of this knowledge simply becomes one with the violence itself.

When the violence peaks, the nature of their relations, "stubbornly denied by the antagonists, is ultimately imposed on them in the course of the shifting of differences—but it is imposed *in the form of a hallucination.*"[31] At the paroxysm of the sacrificial crisis, people see monstrous doubles emerge, and they fall prey to a form of possession that is nothing other than violent reciprocity.

In the collective experience of the *monstrous double* the differences are not eliminated, but muddied and confused. All the doubles are interchangeable, although their basic similarity is never formally acknowledged. They thus occupy the equivocal middle ground between difference and unity that is indispensable to the process of sacrificial substitution—to the polarization of violence onto a single victim who substitutes for all the others.[32]

The victim will then appear as an eminently mysterious being, able to give rise to monstrous doubles and sow confusion among all differences. He or she will seem responsible for the violence and also for the peace that will follow once he or she is put to death. The victim will seem to manipulate his or her own death. The victim will seem divine, sacred. All contradictory feelings will converge on the victim: fear of destructive violence, gratefulness for renewed peace. Girard says that only this experience can explain the ambivalence of the sacred, which is both helpful and harmful, both danger of death and source of all life.

The loss of differences and the obscurity of the outcome make the victim sacred. The victim seems to control the action. The mimetic crisis is experienced as a visitation, as the coming of an all-powerful being that destroys the cultural system and then reestablishes peace upon leaving. The mechanism through which the crisis is resolved places the entire responsibility for the violence on the victim's shoulders, and this transfer guarantees the mechanism's efficiency. When the victim is made sacred, a certain form of misapprehension is created, or rather, people's original misapprehension of their responsibility for their own violence is perpetuated. People place their violence under the sign of the sacred—in other words, they project it onto an entity that is exterior to them, foreign to the simple reciprocity of their relations. They turn it into an entity that transcends the social body and establishes cultural order.

Of course, the sacrificial crisis and resolution is an extremely traumatizing, obscure experience. At the end of the sacrificial crisis, we can suppose that people's first concern will be to extend the happy respite that they have been granted, and to keep the sacred—in other words, violence—outside of the community. In the effort to prevent violence, which constitutes a veritable prayer addressed to the sacred to leave the community, and in the necessarily related attempt to understand what has happened, Girard sees the genesis of myths, rituals, and prohibitions.

The attempt to maintain peace will be handicapped by the essential misapprehension that constitutes the very efficiency of the sacrificial resolution. Incapable, for good reason, of discovering the true functioning of the victim mechanism, the sacred will be condemned to two contradictory imperatives that are both equally categorical. On the one hand, the actions that were at the origin of the crisis and that precipitated its occurrence must not be repeated. On the other hand, the actions that led to the resolution of the crisis and the desired peace must be repeated. The contradiction lies in the fact that the actions in question are the same: violence and rivalry. Indeed, there is no specific element that, in principle, distinguishes the sacred from the violence that precedes it, and the action that establishes order is still only one more murder, even if it is the last, the one that puts an end to all the others. The identity of violence and the sacred is what makes it fragile but also what makes it effective. The sacred is effective only at the price of this fragility.

Prohibitions, rules, and obligations result from the need to avoid repeating the actions that were at the origin of the crisis. Rituals result from the opposite imperative, namely, to repeat the actions that brought about the end of the crisis. Sacrifice is the ritual par excellence, the key institution of all primitive religions.

Through the veil of sacred misapprehension, sacrifice reproduces the resolution of the crisis and seeks to reactivate its ordering and cathartic effects. It is based on a substitution similar to the one by which the surrogate victim replaces all the antagonists and polarizes the whole community's violence against himself or herself. A substitute victim is employed in place of the original surrogate victim, and violence's propensity for replacements allows the community to purge itself of violence by converging against the new victim. Sacrifice is of course less efficient than the resolution of the crisis, but it does indeed work. Its efficiency is what makes it the central institution of primitive religion. By once again purging the community of violence, it strengthens prohibitions.

In their own manner, myths tell the story of what has happened. They anchor rituals and prohibitions in the history of the crisis. However, they also sanction misapprehension of the sacred because myths consecrate the gods' divinity and the people's irresponsibility. Beyond and through religion, all of primitive culture springs from the surrogate victim mechanism. Myths tell the story of the birth of peoples. The social structure, differentiated hierarchical system, and kinship divisions that organize the community were established on the first day in mythical time, on the day when the sacrificial crisis came to an end. This is so even according to primitive peoples. Girard invites us to reread the origin and development of all human culture.

Between scarcity as we have described it so far and the sacred from Girard's point of view, there are many clear echoes. Scarcity's relationship to violence, its ambivalence, its construction into an independent entity that is exterior and foreign to people even though it is only the pure result of their reciprocal relations, and finally the position of this ambivalent entity as the foundation and origin of social order (the sacred establishes religion, while scarcity establishes the economic system) so closely resemble the phenomena described by Girard that the connection has to be made.

Of course, we also have to avoid facile analogies and superficial similarities. The sacred's ambivalence comes only from the sacrificial resolution, unanimity, and return of peace. The sacred's ambivalence is cosubstantial with the strength of prohibitions and the permanence of ritual. The sources of the ambivalence of the sacred are both the fact that the sacred and violence are one and the same, and the conversion of violence into order. Both are indispensable.

Scarcity provides no resolution of this kind. As we have seen, scarcity supposes a situation that is impossible in primitive societies. Transcribed into Girard's language, the conditions necessary for the emergence of scarcity seem to create an unsolvable problem.

Indeed, Girard enables us to understand the exact, mimetic nature of the danger that threatens primitive societies. He describes the origin, functioning, and surge of violence against which the prescriptions that regulate exchange and primitive economic activities are directed. He thus confirms and completes what Sahlins has already shown, and he invites us to insert back into the sacrificial system, into primitive religion, to which they probably belong, the solidarity obligations that prohibit the emergence of scarcity.

Scarcity thus corresponds to the loss of antimimetic prohibitions, to the sacrificial crisis. However, clearly, this crisis has no sacrificial resolution because the rediscovered unanimity and peace would eliminate scarcity. The ambivalence of scarcity supposes a state in which the paroxysm of the crisis coincides with a stable system that is not based on the mechanism of founding unanimity.

How is this possible if mimetic desire and the sacrificial crisis are indeed what Girard says they are? The ambivalence of scarcity requires a simultaneity of opposites that is so evident that it seems unthinkable.

It is useful to note that this state, which is indispensable to the emergence of ambivalent scarcity, corresponds precisely to Girard's definition of modern societies:

> If the history of modern society is marked by the dissolution of differences, that clearly has something to do with the sacrificial crisis. . . . It should

be noted, however, that the modern world manages to maintain its balance, precarious though it may be; and the methods it employs to do so, though extreme, are not so extreme as to destroy the fabric of society. As my previous chapters indicated, primitive societies are unable to withstand such pressures; violence would quickly get out of hand and trigger the mechanism of generative unanimity, thus restoring a social system based on multiple and sharply pronounced differences. In the modern Western world, nothing of this kind takes place. The wearing away of differences proceeds at a slow but steady pace, and the results are absorbed more or less gracefully by a community that is slowly but steadily coming to encompass the entire globe.[33]

In many places in Girard's work, we find this definition of modernity as a kind of "crescendo of mimetic rivalry,"[34] among individuals and in history "with no catastrophic outbursts of violence and no resolution of any kind."[35]

This definition of modernity implies that Western civilization is in a strange, privileged position in relation to the essential violence of the crisis. Western civilization "has enjoyed until this day a mysterious immunity from the most virulent forms of violence—an immunity not, it seems, of our society's making, but one that has perhaps resulted in the making of our society."[36]

Of course, Girard describes modern Western society's protection as mysterious because he does not explain it. It is not that he does not spend time defining the special nature of the modern world in relation to all the cultures that preceded it, since he devotes most of *Things Hidden since the Foundation of the World* to demonstrating the uniqueness of modern mimetic phenomena. However, he takes for granted the change in mimetism that produces the distance from essential violence that is characteristic of the modern world.

Clearly, this change in mimetism and the momentary silence of essential violence are not automatic, especially if modernity is defined by precarious levels of balancing that are accompanied by ever more intense rivalry and if modernity is the condition for scarcity's emergence—in other words, the condition for the crisis' paroxysm to coincide with a stable system. While Girard never asks this question, it is certain that this problem arises with respect to his theory.

Scarcity and the Mimetic Crisis

Scarcity is a social institution and is socially instituted. It establishes the modern world just as the sacred established primitive societies. Like the sacred, it protects the community from essential violence. Its operation, which is both very similar to and very different from the sacrificial resolution of the crisis, is based on the same mechanisms. A mutation within the sacred is the sole cause of the change in level and system.

Scarcity is the universalized abandon of the solidarity obligations that used to unite the community. It is the systematic transgression of traditional prohibitions. It is the voluntary rejection of the antimimetic protection offered by the sacred and the sacrificial. This change in point of view with respect to the sacred constructs, socially, a set of goods and resources such that the needs and desires of all cannot be met. The simple definition of the set of goods suffices to explain our obsession with counting and increasing it. Thus, a religious event shapes the illusion of the determining role of economic infrastructure.

The religious event that caused this reversal with respect to the sacred is the appearance and slow spread, in the West, of knowledge about the role and function of the surrogate victim. Indeed, according to Girard, the Judeo-Christian religion is different from the sacred and the sacrificial in one way: among biblical writers there is a clear tendency to take the moral side of victims, to take up the cause and defense of victims.[37] This tendency, which is easy to overlook in the usual context, acquires special importance with respect to the surrogate victim and founding violence. If myths are narratives about the crisis and its resolution warped by the murderers' belief in the guilt and divinity of the victim; if the murder appears in the narratives as a sacred, reconciling action that is required by the god itself and that should thus not be criticized or condemned, then "we can hardly regard as insignificant a change in perspective that consists in taking the side of the victim, proclaiming the victim's innocence and the culpability of his murderers."[38]

The mechanism that resolves the crisis is based on a misapprehension of how it works. The misapprehension is indispensable to the collective transfer mechanism that projects the violence of the entire community onto the surrogate victim. It is the murderers' ignorance about the simple humanity and perfectly arbitrary choice of victim that guarantees the effectiveness of the transfer and allows it to be achieved. The rediscovered peace then confirms the singularity of the victim with his or her unique responsibility for the violence preceding the murder and for the peace that follows. The victim seems to have been behind his or her own immolation. Through the veil of this misapprehension, myths reenact and sanction the crisis. In myths, the crisis appears as a play that the god has enacted with people. When the god goes away, the people are left with prohibitions so that they will not offend the god, and rituals so that they will honor him or her. Thus, the god will stay out of the community, but remain in contact with it. The god is the cause of all death and the source of all life: the god's return would be terrible. Myths teach that the god is all-powerful and that people are not responsible.

In these conditions, there is knowledge that, by definition, is inaccessible to the sacred and the sacrificial. It is knowledge of the victim's humanity: the revelation of the arbitrary nature of the persecution that the victim suffered.

However, it is also obvious that if this knowledge were to emerge within the sacred, if such a thing were possible, then the sacred's efficiency would be ruined. Knowledge of how the scapegoat mechanism works would prevent the collective transfer. The prohibitions and obligations decreed by the gods would no longer be binding on anyone if the victim's humanity and arbitrary nature were revealed. As soon as people recognize the hypostasis of their own violence in the gods, rituals and sacrifices become meaningless. This knowledge desacralizes. It destroys the sacred's power to protect us from violence.

Christ's teachings and Passion reveal the victim's role. Through his death that is powerless to reconcile the community, Christ reveals the structural matrix of all myths. This returns people to their own responsibility for violence.[39]

According to Girard, this revelation, its slow progression as well as it rejection, has gradually desacralized the West. For, while Christianity truly calls on people to renounce violence, it clearly has not been heard.

Christianity makes impossible, because it makes ineffective, any sacrificial resolution of the crisis, and at the same time destroys the institution of sacrifice, the pivot point of primitive religion, which, by purging the community of its violence, strengthens prohibitions and breathes new life into obligations. Thus, since, over time, Christianity can only weaken and then lead to the abandon of traditional prohibitions and obligations, it clearly establishes the conditions for the emergence of scarcity.

However, this does not yet provide us with the positive value of scarcity, which creates its ambivalence and makes it the foundation of the modern world. In order to obtain it, we have to go back to the sacrificial crisis as it occurs in an advanced cultural era. We need only look at the ambivalence of the sacred, at the identity between violence and the sacred. It suffices to return to the description of the mimetic crisis that can be found in the first three chapters of *Violence and the Sacred*.

The description, which centers on the institution of sacrifice, shows how sacred violence—in other words, the purifying violence of sacrifice—can degenerate into impure, contagious violence, into destructive, disorganizing violence. It shows how sacrifice, celebration, and ritual, instead of purging the community of its violence, can go wrong, contaminating all the participants and setting off a cycle of vengeance and countervengeance that gradually but inexorably spreads. The description shows how, once the crisis has been unleashed, all of the barriers designed to stop it are inevitably used to its advantage. It shows how obligations and prohibitions themselves become the driving forces behind the crisis, just as efforts made to smother a fire can end up feeding it.

It is easy to see how the sacred can turn into violence. No principle distinguishes the sacred from the violence that precedes it. The action that restores order is always just another murder. However, the identity between violence and the sacred is not only in principle and theoretical: it is practical and can be observed in real situations. This is true and obvious with respect to sacrifice so long as it remains human sacrifice, and it is still true when the choice of sacrificial victim shifts to animals. It is also true of ritual because ritual is a mimetic obligation: the actions that led to the end of the crisis have to be reenacted. Even though religion isolates the actions on the ritual stage, which is defined by specific times and locations, the ritual still threatens to slide from the theatrical to the real, and to drag all time and all places into the mimetic frenzy.

The identity of violence and the sacred is also true of prohibitions, which are antimimetic brakes designed to prevent us from repeating the actions that began and then hastened the unfolding of the crisis. Indeed, while prohibitions have a negative aspect, they also have a positive face, which is made up of the obligations from which they are indistinguishable. The prohibition on spilling human blood is also the obligation to take revenge for blood that has been spilled. The prohibition against leaving a member of the community to his or her fate is equivalent to the obligation to defend that person. The prohibition against committing adultery is inseparable from the obligation to kill those who commit adultery. It suffices to look at both aspects of prohibitions at once to see how antimimetic brakes impose on people the duty to commit violence, which can rekindle the crisis.

The identity of violence and the sacred, which is inscribed socially in the religious and cultural organization of primitive societies, facilitates the return to the original violence. It explains why the sacred participates in the crisis through the very efforts it employs to contain it.

The sacred is also the segmented organization of primitive societies, which structure social space in concentric circles, each defining degrees of solidarity and forms of reciprocity. The family, kinship, subclan, and clan ties that warp the perfect circularity of the rings of solidarity centered on the household and home produce the delicate architectures of different forms of solidarity.

The crisis has to be defined as the possible but uncertain result of breaking a prohibition. In order to unleash the crisis, it suffices that the transgression cannot be erased through usual means, such as ritual compensation, sacrifice, or reprisal limited to a single punitive expedition. Transgression supposes the strength of prohibitions, all prohibitions, including the one that has been transgressed. It thus supposes that obligations are strong. Under these circumstances, the slightest affront can initially turn all or much of the community into two opposing blocs. Solidarity obligations, which cross the barriers of time and space, can always draw people who were in no way concerned by the initial affront into a broader conflict. The social structures that create solidarity in the community in normal times petrify it in time of crisis. The crisis is propagated along the links of prohibitions and obligations: they are its paths, they convey the violence. At the beginning, the adversaries are not alone. From the beginning, they are already supported by a whole network of solidarity. From the beginning, each member of the network can be included, and is already partially included, in the conflict.

Thus, in times of crisis, violence flows along the paths of traditional prohibitions and obligations—in other words, it is along this dry wood that the murderous fury spreads throughout the entire community. Doubles occur at the end of the crisis, when it reaches its climax. At that point, violence has short-circuited the usual social structures. Under the dangerously high voltage of the end of the crisis, the prohibitions and obligations that initially conveyed the violence shatter. Differences disappear and everyone opposes everyone. Overintegration of violence erases the differences that, at the beginning, propelled the violence along the paths of solidarity obligations.

The sacred defines an order with respect to which no one can take any distance. Solidarity obligations, which solidify the community into opposing blocs, manifest this order in regard to which no one can be exterior. It is this absence of distance, the impossibility of exteriority, that makes it possible for mimetism to spiral out of control. Scarcity, in contrast, establishes an order in which all are external to all. Scarcity is the exteriority of members of society.

In order to make clear the difference between scarcity and the crisis at its climax, we can return to what we have already said about doubles. (If the adversaries' reciprocity and the doubles' identity come back to haunt them, the antagonists dig in their heels and reject that truth while trying to differentiate from each other, illogically, through the violence that makes them the same. Doubles never really possess knowledge of their identicalness: otherwise they would no longer oppose each other. The knowledge has to be defined as belonging to outside observers: those who are not involved in the dispute, are foreign to the adversaries, and thus are not at risk of being contaminated by the violence.) In primitive societies, it is impossible to be sufficiently outside the adversaries to be able to perceive the duplicity of doubles. From the beginning of the crisis, the rigidity of obligations already traps too many society members in the violent conflict.

The only way of escaping from such mortal solidarity is to reject obligations. However, such rejection of solidarity does not remove one from the circle of violence because such rejection is a transgression of a prohibition. The person who rejects solidarity is immediately sucked into the process of impure violence against which the other members of society are united through their solidarity obligations.

The sacred is entirely enclosed in this circle. From the beginning of the crisis, violence flows along the bonds of solidarity obligations just as fire runs along the beams that it consumes. However, it is impossible to reject such obligations without transgressing a prohibition—in other words, without joining the other side of the dispute and becoming fire oneself. At the end of the conflagration, the carbonized beams crumble away, and nothing remains but transgression.

There are not many ways out of this cycle, especially if it collapses only under the pressure of the climax of the crisis, and then immediately reforms around a new victim/god, who establishes new obligations and prohibitions. For there to be the exteriority necessary to perceive doubles, we have to suppose that the bonds that close the cycle all slowly weaken. In order for members of society to gain a sufficiently exterior viewpoint for them to perceive the identity of doubles, there has to be widespread attenuation of obligations and prohibitions such that failing in one's duty to demonstrate solidarity is no longer an immediate transgression. It is not necessary to think that such weakening happens in the same way everywhere in the network of obligations and prohibitions, or that sufficient distance occurs in all places at once. However, we have to suppose that the weakening is widespread. If it affected only one prohibition, distance would not result; there would be only a variation in the radius of the circle.

Christian Revelation provides the conditions for the emergence of scarcity because, over time, it leads to a general weakening of prohibitions and obligations.

The space inside the community that results from the weakening of obligations and prohibitions, and which, paradoxically, we have to call the exteriority of society members, is sufficient to define scarcity and guarantee its ambivalence—in other words, its ability to protect us from violence. First, it is important to note that the weakening of obligations and prohibitions does not correspond to a weakening of mimetism and the rivalries it causes. In fact, the opposite is true since it is the direct result of the failure of the sacred and the sacrificial to expel violence from the community.

While Christian Revelation provides the interior distance needed for the exteriority of society members, scarcity has to be defined, strictly speaking, as the mechanism through which intensification of rivalry fosters the gradual exteriorization of society members. The transformation of the sacred into scarcity occurs in complete mimetic blindness. For each individual whose actions exemplify it, and who unknowingly produces it, it is simply a case of following his or her desires, in other words, of becoming more and more a victim of mimetic fascination.

In order to understand how exacerbation of rivalries can produce peace and build a new economic order, we have only to see that weakening the sacrificial is equivalent to returning mimetism back to its original universality.

The sacred is entirely constructed on the basis of expulsion: expulsion of the surrogate victim at the point when the crisis is resolved, expulsion of bad mimetism and bad rivalries through prohibitions, expulsion of violence and tensions accumulated in the community through ritual and the sacrificial catharsis. The expulsions are also violent, and are based on mimesis, but, in their case, the violence is oriented toward order and peace. The crisis has to be defined as the return into the community of the violence and mimesis that were originally expelled. Violence and mimesis never have legitimate places inside the community, except in the general, abstract form of prohibitions and rites that govern the lives of community members. The return of mimesis to the concrete level of relations among people constitutes transgression. If a ritual does not succeed in rapidly expelling bad mimesis, it will give rise to a crisis.

The crisis spreads little by little, until it encompasses the whole community. It progresses mimetically, and its growth is that of mimesis. In this concrete sense, the universalization of mimesis occurs only at the peak of the crisis. The universalization of rivalries, the clash of all against all, results from the inclusion of all in the conflict. Such universalization never really occurs except at that point, in the frenzy of differences, and then almost immediately turns into the absolute difference that separates the community from the victim/god and expels the harmful violence and mimesis by putting the victim to death.

Scarcity takes mimesis back to its original universality. Scarcity is a kind of upside-down crisis that begins, little by little, with the universal return of mimesis. Christian Revelation transforms the sacred into a boat with holes and leaks everywhere. Scarcity begins with universalization of mimetic rivalries. This is why, whereas the crisis has a beginning that is transgression, a development in the form of contagion, and an end that is expulsion and sudden fall, scarcity has to be seen as the radical impossibility of beginning. The general weakening of prohibitions and obligations means that everyone has already begun.

In the space that attenuation of the sacrificial introduces between transgression of a prohibition and the duty to fulfill solidarity obligations, the refusal to fulfill obligations does not need to be motivated by the vision of the duplicity of doubles. I do not need to perceive rivals' identicalness to reject my obligations to one of them or to refuse to take sides. The simple fact that I am fascinated by someone else will be just as good. For that to be true of all, it suffices that exteriority be universal, and it is, for it is the attenuation of general, universal norms and rules. Thus, exacerbation of each individual rivalry exteriorizes members of society.

Now, if the trend toward exteriorizing members of society is the very trend by which each is fascinated by Others, it is clear that distance grows in proportion to intensification of rivalry. It follows that the most intense rivalries become external in relation to the general trend toward externality. They thus stand out as if they were located, so to speak, on a stage that makes the adversaries' identity all the more obvious. The result is that such rivalries lose their value and such adversaries are alienated from the community. Intensification of rivalries reduces the chances of convergence and the catastrophic imploding frenzy.[40]

Once given this law, which is the very structure and social mechanism of scarcity, the chances of gradual convergence and frenzied implosion become more or less zero. Indeed, even if isolated and isolating rivalries gradually reduce the differences between adversaries and lead to the disappearance of the objects that originally motivated the rivalries, and therefore facilitate lateral shifts of antagonists that would, in other circumstances, lead to convergence on a single victim, it is evident that no convergence will occur if the lateral shifts are universal. The catastrophic frenzy requires an original imbalance in movements in the direction of one antagonist. If mimesis's power grows with the number of people converging, the intensification of rivalry that results from every beginning of convergence will immediately isolate the rivalry. Once the law of exteriority is stated, any imbalance against an antagonist makes manifest the duplicity of the doubles and immediately reestablishes the stability of the structure.

In these conditions, it is clear that the most intense forms of rivalry will quickly come to be seen as shameful. The growing distance created by exacerbation of mimetic conflicts will make rivalries more underground, more hidden as they grow.

The necessary internalization of rivalries defines the interior/exterior relation as constitutive of the social institution of scarcity. The exteriority of members of society is the circular internal-external relationship. The internal aspect is made of the exacerbation and dissimulation of one's own mimetic rivalries. It is the movement by which each individual becomes more deeply fascinated by fascination. The external aspect is the distance acquired with respect to others, the perception of the duplicity of doubles in the case of others. Since the two movements are the same, just as closing in on oneself is also distance acquired with respect to others, it is certain that dissimulating one's rivalries does not reduce the distance separating one from other members of society. It in no way alters the reciprocal alienation of members of society. However, while dissimulation does not reduce the space between members of society, it does optimize each individual's capacity for action in the intracommunal space of exteriority.

In effect, in the solidarity space of primitive societies, where growing rivalries increasingly converge, rivals gain advantage in making their action and rivalry public, since they will experience the mimetic contagion and frenzy as a rallying to their cause. In contrast, in the exteriority of scarcity, in which intensification of rivalries isolates antagonists and cuts them off from the community, making such action public condemns the rivals to using only their own strength. In such conditions, dissimulation will be the absolute rule of all exacerbated rivalry.

Nonetheless, in order to achieve his or her ends, each rival will look to other people for support. Yet the ability to gain strength and rally others to the cause is proportional to one's degree of compliance with the categorical imperative of dissimulation.

It follows that the adversaries' relations with others, who have to be defined as third parties since exteriority prevents them from becoming the rivals' doubles, will tend to become manipulative. The dissimulation rule requires that third parties be used in an undertaking, the stakes of which they are ignorant. Scarcity thus spontaneously entails that both adversaries reduce third parties to instruments. The great associations engendered by exacerbation of mimetic conflicts will thus take the shape of instrumental rationality.

The internal/external relation explains why scarcity and instrumental rationality coincide. However, it also explains another special characteristic of mimetic phenomena in the modern world: the relative absence of violence with which they occur, despite intensification of rivalry. Since intensification of rivalry supposes dissimulation, open violence will rapidly receive a negative value in society because it is an excessively obvious sign and mark of exacerbation of mimetic conflict. Increasingly, open violence will be excluded from specific rivalries. However, there is yet another reason why there is relative absence of violence in the modern world: given that mimesis's strength grows with the number of people who converge, it is certain that for each individual the threshold of murderous fury will be reached more quickly in a system in which exacerbation of rivalries polarizes and makes people converge than in a system where it isolates and creates distance between them. Scarcity, the exteriority of members of society, raises the relative threshold of murderous frenzy.

The internal/external relation is also the archetype of what is known as bad faith. It is structurally deceptive because it requires being blind with respect to oneself but lucid about others, dissimulating one's own desire and rivalries but denouncing the interests and conflicts of others. Each sees the duplicity of others at the very moment that he or she becomes a double. The observer's exteriority is inseparable from his or her interiority. Moreover, since exteriority is universal, to be an outside observer is always to be the outside observer of an outside observer. It is thus to always be in a position to see in others the alternation of criteria, the use of double standards depending on whether it is applied to one's own conflicts or those of others. It is to be in a position to construct a concept of bad faith and to use it to explain behavior. Yet denunciation of bad faith cannot be distinguished from bad faith itself. Both are given in the universality of exteriority, in the fact that it is the exacerbation of one's own rivalries that sheds light on that of others. Lucidity grows apace with blindness.

Scarcity is the sweeping abandonment of the solidarity obligations that used to unite the community. However, they are abandoned little by little. There is no great rupture, and the process is accomplished in complete mimetic blindness. When Christian Revelation weakened sacrifice, it broke the tie between rejection of an obligation and transgression of a prohibition. Once this minimal space is created, each individual is gradually enclosed in the fascination that fascinates him or her, which produces the exteriority of members of society. The original universality of mimesis ensures that the shift toward exteriority continues.

This mimetic model of social organization "with no catastrophic outbursts of violence and no resolution of any kind" explains the ambivalence of scarcity, its dual beneficial and harmful value, which is nothing other than the ambivalence of mimetic desire itself. This model, with "no resolution of any kind," is simply the pure evolution of modern individualism, the gradual externalization and alienation of members of society.

It manages to provide a consistent explanation of the genesis of many typically modern phenomena, such as the internal/external relation, the spread of instrumental rationality, and bad faith. However, the model also explains the relative absence of violence in which modern mimetic phenomena occur, despite exacerbation of rivalries. It shows us how scarcity protects us from our own violence and how the growing exteriority of members of society eliminates any risk of convergence because exteriority is the exacerbation of rivalries. The model explains both how violence and scarcity are identical and how this violence can protect us from the essential violence of the mimetic crisis. Finally, it explains why scarcity cannot occur in primitive societies.

Since this mimetic model is produced by abandoning the solidarity obligations that used to unite the community, it leads to the emergence in society of a set of goods and resources such that the needs and desires of all cannot be met. Moreover, since the obligations were antimimetic brakes, the model makes scarcity even worse. Contrary to the liberal tradition, which believes that limited resources make desires converge on the same objects, our hypothesis shows that the mimetic convergence of desires on the same objects creates the parsimony of nature. Only this mimetic explanation of scarcity can explain its aporia, the fact that scarcity never corresponds to a real quantity of available goods and resources.

Attentive readers will already be protesting! The whole preceding demonstration was designed to prove that scarcity can protect us from our own violence, and to show how a stable order can coincide with ever-increasing rivalries, but it was based on the idea that the exteriority of members of society causes rivalries to diverge as they exacerbate. It seems that I am trying to construct both scarcity and the aporia of scarcity using the convergence of mimetic desire on the same objects. Is there not a contradiction? Does not mimetic theory force us to choose between these two scarcities, between the one that protects us from violence by making conflicts diverge and the one that establishes the parsimony of nature by making desires converge? Does not the fact that these two scarcities cannot be joined prove the failure of the mimetic explanation of the parsimony of nature?

In reality, only the exteriority of members of society makes it possible to mimetically construct the parsimony of nature. Scarcity is impossible in primitive societies: its emergence is equivalent to destruction of the social space, the sacrificial crisis, violence. However, the mimetic frenzy, which culminates in the loss of all prohibitions and obligations, does not produce scarcity, but conflict and violence, pure and simple. Jean-Pierre Dupuy has pointed out that in Girard's writing, the object is always unique and has no equivalent, whereas economic objects, merchandise, are always equivalent to something.[41] The concept of scarcity, as it is construed and constructed in economic science as the set of available goods and resources, supposes that anything can be exchanged for anything else, even cannons for butter.[42] Girard, however, says: "Place a certain number of identical toys in a room with the same number of children; there is every chance that the toys will not be distributed without quarrels."[43] In this sentence, the important word is of course "identical." Not only is the object of mimetic desire unique and without equivalent, but convergence of desires manages to create a difference among identical objects. In other words, out of nothing. At the limit, mimesis creates the object.

It would be hard to imagine a more complete opposition than that between objects of desire and economic objects, since mimetic desire entails that it is impossible to exchange objects, even if they are identical, while economics supposes that any objects can be exchanged, no matter what their differences.

Defined in this way, mimetic convergence certainly cannot create scarcity, a set of goods and resources such that the needs of all cannot be met. It can only engender conflict and violence. In primitive societies, this is always how things appear because mimesis causes two or more antagonists to converge on a single object. In such cases, the convergence makes it logically impossible for a set of objects to emerge, even if they are identical.

Clearly, under the mimetic hypothesis, the problem of how we can obtain scarcity, defined as the convergence of desires on the same, universally equivalent objects, is identical to the problem of how abandoning anti-mimetic brakes can prevent the catastrophic frenzy, since it is the gradual convergence that creates and sanctions the uniqueness and singularity of the object. The answer to both problems is the same. Scarcity takes mimesis back to its original universality.

Scarcity makes rivalries diverge, but it also makes desires converge. These two processes are the same. It makes rivalries diverge by making desires converge. Why and how does it do this if desire is imitative? Because, from the beginning, it takes mimesis back to its original universality since there are as many mediators as there are members of society. Free reign of mimesis will pair people into individual, reciprocal rivalries. The universality of these pairings ensures the exteriority of members of society. Indeed, if universality is given from the beginning, there is no reason to think that people will want to change mediators. On the contrary. This is because, on the one hand, the identicalness of the rivals is not given from the beginning, but manufactured as the conflict exacerbates. On the other hand, each individual sees the conflict as rooted in a belief in the perfect uniqueness of his or her mediator and of the desired object. Since the belief is true of all, no one has any interest in changing mediators. In other words, no one has any reason to get involved in other people's conflicts, to trade the "absolutely unique" for something with no special features.

This means that scarcity institutes from the beginning a plurality of rivalries and thus a number of mediated objects, a set. As soon as it becomes possible to reject the obligations that force us to get involved in other people's conflicts, without at the same time violating a prohibition—in other words, without being forced to integrate that same conflict from the other side—it is clear that, if such obligations still have some strength, all will try to reject them. All will thus soon discover the reciprocity of other people's adversarial relations. However, since that discovery results from the exacerbation of each individual's rivalries, no one will see the mimetic truth of desire because that would be equivalent to demystifying one's own conflicts.

In this situation of exteriority, in which there are many objects, conflict-causing convergence, personal dissatisfaction, and the inability to see the mimetic truth of desire, each individual will conclude that the set of objects available is insufficient. This immediately leads to the conclusion that insufficiency is the driving force behind and cause of conflict. We thus find spontaneous generation of the economic concept of scarcity and its ambivalence, as well as the horizon and insuperable illusion of economic growth that accompanies it. We also find the aporia of scarcity, the fact that the constraint of scarcity is not determined by the real quantity of available goods and resources. Since scarcity is constructed by the mimetic convergence of desires in the mimetic divergence of multiple rivalries, the real quantity of available goods and resources has no impact on it. The mimetic play of converging desires and diverging rivalries makes it possible to construct a set of goods and resources that is insufficient to meet the needs and desires of all, and yet is independent of the real quantity of goods and resources, in other words, no matter what the size of the set.

As rivalries grow, the antagonists become more and more alike. This occurs at the same speed as their exteriority increases. The growing identity of the doubles occurs in the external space through the pure play of mimesis's universality. It universally facilitates antagonists' lateral shifts. As more lateral shifts occur, the unique nature of the mediated objects is destroyed, and a set of perfectly equivalent objects is created. In a mimetic system where there are many diverging rivalries, lateral shifts of antagonists and models will, depending on their frequency and speed, create rates of equivalence among objects. The set will be composed of interchangeable, exchangeable objects. To outside observers, the many rivalries will look like an equivalency of objects. The exterior nature of members of society means that everyone is an outside observer.

The reason the economic order succeeds in establishing rates of equivalence among all objects, which is something that never occurs in primitive societies, is not because the objects have changed, but because the order transforms relations among people. In a given situation of exteriority, the play of reciprocal substitution of antagonists, rivals, and models destroys the uniqueness of objects and makes it possible to establish equivalencies between them. The interchangeable nature of models/rivals, the fact that virtually anyone can become the mediator for anyone else, establishes the perfect equivalency of objects. It is the development of what, in *Deceit, Desire and the Novel*, Girard calls "internal mediation" that engenders exchange values.[44]

We have now come back to the starting point: ambivalent, aporietic scarcity and the liberal tradition. This brings us back to economic reality, which builds on the parsimony of nature and ensures public order by referring everyone back to private interest. However, we have returned armed with a mimetic model that enables us to speak coherently about the political value of the economic system and to see why and how economic logic has gradually invaded all areas of public and private life.

We now have to return to Earth and test our hypothesis. We began by employing a few concepts to reveal the ambivalence and aporia of scarcity, and to show the moral and political value of the economic system. Now, we have to put flesh on the bones of our mimetic skeleton and describe how it determines the shapes life takes. We need to test our hypothesis against the liberal tradition and the contemporary social transformations that have accompanied its evolution. This alone will tell us whether the internal consistency of the system is an indication of its historical and social truth.

Violence and Economics

In the following pages, I show how the ambivalence of scarcity structures certain texts in the liberal tradition into a single, consistent, continuous text, despite the various authors and their personal positions. We will also see that these texts promoted social transformations that were later achieved. Thinkers in the liberal tradition wrote the eleventh thesis on Feuerbach long before Marx. Like Marx, they believed that philosophers had only interpreted the world in various ways and that the point was to change it. For better or worse, they have succeeded.

Next, I show how these social transformations have established scarcity—in other words, as far as people are concerned, misery. I argue that they have instituted scarcity by destroying traditional solidarity obligations and by separating and creating an opposition between the social and individual consequences of human actions. We will see that these social changes are those that, according to the brilliant study by Karl Polanyi,[45] have transformed society into a market society.

I will not perform an empirical verification of the mimetic model that we are proposing. This study is too short for such a vast undertaking. My goal is instead to counter the false impression that inevitably follows when the model is presented: the elimination of certain problems. My goal is to show, beyond scarcity's extraordinary power to protect us from our violence, the fact that scarcity and violence are the same thing. This involves showing how the disjunction between individual and social consequences of actions is a mutilation of life that is by far more terrible, insidious, and complete than any of the voluntary mutilations performed in the rituals of strange savages. My purpose is to show that, unlike the sacred, which banishes and expels violence, scarcity excludes people because it is the contemporaneity of violence and a stable order. Despite what we think, since each thinks only about himself or herself, what threatens us and causes problems is not that economic order is ineffective in protecting us from violence. The danger lies in its very efficiency, for its efficiency is nothing more than violence.

The point is to show what political philosophy has always been teaching: "Eliminating violence is not, in itself, a political action. All that is needed is greater violence. However, simple power relations do not constitute human relations. There is no politics or human society unless freedom is what is at stake in those relations."[46]

The social institution of scarcity is the social institution of misery. In homage to Charles Péguy's brilliance, we have to say "misery" instead of "poverty," and return to the distinction between misery and poverty that, in his eyes, separates economics from morals.

Scarcity is constructed by rejecting traditional solidarity obligations, by abandoning each to his or her fate. The general exteriorizing trend that characterizes scarcity is accomplished by aggravating individual rivalries. The exteriority of members of society is equivalent to the possibility for anyone to become a sacrificial victim, in the sense in which Girard defines this term in his explanation of human sacrifice in *Violence and the Sacred*.

Indeed, insofar as sacrifice tries to reproduce the resolution of the crisis by immolating the surrogate victim, its initial form is often human sacrifice. Given the solidarity obligations that structure primitive communities, primitive religions have a hard time identifying a category of individuals who can be sacrificed—that is, individuals who can be immolated, if needed, in order to purge the community of its violence, but without running the risk of setting off the cycle of vengeance and countervengeance. Otherwise, purifying violence could turn into impure violence. This is a dangerous, sensitive classification problem because the victim has to be close enough to the community for the collective transfer of violence to be effective. Girard shows that the difference between victims that can be sacrificed and those that cannot is defined by the degree of membership in the society. More specifically, between "these [ritual] victims and the community a crucial social link is missing, so they can be exposed to violence without fear of reprisal. Their death does not automatically entail an act of vengeance."[47]

The exteriority of members of society transforms all individuals into potential sacrificial victims. By abandoning traditional obligations, we ensure that no one will avenge those who are the objects of our violence. Yet despite this abandonment, violence does not spread. The growing distance separating people devalues the social worth of open violence between antagonists. Moreover, the threshold of violence and murderous frenzy is reached less quickly in a system with diverging rivalries. Finally there is an institution that prevents the appearance of open violence among rivals: the justice system—in other words, the certainty that the law will avenge the first murder once and for all.

We know that, in *Violence and the Sacred*, Girard insists on the effectiveness of the justice system in protecting us from violence. Girard says that the justice system "serves to deflect the menace of vengeance. The system does not suppress vengeance; rather, it effectively limits it to a single act of reprisal, enacted by a sovereign authority specializing in this particular function. The decisions of the judiciary are invariably presented as the final word on vengeance."[48] Surprised readers will wonder whether we have not made a mistake, whether we have not created an artificial problem that Girard has already solved. Does not the justice system alone suffice to explain the West's ability to avoid the most virulent forms of essential violence?

I do not think so. Sociology teaches us that a justice system cannot repress violence efficiently unless that violence is sporadic, isolated, and marginal. History shows that as soon as violence spreads even a little bit, the justice system is impotent to curb it. Yet in any system where rivalries polarize and lead to convergence, violence will spread rapidly in the absence of traditional restraints. Moreover, it is easy to see that the justice system can function efficiently only if minimum exteriority among society members is already given. Otherwise, traditional solidarity obligations will distort its operation. Every network of solidarity will try to turn the justice system to its advantage, and since every officer of the system is linked to a network, he or she will try to make each judicial decision lean in favor of his or her traditional obligations. In short, the state will never be able to acquire a power—in other words, an exteriority that is sufficient—to have the last word on vengeance. It is scarcity, the exteriority of society members, that is clearly the condition of possibility for the justice system, at least in the universal form that such systems have in modern societies.

Relative absence of open violence among antagonists does not mean that violence has disappeared. Indeed, the nonoccurrence of brutal force between rivals is, paradoxically, only the quasi-automatic result of universal exacerbation of rivalry. Violence does not disappear, but shifts and changes, and, above all, becomes institutionalized in a very special way. Since it cannot be expressed directly, violence transforms into envy, jealousy, impotent hatred: it turns into resentment. It silently destroys rivals, from the inside. However, it also shifts and expresses itself in new ways.

In primitive religion, the fact that violence and the sacred are one and the same was obvious everywhere, including in the obligations that forced people to discharge violent duties whether or not such duties were chosen or desired. In contrast, in social organizations based on scarcity, the abandonment of solidarity obligations institutionalizes the identity of violence and scarcity by transforming all individuals into potential sacrificial victims.

We know that scarcity involves neither frenzy nor resolution of any kind. It is manufactured out of thousands of small, independent, isolating rivalries, each exterior to the others, occurring in relative absence of violence, but so externalizing when violence appears that others who are not involved in the conflict turn away rather than become polarized. Yet while scarcity involves no resolution, the many rivalries that constitute it have many repeated temporary endings (and a few definitive ones) that are more or less serious and dangerous for those involved. There are outcomes that involve defeat of one of the doubles and a victory for the Other. Since solidarity obligations no longer count and each is abandoned to his or her fate, scarcity is purely and simply equivalent to "might is right." Since all have avoided their solidarity obligations because they were fascinated by something else, they will turn away from the loser, just as they refused to get involved in the conflict that preceded his or her defeat. Scarcity is the social construction of indifference to the misfortunes of others.

Scarcity also does not involve an institution like sacrifice, which has the function of periodically purging the community of violence. Since the law of dissimulation requires us to inhibit violence, the community always contains a large amount of unreleased violence and unappeased resentment. Clearly, psychological transfer mechanisms will encourage us to abandon others to their fates. The propensity of violence to employ substitute victims will find the victims of others highly convenient.

The transformation of every individual into a potential sacrificial victim means that the victims of specific outcomes of the many rivalries that compose scarcity will indeed be sacrificed. It will not be by the open violence of their enemies, but by the indifference of others, who will abandon them to their fates.

Surprisingly, but logically, it will not be the relations between rivals, in other words, doubles, that will be the most violent, but the relations of each individual with all the others—in other words, relations between third parties. They will involve the greatest subjective violence because the blows of our enemies seem more understandable to us and those that we inflict on them more justified than the indifference and disdain of third parties watching our fall without flinching and perhaps even without seeing it, when all they had to do to save us was lift a finger. They will also involve the greatest objective violence because, in a world where relations between rivals are characterized by relative absence of open violence, the conclusion of conflicts engendered by the mimesis of appropriation will consist more often in material loss than in physical violence. This is when the refusal of third parties to help and support the loser will confirm his or her failure and transform it into a real death sentence. Their indifference is much more deadly than the blows delivered by the winner.

The more intense violence that characterizes relations among third parties creates the social invisibility of violence. Third parties do not see the violence that they do to one another. There are a number of reasons for this: while the violence is not involuntary, it is also not the result of a clear-cut intention with respect to those who suffer it. It results from simple indifference. Third parties are too busy with other things to worry about those around them or simply those in need. The violence is faceless; we do it with our eyes closed, and we refuse to see.

Another thing that fosters the invisibility of violence and the little open violence in even the most intense rivalries is that, since exacerbation of conflict inhibits violence, people do not see what harm can result from simple indifference when even a clear intention to destroy the Other is powerless. The crucial condition for people to become aware of the veritable violence of their indifference is necessarily absent. The indifference of third parties upholds the law that might is right. For losers to be able to show third parties the violence of the indifference that they suffer, solidarity obligations would have to play in their favor and those close to them would have to give them enough strength to make themselves heard. However, in such circumstances there would never have been indifference. In fact, there might have been a mimetic crisis.

The invisibility of violence does not entail the invisibility of its consequences. Third parties are violent to one another in ways that they do not see and that are, paradoxically, the worst forms of violence that occur inside the system. We see around us the emergence of impoverished, miserable, excluded people to whom we have done nothing and never wished harm. Sacrificed victims appear, and we are the ones who have sacrificed them, by our indifference. Yet they are not generally our own victims. Since we do not see the link between our actions and these consequences, between our indifference and the poor, this strange phenomenon puzzles us.

The positions of double and third party are universal and simultaneous. They do not designate exclusive points in space. They define the relations that we all have with certain people. In fact, the double/third party distinction maps perfectly onto the interior/exterior relation. In other words, each of us always plays both roles at once, and indifference is only the flip side of the fascinated desire of doubles. The positions of conqueror and conquered are also universal, but not simultaneous. Moreover, the transformation of a conquered person into a sacrificed victim is often determined by contingent, exogenous factors, such as social milieu, the size of the failure, and so forth.

The universality of double/third party relations and the potential universality of winner/loser positions turn indifference and rejection of traditional obligations into laws. They are independent of anyone's will or choice. For some social groups, the rivalries engendered by the mimesis of appropriation will turn into a struggle for survival, pure and simple: if they lose, they lose everything. No one will help them. For them, indifference and rejection of solidarity obligations become an absolute imperative, a new negative obligation to which universal rejection of traditional obligations condemns them. They are obliged to play the indifference and fascination game, just as primitive people were forced into the cycle of violence and vengeance.

Naturally, people will consider the violence that they do one another—in other words, their reciprocal indifference—to fall into the category of needs and necessity. This is because the indifference of all transforms each individual's indifference into an obligation. Since rivalries focus on objects and those who are sacrificed are abandoned to their fates, we spontaneously believe that it is the real quantity of goods and resources that determines the convergence of desires and brutality of human relations. Since no one sees that indifference manufactures sacrificed victims, because the violence is invisible, all think that a lack of objects is the cause of the fate of the unfortunate.

The relationship between doubles means that each desires to own more objects, or at least an object that he or she does not yet own. Each double thus imagines that only pursuing and intensifying the relationship will solve the problem of misery because each thinks this will reduce scarcity. However, since this relationship is the other side of the murderous indifference that manufactures the poor, scarcity is produced by the very actions that we imagine will reduce it. The paradox that so struck observers at the beginning of the industrial age, namely, that the wealth of nations and number of poor increase in parallel, is thus solved.

This time, the infernal machine is working: the social apparatus for producing misery is ready to operate. The disjunction between the social and individual consequences of people's actions is almost total. The abandonment of solidarity obligations prevents polarization of conflict and produces misery. The other side of this abandonment is both conflict and a means of subsistence. The individual consequences of mimetic desire and exacerbation of rivalries are envy, jealousy, impotent hatred, and resentment. However, the consequences also include real or desired wealth and abundance. The social consequence of mimetic desire and exacerbation of rivalries is protection against the catastrophic frenzy and open violence. However, the social consequence is also misery and abandonment of every individual to his or her fate. Finally, because all believe that conflict and misery stem from scarcity, all throw themselves blindly into seeking self-interest, believing that they are thereby curing the evil, but in fact they are only perpetuating and increasing it.

The reciprocal violence that people inflict on one another is instituted under the auspices of scarcity, the parsimony of nature, necessity, and needs. Paradoxically, this reciprocal violence is always established in order to eliminate violence and misery. The multifarious nature of mimetic rivalry and the disjunction between individual and social consequences of people's actions construct an independent entity that is external to their simple relations: the parsimony of nature that transcends the social body and founds the cultural order. Scarcity is the means that people use to defend themselves against their violence and to project it outside of themselves.

The action that constructs scarcity also creates what has to be called the unreality of evil. Scarcity is above all characteristic of relations among third parties, while the unreality of evil is symptomatic of relations between doubles. The unreality of evil is the belief that evil does not do harm, and just as scarcity is related to the development of economic thought, the unreality of evil cannot be dissociated from the development of intention-based, internal morals.

The unreality of evil is the certainty that envy, jealousy, desire, unbridled acquisitiveness, and resentment do not cause any evil. (How incredibly naive! Everyone does that!) This certainty is supported by the idea that these vices create wealth, that they are economic incentives. It is also the idea that actions are to be judged by the intent, good or bad, and that only intent, independent of the contingent consequences, determines the value of an action.

At first sight, the two things seem to be in contradiction. One attitude confines evil to intent, while the other sees nothing bad in the evil feelings that gnaw away at the heart, so long as the consequences are good. Yet, clearly, these are only two aspects of the same disjunction between social and individual consequences of actions. Since intent inevitably stumbles over this disjunction, since the greatest violence occurs in relations among third parties, since everyone sees evil but no one sees violence, the social effectiveness of traditional morals crumbles. Moral sentiments thus seem to be unfounded or enclosed in the nonspace of interiority. One way or another, human evil becomes unreal. Either it flows from the parsimony of nature or it is reduced to that inconsequential nonsense: bad intentions. One way or another, scarcity, the disjunction between individual and social consequences, sanctions people's irresponsibility.

◆ ◆ ◆

Péguy thought that poverty and misery were located on two sides of a line separating economics from morals. "The economic boundary is the one beneath which economic life is not ensured and above which economic life is ensured."[49] The social institution of scarcity is the social institution of misery because abandoning traditional solidarity obligations makes the line ubiquitous. In the social world of scarcity, the boundary is everywhere, and everyone is always in danger of crossing it, no matter how many goods and resources are really available, because the guarantee of life does not depend on material wealth or on the number of objects one owns, but on the relationships that one has with others. Material and psychological misery always comes in the shape of exclusion and solitude. It always takes the form of victims sacrificed to the indifference of third parties. Those who have been sacrificed are fascinated and indifferent, yet not indifferent to the indifference of others. Misery always takes this contradictory, weak form, which is the other side of the falsehood of absolute autonomy that the fascinated doubles loudly proclaim. If, in rich societies, the white plague of suicide replaces the microbial epidemics and famine that accompany material misery, it is because violence's identity with scarcity is not just in principle and theoretical. Irresponsible indifference kills invisibly.

Of course, there are true differences. Between the exclusion of an unfortunate condemned to precarious, hopeless survival and the failure and solitude of someone whose wealth guarantees that he or she could, if he or she wished, return to the world of reciprocal fascination of doubles, which we call life, there is just as great a distance as that separating human from animal sacrifice. Yet this difference does not separate economics from morals, and it warps our understanding of the phenomenon. We are immediately brought back to the illusion of scarcity, the illusion that the real quantity of goods and resources is the problem that inevitably produces miserable, unhappy people. If we do not see that scarcity takes the same form, no matter what the quantity of goods and resources, we will expose ourselves, like Sisyphus, to pushing a boulder up a hill for all eternity. We will expose ourselves to seeing misery reborn out of our very attempt to eliminate it. One can *only imagine* that Sisyphus was happy![50]

The moral change in character and life, which is the indelible mark of misery, is universal in the social institution of scarcity. This is because it marks the disjunction between the individual and social consequences of people's actions. We have to see that the exteriority of members of society is the shape of the social world established by scarcity in order to understand how the economic order manufactures misery in the strict sense, how it has spread a new form of poverty that is unknown and impossible in primitive societies.

The exteriority of members of society is the abandonment of traditional solidarity obligations. For this reason, the social institution of scarcity establishes a special form of destitution, which combines material poverty with being left to one's fate. This combination of material need and socially sanctioned personal impotence is what has to be called misery. Misery never occurs in primitive societies because solidarity obligations prevent it from existing, just as they make scarcity impossible. While primitive peoples are often poor, terribly poor, they do not experience the change in character and life that is produced by misery. It is the exteriority of members of society that guarantees that the destitute have the sad privilege of being abandoned to their fates, and it is exteriority, exteriority alone, that guarantees that they are destitute because the exteriority of members of society constructs a set of goods and resources that is insufficient to meet the needs of all.

The disjunction between the social and individual consequences of actions is the ubiquity of the boundary below which material life is not guaranteed. The exteriority of members of society condemns the entire economic system in the eyes of ethics and political philosophy because misery, in the constant form of exclusion no matter what goods and resources are available, is inseparable from misery in its specific form of insufficient goods. We cannot provide for the needs of the poor without reducing society members' exteriority—in other words, the exteriority that produces scarcity.

There are real differences. There are people who are miserable, who have lost and been beaten once and for all, beings who have been confined forever to the position of third party, people who cannot return to the struggle between doubles. There are social categories that carry the pure weight of the violence of scarcity, for whom the stable order of the economic world is only violence, for whom ambivalent scarcity has only its negative value of lack and need. There are excluded third parties who are like the reification and personification of the exteriority of society members, even though those third parties may have among themselves the relations of doubles.

To say this is to say that the social institution of scarcity entails, at the macrosociological level of relations between groups, the same form of exclusion and exteriority that defines relations between persons at the microsociological level. However, since the positions of double and third party are universal and simultaneous, since the positions of winner and loser are universal and successive, we can and must ask how such broad, stable social lines are drawn and determined.

The universal return of mimesis, characteristic of scarcity, does not take place in an undetermined vacuum. It is the imperceptible degeneration of a hierarchical system. Mimetic rivalries arise everywhere at once, but within each hierarchical level and not between levels. For them to arise between levels, the entire system would have to have collapsed already, but it is only the evolution of rivalries that destroys it.

So long as the differences between people remain real, provide some power, the rivalries between the hierarchical levels will remain few, and we can establish as an absolute rule that the most powerful will never try to rival with their inferiors. So long as the differences remain real, for, as they fade away, this rule will be overturned, or, more precisely, no longer work. Anyone will be able to become the mediator of anyone else. Exacerbation of rivalries leads people to choose mimetic models in accordance with those models' ability to create obstacles for them. It is an absolute rule that subordinates will try to rival their superiors, at least if the social distance between them is not too big.

The positions of double and third party are universal and simultaneous. Each is both the double of his or her rival and an exterior third party with respect to others, those with whom he or she is not in conflict. Yet despite this universality of positions, there are people who have to be socially defined as third parties. If rivalries occur within hierarchical levels and if exacerbation of rivalry gradually pushes them upward, the social third parties of each hierarchical level will be lower-ranking people. If each has a relationship as a double with his or her rival and as a third party with others, each individual's social third parties are those with whom he or she does not risk coming into conflict owing to their social inferiority. The absolute social third parties are those who are at the very bottom of the social scale. Of course, this does not prevent them from having relationships as doubles among themselves. Indeed, it is because such social third parties have abandoned their traditional solidarity obligations to one another that they are miserable and not poor.

Those who have greatest need of help from others and who depend most on traditional solidarity obligations are the special victims of scarcity, those who have been most completely sacrificed to the indifference of others. Clearly, they will not let go of their obligations easily, or at least not the ones they depend on, and they will remind others, insofar as they can, of their duties to them. The social institution of scarcity will then be noticeable in history as the action by which social doubles expel from the social body third parties who then have the right to nothing but indifference. This thus institutes misery, in the proper sense of the conjunction of material destitution and abandonment to one's fate.

The exclusion of those who are miserable is not the result of a mimetic conflict in which the poor and those who reject them from the social body are rivals properly speaking—in other words, mimetic doubles. The greatest violence and institutionalized violence occur between third parties, at the level of major social divisions, between doubles and those who can be called social third parties. The exacerbation of rivalries between doubles leads to exclusion of third parties. If third parties' resistance leads to a struggle between them and doubles, the dispute will be seen by the doubles as an activity that is instrumental in the struggle between themselves. This is important. In the modern world, the greatest violence is always committed under the banner of instrumental rationality, and is perceived by those who suffer it as exploitation. This analysis is accurate, and the violence it describes is very real. However, we have to look beyond it, to the omnipresence of mimesis that produces, like the flip side of specific fascinations, the dehumanization of the world, the cold, indifferent rationalization of human relations.

The Liberal Tradition

Nothing is more difficult to read than a text we know well, nothing more invisible than our own thoughts. We encounter them without seeing them, and we blindly agree to what we have always known. The texts in the liberal tradition speak so well a language that we all know that it is difficult to imagine what light could be shined on them to return them to their original strangeness. Their nonsense and contradictions are so much a part of our common sense that we risk understanding them without grasping that they phrase our everyday ideas and the thoughts to which we always return. However, we have to make an attempt and start again from the beginning, from the ambivalent scarcity that is the foundation.

There is a text by Hume that seems to have been tailored to this purpose.

It is found in *An Inquiry Concerning the Principles of Morals*, and includes most of Part I of Section III, which is devoted to justice.[51]

Hume seeks to show that social utility is the only origin of justice and justice's unique source of merit. For this, he proceeds by elimination, and imagines four situations in which, because it would be useless, justice would not exist. This method allows him to define the conditions or "circumstances of justice," namely, moderate scarcity and self-love, in other words, self-interest.

The first situation:

> Let us suppose that nature has bestowed on the human race such profuse *abundance* of all *external* conveniences, that, without any uncertainty in the event, without any care or industry on our part, every individual finds himself fully provided with whatever his most voracious appetites can want, or luxurious imagination wish or desire. . . .
>
> It seems evident that, in such a happy state, every other social virtue would flourish, and receive tenfold increase; but the cautious, jealous virtue of justice would never once have been dreamed of.[52]

What would be the point in establishing property rights in a situation where there can be no conflict, where when another takes something of mine, all I have to do is reach out with my hand to grasp a good of equal value? Why divide goods up if every individual has more than he or she needs? Since it would be perfectly useless, justice would never have found a place in the catalog of virtues.

The second situation: Suppose this time that every individual's needs remain the same, but that his or her

> mind is so enlarged, and so replete with friendship and generosity, that every man has the utmost tenderness for every man, and feels no more concern for his own interest than for that of his fellows; it seems evident, that the use of justice would, in this case, be suspended by such an extensive benevolence, nor would the divisions and barriers of property and obligation have ever been thought of. . . . And the whole human race would form only one family; where all would lie in common, and be used freely, without regard to property; but cautiously too, with as entire regard to the

necessities of each individual, as if our own interests were most intimately concerned.[53]

Hume goes on to imagine situations in which the above suppositions are inversed and also taken to extremes.

The third situation:

> Suppose a society to fall into such want of all common necessaries, that the utmost frugality and industry cannot preserve the greater number from perishing, and the whole from extreme misery; it will readily, I believe, be admitted, that the strict laws of justice are suspended, in such a pressing emergency, and give place to the stronger motives of necessity and self-preservation. . . . The use and tendency of that virtue [justice] is to procure happiness and security, by preserving order in society. But where the society is ready to perish from extreme necessity, no greater evil can be dreaded from violence and injustice.[54]

The fourth situation:

> Suppose likewise, that it should be a virtuous man's fate to fall into the society of ruffians, remote from the protection of laws and government; what conduct must he embrace in that melancholy situation? He sees such a desperate rapaciousness prevail; such a disregard to equity, such contempt of order, such stupid blindness to future consequences, as must immediately have the most tragical conclusion, and must terminate in destruction to the greater number, and in a total dissolution of society to the rest. . . . And his particular regard to justice being no longer of use to his own safety or that of others, he must consult the dictates of self-preservation alone, without concern for those who no longer merit his care and attention.[55]

Finally, Hume concludes:

> The common situation of society is a medium amidst all these extremes. We are naturally partial to ourselves, and to our friends; but are capable of learning the advantage resulting from a more equitable conduct. Few enjoyments are given us from the open and liberal hand of nature; but by

art, labor, and industry, we can extract them in great abundance. Hence the ideas of property become necessary in all civil society: Hence justice derives its usefulness to the public: And hence alone arises its merit and moral obligation."[56]

Hume also adds that the poets have not been mistaken in this respect. In their descriptions of the golden age, they associate abundance of material goods with great goodness of soul. "This *poetical* fiction of the *golden age*, is in some respects of a piece with the *philosophical* fiction of the *state of nature* . . . a state of mutual war and violence, attended with the most extreme necessity."[57] The empiricist weighs the poetical and philosophical fictions, and finally opts for moderate scarcity.

This text is perfect. Everything is there. Scarcity is the foundation; it is the condition for justice, but only in its moderate form, as a middle between extremes. The positive value of scarcity is there: through art and industry, we can extract great abundance. However, the negative value of scarcity also colors the text: when society is about to perish from extreme necessity, no greater evil can be feared from violence and injustice. Extreme scarcity corresponds to disruption of the social fabric under the pressure of needs. Moreover, both values of scarcity are kept separate through the distinction between extreme and moderate scarcity, between need and scarcity.

In Hume's text, scarcity is not ambivalent, or at least it is not openly ambivalent: the distinction between extreme and moderate scarcity prevents this. Yet if we managed to find, for example, that need is the foundation of social order, the need that annuls the strict laws of justice, we would then discover the ambivalence of scarcity in Hume's text. This ambivalence would be a contradiction that would destroy any possibility of differentiating justice, whose goal is to procure happiness and security by maintaining order in society, from violence and injustice, from which no greater evil can be feared. This is precisely what we are going to find.

Moreover, the conditions of justice are also those of economics: moderate scarcity and self-interest. The third situation implies that justice is subject to economics, or at least to the struggle against scarcity, since such extreme emergency annuls the strict laws of justice. The social utility of justice is the unique origin of its moral value and its only source of merit. Yet it is possible to show that, although the goal and tendency of this virtue is to create happiness and security by maintaining order in society, the social utility of justice is inseparable from the fight against scarcity.

This is because, first, all the specific laws that shape justice and determine property tend toward the goal of fostering economic activities. Hume says:

> Who sees not, for instance, that whatever is produced or improved by a man's art or industry ought, for ever, to be secured to him, in order to give encouragement to such *useful* habits and accomplishments? That the property ought also to descend to children and relations, for the same *useful* purpose? That it may be alienated by consent, in order to beget that commerce and intercourse, which is so *beneficial* to human society? And that all contracts and promises ought carefully to be fulfilled, in order to secure mutual trust and confidence, by which the general *interest* of mankind is so much promoted?[58]

Second, the social utility that determines the moral and political value of actions is the struggle against scarcity. In Hume's text, the struggle involves things that are improved by and benefit from art, care, and industry, thanks to which we can extract great abundance from nature.

> Luxury, or a refinement on the pleasures and conveniences of life, had long been supposed the source of every corruption in government, and the immediate cause of faction, sedition, civil wars, and the total loss of liberty. It was, therefore, universally regarded as a vice, and was an object of declamation to all satirists; and severe moralists. Those, who prove, or attempt to prove, that such refinements rather tend to the increase of industry, civility, and arts regulate anew our *moral* as well as *political* sentiments, and represent, as laudable or innocent, what had formerly been regarded as pernicious and blameable.[59]

Is it possible to be more clear? Yes, of course.

> Giving alms to common beggars is naturally praised; because it seems to carry relief to the distressed and indigent: but when we observe the encouragement thence arising to idleness and debauchery, we regard that species of charity rather as a weakness than a virtue.[60]

Thus, Hume's justice, and all of its moral and political worth, is subject to, and absorbed by, economics. The texts that I have just cited show again how the two senses of scarcity are used to establish the moral value specific to the economic system. The distinction between moderate and extreme scarcity gives scarcity two contradictory values, which are, according to Hume, indispensable to establishing the economic system and justice as a social ideal.

Trapped as it is between violent necessity and peaceful abundance, justice shares a little of each, and acquires a degree of legitimate ambivalence in accordance with the logic of the text. Its ambivalence is legitimate in relation to the illegitimate ambivalence of extreme scarcity. Thus, we can and must find ambivalence in justice: it is both beneficial and harmful, both useful and pernicious.

In appendix 3 of the *Inquiry*, entitled "Some Farther Considerations with Regard to Justice," Hume delivers the secret of the normal ambivalence of justice.

> The social virtues of humanity and benevolence exert their influence immediately by a direct tendency or instinct, which chiefly keeps in view the simple object, moving the affections, and comprehends not any scheme or system, nor the consequences resulting from the concurrence, imitation or example of others. A parent flies to the relief of his child; transported by that natural sympathy which actuates him and which affords no leisure to reflect on the sentiments or conduct of the rest of mankind in like circumstances. . . . In all these cases, the social passions have in view a single individual object and pursue the safety or happiness alone of the Person, loved and esteemed. . . .
>
> The case is not the same with the social virtues of justice and fidelity. . . . The benefit resulting from them is not the consequence of every individual single act; but arises from the whole scheme or system, concurred in by the whole, or the greater part of the society. General peace and order are the attendants of justice or a general abstinence from the possessions of others; but a particular regard to the particular right of one individual citizen may frequently, considered in itself, be productive of pernicious consequences. The result of the individual acts is here often directly opposite to that of the

whole system of actions; and the former may be extremely hurtful, while the latter is, to the highest degree, advantageous.[61]

Justice is a strange virtue that can contradict itself. The specific result of a specific court decision can be harmful and evil, but obedience to law and application of general rules benefit the whole society. Can we say that justice is a lesser evil in a world where perfect goodness cannot prevail? In any case, we cannot avoid the specific contradiction that we find here, namely, that justice is sometimes unjust when delivering justice. This is because what is at stake, independent of the number of acts of justice that have unjust consequences, is the possibility that specific actions can enter into contradiction with the final outcome of the entire system of action.

In Hume's work, the normal ambivalence of justice takes the form of dissociation of the immediate and the social consequences of acts of justice. This means that the structure of society is such that the combination of individual actions can contradict their individual outcomes. The consequences of the system can be in opposition to the consequences of the actions that compose it. This is the logical structure that underpins the strange injustice of justice in Hume, and thereby makes it less scandalous.

Hume indeed says that "the particular consequences of a particular act of justice may be harmful to the public as well as to individuals."[62] This is important because the contradiction takes place between the specific and the general, between immediate consequences and social consequences. A specific act of justice that has a pernicious public consequence nonetheless can have beneficial social consequences because it is part of a system of action. It is at this level that the disjunction occurs, and this is why Hume's ambivalent justice supposes a disjunction between the individual consequences, in the sense of the immediate consequences, and the social consequences of people's actions.

Hume's justice, born of scarcity, possesses the disjunctive form of the economic system. By separating and opposing the social and immediate consequences of actions, it ensures order. This disjunctive form is the shape of its specific, legitimate, normal ambivalence, which flows from moderate scarcity, halfway between violent necessity and peaceful abundance.[63]

What more could we ask? Hume is a tailor-made author. Is this pure

chance? Everything is in his text, or almost. There is only one thing missing
... the essential, the centerpiece, the non-disjunctive ambivalence of scarcity,
the ambivalence of extreme scarcity, of the necessity that founds the social
order. We already have the negative value of necessity; now we just need its
positive value. This should not be too difficult. In fact, the attentive reader
has already seen the influence of this obliging necessity because, if by giving
beggars money I encourage them to be lazy and debauched, it is, I suppose,
because moderate scarcity does not provide them with much incentive to
engage in art and industry.

It is thus possible to pull Hume's text apart, in cold blood so to speak,
in order to find beneficial necessity. However, if we do it in cold blood, this
exercise might not be very conclusive because demonstrations sometimes
lose, owing to obviousness, what criticism gains from virtuosity. I thus propose to do better, and invite the liberal tradition to read itself. After all, a
tradition is a text that is read and reread, that is reworked again and again,
and that gradually becomes deeper so that it becomes visible to itself, little
by little. I propose to read Hume based on other texts in the liberal tradition,
or, if you prefer, based on other versions of the text that we have just found
in Hume. The tradition will make us sure of our reading of Hume, and our
reading of Hume will make us sure of the unity of the tradition.

Our journey will be both long and short. Short in terms of texts, and
long in terms of time: over a century, which is a relatively lengthy period
for the liberal tradition. We will be short in terms of texts because we will
use few authors and writings. In fact, I am seeking something specific:
beneficial necessity in Hume. And I am taking the shortest path to get there.
However, the underlying hypothesis is that, once the text is completed and
the ambivalence of scarcity rediscovered, we will see it in all authors in the
liberal tradition; their writings all involve the play of the ambivalent, violent
scarcity that founds the social order. This applies to all authors in the liberal
tradition, plus Marx.

◆　◆　◆

More than forty years before Hume's *Inquiry Concerning the Principles of
Morals* appeared, a certain Bernard Mandeville, physician by trade, pub-
lished in London a cheerful but provocative little pamphlet in verse, entitled
The Fable of the Bees.[64] Thanks to the controversy it raised, the pamphlet

became a voluminous treatise. To the original poem, Mandeville added an *Enquiry into the Origin of Moral Virtue*, a series of twenty-two long *Remarks*, identified by letters, intended to explain the meaning of certain verses, and then an *Essay on Charity and Charity-Schools*, a *Search into the Nature of Society* and a *Vindication of the Book*. Finally, in a second volume, he published six *Dialogues* in which two gentlemen discuss the contents of the first volume of *The Fable of the Bees*. The poem appeared for the first time in 1705, and the second volume in 1728.

The *Fable of the Bees* contains the following thesis: envy, jealousy, greed, vanity, desire for unlimited gain, luxury, pride, and all related vices are the solid foundations of a wealthy, powerful society and a stable, well-policed state. Goodness, generosity, humility, and charity, in contrast, lead straight to poverty and disorder, impotence and indigence. Thus, the latent violence in vanity, greed, envy, pride, and desire for wealth, far from creating conflict and dividing people, unites them with the strong chains of wealth and economic growth. The subtitle of Mandeville's treatise is significant: *Private Vices, Publick Benefits*.

Mandeville is thus one of the authors who, according to Hume, renew our moral and political sentiments, and he does so in the same sense as Hume. Moreover, it is clear that public utility is the only source from which private vices gain the merit that they are accorded. However, the similarity between Hume and Mandeville does not stop there. Private vices, public benefits, the happy array of rivalries, and the latent violence that promotes economic activity in *The Fable of the Bees* and thereby builds a strong, well-policed nation, requires a disjunction between the immediate consequences and the social outcome of actions.

Mandeville explains that he

> will now without loss of time proceed with my Argument in artless dull Simplicity, and demonstrate the gross Error of those, who imagine that the social Virtues and the amiable Qualities that are praise-worthy in us, are equally beneficial to the Publick as they are to the Individual Persons that are possess'd of them, and that the means of thriving and whatever conduces to the Welfare and real Happiness of private Families must have the same Effect upon the whole Society. This I confess I have labour'd for all along.[65]

This has been Mandeville's purpose all along: to demonstrate that the happiness, order, and stability of a well-policed society do not come from simply adding together private good deeds, from the accumulation of individual virtues. His goal has been to show the social ineffectiveness of traditional morals and the fact that exacerbation of private rivalries makes nations great, that envy and vanity are ministers of industry (remark N, p. 134), that bandits are no different from industrious workers (remark B, p. 61), that the worst among us does something for the common good (remark G, p. 86). He has been trying to show that there is a disjunction between the individual consequences of actions and their social consequences, that the outcome of a system of action can contradict the results of the actions that comprise it. Of Mandeville's envy, jealousy, vanity, and greed, we can say what Hume said about justice and fidelity: "the benefit, resulting from them, is not the consequence of every individual single act; but arises from the whole scheme or system, concurred in by the whole, or the greater part of the society."[66]

The same social structure, in which the result of the system of action can be in contradiction with the results of the actions comprising it, supports Hume's justice and Mandeville's beneficial "vices." Private vices, public benefits: the ambivalence of desires is obvious in Mandeville's writing. Just as Hume's justice is both just and unjust, Mandeville's desires are both private vices and social advantages. However, while in Hume's theory justice's normal ambivalence is legitimated by the middle position of moderate scarcity, which is a condition for justice and is located halfway between violent necessity and peaceful abundance, there is nothing to attenuate the scandal of the disjunction in Mandeville's work. This was the source of the general indignation that the good doctor's thesis raised.

However, Mandeville's rivalry-based approach has the advantage of shedding brighter light on the noncumulative nature of such a system: it cannot be obtained by adding together the specific actions that comprise it. If the social consequences of actions can come into contradiction with their immediate consequences, the general outcome of the system of action is not the sum of individual results. Mandeville's text shows this very well: it is not by amassing kindly virtues conducive to family harmony that we obtain the nation's happiness. It is also not by accumulating private vices that we obtain social order. There has to be a disjunction between the immediate consequences and the social consequences of actions. The noncumulative nature of the system of action produces the idea of a whole that is other or more than the simple sum of its parts.

It is clear that it is in this more abstract form that Mandeville's thesis was passed on to posterity, or perhaps we should say thanks to this form. In fact, the idea that a whole is greater than the sum of its parts is very frequent in modern thought, and all of sociology uses it to explain why society cannot be reduced to the sum of its members—in other words, it is employed to constitute society as an object. This idea raises the problems engendered by the ambivalence of desires in Mandeville's theory. The ambivalence supposes a dual contradictory value in the same relation. Yet if the whole is greater than the sum of its parts, then from the individual to the general, from the parts to the whole, there is a qualitative jump, a veritable passage from one world to another, in which the same laws do not apply. This shows why in Mandeville's work the desires—private vices, public benefits—do not produce the same effects at the individual and social levels. They do not obey the same laws.

As impressive as the idea that a whole could be more than the sum of its parts may be, and despite the many useful findings that it produces in many areas of knowledge, it is clear that here it explains nothing at all, and that it is in fact the thing that needs explaining. We need only read Mandeville through Hume in order to see this. The noncumulative nature of the system of action is present in Hume, but the middle position of moderate scarcity hides its strangeness. As soon as we notice it, Hume's argument crumbles. The noncumulative nature of individual actions is an inexplicable privilege bestowed upon the situation of moderate scarcity. Extreme scarcity engenders violence and the destruction of the social body through the pure addition of individual actions. The peace flowing from abundance is also a result of pure addition. If we grant that, in both extreme situations, the results of the actions that comprise the system of action can contradict the outcome of the system as a whole, nothing remains of Hume's demonstration.

To say that this special privilege is equivalent to the institution of society is to say nothing at all because this is specifically what is in question: why is there society rather than nothing at all?

However, let us grant for a moment the legitimacy of the ambivalence of desires in Mandeville, and of the ambivalence of justice in Hume. Let us grant them as if they were consistent, integral parts of the texts' logic, as if they did not contradict the arguments, even though the two authors do not quite manage to explain them.

We begin, thus, in Mandeville, with the disjunction between the social and immediate consequences of actions. We could say that this is the fundamental intuition of all of his work. Compared with Hume, the text is written backward. We thus have to return to the foundation of society to see if we can find the positive value of extreme scarcity, which is what is lacking to complete our text.

How does Mandeville explain the origin of society? In *The Fable of the Bees*, we find a *Search into the Nature of Society* and an *Enquiry into the Origin of Moral Virtue*, in which Mandeville presents the exact content of his theory in greater detail.

Mandeville writes: "the Sociableness of Man arises only from these Two things, *viz*. The multiplicity of his Desires, and the continual Opposition he meets with in his Endeavors to gratify them. The Obstacles I speak of relate either to our own Frame, or the Globe we inhabit."[67] Mandeville insists on this over and over again. The multiplicity of human desires is what establishes human sociability, and everything that increases the number and strength of human desires fosters the building of wealthy, powerful, well-policed societies. The more numerous and varied people's desires are, the easier it will be to bring them together into large, strong societies. This is why private virtues, such as charity, generosity, kindness, anything that asks people to renounce or reduce even a few of their desires, are not public virtues: they are not beneficial and do not promote social order. This is also why private vices, such as greed, vanity, envy, and desire for unlimited gain, are public goods. They reproduce and maintain the original multiplicity of desires.

Clearly, this situation is very close to that which establishes the economic system, except that Mandeville insists more on the multiplicity of desires than on scarcity of resources. Mandeville, like Hume, also mentions in passing the possibility of a golden age in which people would be entirely satisfied and would lack nothing. He concludes that "it is impossible to name a Trade, Art, Science, Dignity or Employment that would not be superfluous in such a Blessed State."[68]

Attentive readers of *The Fable of the Bees* go from one surprise to the next. After having spent pages showing that the evil of private vices such as envy, jealousy, covetousness, and desire for unlimited gain is very small in comparison with the public benefits that they produce, Mandeville suddenly claims that, in certain very special cases, private vices are also public vices. Envy, mother of all wealth, suddenly undermines law and order, and risks destroying all of society. Just as day and night are opposites, harmful, destructive desires are the opposites of beneficial, constructive desires. There is no way of telling the difference between these two types of private vices, except for the fact that they do not affect the same people.

The evil private vices that Mandeville loathes to the same degree that he loves good vices are the private vices of poor people, the increase in desires among the rabble—for example, a servant's envy of his or her master. Rich people's envy, vanity, and greed are productive vices that give work to craftsmen and encourage businesspeople to strive to increase their profits. On the contrary, among the poor, envy, vanity and greed lead people to believe that they can bargain with their employers to determine their wages. Envy, vanity, and greed are both public and private vices among workers, and they whisper to workers that they can try to equal their masters. In this case, what are under attack are the very foundations of society, hierarchy and subordination. When private vices and multiplication of desires penetrate into the hearts of poor people, workers shun labor and servants refuse to obey. Soon everyone, rich and poor, is reduced to misery. The state is impoverished, and disregard for the law is added to the powerlessness of the police.

The contradiction is even more obvious. The following cheerful, orthodox remarks on the well-foundedness of our good qualities and the public utility of our private virtues are found in his *Essay on Charity and Charity Schools*. In the essay, Mandeville tries to show his contemporaries that the madness that has seized them, namely the plan to establish in (almost) every English parish a charity school in order to educate the children of the poor, is dangerous lunacy that threatens to destroy the nation. The contradiction is blatant because the good doctor's demonstration is based on the following reasoning: education will increase and diversify poor people's desires, suggest to vulgar commoners desires that they would not otherwise have, and thereby make them unfit for life in society, unable to assume the positions and roles that they must take in society. Their roles are to perform the "Abundance of hard and dirty Labour [that] is to be done"[69] because the "whole Earth being Curs'd, and no Bread to be had but what we eat in the sweat of our Brows, vast Toil must be undergone before Man can provide himself with Necessaries for his Sustenance."[70]

We thus find that desires are truly ambivalent in Mandeville's work. The ambivalence is nondisjunctive: private vices are sometimes, as here, public vices, and sometimes public benefits, though what separates the two possibilities is not based on solid foundations. This is an illegitimate ambivalence, in which the multiplication and diversification of desires sometimes elevates people into powerful societies and vast Leviathans, and sometimes threaten to destroy order and subordination.

Interestingly, when Mandeville seeks to demonstrate the woes caused by humble workers' private desires and vices, he bases his arguments on the needs and large quantity of goods necessary for life in society. Even more interestingly, in order to cure poor people of their private vices and get them to work, Mandeville proposes to reduce them to the strictest possible necessity.

> When Men [the poor] shew such an extraordinary proclivity to Idleness and Pleasure, what reason have we to think that they would ever work unless they were oblig'd to it by immediate Necessity?[71]
>
> The absolute necessity all stand in for Victuals and Drink, and in cold Climates for Clothes and Lodging, makes them submit to any thing that can be bore with. If no body did Want no body would work; but the greatest Hardships are look'd upon as solid Pleasures, when they keep a Man from Starving.[72]

The *Fable of the Bees* is full of surprises. When the ambivalence of the foundation of social order appears in Mandeville, a beneficial necessity suddenly emerges, which transforms insolent, corrupt servants into honest workers. This positive necessity socializes the paupers while reducing the number and diversity of their desires. However, this necessity also attenuates the contradiction between the increase in desires that form the foundation of social order and the increase in desires that are dangerous to the nation. Indeed, this is an unsolvable aporia in Mandeville's work: necessity corresponds to no real quantity: "the more extensive their Knowledge is, the higher their Quality, and the greater their Possessions are, the more necessitous and helpless they are in their Nature."[73] This little sentence makes it possible to translate the increase in desires into needs, and the growth of wealth into extreme necessity. "As his Knowledge increases, his Desires are enlarge'd, and consequently his Wants and Appetites are multiplied."[74] From this it appears completely clear that necessity, and necessity alone, is the foundation of the social order and fashions strong Leviathans. This also shows that it is ambivalent, since necessity, and it alone, requires us to labor hard and long in order to subsist, and changes the private vices of the poor into public vices, just as the increase in needs changes the private vices of the rich into public benefits.

◆   ◆   ◆

We have not finished; the demonstration is not complete. It is true that we have found the positive value of necessity, the founding value of extreme scarcity, even though the meaning of this necessity slides to hide its contradictions, just as scarcity splits into extreme and moderate in order to dissimulate its ambivalence. We now have to read and reread the positive value of necessity until it brings us back to Hume and the foundation of society in his work.

Nondisjunctive, true ambivalence of desire corresponds to the emergence of beneficial necessity in Mandeville. Private vices reveal themselves to be sometimes public benefits and sometimes public evils. This is illegitimate, contradictory ambivalence, and an understandable consequence of the ambivalence of necessity, which is necessary but impossible to admit. We can thus predict that the extreme scarcity that founds society will also engender illegitimate, contradictory ambivalence in justice: nondisjunctive ambivalence in justice. If the social seat of this ambivalence turns out to be the same as that of the ambivalence of desire in Mandeville, it is obvious that we have additional confirmation of the unity of the text of the liberal tradition.

In Mandeville, the contradiction is found in his *Essay on Charity and Charity Schools*—in other words, in an essay that discusses poverty and social measures for helping the poor. Indeed, the liberal tradition and political economics are overflowing with texts on poverty and the poor. From the end of the eighteenth century to the beginning of the nineteenth century, England was plagued by poverty. From the beginning of the Industrial Revolution, poverty was the national tragedy in England, and the paradox that challenged the best minds of the richest, most powerful nation. The problem was not new, but it got only worse throughout the eighteenth century. From around 1780 to the 1830s, the problem of poverty was at the center of all private and public discussions, and all philosophical and economic debates.

Mandeville's text preceded by a little more than fifty years the major wave of the debate, which focused on the Poor Laws and continued until 1834, when they were reformed. The 1834 Reform Bill more than amended the law: it was primarily pure and simple abolition of assistance that used to be provided for poor people and indigents. Contributors to the debate included Bentham, Townsend, J. S. Mill, Malthus, and Ricardo—in short, the most illustrious representatives of the liberal tradition at the time.

Generally, the Poor Laws were criticized for encouraging sloth and for threatening the nation's prosperity by turning workers away from their duty. Theoretically, the laws were above criticism because, while they gave the poor subsidies, they also forced them to work. Of course, the laws had been poorly administered, and the clauses concerning poor people's work had not been enforced very well. However, bad management clearly could not explain everything, certainly not the growing number of poor people, the ineffectiveness of subsidies in relieving their misery, or the law's impotence with respect to forcing them to work. Something better had to be found.

Attacking the agents of justice, accusing them of incompetence and corruption, was pointless since that would have indicated that reforming that part of the administrative apparatus was the solution to the problem. Liberal thinkers wanted the law abrogated: they rejected the very principle of the law. They thus had to show the law's necessary uselessness.

There are not many solutions to such problems. The simplest and most obvious consists in showing that, in this specific case, the law is in contradiction with a higher law that establishes the legality of laws regulating political societies.

Thinkers in the liberal tradition would say that the Poor Laws encourage indigents to be lazy, and instill envy and jealousy in the hearts of the miserable. They impoverish the entire nation in their attempt to combat misery. But why?

Hunger, poverty, misery, and extreme scarcity are nothing more than remnants of nature in human societies. By trying to solve the problem of poverty, human laws have overstepped their jurisdiction. It is not surprising that their effects are in direct contradiction with their aims. The Poor Laws "proceed upon principles which border on absurdity, as professing to accomplish that which, in the very nature and constitution of the world, is impracticable."75

The Poor Laws are a form of illicit intervention by human justice in a domain where it does not belong, namely, nature and necessity, the natural laws of economics.76 The Poor Laws sabotage order because they try to change "the laws of nature which regulate property as well as all civil laws."77 The laws of civil society are based on the laws of nature, and the latter define a domain in which justice has no jurisdiction. Natural necessity is the foundation of the legality of political laws. "Economic society is subject to laws that are not human laws."78 Misery and poverty are manifestations within civil society of the persistence of natural necessity. Laws are powerless in that realm.

Now, remember Hume's third supposition: "Suppose a society to fall into such want of all common necessaries, . . . that the strict laws of justice are suspended."79 This is how Malthus, Ricardo, Bentham, and Townsend define the realm of the natural laws of trade and economics, in which any intervention by the legislator is a priori bad. This is because economic society is subject to laws that are not human.

Yet there is nothing to distinguish between areas where justice is always bad and those where it is good. Indeed, if the primary purpose of justice is to establish property laws and divide goods, it is difficult to see how the area it governs is different from that in which the natural laws of economics and trade apply. It is just as impossible to distinguish the bad envy of the poor from the good envy of the rich, or to assign to different parts of the social body the good justice that divides goods and establishes property laws and the bad justice that contravenes the natural laws of economics. It is in relation to the same things that justice is both beneficial and harmful.

Who cannot see that this place where the disjunction of consequences fades away, where justice acquires true ambivalence, is also where we find the founding necessity of the social body? Listen to Townsend:

Hunger will tame the fiercest animals, it will teach decency and civility, obedience and subjection, to the most brutish, the most obstinate, and the most perverse. . . . In general it is only hunger which can spur and goad them on to labor; yet our laws have said, they shall never hunger. The laws, it must be confessed, have likewise said that they shall be compelled to work. But then legal constraint is attended with too much trouble, violence, and noise; creates ill will, and never can be productive of good and acceptable service: whereas hunger is not only a peaceable, silent, unremitted pressure, but, as the most natural motive to industry and labor, it calls forth the most powerful exertions. . . . The slave must be compelled to work; but the freeman should be left to his own judgment and discretion; should be protected in the full enjoyment of his own, be it much or little; and punished when he invades his neighbor's property. By recurring to those base motives which influence the slave, and trusting only to compulsion, all the benefits of free service, both to the servant and to the master, must be lost.[80]

Townsend's text asserts the superior power of the pressure of hunger in comparison with the force of law. He had already noted, concerning the use of courts to force paupers to work, that the "appeal in this case to a magistrate is from a superior tribunal to the inferior, from the stronger to the weaker."[81] In this he was in agreement with the liberalism of Bentham, who, in his *Principles of the Civil Code*, wrote: "The force of the physical sanction being sufficient, the employment of the political sanction would be superfluous."[82] Furthermore, Townsend identifies suppression of the Poor Laws with the idea that "the freeman should be left to his own judgment and discretion."[83]

In order to force paupers and indigents to work, Townsend suggests nothing less than reproducing the foundation of civil society at their level. Townsend says that in order to teach ferocious beasts decency and civility, obedience and submission, in order to reintegrate poor people into civil society, in order to take them out of a veritable state of nature and get them to enter the social contract, we must and must only reproduce in the present day the original, atemporal institution of society.

By letting the laws of trade and economics take their course, Townsend and Bentham force, though do not constrain, poor people to comply with the social pact. The pressure involves no violence and comes from the exercise of reason because civil society and justice are natural to people. Evil flows from the fact that the Poor Laws prevent workers from seeing the natural, rational nature of political society. Townsend clearly saw that abolishing those laws would put the poor in a situation similar to that described by philosophers to explain the natural generation of society. Abrogating the Poor Laws would

reproduce the original conjunction of natural necessity and human rationality from which political society emerges.

The reason Bentham, Townsend, Ricardo, J. S. Mill, and Mandeville all
suggested reducing the poor to the most extreme necessity in order to cure
them of their private vices and incite them to work was because they knew
that contact with harsh reality would teach the miserable and the poor what
philosophers always keep in mind: the usefulness of laws and the "necessity
of justice to the support of society."[84]

Hume says,

> Had every man sufficient *sagacity* to perceive, at all times, the strong inter-
> est which binds him to the observance of justice and equity, and *strength
> of mind* sufficient to persevere in a steady adherence to a general and a
> distant interest, in opposition to the allurements of present pleasure and
> advantage, there had never, in that case, been any such thing as government
> or political society.[85]

Hunger, need and lack are the wisdom and strength of character of the poor,
but they are also the wisdom that led the first men to enter into the social
pact in accordance with the eternal standards of reason. According to Hume,

> If self-love, if benevolence be natural to man, if reason and forethought be
> also natural, then may the same epithet be applied to justice, order, fidelity,
> property, society. Men's inclination, their necessities, lead them to com-
> bine, their understanding and experience tell them that this combination
> is impossible where each governs himself by no rule and pays no respect
> to the possessions of others. And from these passions and reflections con-
> joined, as soon as we observe like passions and reflections in others, the
> sentiment of justice, throughout the ages, has infallibly and certainly had
> place, to some degree or other, in every individual of the human species.
> In so sagacious an animal, what necessarily arises from the exertion of his
> intellectual faculties may justly be esteemed natural.[86]
>
> Human nature cannot, by any means, subsist without the association
> of individuals; and that association never could have place were no regard
> paid to the laws of equity and justice.[87]

Our journey is now complete, the text is closed, the ambivalent necessity that annuls the strict laws of justice creates the association of individuals. Extreme scarcity makes justice inoperative, and excludes the poor from civil society, for it is extreme scarcity that is responsible for the law's impotence and poor people's disobedience. However, extreme scarcity alone is also what can bring them back into society. Necessity, and it alone, forces the poor to work, makes them disciplined and industrious. Necessity destroys what it has erected, and rebuilds anew what it has just torn down. It is ultimate power, the foundation of all laws and the cause of all violence.

Texts in the liberal tradition are secular legends that tell the story of the birth of godless societies. They are atheist myths that describe the institution of eternal, atemporal scarcity and the fall of primitive religion. They are riteless commemorations of the time when the exteriority of members of society prevailed against the sacred *religiare*; times without heroes, in which the parsimony of nature was responsible for human violence. In the end, small-minded private vices produce public misery in the name of abundance. Behind the calm reasoning of liberal philosophers hides terrible, terrifying violence achieved socially in indifference, in the name of abundance and under the sign of instrumental rationality.

The Social Institution

The social institution *of the text* of the liberal tradition does not mean that *that text* has been put into practice, realized in society, or used as a guide or model for social changes or transformations. *The text* of the liberal tradition has never been socially fulfilled. The social institution of *the text* of the liberal tradition means exactly the opposite. Some social transformations have established *that text* as a text. Rejection of traditional solidarity obligations revealed new social phenomena, which gave birth to *that text* as a set of possible meanings of those phenomena. The social institution of scarcity is the historical realization of the mimetic model described above in sections "Scarcity and the Mimetic Crisis" and "Violence and Economics." It is also this founding institution of the modern world that establishes *the text* of the liberal tradition.

The social institution of scarcity combines two things: *the text* of the liberal tradition and the object that it concerns, what we call economic and social facts. It produces these two things in parallel: *the text* and its object. It produces them in a way that makes them indivisible yet also eternally distanced from one another, and each one produces the other. This is a strange phenomenon: the social construction of reality or, if one prefers, the social construction of social reality. This social construction is what Lukács, like others, called reification: the transmutation of human activities into an entity that is foreign and exterior to people, into a set of objects subject to rational, universal laws that are independent of human will.[88]

Without reification, there is neither social reality nor economic and social facts. There is nothing surprising about this assertion because everyone knows that social facts are things (this is the price we have to pay to have social sciences) and that these things are governed by laws that escape human free will and of which the first is probably the law of scarcity. Goods are available to people in limited quantities and numbers.

Yet to construct something real, a reality, we need at least two things. We need information, knowledge, some thought, and also something else, something ineffable and indefinable, an irreducible residue that transcends thought, a stubborn unknown that constantly evades knowledge. In order to construct the real, we need knowledge and an unknowable X, an inconceivable but necessary noumenon that establishes the reality of phenomena. For centuries, philosophers have been seeking in vain to know its nature, and, paradoxically, to establish its reality.

This should be obvious. Take away knowledge, and you have nothing at all, especially not the real, of which we should know at least this: that it is. This is the minimum knowledge possible. Being is the emptiest concept, the concept that brings us no knowledge. Remove the irreducible, unknowable X, and you still do not obtain the real, but knowledge, discourse, the textual, idealism, reabsorption of the world into thought. Without the residue that transcends knowledge, the real loses its reality. It merges into thought to which it then becomes identical. The foreignness of the real to the thought that apprehends it is the indelible seal of its reality. Reality asserts itself as real through the way it escapes the knowledge that seeks it. It thus reveals itself to be something other than a pure product of the mind.

In order to construct reality, we need two things: knowledge and the unknown, knowledge and an irreducible residue. If either of the opposing extremes is removed, reality disappears. In order to produce social reality, we need these two things, and this is what is produced by our mimetic model of the social institution of scarcity: knowledge and the unknown, knowledge and some residue that this knowledge finds irreducible.

The text of the liberal tradition is the knowledge component of social reality. As such, it is constitutive of that reality. It is indivisible from the other component, the unknown that cannot be reduced to knowledge but that is also not in itself, alone, social reality, though it is the mark of its reality. Social reality results from these two things: *the text* of the liberal tradition and the unknown that cannot be reduced to that text. Yet while these two things are opposites, the known and the unknown, it is certain that this is a very special opposition since it is an opposition/collaboration that produces social reality. It is thus not possible to oppose the liberal tradition's *text* to the residue that cannot be reduced to it in the same way as we can oppose discourse on the social to the reality that it is supposed to describe. *The text* of the liberal tradition is not a discourse on the social, but the knowledge that is constitutive of the social. This is something completely different.

Concerning the knowledge that constitutes the real, the knowledge component of social reality, the classical question of truth in terms of correspondence between knowledge and reality obviously cannot be asked. Or at least it does not arise and cannot arise between knowledge and the social reality that it produces. Since the two things are indivisible, there can be no question of representation. Knowledge and the unknown produce each other reciprocally as the social reality, and they have no form outside of that reality, which they form together. They thus cannot be seen as opposites, as if they existed independently. They cannot be placed side by side to see how they differ. The distance that unites them is their reality itself.

The text of the liberal tradition, the continuous *text* above and beyond the various authors and their differences, *the text* that we reconstituted in chapter 6, is not something that all liberal economists have said, or even the sum of all their statements. The distinction between *the text* and what they have said may seem strange, but it is nonetheless rigorous.

The text of the liberal tradition, which we presented in the previous section, is entirely organized and structured around ambivalent scarcity, but Hume, Mandeville, and Townsend never read it, nor did any of those who have taken it to be true. The reason is simple. For each author, what shows and unveils the ambivalence of scarcity appears in the form of inconsistency or a contradiction with his or her general thesis. When we realize that these specific contradictions are not accidental mistakes or unmotivated disorder, but that they form a coherent whole, we discover *the text* of the liberal tradition and the ambivalence of scarcity that structures it.

We then become astonished witnesses to a strange event. The thesis of the ambivalence of scarcity is the consistent articulation of a series of contradictions, and their reduction and reference to an initial contradiction that establishes and explains them. However, the initial contradiction, the ambivalence of scarcity, and it alone, both explains the contradictions in each author's work and gives meaning to each author's thesis. In the above sections "Scarcity and Violence" and "The Liberal Tradition," I showed that the many proposals for economic organization of society find meaning by basing themselves on the two contradictory values of scarcity. Hence this proposition, which is certainly paradoxical, but I can do nothing about it: the ambivalence of scarcity is a contradiction that gives meaning.

It gives meaning in every sense. On the one hand, it gives meaning to each author's thesis. Thus, in Hume, the edifice is based on the two values of scarcity, which are introduced thanks to the concept of moderate scarcity. However, the ambivalence of scarcity also explains the contradiction expressed by the positive value given to necessity. This positive value undermines all of Hume's arguments because they are based on the distinction between the two values and on attributing only negative value to necessity, while giving moderate scarcity positive value. The ambivalence of scarcity creates the meaningful meaning and also, it might be said, the nonsensical meaning of the texts. We thus see that the meaning of the authors' consistency and that of their inconsistencies are the same, that consistency is possible only through this paradox: the presence/absence of the ambivalence of scarcity, and that inconsistencies are nothing other than the simple presence of ambivalent scarcity.

The text of the liberal tradition is this backdrop: the ambivalence of scarcity gives meaning to all the sense and nonsense of the liberal tradition, and forms of the ambivalence of scarcity are deployed in all texts of the liberal tradition. Clearly, liberal economists have neither seen nor read *this text*. They have believed that what they say is consistent. They have seen neither their inconsistencies nor a fortiori that the meaning and reason for those inconsistencies was the very thing that gave meaning to what they said. They have thus written the text of the liberal tradition without knowing it. From this flows the rigorous distinction between their statements, what they have seen and said, and *the text* of the liberal tradition, which they have unknowingly written, and yet which gives meaning to their statements.

I have now come back to my two earlier propositions. First, no one has ever tried to achieve *the text* socially for the excellent reason that no one has ever read it. Second, *the text* is not a discourse about the social. It does not portray social reality. It is not a model of society. On the contrary, it is the semantic framework that gives meaning to the different models of economic organization of society.

Now, if this is true *about the text* of the liberal tradition, things are very different when we come to various theses by liberal economists, which are, in both senses of the word, models of society. They are simultaneously types, abstract descriptions of nature and of the way societies operate, and models of society, theoretical ideals of social organization. Moreover, history shows[89] that such theoretical models have been implemented, that we have tried to achieve them socially. Furthermore, if we abstract from the imperfections of our knowledge, we all agree that our economic models describe social reality. In other words, they tend toward accuracy, subject to the restriction that social reality never equals what we say about it.

The following problem arises. If the discourse is inconsistent, on the one hand, and if, on the other hand, it has no meaning except through *the text* that establishes it and which is unknown to it, then how could this discourse be achieved in society? What does putting it into practice mean? In other words, since this new question is the same, if this discourse has no hold except through *the text* of the liberal tradition, from where does its strange ability to apprehend the real come?

When we say that our discourse on social reality does not equal that reality, we mean to say that, from the discourse to the real, there is no pure and simple identity relation or adequate representation. However, we also recognize that they are not totally unrelated, that the discourse is not pure nonsense with no grasp on what it is supposed to describe. Neither truth nor madness: between the discourse and the real there is the complex relationship of approximate apprehension, growing accuracy, subject to an irreducible residue, a stubborn unknown that foils theoretical predictions and resists manipulation.

The relationship between *the text* and the discourse is quite similar to this: neither identity nor, of course, absence of relationship. Moreover, the relationship between *the text* and the discourse is such that, no matter what is said, *the text* always contains an irreducible residue in relation to the statement, the other value of scarcity. Finally, this relationship makes it possible to understand the relative efficiency of the economic and social propositions of liberal thinkers and their necessary malfunctions. The ambivalence of scarcity establishes both the meanings and the contradictions of political economics.

My thesis is thus relatively simple. *The text* of the liberal tradition is the knowledge that constitutes the social reality, and the statements of liberal economists are a discourse on that reality, a social science, political economics, if you like. We have to reformulate this thesis immediately if we want to avoid a major misunderstanding. Rather than saying: "*the text* of the liberal tradition is the knowledge that constitutes the social reality," we have to say: "the knowledge that constitutes social reality is initially written as *a text* of the liberal tradition." However, it is also stated in other places and in other ways. It cannot be reduced to the liberal tradition, but it is especially noticeable when it is written as a continuous *text* through the diverging statements of liberal thinkers.

It now remains to demonstrate this, to find in a sequence of historical events the establishment of the mimetic model and the necessary emergence of *the text* of the liberal tradition.

◆ ◆ ◆

Scarcity has no beginning, neither start nor origin; no abrupt action marks its institution. On the one hand, this is because the new order that it establishes is only the imperceptible decline of the preceding order. On the other hand, it is because it is the universal return of mimesis. Nothing inaugurates what occurs everywhere at once. The historical demonstration thus has to solve this problem: Where is the beginning of what happens in the universal? How can we show the establishment of something that does not begin?

Our model provides an answer to this question. Despite the universality of the positions of doubles and third parties, the overall model defines areas.

It divides up the major social areas in which the positions of doubles and third parties, through the play of their universality and structural elements of the former system, acquire a degree of social specificity that makes it possible to identify them. The social institution of scarcity is then visible historically as the action by which doubles socially exclude third parties from the body social. The excluded parties then have the right only to disregard. This social arrangement is not first because it presupposes that obligations and prohibitions have been weakening. The positioning that it performs specifically supposes the universality of the double/third party positions, but as we will see, it nonetheless creates a set of goods and resources that is insufficient to meet the needs of all.

There is an excellent, particularly clear, even luminous example of such exclusion of third parties by doubles in the social and economic history of England. It was a strange event, a prelude to the Industrial Revolution, and a stage in the establishment of a market economy: the systematic destruction of the village communities inherited from the Middle Ages. This is a well-known fact. It was the enclosure movement, a vast undertaking to turn open fields and commons into lots and enclosed spaces that, in two waves, at the end of the fifteenth century and in the mid-nineteenth century, transformed both villagers' lives and the landscape of the English countryside.

Enclosures were a reworking of land ownership and involved reorganizing all parish land into new lots and redistributing those lots. In order to fully understand what was involved in the territorial reorganization, we have to keep in mind the earlier land ownership regime of lots and commons.[90]

English texts use two different series of terms to define types of property under the former land-use regime. On the one hand, we find "open fields" and "common fields," which were synonymous, and designated fields composed of small lots over which many different people had rights. Such fields were open and common because the various lots were enclosed by neither hedges nor fences. On the other hand, there were "common lands," "common wastes," and "common pastures," which referred to land that was shared.

Open fields were composed of pieces of land belonging to many different people. No property formed a continuous, undivided whole: parts of it were scattered here and there across the entire parish, randomly neighboring other pieces of land belonging to other people. Most often, lots were rectangular and measured around 200 meters long by 20 meters wide. They were separated by thin strips of grass. Sometimes the rectangles were further divided into two equal pieces. Furrows were plowed in the direction of the long side of the rectangle, and space was kept at each end to turn the plow. While the lots were often identical in size, the amount of land owned was often completely different. Some landowners had yardlands composed of around sixty lots, while others had barely half a lot. There were also different kinds of property titles: some people were yeomen or free farmers, others were copyholders, who had a kind of perpetual lease that gave them an unalienable right to earn a living from the land.

The primary feature of the open field system was the extreme division of land between landowners and the extravagant scattering of lots. A paradoxical consequence of such division into scattered lots, when taken to its greatest extreme, was that the only way the land could be tilled was according to shared rules. Since lots were scattered across the parish, landowners had to travel huge distances simply to check on their property. They had to cross their neighbors' lands, and their neighbors had to cross theirs. If everyone had tried to do as they wished, there would soon have been total confusion.

One farmer might decide to plant while neighbors might leave the surrounding lots fallow and send their animals there to pasture. Another might delay harvesting, preventing others who had finished harvesting from using their neighboring land as pasture. Yet another might decide to build fences, forcing neighbors to take huge detours in order to get to their land. From obstacles to damage, the division of land into tiny lots transformed personal initiatives into opportunities for conflict and sources of disorder.

Thus, all obeyed common, traditional rules. All of the farmable land in the parish was grouped into three (sometimes two, sometimes four) open fields in which planting rotated in accordance with a very ancient method. One field was planted with wheat or barley, the second with peas, oats, or beans, and the third would be left fallow. After a year, the field that had been left fallow would be planted again, the one that had produced its first harvest since being left fallow would be prepared to be seeded again, and the field that had produced for two years would be left fallow.

For a long time, farming was done in common, and each contributed according to his or her means: manure, seeds, plows, draft animals. However, in the eighteenth century, this method fell into disuse almost everywhere. Yet at the same time fertilization, plowing, sowing, and harvesting continued to be done in common across the whole parish. The lots, which were separated by thin strips of grass, remained perfectly distinct, and even where farming was done in common, the harvest from each lot was the unquestionable property of the lot's legal owner.

Once the harvest was finished, the fields formed a common pasture for large livestock, and all of the open lots became pasture where landowners sent their geese, pigs, and sheep to graze and forage together. Thus, between harvest and planting, the land remained undivided, and maintenance of each landowner's exclusive rights was pointless.

However, the open fields were only part of the land in a parish: they composed the private property. The rest of the land was the commons, which were communally owned, though not by all villagers equally. The commons were the shared property of the landowners only, at least as a general rule. According to custom, ownership of land in a parish gave one the right to have access to the commons. Use of the commons flowed from the customary links between landowners. After having farmed their land together, they used it in common as pasture. Their rights to access the open fields for pasture were in proportion to the amount of land they owned. Access to the commons was subject to the same system. It was in function of their property rights over the open fields that landowners could put their livestock to pasture on the commons. In this sense, the English system of commons maintained inequalities among villagers.

Sometimes, the right to have access to the commons was connected to a person rather than to property, and was thus a personal right independent of any landownership conditions. Indeed, the commons actually belonged to the lord, who had a kind of eminent right over the entire parish, and it was he who traditionally gave various individuals the right to use the commons. Such rights could also result from the fact that two neighboring parishes did not have clearly defined borders.

The commons remained undivided all year. They were not farmed and were not considered to be worth much. Yet peasants benefited from them in many ways. In addition to having the right to pasture their livestock on them, they had the right to cut wood to repair their homes if the commons included a forest or trees, the right to gather dead wood for heating, the right to catch fish if there was a river or pond, and the right to cut turf if there was a marsh.

Even when the commons were by law the property of landowners only, custom and usage generally authorized all the parish's inhabitants to access and use them. Access was set out in no law, but flowed from age-old usage. The commons thus rendered many services to the poorest, most underprivileged members of the community, who were often also the most numerous: farm workers, people involved in cottage industries, and all those who did not own land.

Generally, anyone occupying a house in the parish was authorized to put two or three animals to pasture on the commons. This was a major advantage for those whose entire fortune consisted of only a cow, a pig, and a few chickens. Poor weavers also used the commons to spread out their fabric after dying or bleaching. The homeless built humble shelters on the commons with materials they found there. In some places, it was the custom that if from sundown to sunrise a person succeeded in building a house and if at dawn there was smoke coming from the chimney, he or she could then live in it without paying anything to anyone.[91] Finally, the right to gather turf and dead wood extended to all inhabitants of the parish.

Thus, thanks to the flexibility of the way they were used, the commons were highly useful to nonlandowners. They made it possible for an entire population to survive thanks to a precarious balance between a subsistence economy and poorly paid work. Access to the commons was vital to those who had no legal rights to it and in fact acquired the least advantages from it.

Yet we do not have to spend much time pondering to see that the ancestral way of using the land was much more than that: above all, it was not simply a way of organizing land. It was like a material precipitate of the community itself. Even when many customs had been forgotten or abandoned, the system of open fields and commons, simply by existing, ensured the survival of the village community. Thanks to the commons, on which they often lived and to which they always had access, the poorest, outsiders, and indigents had a safe haven on Earth and, at the same time, found places within the community. The commons were like a material embodiment of the solidarity ties that united the village community. Their presence sufficed to ensure that they were used exactly as they were. In order to prevent the needy from using the commons, a form of policing would have been required that villages could not afford. Moreover, the arrangement was advantageous for everyone. Small landowners had nothing to lose by authorizing the farm workers whom they hired to use the commons. Since they were unable to pay them enough to live on their salaries alone, access to the commons, even though it was by tacit agreement among landowners and farm workers, was like an indispensable clause in their contract. It was necessary to all. It ensured that landowners had access to a labor supply that they needed.

The question thus arises: how and why was such a good balance—and an apparently relatively stable system—destroyed? How, why, and by whom? Small landowners and farm workers did not benefit in any way from its elimination.

Let us go back to enclosures: what were they? A reorganization of the land ownership system. In fact, this involved two things: parceling and enclosing. Parceling meant combining into a single property held by only one owner all of the lots belonging to that owner as well as his or her share of the commons. Enclosing meant growing hedges and building fences to separate from others the lots that had been grouped together.

Uncomplicated in appearance, the enclosures were an obvious simplification. From then on, each person was at home on his or her reunited lands. There were no more long treks from one end of the parish to the other. Each could do as he or she wished, change the way of rotating crops, experiment with new crops, turn arable land into pasture. Everyone was freed of the easements and reciprocal obligations that resulted from the former system.

It is clear that everywhere that farming was no longer done in common—in other words, almost everywhere in the eighteenth century—the enclosures were a means of making agriculture more efficient. They were also a precursor for all later rationalization. The reason for this is simple. When land was divided into small lots, farming had to follow communal rules, even when each farmer cultivated his or her land independently. Any agricultural innovation thus had to be implemented by the whole parish. This required everyone's agreement, or at least the agreement of what constituted the majority in a traditional parish assembly: that of the landowners whose holdings totaled at least four-fifths of the area of the open fields. All had to consent to the risk and investment that such innovation would involve. In places where land was not farmed in common, the parish was not an economic association, and each individual thus had to pay his or her whole share of the costs. It was not certain that all could do so.

In short, the former system only created obstacles to attempts to implement new agricultural practices. Those who desired such changes quickly came to the conclusion that the system had to be eliminated once and for all, and they sought to obtain the village assembly's final agreement on the principle of enclosures.

Enclosures are an obvious way of rationalizing farm work because it is preferable and easier to have all one's lots grouped together rather than scattered in different places in the parish, often many kilometers apart. However, even here, at this very elementary level, the question arises: for whom? Rationalization of farming, increase in productivity, simplification of tasks, less effort per output, elimination of needless travel: it seems to go without saying that these are advantages. This seems basic and obvious. Yet such rationalization makes sense only under certain conditions. We do not generally notice this because in the modern world these conditions are always satisfied. In traditional village communities, things were quite different.

Increasing production made sense to farmers only if they had markets where they could sell their excess production. If elimination of the commons was a condition for the increase, then the money from the new sales had to compensate them for losing their rights to use the commons.

In even simpler terms, rationalizing labor makes sense only to those who are no longer in a subsistence economy. Rationalizing work means making it a better instrument with a view to some end, to produce more at lower cost. In a subsistence economy, work is nothing but life itself, and life is not a means to something else but the end toward which all means are directed.

For whom did the rationalization make sense? For those who were already selling a large part or most of their production. In other words, for those who were the richest and at the top of the social scale defined by the land-use system: large landowners and lords.

Now, let us look at the problem in a different way. The former land-use system was hierarchical, and at the top were the large landowners and lords. They were the ones who destroyed the system. Why and for what reason? Why destroy something that is entirely favorable to you? For even greater advantages? This is an ambiguous answer because you already receive all the advantages. The proof is that you will soon succeed in destroying the system, despite opposition from the other stakeholders. Therefore, it is only in relation to another related system that you can gain either more of less from this one and especially in relation to someone who occupies, in that other system, a position that is equivalent to yours. In other words, the reasons that led rich landowners and lords to enclose parishes did not have anything to do with their relationships with their peasants, but with rivalries that opposed them to one another. Q.E.D.

The expulsion of third parties by social doubles was the result of rivalries that opposed the doubles to one another. The expulsions were accomplished with indifference through the abandonment of traditional solidarity obligations and under the sign of instrumental rationality.

Open any book on the history of eighteenth-century England and you will find exactly the same thing. The enclosures were achieved by land-owning members of the upper and lesser nobility who sought to increase their wealth and were jealous of the growing prosperity of the new merchant bourgeoisie. Now, take a slightly more specialized book, such as *La révolution industrielle au XVIIIe siècle* by Paul Mantoux,[92] and you will find that the arguments employed to justify the enclosures were essentially rationalization of farm work and increase in production.

Yet this is only a first point. We also have to show that the enclosures created scarcity, and how they did so. First, then, the lords and large landowners were in rivalry among themselves and with the closest neighboring social category: the merchant bourgeoisie. The members of all of these groups were vying for the same things: the bourgeois were buying land, and the lords were trying to get wealthy. This is all very simple and humdrum: this is the story of very ordinary relationships among people.

In order to get wealthier, lords and large landowners tried to improve the yield of their primary source of income: land. They could do this in two ways: by increasing agricultural production or by increasing rent. The two things were related. It was impossible to increase rent without increasing agricultural productivity, and especially without selling what was produced. In fact, commercialization of production was crucial. In order to increase income from renting land, what is important is not the parish's total production, but the portion of that production that can be sold. If everything that is produced is consumed by the producers, no money is brought in. It is not possible to procure high rents from people who eat almost everything they produce, even if there are a lot of them. In contrast, it is possible to get a lot of profit out of two or three large undertakings that sell all of their production.

This is only the first point; the next point is much more interesting. Let us see what happens with respect to doubles and third parties. Drawing new property lines and enclosing, grouping into a single lot, each individual landowner's pieces of land is much more than simple reorganization. Giving each person a share of the land equivalent to his or her former rights over the commons is much more than transforming ancient, multiple, complex rights into a simple, singular modern right, the right to private property, an exclusive right, the right to sell and enclose. It is to create scarcity and institute misery.

Once the commons had been divided into private property, where were the farm workers who had built their homes on the commons to live? Certainly not in rented houses because their choice to live on the commons stemmed from the fact that they were unable to pay rent. Note thus something simple: even though there was no change in the real quantity of land (obviously), land suddenly became something that was insufficient to meet the needs of all. There was not enough.

Before land was enclosed and private property fenced, land was not even a set of objects. It was the world, Mother Earth, people's home, the place of ancestors, nature and life, where everyone had a spot, good or bad.

Allocating and enclosing the commons and open fields destroyed the human habitat and replaced it with a set of objects that was insufficient to meet the needs of all. At the same time, the ancient village community was also destroyed. Open fields and commons used to form a res publica, a public thing, in which all villagers normally had interest. Everyone was concerned by the general farming rules, decisions concerning the commons, and even individual disputes between landowners. The openness of the fields, the fact that lots were interlocking, and the practice of putting the livestock of all landowners to pasture together on the open fields and commons meant that, if a quarrel arose over a cow that had disappeared or a property marker that had been moved, the entire community felt concerned.

Sending everyone behind the hedges and fences of private property, where each reigned as absolute master, destroyed the common interest and eliminated the village assembly's reason for being. The new way of occupying the land made villagers exterior to one another. The parish no longer had a common object that could bring it together into a community. It became nothing more than an administrative unit, and the exteriority of the villagers could not be separated from their new obligation to produce more in order to compensate for the loss of their right to use the commons.

Under the former land-use system, landowners agreed to respect tradition and give each a right to use the commons. There was a form of communal, traditional, institutionalized solidarity in the very existence of the commons. The disappearance of the commons was thus the abandonment of traditional solidarity obligations. The exteriority of the members of society that resulted from the enclosures made that abandonment acceptable. It is one thing for landowners to extend to others, who do not really have the right, the privilege of using common lands. It is quite another for each individual to agree to welcome the needy onto his or her private land when he or she is often also in need. Moreover, anyone who agrees to do so will soon be overwhelmed by a flood of needy people. The new system even makes generosity scarce.

In the eighteenth century in England, the enclosures gave rise to much debate and controversy. Those in favor of enclosures were accused of stealing the commons' meager goods from the poor and indigent, who were already the most underprivileged. Enclosure promoters unanimously answered that the poor had no legal right to use the commons. In other words, they did not care what happened to the poor, and felt they had neither rights nor duties in their respect. It was with indifference that the greatest violence was done within the system, and the violence was invisible because once the commons were destroyed, the poor were obliged to leave. Where did they go? That was their business.

It was not only land that the enclosures made scarce, but everything. If a peasant needed wood to repair his or her house, where would he or she get it once the communal forests had become private property? Wood became scarce. If the peasant bought it, then money became scarce. What about heat? Fuel became scarce. If the pond was enclosed on a neighbor's land, where was the peasant to fish? What did he or she care about the few meters of land, equivalent to his or her right of access to the commons, that had been added to the peasant's original land? They were insufficient to feed his or her few cows and twenty sheep. Of course, part of one's agricultural land could be transformed into pasture, but that would mean that there would not be enough wheat, barley, or oats. He or she would have to sell his or her livestock, but that would make milk and meat scarce.

Moreover, enclosures were expensive. Often extensive legal proceedings were required to achieve them, and the cost of the proceedings had to be shared by all landholders in accordance with the size of their property. Nonetheless, once again, the poor were at a disadvantage. The enclosures were expensive for another reason: they required enclosing—in other words, fences. This required investment in labor and materials that was often beyond the means of small landowners. They could neither buy the materials they needed nor pay workers. They also could not build fences without neglecting their farm work. All that remained was for them to sell their property and leave, and with the money from the sale, seek their fortune elsewhere in the city or in the Americas.

Mantoux[93] estimates that in less than fifty years, there were 40,000 to 50,000 private transactions through which, following the reorganization of land use, large landowners acquired the land of small peasant landholders. The private transactions completed the work of the enclosures, the destruction of traditional village communities, the concentration of land ownership in the hands of a wealthy social class, and the establishment of scarcity. From 1714 to 1810, the English Parliament passed over 3,000 acts ordering the division, allocation, and fencing of the fields of various parishes.[94] However, those documents concern only parishes where a parliamentary decision was necessary to force the village assembly to fence open fields and eliminate the commons. The parishes where the lords' authority alone was sufficient were at least as numerous.

Thus, scarcity was established, imperceptibly, parish by parish, but on a very large scale. Excluded people appeared in every parish, and everywhere the land became a set of goods and resources that was insufficient to meet the needs of all.

Moreover, the increase in agricultural production changed nothing. It mattered little that the total production of the village had doubled or even quadrupled since the enclosures. The poor and the uprooted small landowners gained nothing. The new farms employed fewer people, and all those who no longer had a place on the land found that not only land but all goods and resources indispensable to life had become scarce.

Let us go back a few pages. The enclosures were the necessary condition for rationalization of farm work and increase in production. The conclusion is immediate: the procedure by which farm production was increased is what instituted scarcity. My model has been found again: the very means by which we think we are fighting against scarcity (the means by which we increase the real quantity of goods and resources) is what produces scarcity. I thus find again the aporia of scarcity: scarcity is perfectly independent of the real quantity of goods and resources.

The greatest violence produced within the system results from the doubles' simple indifference to third parties, and that violence is invisible. In enclosed parishes, this is clearly what happened. Violence was invisible because often, after the enclosures, the parish purely and simply disappeared. Houses were torn down, and where there was once a village there were then simply immense pastures as far as the eye could see. The violence was invisible also because large landowners did not particularly dislike the farm workers and poor who were displaced by the enclosures: they were simply not interested in them. Anyway, they said, the poor will certainly benefit from the increase in farm production. Is producing less a way of feeding more people?

The misery of the poor did not prick their consciences. As for the impoverished small landowners who swelled the ranks of the poor and homeless, had they not sold their property by contracts into which they had freely and voluntarily entered? Had they not been duly paid? The violence was invisible because it occurred in indifference and no one had the impression they were involved.

Now the model was in place, and institutionalized scarcity would function according to the laws of economics. However, scarcity was also to reveal itself as ambiguous, as both a source of disorder and the foundation of the economic system. Let us see what happened next, which is only one page in the history of England, toward the end of the eighteenth century and the beginning of the nineteenth century.

While the violence was invisible, its consequences were not. The homeless, out-of-work farm laborers, indigents, and people living in misery did not disappear as easily as the commons, from which they had been expelled, or as their houses, which had been destroyed. They reappeared everywhere, in cities, in the countryside: famished vagabonds, poor itinerants, and in every parish there were increasingly numerous indigents whom the law tried to settle by making help available through poorhouses, which were public parish aid institutions.

Throughout the entire eighteenth century, the English asked: where do the poor come from? Unable to find a good answer and encouraged by their growing prosperity, they concluded that poverty and progress go hand in hand, and that the richest countries were the ones with the most people liv-ing in misery. Yet this was not a solution to the problem, and those living in misery soon became so numerous that they threatened public order. Scarcity proved to be a cause of violence. In 1795, in order to reduce the danger, an amendment to the Poor Laws was adopted, instituting the Speenhamland System.

The Speenhamland System guaranteed poor people a minimum income, independent of their salary, and provided that they would receive benefits, whether or not they had salaries, so that their total income would be in accor-dance with a rate established in function of the price of bread. The benefits were either in addition to the salaries of poor people up to the established rate, or constituted the poor people's only income. However, since most farm workers' salaries were lower than the rate set by law, no one had interest in working. The money for the benefits came from legally required contribu-tions from all landowners and tenants in the parish. Their contributions were based on the value of their land or the rent they paid to the owner. Nonetheless, the law was very popular among farmers and large landowners because, since it forced the poor to work, its immediate result was to make farm wages lower than the rate set by law. Farmers and large landowners thus had access to a cheap pool of labor that they could pay whatever they liked since the Speenhamland System benefits ensured workers received a mini-mum income. Under the cover of ensuring that poor people had a minimum income, employers gave themselves subsidies to pay their employees' salaries.

However, the Speenhamland trap was even more infernal that it seems because it led to the downfall of free tenants and small landowners, and completed the work of the enclosures. Indeed, if one held any land in the parish, one had no right to help from the parish. Clearly, the first victims of the Speenhamland System were honest workers who clung desperately to a miserable patch of land and tried to subsist with dignity. The subsidies low-ered salaries so much that they were unable to find any work that paid well enough for them to survive. They soon had to sell the little they owned and found themselves among the ranks of the assisted poor. Tenant farmers were not much better off. They had to contribute to the fund for the benefits for poor people. In exchange, the law provided them with cheap labor. However, the forced laborers knew that their income was guaranteed, so they worked little and poorly. Moreover, the farmer had no authority over them. They damaged his or her land through negligence, and farm productivity dropped while the farmers, ruined by their contributions to the benefits, in turn found themselves among those receiving aid.

Only large landowners could seem to profit from the arrangement, but they also suffered from the drop in farm workers' productivity. Thus, a law that was originally very popular and satisfactory to everyone, both workers and employers, turned into a machine that disrupted the lives of honest people and produced physical and moral misery. Clearly, the Speenhamland System dissociated the individual and social consequences of workers' actions. Those who sought to keep their dignity and independence through constant work were inevitably pushed into misery and dependency. The lazy and indolent, on the contrary, had only to cross their arms and take advantage of the law. This kind of arrangement gradually but inevitably destroyed any feeling of personal responsibility.

This brings me back to the texts of the liberal tradition and the ambivalence of scarcity. When Townsend, Bentham, and Malthus complained about the Poor Laws, they were targeting the Speenhamland System, and that system was repudiated in 1834. Clearly, the Speenhamland System encouraged laziness, and it is evident that once scarcity is institutionalized, only necessity, or almost, forces us to work. However, while Townsend, Malthus, and Bentham were right about the positive value of scarcity as the foundation of the economic order, were the magistrates in Speenhamland, who were trying to ensure public order, really wrong?

Historians generally reproach economists for their criticism of the Speenhamland System. They say that economists forget that Speenhamland was for England veritable insurance against revolution, and that it saved England from something similar to what erupted in France in 1789.

Indifference and Envy

Girard and the Anthropological Analysis of Modern Economy

Girard and Economics

René Girard himself has not written very much on economics, at least explicitly, though his works are full of insights into and short remarks on the sacrificial origin of different economic phenomena or the way in which mimetic relations and commercial transactions are often intertwined and act upon each other.[1] Unlike religion, psychology, psychoanalysis, literature, and anthropology, the analysis of modern and traditional economies from the point of view of mimetic theory has never been carried out by Girard himself, but for the most part by other people—for example, in the French-speaking world, which I know best, essentially by Michel Aglietta and André Orléan in *La violence de la monnaie* (1982) and by Jean-Pierre Dupuy and myself in *L'enfer des choses* (1979), as well as by others, such as Mark Anspach, Andrew Feenberg, Pierre Lantz, André Orléan, Georges-Hubert de Radkowski, and Lucien Scubla in various works on economy, economic anthropology, or the place and role of money in literary texts.[2] In a way, this is somewhat surprising since the relationship between mimetic and economic phenomena, at least in a broad sense, was seen quite early on. For example, soon after the original publication of *Mensonge romantique et vérité romanesque* (1961), the

French Marxist Lucien Goldmann wrote in his *Pour une sociologie du Roman* (1964) that Girard's work was the most important book to read in order to understand the effects of economic alienation on literature since Georg Luckas's *Theory of the Novel* (1920). Moreover in a footnote in *Les origines du capitalisme* (1971), Jean Baechler suggested that those wishing to understand the nature of the infinite desire for acquisition that capitalist economies have institutionalized should read Girard's book.[3] Whatever the reason for Girard's relative disinterest in economic phenomena, others have not been prevented from tackling this problem, and it bears witness in a special way to the dynamism and intellectual power of the mimetic theory that its application to the field of economics has essentially, if not entirely, been due to the work of others rather than to the efforts of Girard himself.

The Substantivist-Formalist Debate

In the late 1940s and early 1950s a debate began that divided (and still divides) the community of economists and of anthropologists interested in economic phenomena. It concerns the nature of economy and is generally referred to as the substantivist-formalist debate. It was first formulated in the works of the Austrian economist Karl Polanyi.[4] In *The Great Transformation* (1945), a book on the history of the formation and organization of the market economy in Europe from the late eighteenth to the early twentieth centuries, Polanyi already argued that the modern market economy was a rare historical accident. Furthermore Polanyi said that, unlike what liberal and economic ideologies pretend, there is nothing natural about the market. It does not correspond to any spontaneous human tendency to barter and exchange, and it does not arise by itself as soon as certain conditions are satisfied. On the contrary, modern markets have been put into place through sustained and voluntary state policies that consciously destroyed traditional solidarities, authorized the unlimited sale of land, and labor and literally created the labor market—for example, in England through the Reform Bill of 1834, which repealed the existing Poor Laws, which had prevented the free circulation of labor. The system formed by market economies, the balance of power among European states, and the gold standard granted Europe one century of unprecedented economic growth and relative peace, from the end of the Napoleonic wars to the catastrophe of 1914. Yet that First World War, as well as the Second World War and the authoritarian political movements that led to it, were, according to Polanyi, the result of the inevitable collapse of a system wrought with contradictions. The collapse was inevitable because the market system rested on some very particular political and economic conditions—the balance of power and the gold standard—and because neither that dependence nor those conditions were clearly understood by the system's proponents. However, the main reason the breakdown of the market system could not have been avoided is because it is a highly unnatural economic system that replaces the normal function of economic activities, which is to ensure the livelihood of man (which is the title of Polanyi's last book)[5] by the unlimited search for profit. Furthermore, theoretically it is based on the idea of *homo economicus*, an abstraction to which no reality whatsoever corresponds in spite of economic and political efforts to create a world consistent with economic theory. In later years Polanyi, with the help of many collaborators, went on to document his claims with historical and anthropological studies of trade in various archaic and traditional societies.[6]

Such claims were bound to generate controversy. They challenged classical economic theory on at least three points. The first point is that of the naturalness of the market, which is, to some extent, both an empirical and a conceptual question. Whether or not the market is natural, whatever that may mean when one really comes to think about it, is a question of knowing if it is rare or frequent, if it arises spontaneously as soon as certain "natural" conditions are satisfied or if these conditions need to be explicitly and voluntarily created as Polanyi affirmed. These are empirical questions. But then even if market economies are rare, perhaps even unique in the history of humankind, does it follow that markets are "unnatural" in any other sense than that they are rare? Jean Baechler, for one, believes that capitalism is rare and, in a way, that our present experience is unique in the history of humankind; yet he asserts that it is the only natural form of economic organization.[7] Second, Polanyi's claims challenge the universality of economic theory. Since Adam Smith, at least, economists have believed that their discipline is founded on some universal traits of human nature and therefore that their discipline applies at all places and at all times, that economics defines efficient or economic behavior independent of all historical or cultural contingencies. This is precisely what Polanyi and many anthropologists reject.

They argue that it is an illusion that induces the economists, and anthropologists who adopt it, to view nonmodern economies as failed attempts to create rational and efficient markets, while they are often actually very successful institutions in their own right, in view of their different goals. However, the main point is that market economies are the exception rather than the rule, and economic man is nowhere to be found; economic laws are not universal theorems of efficient behavior and are only true within the economists' formal models and perhaps, at times, within modern economies, which have been artificially transformed in order to be consistent with economic theory. Finally, and perhaps most important, Polanyi's claims challenge the moral neutrality of modern economic theories, in which exchanges are by definition fair if they are free; otherwise, say the economists, they would not have taken place. Modern market economies, argue the substantivists, are socially destructive. Traditional economies, according to Polanyi, were embedded in the social structure. He meant by that, first, that in traditional societies economic activities were not separated from other types of social relationships, but were present in various forms of ritual, political, domestic, or cultural activities. The economy did not constitute an independent sphere of activity, but existed as an aspect of different types of social relations. Second, as anthropologists have known since Marcel Mauss's famous *Essai sur le don* (1923–1924), exchange in traditional societies is not a way of making profit but a means through which the social bond is continuously created and relations of solidarity enacted. Modern market economies are, in contrast, characterized by the independence of the economic sphere. This means that economic transactions constitute a domain of activity in itself, separated from other forms of social relationships. It is claimed that economic exchanges constitute a type of activity whose rationality and efficiency require it to be free of all restraints from traditional beliefs or obligations. Furthermore, this economic model of interaction tends to invade all social relations and to replace the personal bond of traditional exchange by abstract connections between individuals that are established only through money and the division of labor.

The debate has been going on since it was first initiated in the 1940s. It flares up once in a while, but is pretty much continuous, with each camp holding its position. The formalists generally ignore the substantivists and simply refuse to discuss the issue, claiming "that the proof of the pudding is in the eating," that the system works in spite of its failures and difficulties, and that market economies have led to unheard-of levels of economic and demographic growth. Though the substantivists are very active in economic history and economic anthropology, and often produce remarkable studies, they have always failed to make any significant inroads into classical theory. Of course I am not presumptuous enough to believe that I can convince an economist, but I do think that mimetic theory can allow us to reformulate the problem—that is, the question of the radical novelty of market economies and whether they are an unnatural exception—in a way that may throw some light on this debate. Of course, as it should be clear to everyone by now, this is not just some scholarly debate in economic theory; what is at stake is our own attitude toward the modern economy. I suspect that each and every one of us can recognize himself or herself in the substantivist or the formalist position, and, if you are like me, in both at different times.

The Ambivalence of Scarcity

In *L'enfer des choses* (1979) I argued that scarcity functions in the modern world in the way the sacred does in traditional societies. That is to say, it is a means of protection against violence. Like the sacred according to Girard, scarcity contains violence in two senses of the verb "to contain." First, in the sense that it limits and controls violence: it keeps it in check. It is, as I said, a means of protection against violence. Second, in the sense that it incorporates or embodies violence within itself, in the sense that to some extent it consists of violence. Hence, like the sacred, scarcity is a violent way of protecting ourselves against our own violence. This presupposes that scarcity is not a natural condition, just like the sacred is not divine, but something that we make and, in a sense, an institution, or, better, a matrix out of which modern institutions are made, starting with the market. Some may consider it obvious that we make scarcity. That is, I suspect, because they confuse what I call scarcity with inequality. Some may consider the claim to be preposterous. Scarcity, they will say, refers to the fact that resources are finite and the multiplicity of ends open to us entails that we must choose and decide how we will use our resources and which resources will go to what end. Economics is simply the science of the rational or efficient allocation of limited resources.

This, though in itself unobjectionable, misses the point. Socially, scarcity is not the fact that resources are limited, but the fact that, no matter the real quantity of resources, they are deemed insufficient to satisfy the needs and desires of all. This is a quite different problem, for the social allocation of limited resources does not in itself entail that the needs, and even the desires, of all will not be met. Scarcity is the mimetic mechanism through which these further conditions are satisfied, and this protects us from our own violence.

It has long been known that increasing one's income is not the only road to abundance: one can also limit one's needs and desires. In *Stone Age Economics* Marshall Sahlins reminds us that this solution was preferred by many traditional and primitive societies. Yet contrary to what Sahlins sometimes seems to suggest, we should not think that this solution was an individual one, or even a "cultural" solution in the sense that noble values, such as a certain sobriety in desire, were internalized by agents. In fact, many very simple and poor societies show large discrepancies in wealth and power and intense rivalries between agents, which suggests that the "*bons sauvages*" are not particularly more restrained in their desires than we are ourselves. Sahlins's remark makes sense only if we think about it socially. The restraints and limits in question are established by bonds of solidarity, prohibitions, and obligations—that is, by the sacred. They are set by sacrifice and by the sacrificial mechanism that unites everyone, except the victim, in one and the same community. Under those conditions, to refuse help to one whose fundamental needs are not fulfilled is to cast him or her out of the community. That is why help of some sort is never refused in normal circumstances. Yet for those who receive that help, to question the amount, or to ask for more, at least repeatedly, is generally, as we commonly say, "to ask for it." That is to say, it is to expose oneself to a refusal that will not be for this time only, but forever; in short, it is to expose oneself to the risk of being cast out of the community. Though this will certainly happen often, it is perfectly consistent with the fact that there is no one within the community whose basic needs are left unattended. Bonds of solidarity, obligations, and prescriptions restrain the desires of those who have, by imposing upon them a duty to give, and of those who have not, for they must be satisfied with what they get. Thus "abundance," so to speak, is achieved at the same time that the existing hierarchies of wealth and power are reproduced. It is achieved through the normal functioning of the sacrificial system—that is to say, by the violent mechanism that protects traditional societies from their own violence.

Scarcity is the result of the demise of that system of protection against violence. More precisely, it is the result of the progressive rejection of these various bonds of solidarity. There is a long and interesting story to be told as to how and why such an evolution took place, too long for the space allotted here. By rejecting traditional obligations of solidarity, or rather by the general weakening of such obligations, a new social space was created in which those who were left to fend for themselves could live, that is, those who were neither helped nor eliminated from the community. Progressively, this space was extended to all of us. The mechanism for this is relatively simple. The weakening of the obligations of solidarity can either be a curse or a blessing depending on your present situation. If you are well off, to be able to say that you have no duty to help, that these are neither your poor nor deserving poor, is no disadvantage. Given this, some were always ready to extend this independent status to themselves in spite of the precariousness it entailed. In a sense, scarcity is nothing but a social organization where this status of independence has become general. As a consequence, the problem of how to allocate limited resources now arises. It concerns each and every one of us. Because of the uncertainty typical of this independent status, but also because since there are now no binding rules to prescribe a specific reallocation of resources in times of need, the problem is now everyone's individually not only on the receiving end but also on the giving end. Scarcity is socially constructed because whether or not resources are sufficient to satisfy the needs of all does not depend primarily on the size of the resources available, but on the social bonds, obligations, prohibitions, and prescriptions that link the members of the community. It depends on the type of social organization.

But how does this new form of social organization protect us from our own violence? In at least two ways, I think. First, by rejecting traditional bonds of solidarity. This may seem strange since obligations of solidarity are fundamental to the sacrificial system's ability to protect traditional societies from their own violence. Yet bonds of solidarity are also means through which, in a traditional society, whenever a conflict erupts, many people—that is, a whole family, a clan, or a tribe—are immediately concerned and in danger of being engulfed in the dispute. Traditional bonds of solidarity impose obligations of violence and duties of revenge. They expose one to being the next victim of a conflict in which one has never taken part "personally." Traditional bonds of solidarity are a violent form of protection against violence. That is why they can always ultimately end up feeding the violence they aim to stop. Scarcity isolates conflicts. Just as it allows us not to help those whose basic needs are not satisfied, it allows us "not to get involved" in other people's conflicts. Scarcity generates, to borrow an apt phrase from Norman Geras, a "contract of mutual indifference."[8] Such indifference, just as it creates a situation where resources are insufficient to satisfy the needs and desires of all, also liberates us from our traditional duties of violence. This isolation of conflicts makes it more difficult and less likely for violence to converge in a unique dispute that engulfs the whole community. Thus scarcity protects us from our own violence first by providing us with a form of social organization that makes it more difficult for violent contagion to converge upon a unique enemy. The sacred is built on the sacrificial crisis itself. It reproduces and forces agents to reproduce, as Girard reminds us, the very actions that led to its violent issue. It is therefore not surprising that the same obligations and prohibitions that protect the community in normal times can serve as a channel through which violence travels. Scarcity, to the contrary, because it rests on the abandonment of these same obligations, cuts off that path to the propagation of violence. Furthermore, since it is not permanently threatened by the danger of a general conflagration, scarcity can remain a relatively "nonpacified" social situation where many local, more or less violent conflicts cohabit within the stable order of society.

Scarcity also protects us against our own violence in a more dynamic way. Fascination with one's own mimetic conflict and rivalry makes one indifferent to the needs and conflicts of others. The plurality of conflicts present within scarcity actually encourages each individual to renege on the obligations of solidarity in order to pursue more intensely his or her own cherished and hated privileged rivalry. To put it in another way, the more one is fascinated by one's own conflicts the less one will be easily fascinated by the conflicts of others and tempted to join them, so the plurality of conflicts actually makes for the divergence of rivalries rather than for their convergence against a unique antagonist. This is why in scarcity also it is by their own violence, or at least by their own mimetic behavior, that agents are protected from the more disastrous consequences of mimetic fascination. Furthermore, because in these conflicts there are necessarily winners and losers, scarcity cannot but create large amounts of frustration and resentment, which, in the absence of the catharsis provided by sacrifice, must at some point, it seems, erupt into a society-wide sacrificial crisis. Yet over the last centuries our modern forms of social organization have shown a remarkable degree of stability in spite of the high level of rivalry they contain. The reason, I believe, is that though scarcity does not possess any proper sacrificial ritual, it does not lack substitute victims to whom agents can transfer their resentment. In fact, they are everywhere. They are the "poor losers" who inhabit the gaps of our social security systems and the streets of our cities. They are all those who, having been rejected by the fair and impersonal functioning of the market, are now left to their own devices to fare as best as they can and who face our general indifference, when it is not our silent suspicion that they must in some way deserve what has happened to them. Our indifference is not just the counterpart of our fascination, the reverse side of the coin whose other face is our own envy; it is also our form of "ritual immolation."

It should be noticed, though, that the essential condition for this system to exist is a negative one. It rests on an absence, on the rejection and refusal of bonds of solidarity and spontaneously arises when there is nothing to replace them and mimetic relations are let free to play. This means that scarcity is not properly an institution, but, like the sacrificial crisis, a spontaneous mechanism that can serve as a matrix for different institutions.

The Debate Revisited

Central to Polanyi's argument is the empirical finding that market economies are the exception rather than the rule, and that they did not arise spontaneously. Though his claims are well documented they leave open one question: Why did this exception occur? Why did modern market economies arise precisely there and then? If market economies are such an "unnatural" economic system, through what rare and unlikely accident did they ever appear? Mimetic theory provides at least a plausible general answer to these queries. Given that the historical effect of Christianity is to progressively ruin the sacrificial system and that scarcity spontaneously emerges as traditional bonds of solidarity are abandoned, then we should expect this system to arise in a region where Christianity has long weakened these bonds. Why it emerged precisely where and when it did, as well as the role of the state in this process, is a question too complex to even begin to answer in the present context. Nonetheless, what mimetic theory gives us is a means for understanding the radical novelty of modern market economies and a reason for their "unnaturalness." Their historical specificity is related to the unique breakdown of the sacrificial system caused by Christian Revelation. It is also linked to rejection of that Revelation. Scarcity is what we live in, which is neither the sacred nor the Kingdom of God.

From a purely secular and scientific point of view, mimetic theory allows us to understand the particularity of modern economies. They are neither natural nor unnatural, but rest on a different regime of human mimesis, which is made possible by the absence of traditional bonds of solidarity. Or, to put it in another way, scarcity constitutes, like the sacred, a fixed point in the space of collective mimetic behavior. This explains its remarkable power of attraction. It also explain why it was hitherto unheard of, without having to conclude as the substantivists do that it is in some way against nature. Mimetic theory also allows us to understand why substantivists and formalists are talking at cross-purposes. They are not really talking about the same thing. Substantivists claim that at all places and at all times economic processes have been embedded in the social structure and that it should be so here also. They argue that modern economies with their abstract market systems are not the rule but the exception. Formalists counter that traditional rules of solidarity are irrational in view of the optimal allocation of rare resources. Both are right. The substantivists' empirical claim is correct, though not the normative conclusion they derive from it. The formalists' theoretical response is accurate, except that they remain unconscious of the specific conditions necessary for the empirical application of their theory. Ultimately both are wrong because they believe that they are essentially dealing with economic phenomena. Substantivists observe, but cannot explain, that economic processes are always embedded in the social structure, while formalists take for granted the independence of such processes, unaware of the mimetic mechanism through which they gain their modern autonomy. Behind these different types of economies are distinct regimes of mimetic behavior that explain their particularities.

Mimetic theory also provides us with a different outlook on what may be called the moral dimension of this debate: an outlook that some may find relatively uncomfortable. Let me explain. There are two sides to this moral debate. One is that of the formalists. According to them the market is by definition fair. Given ideal conditions of perfect information, where exchanges are free, in the sense that no one is forced to exchange but can refrain from concluding a bargain until he or she finds a satisfactory price, and where agents are rational, exchanges are by definition fair or they would not take place. Of course we may want to retort that these "ideal" conditions are generally not satisfied. To which the formalists will usually answer, not without reason, that this is probably true and therefore that it is not the presence but the absence of market conditions that are to be blamed. The substantivists, on the contrary, will claim that modern market economy has historically been destructive of traditional bonds of solidarity; it has instituted indifference to the suffering of others as a way of life. They will claim that the exclusive rule of market transaction progressively destroys the moral fiber of a society, no matter how "fair" the market may be in principle.

Mimetic theory suggests that we can share neither of these points of view. The destruction of sacred bonds of solidarity periodically strengthened by sacrificial rituals cannot be such a bad thing. Substantivists also fail to see that our indifference, which they condemn, protects us from our own violence, and that by condemning it they condemn our own violence but fail to renounce it. Formalists are right that in ideal conditions market exchanges are fair, but they fail to see the violence that is embedded in this fairness. A fair exchange is one about which neither of the parties has any reason to complain afterward. It lasts for an instant and leaves no bond or obligation between the agents afterward. That is precisely what it means to say that it is fair. A fair exchange is a relation which of itself gives to its participants no reason to enter into another relation later on. Justice as fairness is justice among those who are indifferent. Yet we should not condemn it, for until everyone has renounced his or her own violence, it is what protects each individual against all those who are not indifferent. The ambivalence of scarcity is our own ambivalence.

A Mimetic Rereading
of Helmut Schoeck's *Envy:*
A Theory of Social Behaviour

I n spite of its title, Helmut Schoeck's *Envy: A Theory of Social Behaviour*[1] does not so much constitute a *theory of envy* properly speaking as
an attempt to establish what could be called the case for envy. In fact,
Schoeck's book contains very little about envy from a theoretical point of
view. He does tell us something about the origin of envy, about its cause
and function within society, but everything he has to say about these topics accounts for less than 10 percent of his more than 400-page book. For
example, Schoeck tells us, as far as its origin is concerned, that envy is a fundamental human disposition rooted in our biological makeup. Concerning
the cause of envy as a psychological trait of certain individuals, he points in
the direction of depth psychology and rivalry among siblings. Though he
often repeats that envy plays a fundamental role in human society, what he
has to say about what that role is and how it is played is not only very limited
but at times apparently contradictory. However, what his book does contain
is a wealth of information on envy, its place and its importance in various
human institutions and different societies. It is rich in examples of envy
taken from numerous cultures and different time periods. Furthermore, it
documents the importance of envy in literature, philosophy, and many social
sciences. The case for envy is the claim that envy occupies a fundamental

place in human life and that the social sciences must recognize this if they are to offer plausible explanations of our social existence and institutions. That point is very forcefully and to some extent convincingly made in Schoeck's book. What his book lacks, though, is precisely a theoretical framework that allows the reader, and which would have allowed Schoeck himself, to organize into a coherent whole the rich information and many observations he has assembled.

A mimetic rereading of Schoeck's *Envy: A Theory of Social Behaviour* can bring a theoretical framework—namely, one found in René Girard's theory of mimetic desire—to Schoeck's observations and insights into envious behavior. As one might suspect, such an enterprise is in many ways critical of Schoeck's work. It is also difficult because it requires one to separate the wheat from the chaff in the Austrian sociologist's reflections on envy. Of course, mimetic theory will be used to separate Schoeck the good observer of envy from Schoeck the confused analyst of its causes. One difficulty remains: the criticism rests on, or at least suggests, one specific interpretation of Girard's theory in relation to the sensitive issue of social justice. The remainder of this text will proceed in the following manner. Part one presents the essentials of what I take to be Helmut Schoeck's theory of envy. Part two recalls his criticism of egalitarianism and socialism. Part three reinterprets and criticizes Schoeck's finding in light of mimetic theory. Finally, part four draws the consequences of this rereading for the issues of equality and social justice.

Envy: A Theory of Social Behaviour

Central to Schoeck's research on envy is a twofold intuition. First, envy plays and has always played a central role in human societies; second, the role of envy in human societies has to a large extent always been dissimulated, and perhaps it must remain hidden in order to work efficiently. Put another way, Schoeck's claim is that envy inhibition has played just as important part in human history as envy itself. In order to understand this, we must first turn our attention to Schoeck's very precise definition of envy as opposed to other closely related emotions, desires, and interpersonal phenomena, such as jealousy, rivalry, and emulation. According to Schoeck, what distinguishes envy from jealousy is that envy is not transgression specific. One feels jealous only when another person lays claim to something that we believe is ours for whatever reason. The important points here are that in jealousy, first, there is an object or asset of some sort that is at stake, and second, that the meaning or goal of the conflict is to acquire or to retain that object. The structure of envy is completely different, according to Schoeck. What is at the heart of envy is not an object or transgression, but another agent. On this view, the envious agent is primarily preoccupied with his or her rival. It is the other person as such that is the object of envy, rather than the other's talents, assets, success, belongings, or whatever else could be invoked by the envious person to justify his or her feeling of enmity toward the other agent. More precisely, the object is still present in envious relations, but it occupies a different position. While in jealousy the rivals compete to obtain something of value that they cannot or will not share, the envious person would rather see the object of the dispute destroyed than allow the rival to be victorious. In fact, according to Schoeck, the goal of an envious person is precisely the destruction of the goods, assets, or talents of the other. What motivates an envious agent is not to have what the other has, but the fact that the other has it. The envious agent's goal therefore is not so much to possess the object as to deprive the other of it, to take it away from him or her. In consequence, envy is, for Schoeck, a purely negative and destructive impulse.

Because envy is not transgression specific, according to Schoeck, it follows that it cannot have its cause in any particular distribution of goods, assets, or social benefits. Unlike jealousy, rivalry, or emulation, which Schoeck says are caused or fueled by material differences between agents' assets, envy does not have any objective cause. Envy comes from a comparison between equals (or between those who are nearly equal), and it takes advantage of the slightest difference to justify its resentful claim. In fact, Schoeck insists that envy is more frequent when the proximity between the envious and the envied is greater. Like Girard in *Deceit, Desire and the Novel*, and like Tocqueville before him, Schoeck argues that the rise of egalitarian principles and politics since the French Revolution has facilitated the spread of envy in the modern world.

If envy proceeds from comparison between equals, one would expect it to be a symmetrical relation. Yet it is clear and important that, for Schoeck, envy is an asymmetrical relation. The first aspect or dimension of this asymmetry is cognitive: the "envious man . . . may have hostile feelings towards a person who may actually be ignorant of his existence."[2] In consequence, between the victim of envy and the envious agent there is, or at least can be, one fundamental difference, which is envy itself. Rivals may have more or less legitimate claims to whatever is the object of their dispute, but they are equals in the conflict that opposes them in the sense that they share the opposition that divides them. On the contrary, according to Schoeck, those who are envied can be pure victims. They are hated without reason. There is no objective cause of the evil that pursues them, for it proceeds from an envious comparison that is without reason, a form of comparison that is all the more frequent, according to our author, now that there are fewer social differences between the agents involved.

Given that envy does not have any objective cause in the exterior world, its origin, according to Schoeck, can neither be in the distribution of social benefits nor in class or caste differences. In fact, we have just seen that reducing such differences tends to exacerbate envy. It follows, concludes Schoeck, that the source of envy can be found only in the envious agent. Ultimately, envy is rooted in the envious character of the envious person. Schoeck is aware that this is not a very enlightening answer, and he attempts to ward off the impression of excessive circularity by suggesting that the origin of the envious character of certain individuals is to be found in their childhood and is most likely related to sibling rivalry. Leaving aside for now the question of the value of this explanation, it is clear that Schoeck adopts toward envy what must be described as an essentialist attitude. According to him, envy is something in itself, a characteristic of some individual, and it is in relation to that intrinsic characteristic that envious behavior is to be explained. An immediate consequence of this essentialism and of the above-mentioned cognitive asymmetry is that the enviousness of the envious constitutes an essential ineradicable difference between the agent who envies and the person who is envied.[3] The asymmetry between the envious and the envied is in final analysis a moral asymmetry. The envied is, or at least can be, a pure victim, and the enviousness of the envious is never explained but simply constitutes an evil or, as Schoeck sometimes says, an immature personality trait of the envious agent. The second form of asymmetry in the relation of envy is therefore moral or ethical. Victims of envy can be purely innocent, but the envious are guilty, without any mitigating circumstances.

An important consequence of the above explanation is that envy constitutes a permanent feature of the human condition. Given that envy stems, according to Schoeck, from invidious comparisons with roots in a person's childhood, there is no social arrangement that can solve the problem of envy, and there is no possible redistribution of wealth and privileges that can placate the envious agents' resentment. Envy is here to stay, and as Schoeck insists later on, to believe that there can be a society that is free from envy is a dangerous utopian dream.

Yet Schoeck says that because envy is such a negative and destructive feeling, all societies have invented means of defending themselves against envy, as well as ways to repress public expression of it. Because of its cognitive asymmetry, envy, unlike many other emotions and most forms of rivalry, can remain hidden and silent; because envy typically acts in the dark, fear of envy has always been a major motive of human behavior. According to Schoeck, many aspects of both traditional and modern societies can be explained by the fear of causing envy, by the fear of becoming the target of the envy of others. Following Evans-Pritchard, Schoeck reminds us that in many traditional societies envy and the perceived need to defend oneself from envy constitute the main reasons why individuals resort to magic. In such societies, when an agent suffers a personal misfortune, he or she views it as a result of the usually magical intervention of some other agent. In consequence, the alleged victim takes countermeasures to protect himself or herself, and often even attempts in return to hurt his or her perceived attacker.[4] According to Schoeck, the fear of envy and measures taken to protect oneself from the envy of others combine to form the single most important obstacle to the economic development of such societies. Implicit in this bold diagnostic is the idea that the economic success of the Western world is to a large extent due to its greater ability to tolerate envy. Schoeck will argue that our increased capacity to withstand the envy of others and our superior ability to not give in to the fear of envy has been a major, if not the main, factor in the economic growth of the West. Furthermore, he credits Christianity with the enhanced resistance to the fear of envy, arguing that the Christian God, contrary to ancient deities, is not envious of humans.

By the time we come to the last chapter of his book, Schoeck has drawn a picture of envy that is so completely negative that the question arises as to why nature has preserved such an entirely harmful disposition among humans. Or to put it in another way, how could this wholly destructive trait have escaped the optimizing hand of natural selection? The Austrian sociologist offers two different answers to this question. It is interesting to analyze them briefly since they clearly reveal the limitations of his theory. His first answer starts from the observation that every human society needs a number of rules and regulations in order to function. It is in relation to these that our author sees the usefulness of envy. Envy, he argues, keeps us in line. It is the great guardian of everyone's honesty, our best means of protection against free riders. Fear of the envy of others makes us good citizens, and envy transforms each and every one of us into a police officer watchful of his or her neighbors' behavior.

> The individual scope for action of a being who has outgrown instinct must once again be so restricted as to permit the proper functioning of a larger social group. No motive . . . ensures conformity more certainly than the fear of arousing envy in others and the sanctions this entails. To the degree, therefore, that man has developed the capacity of mutual control out of suspected envy in the other, larger social groups with division of labour for their members have become socially possible.[5]

Envy is thus an indispensable part of every human society and plays a fundamental role, for only envy, and the fear of envy associated with it, makes us accept the social and moral code of behavior indispensable for the existence of large and complex societies.

Yet as Schoeck acknowledges, there can also be too much envy within a community. A society that does not limit and control the expression of envy among its members will be condemned to a life that is, in Hobbes's famous words, "nasty, brutish and short." In order to illustrate this danger, Schoeck gives the example of the Siriono tribe of eastern Bolivia studied by A. Holmberg.[6] According to Schoeck, the Siriono, who live in hordes of twenty members or so, "out of fear of the others' envy seldom eat except when they believe no one is looking: usually alone at night."[7] Schoeck offers this as an example of the social disruption that excessive envy can bring about, and he concludes that smaller groups "whose members *failed* to develop sufficient sensitivity towards the threat of envy in others, fell behind phylogenetically because they were unable in the long run to form themselves into the larger groups necessary for the mastery of their environment."[8] But in the case of the Siriono tribe, it is not so much fear of envy that is missing; they clearly have not failed to develop sufficient sensitivity to the envy of others. Rather, it seems it is an excessive fear of envy that condemns them to fasting most of the day.[9] Both Schoeck's discussion and the above example suggest that it is not envy itself or envy alone, and probably not even envy and the fear of envy only, that is indispensable for the existence of large complex societies, but a combination of associated dispositions. It seems envy will not produce its beneficial social effects unless it is accompanied by other character traits that transform its destructiveness into compliance with noninstinctual rules.

A somewhat related difficulty is also present in Schoeck's other example of the beneficial effect of envy. While discussing the negative and destructive effects of envy, Schoeck claims that one of the two social processes in which envy plays a fundamental role is the "inhibiting process, which serves tradition by thwarting innovation."[10] Yet a few pages earlier, consistent with H. G. Barnett's theory of innovation, he argues that envy is often a positive factor determining the acceptance of innovation.[11] Schoeck is aware of the apparent contradiction between these two claims and tries to spell out the particular circumstances that explain why in some cases the generally conservative motive of envy can become the motor of social innovation.

Both examples—that is, the Siriono tribe's eating habits and the role of envy in economic innovation—reveal the same difficulty. When he is confronted with what can be called the ambivalence of envy, Schoeck resorts to particular circumstances or rare accidents that explain how a purely destructive impulse can at times have positive consequences. When faced with the difficulty of explaining why natural selection has retained this wholly negative characteristic, which succeeds only in making everyone, including the envious person, worse off, he is suddenly led to respond in terms of associated traits that form a cluster with a net beneficial effect. What lies at the heart of these two problems is Schoeck's essentialism concerning envy. His belief that envy is a particular impulse or emotion that is completely unrelated to other apparently similar phenomena like jealousy and rivalry is incompatible with his explanation of why it was preserved by natural selection. His belief that envy is completely harmful is dissonant with the positive role it plays in the acceptance of innovation. But before offering a diagnosis of these difficulties and suggesting how they might be solved, we must turn to a second aspect of Schoeck's work: his criticism of socialism and egalitarianism.

Envy and the Modern World

Helmut Schoeck wants to convince us of the importance of envy in social life, of the central role it plays in human behavior and institutions, as well as of the fact that envy cannot be eliminated. He also has another goal, which gave his book a sense of urgency when he wrote it and a political tincture that it still retains today. According to Schoeck, our present society is in grave danger due to false beliefs concerning envy propagated by socialists and advocates of egalitarianism. His book therefore should not be seen as a purely scientific enterprise. It is also an attempt to set straight the political record concerning envy. He tells us that *Envy: A Theory of Social Behaviour* aims at unmasking the errors of socialism and the "mirage of social justice,"[12] just as much as it aims at contributing to our scientific understanding of envy. Like his compatriot Friedrich Hayek, Schoeck is clearly convinced that these two aspects of his work are inseparable. Fighting the political mistakes of the friends of social equality rests on an exact science of social behavior where the role of envy is correctly identified.

According to Schoeck, socialist ideology and claims to social justice are determined, in the best of cases, by three closely interrelated false beliefs concerning envy, its nature, and its cause. In the worst cases, they are motivated by envy itself. In order to see how the latter conclusion is reached, it is better to start from what Schoeck considers false beliefs concerning envy, which are central to the socialist movement and egalitarian claims. The first one, and to Schoeck's eyes the most damaging because he (falsely) believes that it implies the two other false beliefs concerning envy, is that envy can be eliminated. It finds its expression in the opinion that it is possible to devise a society, a socialist society, or a just society, from which all causes of envy will have been removed. Such a society would therefore be entirely free from envy.[13] It is, according to Schoeck, this false belief concerning the elimination of envy that fuels the socialist dream of a classless society, conceived as a society from which all causes of envy have been removed. It is false, according to Schoeck, because the real cause of envy does not lie in differences of income or class, but in a psychological disposition that is acquired during early childhood through experiences of sibling rivalry. The independence of envy from objective causes is clearly visible in the fact that an envious person will take advantage of any pretext, real or imagined, in order to justify his or her envy. It is also revealed by the fact, which Tocqueville noted long ago, that the disappearance of social hierarchies and reduction of class differences do not reduce but rather encourage envy between the representatives of different social classes. We must therefore, Schoeck argues, renounce the fantastic dream that it is possible to create a society that is completely free of envy.

Closely related to the first false belief is the belief that objective differences in revenue and social differences are the causes of envy. Once again the same evidence that was used to demonstrate the falsehood of the previous belief can be used to reveal the error of this opinion. The third false belief that propels socialist and egalitarian claims is the conviction that the moral responsibility for envy lies with those who are envied rather than with the envious. Clearly, if one thinks that there are objective causes for envy, then it seems reasonable to conclude that persons who cause envy in others should to some extent be deemed morally responsible for the envy that targets them. They could, in principle, have taken steps to prevent the appearance of the evil of which they are victims. However, according to Schoeck, such a conclusion is wholly unacceptable. Surely if envy does not have any objective source in social inequalities, envious agents must be wrong to blame the rich and successful for the invidious hatred that they feel. Furthermore, this groundless accusation suggests that what lies at the heart of their claim to social justice and equality is nothing else than their own envy. We have now reached Schoeck's second conclusion.

To understand the dangers to our civilization that, according to Schoeck, these three false beliefs constitute, it is better to work our way back from the third belief to the first. The conviction that the victims of envy are responsible for the envy that targets them tends to legitimate envious behavior. That is to say, it encourages invidious attitudes and renders acceptable to some extent all and every resentful claim of social justice. Yet if relaxing the fear of the envy of others is necessary for economic growth, this justification of envy can endanger our way of life, for it promotes and legitimizes the expression of envy. The resulting multiplication of envious behavior can in time lead only to a renewed and more intense fear of envy. The second false belief—namely, that objective differences in revenue and assets cause envy—provides envious resentment with a clear-cut target: social equality. Thus, according to Schoeck, it is not only the justification of envy that is dangerous for our social achievements but also the content of the claims motivated by envy. The idea that a society without envy can exist justifies in turn the cynical politician who stirs the envy of his or her fellow citizens in order to attain that utopian goal and forward his or her own petty ambition. Finally, in view of the fact that there are no objective causes of envy, this system of false beliefs contains a built-in mechanism that exacerbates the demand for equality, leads to endless claims, and can only spell disaster. Given that it is not possible to satisfy the demands of the envious person, those who believe that envy has an objective cause in social differences will take advantage of the failure of every concession to social justice to reduce envy to demand an ever greater equalization. On Schoeck's view, this dynamic of envious claims always gaining force and speed can only lead to the destruction of our civilization.

Unfortunately, unpleasant political opinions are not proof of scientific error. Yet anyone who wants to evaluate Schoeck's contribution to our understanding of envy must address the political consequences that he believed derived directly from his scientific work. This I do in the next two parts. My strategy will be to argue that Schoeck's political conservatism is inseparable from his essentialism concerning envy. However, in order to carry out this demonstration, we need to resort to some of the analytical resources of the philosophy of science. This is the first task to which we now turn.

Envy and Mimesis

Mimetic theory argues that envy is not something in itself. Envy, jealousy, rivalry, emulation are not independent substances or psychic atoms that are unrelated to one another. They are moments in a dynamic process of relation and correspond to greater or lesser intensity of mimetic desire. Many years ago, in an analysis of Girard's *Mensonge romantique et vérité romanesque*, Jean-Pierre Dupuy showed that mimetic desire gives rise to stable figures of rivalry.[14] Schoeck's definition of envy as a form of rivalry in which the agent would rather deprive himself or herself of the object of the conflict than let his or her adversary win the prize could very well constitute such a stable figure of rivalry. But we should not forget that these stable figures are not independent entities. They are various forms that mimetic desire can take. It follows that in the context of mimetic theory, the definition of envy is fundamentally conventional or, as John Locke would have said, "nominal." That is to say, the term "envy" is useful inasmuch as it allows us to reidentify a recurring figure of mimetic behavior and isolate it for purposes of description, prediction, or explanation, but we should not believe that it refers to a particular independent entity in the world. It does not designate a self-subsisting reality that is essentially different from any other object. Furthermore, it must be remembered that in mimetic theory, envy is not an explanatory category. On the contrary, it is itself a form of behavior that is to be explained by mimetic desire. According to Girard, envy is neither a biological impulse nor a fundamental drive with origins in childhood experiences of sibling rivalry. It is a descriptive category, and one with a utility that may very well be culturally limited. That, I take it, is the first and fundamental difference between Helmut Schoeck's and René Girard's treatments of envy.

In *Mensonge romantique et vérité romanesque* (1961) Girard, following Stendhal and Tocqueville, suggests that we should reserve the term "envy" to describe certain aspects of mimetic rivalry in the modern world. In that book, he traces the parallel evolution of the novel as a literary form and the transformation from external to internal mediation as the socially dominant mode of mimetic desire. Envy corresponds to a stage of internal mediation, once the rivals have lost sight of the object that originally motivated their conflict and become exclusively fascinated by each other. Furthermore, Girard would probably agree that what we call envy in everyday life is generally associated with the behavior and attitude of the losers in mimetic conflicts, like Dostoevsky's man from the underground, rather than with the behavior and attitude of the masters of mimetic desire, like the army officer he simultaneously admires and despises. Because mimetic theory construes envy as a moment in a dynamic relationship of conflict, it is able to explain what appeared to Schoeck as brute, intrinsic characteristics of a particular psychological disposition. For example, the fact that envy is not transgression specific but directed toward the other person is in a mimetic context a very straightforward result of the passage from external to internal mediation and the subsequent intensification of mimetic desire. It is often claimed that an envious person, unlike a jealous rival, is often ready to adopt a course of action that is harmful not only to his or her rival but also to himself or herself, if only it can bring some destruction upon his or her hated enemy. In fact, Schoeck and many other authors consider this trait to be a defining characteristic of envy. Mimetic theory allows us to understand that such behavior is not the sign of a strange disposition or particularly perverse frame of mind but, on the contrary, the normal result of the intensification of mimetic rivalry. Interestingly enough, readiness to suffer damage in order to harm one's adversary has also been considered by some authors as *the* trait that distinguishes hate from simple enmity[15] or as a peculiarity of irrational anger.[16] Construing this "defining characteristic of envy" as a moment in dynamic process of relationship, rather than as an intrinsic trait of a particular psychological disposition, renders perfectly understandable what would otherwise be either an incomprehensible anomaly or simple contradiction. Mimetic theory allows us to understand how this "defining characteristic of envy" can also have been considered as *the* trait that distinguishes hatred from enmity or a sign of irrational anger. From a mimetic perspective, the fact that various authors resorted to the same trait as a defining characteristic of what are for them very different emotions such as envy, hatred, and anger illustrates their shared failure to perceive the dynamics of conflict that lies behind the agents' apparently stable "psychological traits." It is a sign of the all too common tendency that transforms fleeting moments of rivalry into permanent essences. Mimetic theory inverts this point of view. Rather than starting from well-defined psychological dispositions in order to define the behavior of agents, it begins with social relations between agents and explains the psychological characteristics of each as responses to their interaction.

According to Schoeck, in spite of the fact that it rests on comparison between equals, envy is an asymmetrical relationship. The asymmetry is both cognitive and moral. Envy, as it is conceived by the Austrian sociologist, entails a strong moral distinction between the envious person and his or her purely innocent victim. Mimetic theory, on the contrary, argues that though envy may constitute an asymmetrical moment in an ongoing process or rivalry, it is part of a dynamic of conflict in which symmetry rules. If envy is defined as the attitude of the loser in mimetic conflict, then subjectively it is asymmetrical. It corresponds to the loser's recognition that he or she has lost. But if envy is seen as a moment in a conflict, rather than as an essential attitude of certain persons, then the asymmetry is only temporary, especially if we agree with Girard that in mimetic conflict, sooner or later everyone loses. It follows that in the long run, if you wait long enough, positions will be reversed, and those who are envied will have the opportunity to be envious. Furthermore, mimetic theory does not acknowledge any moral difference between the losers and the winners in mimetic rivalry. Those who are envied are not any less mimetic than those who envy them. Perhaps they are just luckier, and then perhaps not.

Once envy is placed in its proper mimetic context, the question of why this destructive urge was retained by natural selection no longer arises. Envy is destructive, but its destructiveness can be understood and evaluated only in relation to mimesis, the disposition to imitate others of which it is part. Schoeck understood that the biological and social usefulness of envy taken alone was hard to establish. He therefore built his case around a cluster of dispositions: envy, the fear of envy, the ability to repress the expression of envy, sensitivity to envy, and so forth. But Schoeck did not exhibit or even suggest any social mechanism able to explain how these dispositions are connected to one another. He also did not offer any biological reason for believing that these behavioral dispositions come together and link to each other, and that natural selection therefore can act upon them only as a group. That is to say, Schoeck did not give us any reason to believe that natural selection can promote or disadvantage them only as a unified group and not severally. Mimetic theory, on the contrary, offers a very natural solution to both problems. The social mechanisms that limit and control envy are the self-regulating scapegoat mechanism and the sacred institutions that proceed from it. Because envy is an aspect of mimesis, it is a moment in or a part of the mechanism of protection against violence. Selection for envy is therefore not different from selection for fear of envy or sensitivity to envy. Given that what we call envy corresponds to one of the stable figures of mimetic rivalry, Girard does not have to postulate an independent selection force for each member of the cluster of dispositions that are necessary to make envy a positive element in social life, contrary to what Schoeck would have had to do had he seen the difficulty.

To what extent are René Girard and Helmut Schoeck talking about the same thing when they use the word "envy"? If they are not, then my whole discussion so far has been based on a misunderstanding. Clearly, both Girard and Schoeck are to a large extent targeting the same types of objects. All

of the anthropological and literary examples quoted by Schoeck could find
their place in mimetic theory without any difficulty, and, had he known
about them, Schoeck could have easily used much of the empirical data contained in Girard's books in order to sustain his own theory. In other words,
both authors are trying to explain pretty much the same class or cluster of
phenomena. However, as I argued at the beginning of this section, both the
meaning and the extension of the word "envy" are different in their theories.
The meaning differs inasmuch as, for Schoeck, envy is a psychological disposition, with an origin in experiences of sibling rivalry during early childhood.
For Girard, envy is a stable figure of mimetic rivalry. That is to say, it is a result
of certain interpersonal conflicts, not a psychological disposition. Furthermore, for Girard, envy is a nominal category with primarily descriptive use.
According to Schoeck, on the contrary, envy picks out an essential intrinsic
disposition of certain individuals. The extension of the term is also different
in the authors' writing. According to Schoeck, envy is a universal characteristic of the human mind. He therefore finds examples of envy in every culture
and era. Girard for his part tends to limit envy to the modern world. At least,
that is the impression one gets when reading *Mensonge romantique et vérité
romanesque*, where he recalls Stendhal's trio of typically modern sentiments,
namely "envy, jealousy and impotent hatred" and argues that the advent of
political equality has encouraged the universal vanity from which these proceed.[17] This impression is reinforced when, in the third part of *Things Hidden
since the Foundation of the World*, Girard argues that we should reserve the
term "desire" for the particular forms that mimesis acquires in the modern
world.[18] This suggests that, in spite of the discovery of the scapegoat mechanism and its role in human cultures, we can retain "as is" the distinctions and
terminology of *Deceit, Desire and the Novel*. We can, but it does not follow
that we should or that a student of mimetic theory has to. The decision to
limit the extension of the term "envy" to mimetic phenomena characteristic
of the modern world is, once again, purely conventional.

Therefore, it is clear that when Girard and Schoeck speak of envy they
mean different things. It is also likely that the extension of the term is not
the same in both authors' work. However, it does not follow that the debate
between them is based on a simple misunderstanding, for both Girard and
Schoeck want to explain overlapping sets of phenomena. Furthermore, if
Schoeck is right about the nature of envy, Girard must be wrong, and vice

versa. One cannot consistently accept both René Girard's and Helmut Schoeck's theories of envy. One must choose.

Mimesis and Social Justice

In addition to the scientific differences that oppose mimetic theory to Helmut Schoeck's "theory of social behavior," mimetic theory also suggests a radically different approach to the problem of social justice. One can agree with Schoeck that the three beliefs that he takes to be at the heart of socialism and behind the demands for social justice are effectively false. But does it follow that all demands for social justice can be reduced to envious resentment? That remains at least an open question. Furthermore, even if one grants that envy or, if you prefer, mimetic desire is never absent from demands for greater equality and social justice, does it follow that those claims are always and in every case unjustified?

There are two dimensions to Schoeck's criticism of socialism and social justice. The first is a scientific criticism that is explicit. It argues that demands for social justice constitute an economic danger. Giving in to those demands can put an end to economic growth. The second aspect of Schoeck's criticism is moral. It is implicit and it argues that (all?) such claims and demands for greater social and economic justice are morally unjustified. The reason they are unjustified is that they originate in an envious comparison rather than from objective differences.

Let us turn first to Schoeck's scientific critique of socialism and social justice. The gist of his criticism is that demands for equality and social justice threaten our way of life. They may lead to economic disaster. This danger, he argues, does not come primarily from directly economic reasons. In other words, it is not because satisfying such demands would be too expensive or because it would ruin the state and destroy the margin of profit of most companies. The reasons invoked by Schoeck are only indirectly economic. The danger that such demands represent is, he argues, that they may progressively destroy the cultural conditions of economic growth. Schoeck believes that modern economic growth is possible only in a culture that has succeeded for some reason in reducing the fear of envy. Though, as we have seen, envy can at times facilitate the acceptance of innovations, in most cases it constitutes the major obstacle to the permanent cultural change that is inseparable from economic growth. Schoeck also thinks that in the Western world, Christianity has allowed us to abandon our fear of envy. According to him, because socialism and demands for social justice are essentially fueled by envy and because they legitimate envy as a social motive, they can generate a paralyzing fear of envy similar to what was typical of traditional societies.

Once again, Schoeck's analysis bears striking resemblance to Girard's, but there are also major differences. Girard, like Schoeck (and many other authors), suggests that Christianity has been essential to the birth of capitalism. But where Schoeck sees a reduction of the fear of envy, mimetic theory construes a change in the form of mimetic rivalry and our mode of protection against violence.[19] Furthermore, many of Girard's texts suggest that the modern world can sustain much greater intensity of mimetic rivalry without falling into the generalized violence of the mimetic crisis.[20] In consequence, the presence of mimetic resentment in demands for socialism or equality does not pose the same cultural danger in Girard's analysis as it does in the Austrian sociologist's approach. Even if claims of social justice were only and exclusively motivated by the aspect of mimetic behavior that can be described as envious resentment, as Schoeck sometimes seems to believe (though I think that is highly unlikely), it does not follow that they represent any danger to our economic prosperity. More precisely, it does not follow that such demands threaten our ability to accept continuous cultural change, the ability that Schoeck thinks is the central condition of economic growth. On the contrary, Girard has argued that the capacity of the modern capitalist world to absorb ever greater quantities of mimetic rivalry without triggering the scapegoat mechanism is one of the characteristic traits of our culture in opposition to traditional societies. It is reasonable to suspect that this capacity is not unlimited. Nonetheless, from the point of view of mimetic theory, there is no particular reason to believe that demands for social justice are precisely what will drive the system over the brink. From the perspective of mimetic theory, there are no scientific grounds for Schoeck's antisocialists fears.

Schoeck's moral brief against socialism and social justice is not as explicit, transparent, or straightforward as his scientific criticism. Yet the ground on which it rests is clear. It is the fundamental moral asymmetry of envious relationships for which he argues at the very beginning of his essay.

The envied person, he reminds us,[21] can be the object of another agent's envy without ever knowing it. He or she can therefore be the pure victim of entirely unprovoked envy. This is certainly true; such cases can and do occur, but if envy corresponds to a local asymmetry in a dynamic process of mimetic conflict, rather than to an essential behavior of certain agents, then this moral asymmetry cannot be accepted as a rule. That is to say, this can neither be assumed to generally be the case nor can it serve as a criterion to distinguish envy from other forms of rivalry. From the point of view of mimetic theory, the moral asymmetry between the envious agent and his or her victim is not essential but a transient accidental characteristic. For Schoeck, on the contrary, the moral weight and stigma of envy always lie with the envious person. In mimetic theory, envy is but a moment in a process of mimetic conflict, a process in which we all participate at times. It is a shifting position that anyone can occupy rather than an essence. In consequence, the clear and final distribution of moral responsibilities is impossible. It is impossible at the personal level, and even more so at the social level. Demands for social justice may be fueled by mimetic desire, but the same is true of economic growth and scientific progress. Are these morally reprehensible also?

Homo mimeticus as an
Economic Agent

I n *L'enfer des choses: René Girard et la logique de l'économie* Jean-Pierre
Dupuy and I presented a mimetic reading of the modern economy.[1] Our
goal was to apply Girard's approach to understand the rise and development of the modern capitalist economy. For my part, that endeavor took
the form of an inquiry into the notion of scarcity, one of the fundamental
concepts of modern economic science. Or perhaps rather than a fundamental concept of economic science, it would be better to define scarcity as the
"state of affairs" that is considered necessary in order for economic activity to
take place. Inasmuch as the goal of economics is understood as the (rational)
allocation of rare resources and real economies as the process through which
this allocation takes place, then the precondition for both economics and
economies is a world where abundance is not unlimited. In "L'ambivalence
de la rareté," my contribution to *L'enfer des choses*, reprinted in English as
chapter one of this text, I defended the thesis that scarcity as it appears in
modern economies and economic science is not a natural category, but, to
the contrary, that there is a social construction, or perhaps a more adequate
expression, a *social institution* of scarcity.

This claim can easily lead to many misunderstandings, and it therefore
needs to be made more precise and clear. First of all, it is important to say

what it does not mean. To say that there is a social institution or construction of scarcity does not mean that scarcity does not exist; it does not mean that the limitation of resources is not real, or that the claim that there is such a limitation is only a ruse of the strong against the weak, or of the rich against the poor. It does not mean that claims made about the scarcity of resources are simply ideological, or that they can be reduced to lies seeking to justify unpleasant and unfair policies. Nor does it mean that the world is so abundant in all that we may need that there are no problems concerning the allocation of rare resources. It is clear that we live in a limited world where we are sometimes unable to reach our goals because of insufficient resources.

However, in spite of this age-old limitation of resources, only the modern world has adopted the scarcity of resources as a central tenet of its social and political organization and argues that this situation forces upon us particular behaviors and decisions and that it justifies the creation of a new domain of inquiry whose discoveries promise to bring us a level of wealth and well-being previously unimaginable. The questions that then arise are why and how? First, why did this limitation of resources, which had always existed and had always constituted a problem, suddenly became a central issue around which a whole civilization was to be organized? Especially that historically as time went by and civilization became more and more organized around that fundamental belief in the inescapable scarcity of resources, its wealth grew progressively greater and greater. Second, how did this transformation take place? What brought it about? Through what means did scarcity become so evident and central in our representation of the social world?

The claim that scarcity is socially instituted or constructed constitutes an answer to these questions. It is, I argue, through a number of social changes, changes that did not bear on a domain that we would usually describe as "economic," that the preeminence of scarcity was brought to the fore. More precisely, it is through a transformation of the rules of solidarity between groups and individuals that the limitation of available resources became a central social issue to which attention came to be directed. These rules of solidarity were not primarily economic, though they did have an important economic dimension, as they affect the distribution of wealth and resources, but they do not do so through market exchanges; rather, they determine a social domain that partially escapes market exchange by prescribing rules of nonmarket exchanges. It was through the transformation, more precisely through the relinquishing of these rules of solidarity, that markets became a paradigm of societal organization and that scarcity was both socially realized and promoted as the fundamental problem of our life in common.

Following René Girard, I consider that rules of reciprocal solidarity are an essential part of the sacred, the mechanism that protects us against our own violence.[2] It is therefore a transformation of this mechanism that is responsible for the institution of scarcity and ultimately for the birth of modern economies.[3] Scarcity understood in this way, as a social institution, also constitutes a mechanism that protects us against our own violence. The word "scarcity" thus should not be understood to only refer to the (socially instituted) limitation of resources but must also refer to the social mechanism through which this limitation is instituted. It follows that the economic function of growth and of modern economies cannot be separated from their protective role relative to violence.[4] Modern economies, the constant refinement and development of the social institution of scarcity, play a central role in this mechanism of protection against violence.

Like the sacred, according to Girard, scarcity is a spontaneous self-organizing mechanism of protection against violence. This means first that like the sacred, scarcity as a social construction was neither invented nor planned by anyone. There was no social contract or common agreement that led to its institution. As Hayek said of market economy, it is the result of human actions, but not of human design.[5] Second, to say that scarcity constitutes a self-organizing mechanism of protection against violence implies that violence itself protects us against violence. In consequence, this mechanism of protection against violence is itself violent. There is nothing surprising or paradoxical about the idea that violence protects us from violence. One of the most universally recognized definitions of the modern state is that of a monopoly of legitimate violence over a given territory that protects each associate from the violence of others and all from the violence of outsiders. What is more surprising is to say that scarcity is a self-organizing mechanism of protection against violence that proceeds directly from the violent actions of all, that it is violence limiting itself through the particular way that the violence of each interacts with that of others. What is most surprising of all is to claim that scarcity plays that role! How can the limitation of resources protect us against violence, when want, deprivation, lack of adequate resources are generally viewed as major sources of conflicts? The answer is that it is not the quantity of resources as such that plays a causal role here, but the mechanism through which the limitation of resources is socially instituted.

◆ ◆ ◆

"But man has almost constant occasion for the help of his brethren, and it is in vain for him to expect it from their benevolence only. He will be more likely to prevail if he can interest their self-love in his favor, and show them that it is for their own advantage to do for him what he requires of them," wrote Adam Smith.[6] Even if we were to assume that this statement is universally true, it is only in certain societies that the advantage that an individual may gain from doing what another requires of him or her will generally adopt an economic form and be equivalent to self-interest. We spontaneously, generally, almost unanimously assume that this is the case. Given where this passage is to be found, in *The Wealth of Nations*, it is most likely that this was also what Adam Smith had in mind. Yet it is only if specific conditions are satisfied that the interest I take in my own interest will in many or most cases automatically take the form of an economic interest.

One of the most famous and often quoted passages from Adam Smith says that it is not from the benevolence of the butcher, brewer, or baker that we should expect our dinner, but "from their regard to their own interest."[7] Adam Smith in this assumes that his readers are neither the wife, the son, or perhaps the old grandmother of the butcher, brewer, or baker. More generally, Adam Smith assumes that his readers live in a society where there is no system of reciprocal obligations from which they may expect others to provide them with dinner. Adam Smith's claim can only be true in a society where the butcher, brewer, or baker is not obliged toward those who are looking forward to dinner, by what an anthropologist describes as "obligations to give, to receive, and to return." Of course it may be objected that where such obligations exist, it would still not be from "benevolence" but from the baker's, butcher's, or brewer's self-interest that is involved in fulfilling the obligation that dinner would come. That is most certainly the case, but let us leave for now benevolence to the side, for as I have tried to show elsewhere, it only has a place in a world where such obligations have already to a large extent disappeared.[8] In other words, the alternative of either benevolence or self-interest is a false alternative.

The important point is that where reciprocal obligations of solidarity prevail, the self-interest a person may have in fulfilling them will not generally take on the shape of an economic interest. A hunter may be motivated to share his catch, in conformity with his traditional obligations, by a desire, for example, to enhance his reputation as a hunter and hence his marriage prospects, but it is only in a society where no such obligations exist, or more precisely where they have already to a large extent disappeared, that the self-interest of the butcher, brewer, or baker will automatically be translated, as it commonly is among us, into economic interest. Why is this so? Because only in societies where reciprocal obligations of solidarity have disappeared is it the case that agents generally do not have any interest vested in *other particular people's interest*, or when it is the case that they do, those *particular others* tend to be more or less reduced to a few friends and the immediate family. In such a society each agent's self-interest will take a form that is independent of any specific interest of any particular other agent—that is, a form that is best realized through a medium that has universal currency.

The social institution of scarcity is the result of the progressive abandoning of reciprocal obligations of solidarity. Scarcity, as a set of resources that is insufficient to satisfy the needs of all, is the consequence of abandoning, of relinquishing reciprocal obligations. As Marshal Sahlins argues, a society where reciprocal obligations are still respected may be an extremely poor society, yet no one is in danger of starving unless all are.[9] Reciprocal obligations of solidarity have two very important characteristics. First, like conventions, but even more so, they police themselves. Because refusing to reciprocate is equivalent to exiting the network of solidarity, everyone, unless one is certain of his or her complete autonomy, has an interest in honoring his or her obligations. Second, reciprocal obligations of solidarity create borders. They have limits beyond which they do not extend. They divide the social world between those who owe us something and to whom we owe in return, on the one hand, and those who do not owe us anything and to whom we do not owe anything, on the other. Therefore, scarcity as an object of social perception will appear not only in a society where many agents are exterior to these networks of reciprocal obligations, a society where there are paupers, but where in principle anyone can be left out. The fact that there is not enough to satisfy the needs of everyone only becomes socially evident, it only becomes a fundamental issue that concerns all, when the distinction between those to whom we owe something and those to whom we do not and therefore between those who owe us and those who do not has to a large extent disappeared. Scarcity understood in this way is inseparable from individualism and from modern negative freedom. Being free and independent as we moderns understand it is to live in a world where we have hardly any reciprocal obligations and then only to very few particular others.

How does scarcity protect us from violence or limit violence? Abandoning reciprocal obligations of solidarity changes the logic of violent interactions, for such obligations are not primarily or essentially economic, but concern the whole range of human interactions, from marriage to vengeance. Obligations of solidarity are also obligations of violence. They impose on agents, on the one hand, strict obligations of nonviolence toward other members of their network of solidarity, and, on the other hand, duties of violence to help members when they are in conflict with outsiders. In consequence, any conflict tends to involve more persons than just those who were originally part of the dispute. Distant others who did not have anything to do with the original disagreement become parties to the violence. Through networks of solidarity violence spreads and progressively involves more and more members of the community. Because the abandoning of obligations of solidarity destroys these networks, it isolates conflicts and reduces their capacity to spread to larger portions of the community. Scarcity primarily reduces the contagion of violence; because the intensity of violence tends to augment with the number of participants in a violent encounter, it also tends to reduce violence itself. Furthermore, for the same reason that it abandons the violent parties to themselves, scarcity facilitates the establishment of a central power holding the monopoly of legitimate violence. Scarcity, the progressive weakening of reciprocal obligations of solidarity, allows this central power to intervene in conflicts without facing the danger of being automatically opposed by large subsections of the community.

Why is this mechanism a violent means of protection against violence? What is violent in this rejection and abandonment of traditional obligations of solidarity? This phenomenon is violent first of all, at least in the sense that it does not in any way stop or prohibit violence as such, it simply "disassociates" conflicts, so to speak. The abandoning of obligations of solidarity makes us indifferent to conflicts and violence that do not concern us directly. Second, it is violent mainly because it is *scarcity*—that is to say, because it is a social institution that inevitably condemns some agents to have insufficient resources, it necessarily produces victims, poverty, and social outcasts, those whom in our politically correct language we call "underprivileged." In an individualistic world where reciprocal obligations of solidarity have been abandoned, each one is not only encouraged but, to a large extent, socially forced to rest mainly on himself or herself; in consequence, those who fail are generally viewed as responsible for their own failure. However, what most of the time transforms a passing difficulty into a major crisis is the fact that no one is willing to help.[10] The essential violence of the mechanism is the indifference toward others that it generates. The institution of scarcity is the institution of the indifference to what happens to others. On the one hand, this indifference prevents us from being involved, from being sucked into the conflicts of others; on the other hand, it abandons those who are in need to their own devices, arguing that it does not concern us. These are the two sides of the same coin. The two faces of scarcity are freedom and indifference.

Why is this a self-organizing mechanism? The abandoning of traditional obligations is not a policy that is consciously, intentionally pursued in an effort to reduce violence or to foster economic growth. Actually, what motivates each agent to progressively attenuate his or her commitment to these obligations is the mimetic rivalry in which he or she is currently engaged and which we usually call his or her "self-interest." Maximizing one's self-interest pushes one to renege on his or her obligations toward others. However, these rivalries are precisely what leads to conflict. Therefore the same mimetic interactions that lead to conflict generate circumstances where these conflicts tend to be less violent and contagious because they tend to remain isolated from each other.

◆ ◆ ◆

So far what we have talked about is not quite economy but the type of social conditions that are necessary for something like a modern market economy to be possible. In *L'enfer des choses* this is also essentially what I did; my topic was not economics as such, but rather the social transformations that underlie the apparition of modern economies in the Western world. Now I attempt to do something somewhat different: taking for granted that this model is approximately correct, what does the type of explanation it provides change as far as economic science is concerned? What if anything does it imply for economics? Given that the social institution of scarcity is to be conceived as a real social transformation, rather than as a mere symbolic process, what economists talk about when they refer to the limitation of resources is real, it is not imaginary or false, and there is in consequence no particular reason to suppose that their entire enterprise is fatally flawed. Of course if my explanation of scarcity as a social construct is correct, it can provide interesting suggestions regarding economic history and help explain the disruptive effects of modern economy on traditional societies. However, what consequence does it have on economics itself, on the way we understand and explain economic behavior? There are two closely related issues relative to which we can try to measure these consequences: one is the scope of economic discipline and explanations, the other concerns its basic conceptual structure.

At the heart of this model of scarcity we find *homo mimeticus*, a mimetic agent, how does he compare to *homo economicus*? I take *homo economicus* to be a most standard and simple agent in a classical economic model. He is rational, and his rationality can generally be reduced to maximizing a utility function. Furthermore, *homo economicus* has a complete and well-ordered set of preferences that are revealed through his action. His rationality thus consists in acting consistently with regard to his self-centered preferences. The fact is, however, that since Sen's seminal article "Rational Fools" in 1977[11]—that is, more than thirty years ago—*homo economicus* has been quite sick. Numerous authors have argued that this model of economic agents as only guided by self-interest maximization is not only absurdly simplified, but clearly false. Efforts have been made to remedy this difficulty by giving this rational egoist, for example, a more complex utility function or social preferences, which interest him in the interest of others. Furthermore, entire (and new) disciplines like experimental economics, behavioral economics, neuro-economics, and evolutionary game theory applied to economics are trying to bridge the gap between this simplified model and how real economic agents behave. *Homo economicus* is now seen by many economists as a very imperfect model that needs to be profoundly modified in order to be able to explain the behavior of real economic agents. Simultaneously, these new "economic disciplines" have turned their attention to phenomena that until recently would have been considered as noneconomic—for example, the origin of cooperation and its relation to warfare. In the process such research has simultaneously extended the scope of "economic" explanations or, if you prefer, the explanatory ambitions of economics, and ushered in a new understanding of what is an economic explanation. It is in relation to this incomplete and uncertain transformation of *homo economicus* that we should consider the possible contribution of mimetic theory.

Central to this growing domain of research has been the question of the evolution of cooperation. How is cooperation possible in a population of interacting self-interested agents? How can rational egoists come to act altruistically? How are social preferences or other regarding preferences established? How can they be stable? Interest in these questions has favored the development of a convergence between economics and some aspects of evolutionary biology where the question of the evolution of cooperation is also central. Interestingly enough, the problems of cooperation and of altruism tend to take more or less the same form in both disciplines. Organisms, alternatively economic agents, are viewed as primarily searching to promote their own self-interest over that of others, and therefore, in theory at least, they will not normally engage in behaviors that are costly to them and that profit others. Furthermore, in both disciplines there is a strong tendency to associate cooperation with altruistic behavior, and for ideological reasons, the possibility of *true altruism* is viewed as an important issue.[12] In consequence, both economics and evolutionary biology consider that, in theory, cooperation is unlikely to exist, and that if it does exist, it will only be in certain very particular circumstances. However, in nature cooperation among organisms is frequent,[13] and it also constitutes a fundamental dimension of social life. The difficulty then is to explain the frequency of cooperative and altruistic behavior in both nature and in society in the context of theories that prima facie suggest that it should not be there. In other words, in both biology and economics cooperation and altruism constitute anomalies that need to be explained, or explained away.

Homo mimeticus, unlike a classical economic agent, is immediately interested in others, not because he is altruistic or naturally enjoys cooperation, but because he does not know what he wants, does not know what he prefers. More precisely, it is because what (some) others want and prefer constitute for each one of us the paradigm of what we want and prefer. The main difference between *homo economicus* and *homo mimeticus* is that *homo mimeticus* is a lot less individualized than *homo economicus*, neither his rule of behavior nor his preferences are fixed and determined once and for all, from the outside and from the outset; rather, they depend on the behavior and preferences of others. What is given to *homo mimeticus* is mimesis, which could be described as a "rule" or "function of dependence" on another. This "function of dependence" leads the agents to form some preferences or others and to adopt this or that rule of behavior. Furthermore, this "function of dependence" is itself subject to endogenous change as a result of the history of dependence between agents as well as their past behaviors and preferences.

Mimesis is often construed as a synonym of imitation; however, *homo mimeticus* is not an imitating agent, at least not in the sense in which we usually understand the term "imitation." Mimesis can give rise to behaviors that are very different from what we normally conceive as imitation—for example, what Girard calls "negative imitation," indicates an agent who always chooses or adopts a behavior that is in opposition to the behavior or preferences of another. So that if you vote liberal, I will vote communist; if you play golf, I will hate it and prefer tennis; if you support one sports team, I will support its opponent; if you dress casually, I will dress formally, and so on—so that while I am not properly "imitating" you, my behavior is nonetheless as rigidly determined by yours as if I were. *Homo mimeticus* then should be understood as a hypothesis concerning the extent to which our choices are not autonomous but depend on the choices of others. What we spontaneously and usually recognize as "imitation" is only one of the forms that this reciprocal dependence can take. Rivalry, opposition, and violence are also paradigm examples of types of behavior where the action of one agent is strictly dependent on the action of another. The behavior of *homo mimeticus* then can only be understood in relation to this "function of dependence" on others. It is, however, a complex function that can take many different forms.

While *homo economicus* has a well-ordered complete set of preferences, *homo mimeticus* has a model.

> Behind our desires, there is always a *model* or *mediator* who most often is not recognized by others and not even recognized by the imitator of the model. In general we desire what other people around us desire. Our models can be real as well as imaginary, collective as well as individual. We imitate the desires of those we admire. We want to "become like them" and to appropriate their being.[14]

Having a model means, among other things, that one's "function of dependence" on others is not the same in relation to all others. There are in this respect "privileged others" who exert a greater influence on the agent's preferences and behavior. Agents are therefore always interested in other people's interest and more in some than in others. This interest that we take in each other's interest, according to Girard, leads to conflict, and it also leads to cooperation. At a more general social level it is through conflict that cooperation is established; more precisely, it is the mechanism that limits violence—for example, the mechanism that produces the sacred or scarcity—that underlies the particular forms of cooperation that we find in different societies. Depending on whether the model is real or imaginary, collective or individual, the "function of dependence" that relates agents will be different. It is also fundamental to the ease or difficulty with which in a given culture individuals can change from one model to another, and the extent to which anyone can become the model of anyone. In consequence it is, according to mimetic theory, always impossible to explain the behavior of one agent taken individually. Agents may at times behave as if they were autonomous, perhaps even act "as if" they were classic economic agents and satisfy the predictions of economic models. However, mimetic theory suggests that when this is the case, this particular reduction of mimetic agents to an apparent *homo economicus* is itself to be explained in terms of mimetic relations between agents.

It is never individually and autonomously that an agent determines his or her preferences. An agent's preferences are always under the influence of other agents' preferences. Interestingly enough, "revealed preference theory" is agnostic as to the origin of an agent's preferences. An agent simply has the preferences that he or she has as revealed by his or her choices and actions. In that sense it is quite compatible with mimetic theory. However, and this I believe is where the main difficulty lies, it is unable to deal with situations where agents' preferences undergo changes or agents act inconsistently. It does not follow from mimetic theory, from the fact that agents' preferences are determined through a "function of dependence," that an agent's preferences will always be in flux or that he or she will necessarily act inconsistently. To the contrary, mimetic rivalry, as suggested earlier, can lead to a situation where an agent may appear to have the same order of preferences all his or her life and act to maximize his or her self-interest. Thus mimetic theory offers a general framework to analyze circumstances when such "classic economic behavior" will be the "normal" outcome of interactions between agents and circumstances, which will then lead to changes in preferences and inconsistent behavior. Furthermore it also provides a tool to determine when such changes and inconsistency should be viewed as irrational and when they constitute a progress and gain in rationality on the part of the agent.

Amartya Sen argues in *Rationality and Freedom* that self-interest maximization should not be construed as an actual characteristic of individuals, but is best conceived as the result of a correspondence with a *norm of maximization* imposed over a complete domain.[15] More generally, his argument is that what we usually take as basic characteristics of *homo economicus*—for example, self-interest maximization or a complete well-ordered set of preferences—are the result of circumstances external to the agent taken individually, and that those circumstances explain why, and the extent to which, this behavior manifests itself regularly. This corresponds pretty closely to the way I understand the relationship between *homo mimeticus* and *homo economicus*, except that mimetic theory adds that these circumstances are essentially to be understood in terms of interactions between agents whose choice and behavior are determined by a mimetic "function of dependence." Mimetic theory thus offers a tool to analyze situations when the classical behavior of the standard economic agent constitutes the rule, or at least the expected regularity, and when it does not. It also argues that such situations are social constructions or social institutions rather than that they reflect an intrinsic requirement of rational behavior.

PART 2

On Mimetic Theory

Mimetism and Autonomy

After what has just been said, I think all that there remains for me to do is to try to sew John the Baptist's head back onto the autonomy of the social, and show how the autonomy of society is related to the theories about autonomy that have been presented to us since the beginning of this colloquium.[1]

The Three Meanings of the Autonomy of the Social

Before anything else, however, we have to clarify what we mean by the "autonomy of the social." This expression has at least three meanings, which we will discuss one after the other this afternoon and tomorrow. They are ordered like successive stages in a history of humanity, and while we should perhaps be wary of this apparent order, it is in any case important to be conscious of it.

The first meaning of the autonomy of the social refers to the fact that the social, a system of actions, gains autonomy with respect to the individuals who make it up. In other words, people's actions determine a system that in turn ensures that they perform actions that determine the system. We are thus dealing with a circular system that is closed at the level of its organiza-tion and has a degree of stability or, if one prefers, a form of behavior specific to it. When this system is subject to disturbances from inside or outside, it either crumbles or, sooner or later, if the perturbations are counterbalanced, it returns to itself, it goes back to its equilibrium, in other words, its normal functioning. A system that constantly returns to itself affirms its autonomy, its independence from the disturbances it sustains. It is not determined by them, but by its own internal organization. This simultaneously implies that it is perfectly heteronomous with respect to the individuals that compose it. It counterbalances all of the new actions that they may undertake and thereby maintains its specific behavior as a fixed point, if you prefer its eigen behavior. This autonomy of the social with respect to individuals is related to a certain misapprehension on their part, to their inability to recognize the purely social origin of society. It is easy to see why.

I call "transformation path" the set of compensations through which an autonomous system is counterbalanced as it returns to its eigen behavior or equilibrium. Now suppose that we are dealing with an autonomous social system that has only one point of equilibrium and a unique transformation path, or perhaps a few closely related points of equilibrium and transfor-mation paths that are roughly the same. In both cases, the people who are the components of the system cannot imagine that the social is the pure concatenation of their activities according to specific laws leading to a self-regulated system. Since all of the actions that disturb the system lead to the same specific behavior (the same social organization) according to the same transformation path (the same crisis), it is impossible for them to establish a correlation between the actions that unleashed the transformations and the result. There is an excellent reason for this: the result is the same though the actions are extremely different; in fact, the set of possible actions is potentially infinite. In contrast, it is evident that they will be able to distinguish between actions that are at the origin of transformations and crises (transgressions) and actions that maintain the system's order, actions that are prescribed.

People will then think that the social system results from intervention outside of their action, that prescribes to them what they have to do in order to preserve order: gods regulate the lives of humans as they see fit; they say what humans should and should not do. In other words, in this case the autonomy of the social is the complete contrary of personal autonomy, and these systems are autonomous only for us, who are external observers, not for the people who comprise them. For those people, the social order comes from intervention outside of human action.

This is the ideal model of societies that are said to be "without history," apparently condemned to the eternal renewal of the same, openly engaged in reproducing what they are. Nothing could seem more foreign to the emergence of something new. Yet we will see below that the conditions for something new to emerge are nonetheless met.

The second meaning of the autonomy of the social is also that the system of actions is autonomous with respect to the individuals who comprise it. It looks a lot like the first meaning, except that this time the individuals know that the social organization is simply the result of the automatic, almost natural assemblage of their individual actions according to set laws, which deflect them from their immediate purposes and defy the divergence of individual interests to produce shared harmony. In this case, individuals are external observers with respect to their own society. They know that it is not only the result of their actions but also that the system of actions forms these actions into an autonomous, self-regulated whole foreign to their intentions.

This conception is that of classical political economy, which sees society as a self-regulated system subject to natural laws—in other words, laws that are not human and that delimit the space in which humans have jurisdiction.[2] Civil society has a mode of functioning that is specific to it and naturally balanced, optimal; the role of the state, of the self-reflexive activity of society members, is to get rid of obstacles, eliminate bad legislation on free circulation of individuals and the minimum wage, which perturbs the normal, natural self-regulation of the market and civil society. As Bacon said, we can control nature only by obeying it, and rational action consists in complying with market self-regulation. Individuals know that social organization and order are simply the results of their free activities, but they also know that these results are obtained thanks to a law that is not under their power and which flows from nature.

We may wonder how such awareness of the social origin of the social is possible if the society is autonomous with respect to the people who comprise it. How can individuals become external observers of the autonomous system that they are a part of, and is the idea of an autonomous social system sufficient to explain it?

Reflecting on what was said above about autonomous societies in the first sense, the answer seems obvious. For society members, components of an autonomous social system, to become aware of this situation, the social system has to have and need only have a number (two is enough) of fixed points or specific behaviors that are relatively distant and reasonably different transformation paths leading from one to the other. In these conditions, the actors will sooner or later correlate certain sets of disturbances, transformation paths, and forms of behavior specific to the system. Since they now have two sets of different, relatively independent data, they can do what Varela calls local coupling. They quickly recognize that the state of the system depends on their actions, but in a way that is neither simple nor direct because there is no coincidence between individual actions and the final result. This means nothing more than that their actions are part of a system. Since there are many specific forms of behavior and the sets of disturbances (actions) associated with each of them are sufficiently large and different, heteroclite, they conclude that the system is self-regulated. In other words, it has a degree of spontaneity and some balancing mechanisms. More simply and clearly: because the system combines people's actions beyond their individual purposes and immediate intentions, they recognize that it is self-regulated, autonomous, that it obtains its equilibrium from itself, independent of their regulating plans and disorganized desires. However, if other actions did not result in a different equilibrium, they would not imagine that the system organizes their actions.

As has probably been noticed, the reasoning is historical, and it supposes that members of a society already know how to distinguish between disturbances and actions prescribed in the framework of an autonomous system with only one form of behavior specific to it, and that they then isolate, from within the set of transgressions, a subset that they associate with one of the system's points of equilibrium.

However, it will be objected that the demonstration is contradictory because it is based on a bastardized concept of autonomy. In effect, it requires that members of society come to perceive the social system as an input-output system by performing a local coupling between different sets of disturbances and different forms of system-specific behavior. In short, they have to think that the state of the system is determined by these perturbations. Yet they also have to perceive the social as an autonomous, self-regulated system, since the very strong interconnectedness of their actions, which diverts them from their immediate efficiency and combines them into a system, defies the individual intentions that inspired them. In other words, they have to see the system as having its own behavior independent of those actions. This remark is correct, but it indicates something completely different than that the demonstration is contradictory.

In his talk, Francisco Varela reminded us that the point of view of control and the point of view of autonomy, that considering an entity as an input-output system and considering it as an autonomous system determined from the interior, are not contradictory but complementary points of view.[3] Although he might not agree, I will add that this is a question of two different approaches not to two different systems but to the same system. If, moreover, what is in question is an autonomous social system with many different fixed points, the components of which are also observers, the simultaneous emergence of two points of view is necessary.

Allow me to explain. It has often been noted that there is a certain ambiguity in the modern conception of the autonomy of the social. In effect, the autonomy of the social means, on the one hand, as has just been said, that the system of actions becomes autonomous, that individuals' actions interact according to a law that escapes them but that, on its own, gives order to the society. However, on the other hand, ever since there have been theories about the social contract, the autonomy of the social also means the self-institution of the society. This is the idea that people institute the social order on their own, that the society is what they make it, that it is an object of their will, and that political power takes its legitimacy only through transcribing for all the will of each. These political discourses construct an artifice—social contract, representation, majority—that is used to transmute individual wills into the general will, individual interests into the general interest. The thing is that they do not naturally coincide; in other words, individual actions combine into a system beyond and independent of the individual intentions that cause them. This means that in order to make society what we want it to be, we must occupy the place of legitimacy created by the artifice and control the political, economic, and social variables that determine the course of the social machine.

Clearly, there is no contradiction between these different points of view on the autonomy of the social, which affirm in one case the independence and autonomy of society with respect to human action, and in the other case, control of the social machine by individuals using techniques. In order for an autonomous social system to discourage those who comprise it from any feeble attempt to change or control it, and to render contradictory their efforts to regulate it, there has to be only one form of behavior specific to the system. Then it would convert all their initiatives into the same result. As we have seen, such a system does not allow members of society to see it as an autonomous system. If a system has at least two forms of behavior that are specific to it, then people will inevitably construct two sets of actions, each of which they will associate with a different form of behavior. Insofar as they are the authors of the actions, they are by definition in an external location from which they can try to control society. Since each set is vast and varied, and the actions do not combine in simple, direct ways, they will conclude that the system is self-regulated. Both ideas emerge simultaneously, despite the difficulties society members may have trying to reconcile them.

Thus, while the autonomy of the social, understood in this second sense, corresponds to a social system that, through the intermediary of some technique, gives society members relative autonomy that allows them to become artisans of their society and to recognize themselves as the authors of the social, it is also important to see the limits of this freedom. All techniques are based on the regularities of the objects to which they are applied, and social techniques are based on the regularities of the social system. No social techniques are possible if the regularities disappear, and any social technique will fail if the regularities change in unpredictable or chaotic ways. Social techniques suppose that social organization remains relatively stable, and in this sense they suppose that the social is an object that exists in an autonomous way. This is why social techniques cannot create anything new. They orient the system toward one of the forms of behavior specific to it, toward what was, in a certain way, always already there. They are part of the way that a complex system maintains its identity when faced with disturbances.

The third sense of the autonomy of the social is the autonomous society to which Cornelius Castoriadis invites us. In such a society, people know, or would know, that the social has no specific nature, that society is the pure product of their actions. They know that while the social organization is what it is, it could be completely different. It is not so much the society as people who are autonomous. The third definition of the autonomy of the social means that the system of actions more or less does not become autonomous. People can thus transform society, but in a way other than using a technique based on the regularities of an existing system. They can create something new; it is the system itself that they transform. We can then wonder whether we are still dealing with an autonomous system in the sense that we have spoken about it so far.

In any case, now that things are a little clearer, we will have a closer look at the first meaning of the autonomy of the social.

The Model

We are thus going to try to construct a model of an autonomous social system based on what Girard tells us. It will not be a mathematical model, but a model in the sense of an abstract, simplified scenario that, precisely because it is abstract and simplified, has heuristic value; it makes it possible to understand and incorporate a large amount of data.

We are thus going to give ourselves certain hypotheses and interacting elements. Since what is in question is the self-institution of society, we will say that these elements are apelike automatons with certain set instincts, such as to eat, drink, have sex and imitate. The last instinct on the list occurs in all superior mammals, and we are going to call it "mimesis." These are things that we find in animal societies. Now we are going to postulate one more thing: these specific apes have a more powerful, stronger mimetic instinct than other apes.

Are these apes more mimetic than others to a specific, measurable degree? Yes: we will define it within the system, in relation to other set instincts. We will say that it suffices that the apes' mimesis be or be able to become strong enough to upset the instinctive brakes that prohibit intraspecific murder.[4] Why this relationship between mimesis and violence? For a very simple reason: because this reciprocal imitation concerns all forms of behavior, including acquisitive behavior—in other words, actions designed to acquire objects.

Girard speaks of mimetic desire, but in this case desire in the usual sense is not necessary. Desire is mimetic in the sense in which it is mimesis that creates desire. To say that there is acquisitive mimesis is not to say that there is an original desire to possess. It is to say that, when one apelike automaton performs a very simple action—for example, grasps an object—that action awakens in another apelike automaton the same movement toward the same object. The link between mimesis and conflict is immediately clear. In order to avoid conflict, one or the other has to yield or renounce the object. Yet, since the behavior is imitative, neither can yield because each wants the object in direct proportion to how much the other wants it.

Moreover, this process necessarily has to escalate. Why? The movement that I make toward an object may be entirely spontaneous and unintentional. In other words, perhaps the intention targets nothing in particular, such as when speaking one may, without noticing, pick up a pencil. However, since I am a mimetic being, my grasp on the object will be strengthened by the other's efforts to take it. This will go on indefinitely, with the other's efforts increasing in proportion to my resistance, and my resistance in proportion to the other's efforts.

During this escalation, a strange phenomenon will emerge, though it is easy to see why. The antagonists will lose interest in the object, and become increasingly fascinated by each other. This is easy to understand because, properly speaking, each is for the other the obstacle that prevents acquisition of the object. Girard calls this the model-obstacle: "model" because he or she is the object of imitation, and "obstacle" because he or she prevents the imitation from being successful. Since between ourselves and the goal the obstacle is the focus, sight is quickly lost of the object as rivalry escalates, and the antagonist takes center stage. The antagonists will try to destroy each other, and, given our premises, this can be to the death.

If we now bring together a large enough number of apelike automatons with these relationships, what will happen?

A priori, we can suppose at least two possibilities: either they will kill one another until only one remains, which is not a very interesting scenario, or something else will happen, but what?

Girard constructs his scenario according to the cultural traces that he finds after the fact. He very simply says the following. Since mimetism is a contagion factor, all will be polarized toward a single object in a rivalry of all against all. However, while acquisitive mimesis divides, once it has gone beyond a certain threshold of intensity and becomes mimesis of the antagonist—in other words, once sight has been lost of the object—it brings agents together because all converge on a single adversary. The killing of the unique adversary of all seals the community's unity because all have succeeded in discharging their murderous fury against a single one at the same time. In other words, aside from the victim, they have all achieved the goal they were seeking. The community transforms brutally from the most complete violence and agitation to perfect calm.

What can we say about the mechanism at this first level? Girard says that it is a self-regulating mechanism, and it is easy to see why: because it results from pure escalation of violence. We do not need to bring anything into play but mimetism and set instincts: neither an intention to reconcile nor awareness of what is happening. In fact, it is because each always seeks to kill the other that the mechanism functions, because all ignore that the violence has no object and results mechanically from mimetism. This is to say that none of those who are caught up in it understand its operation. However, it is also a social mechanism insofar as it does not result directly from instinctive dispositions, but is an organization process that occurs at the level of the group.

We are thus dealing with a self-regulating social mechanism for violence.

What will happen next? We can suppose that the mimetic crisis is a traumatic experience for our apelike automatons since they go from a paroxysm of murderous fury to perfect calm, and they have no idea what is happening. We can suppose that they find themselves in a state of heightened attention, but with no object for that attention. To what will their objectless attention turn? To the dead body around which they are all gathered. However, we have to remember that they have just had an experience that is not quite natural, which is social, and the meaning that is attached to the cadaver is that of this experience combined with all the incomprehension that surrounds it. The meaning of the crisis, its escalation and its resolution, will be associated with the dead body. The meaning is ambiguous, both beneficial and harmful. The cadaver is thus quid pro quo, one thing in the place of another, a cadaver in the place of a social experience. Thus, the experience of the crisis and its resolution seems to be related to the first symbolization, to the fact of using one thing to mean another.

This mechanism seems plausible, but can it be demonstrated? The answer is, no. In contrast, and this is where I take you back to John the Baptist's beheading, it makes it possible to understand a huge number of mythical and religious texts that speak of violence, expulsions, and killings, and in which the victim is a god.

Of the First Meaning of the Autonomy of the Social: The Sacrificial System

The autonomy of the social becomes really interesting when we look at it not only in relation to this self-regulating mechanism for violence but especially with respect to all that Girard thinks flows from it. Girard links this mechanism with a number of cultural features and institutions characteristic of primitive societies. They form the core of what, to facilitate discussion, we will call the sacrificial system.

First, myths: they tell the story of what has happened. Of course they provide false, incomplete narratives of the crisis, its unfolding and its outcome. In fact, they even veil and hide the essential. However, this concealment is not voluntary; it does not proceed from any desire to deceive. It results from the misapprehension characteristic of the crisis resolution mechanism. No one understands that the choice of victim is arbitrary, and that each and any of the protagonists could have served the purpose just as well. Indeed, this is what is dissimulated in the myth: the lack of difference and banality of the victim, not the fact that he or she dies for another, that he or she is the victim *in vicem*, in the place of, but the fact that anyone could have played that role just as well, the fact that no special quality, neither innocence nor guilt, no divine nature, predetermines any individual to this role in involuntary reconciliation. Moreover, this cannot be otherwise because it is only insofar as all think that the one in question is indeed the guilty one, the one who is responsible for the crisis, the instigator of the violence, that they can reconcile themselves against him or her by participating in his or her murder, and in doing so transfer onto him or her, truly, all the violence contained in the community. Once the transfer has been successful and peace returns, these are the facts that convince everyone that the belief is well-founded. From then on, the victim can appear only monstrous, beneficial and harmful, the cause of the crisis and its resolution. The victim becomes a god who visited people, played with them, and led them through an obscure experience that they have to decipher.

The misapprehension characteristic of the crisis resolution mechanism, which myths perpetuate by definition, is that the crisis and its outcome are beyond human will and responsibility, that they belong to the divine jurisdiction. What myths hide is that the violence is a purely human affair. Myths shift into the hereafter of the sacred all of the prescriptions and rules of social organization that are designed to prevent violence. This misapprehension makes the social autonomous; it makes the social system an insurmountable given and transforms the pure result of human interactions into a sacred order, imposed forever, against which we are powerless. It is through this misapprehension that the social system is autonomous—in other words, perfectly heteronomous in relation to the agents who produce it.

Second, rituals and sacrifice, which flow from the crisis. They are derived from the sacrifice, the first sacrifice, the killing of the scapegoat victim and the original reconciliation. Like myths, rituals and sacrifice commemorate the original crisis in their own ways. They commemorate it in actions—in other words, they write the story in a corporeal theater. They reenact what happened, and their purpose is to reactivate the beneficial virtues of the resolution of the crisis. For this, they seek to reproduce the actions that led to its resolution. In this sense, all rituals are sacrificial and always end in sacrifice.

All rituals and sacrifice, which is the ritual par excellence, substitute another victim, animal or human, for the original victim. This makes it possible for the community to be reconciled and purged of its violence. So long as they remain living, rituals are an efficient technique in the fight against violence because they provide each individual with an outlet for his or her resentment, a substitute victim who prevents antagonists from resorting to murder among themselves.

Third, prohibitions designed to prevent repetition of the actions that were at the origin of the crisis: violent and acquisitive actions. The point is to prohibit conflicts and rivalries—in other words, to determine and define people's access and right to various goods that may create opportunities for disputes and conflicts, such as land, livestock, game, women, trophies, and the bloody harvest from raids. Since mimetism ensures that anything can become an object of desire, prohibitions tend to regulate all aspects of social life.

Yet a strange contradiction cripples the sacrificial system, threatens its order, and ensures its reproduction. This is a contradiction that takes two forms but that can be summarized as: nothing distinguishes the sacrificial system from the violence that precedes it. Indeed, there is no action, principle, will, or intention that separates the reconciliation from the murderous madness from which it comes. The killing of the scapegoat victim is always only one more murder, and it is not peace but violence that was sought by those among whom peace has returned. This contradiction, this undifferentiation of violence and the sacred, takes two forms. On the one hand, rituals prescribe the very thing that prohibitions forbid. This contradiction has been pointed out innumerable times; rituals not only authorize but prescribe what in normal times is the greatest sacrilege—for example, murder or incest. In sacred times of purifying sacrifice, they order people to commit the sins that have to be washed away. This is why sacrifice, a mimed crisis in the framework of ritual time, always runs the risk of invading all times and returning mimetism to the crisis, of falling back into the violence that it is intended to prevent.

However, this fragility of the sacrificial system is also its strength and ensures that it lasts. This is because the crisis leads only back to itself, to the immolation of a new victim/founding god for new myths, rituals, and prohibitions.

The contradiction also takes another, less well known form. While prohibitions have a negative aspect that is designed to prevent conflict and reduce violence, like Janus, they also have a positive aspect, namely, obligations, from which they cannot be separated. This shackles people to a duty to commit violence. The prohibition against killing is immediately the obligation to take revenge for killing; the prohibition against adultery is also the obligation to kill those who commit adultery. The problem is that we cannot abdicate this duty to commit violence. No one can distance himself or herself from the obligation to kill or to take revenge without immediately violating a prohibition and attracting the violence of others. Thus, beyond the constraints flowing directly from mimetism, obligations freeze the community with fear and set everyone against everyone else through revenge prescriptions that break down spatial boundaries and extend across generations, bringing the crisis back to its tragic repetitive outcome. No one can distance himself or herself from the sacrificial system; all transgressions, through ritual sacrifice or the sacrificial crisis, take the system back to its precarious, unique equilibrium. Its violent fragility is the only form of behavior specific to it; there is no room for innovation. It lives forever in the monotony of vengeance and the gloomy bonds of prohibitions.

Thus, the sacrificial system is stable and autonomous, and has only one fixed point because the prohibitions that are designed to protect against violence have flip sides that are obligations that relaunch the crisis and lead it back to the scapegoat victim mechanism. This is also why, no matter what those involved in the system do, the system cannot escape itself.

Of Novelty

I would now like to rapidly suggest, through a single example, how a system or mechanism that enslaves a society to its past can be, if not the driving force, at least the opportunity for a history, and provide the conditions of possibility for something new to emerge. I would like to suggest how the narrowness of its view and its very stability can deliver more than they can promise.

The example is very simple: animal husbandry and domestication. In *Things Hidden since the Foundation of the World*, Girard shows how the sacrificial system could have been the source of animal husbandry and domestication. Girard says that we cannot really imagine that at some point the first people said: "Let's live near certain groups of animals and attach them to us, and in a few generations, our great-grandnephews and great-grandnieces will enjoy the economic advantages of domestication and the new source of wealth that will flow from animal husbandry." We cannot suppose that this kind of economic reasoning was at the origin of domestication because, first, it presupposes that the result of the undertaking is known in advance; second, it supposes prior knowledge of which species can be domesticated and which cannot; and, third, the result would not emerge until several generations had gone by, so the reasoning requires that we give primitive societies economic wisdom and very long-term plans that are often lacking in our own actions. In short, these are very strong, highly unlikely hypotheses.

Yet to arrive at the same result, namely domestication of animals, it suffices to suppose that people attached themselves to certain groups of animals not in order to draw unpredictable economic advantages from them in the future but to have at hand a sufficient number of surrogate victims always available for sacrifices. Depending on what kind of animals were in question, over time, some became domesticated. Finally, Girard gives as a counterexample of failed domestication, since the animal does not lend itself to it, an Ainu custom in which, for ritual purposes, a bear cub was raised with the children of the tribe.[5]

Girard uses this explanation of the origin of domestication to support his thesis that all human institutions come from the surrogate victim mechanism. I am more interested in the inverse: not in tracking it from the victim mechanism, but in how new things emerge and in their unpredictability. There is nothing in the sacrificial system that makes it possible to predict the domestication of animals. It does not even contain this result as a "perverse effect" in the sense in which sociologists and economists use that term. Domestication looks instead like an event that emerges out of the necessary, but partly undetermined, encounter of a closed, self-defined system, which is in this sense autonomous, and an environment with certain characteristics. This is a necessary encounter because a system that is closed at the level of its organization cannot avoid entering into contact with its environment, if only for energy exchanges. The system is partly undetermined because it does not entirely specify the nature of the encounter. Domestication sometimes emerges from the encounter, but sometimes it does not. It all depends both on transformations internal to the system (human or animal sacrifice) and on characteristics of the environment (whether or not the animals can be domesticated).

The result is thus truly new for the system, and for the environment, because what has just been defined as a characteristic of the environment is the result of the system's action on it. We can thus see how a closed system that is foreign to change can, for these very reasons, provide the necessary if not sufficient conditions for something new to emerge—in other words, for there to be history. Why for these very reasons? Because if the system had many eigen behaviors specific to it but very distant from one another, there would be no domesticated animals.

Violence and Nonviolence

The following is a revised version of an article that was originally meant to be published in *Alternatives non-violentes* (ANV). In March 1979, that journal organized a roundtable with René Girard and four activists from the *Mouvement alternatives non violentes* (MAN) on the possibility of effective nonviolent action in the political arena.[1] In July 1979, the editors of the journal asked me to write an article, note, and critical reaction to the roundtable and to a postscript written by another MAN activist, F. X. Verschave. All of these texts were to appear in a special issue on Girard.[2]

Though the article was written upon request, it was considered by the editors to be too critical, and they refused to publish it. This anecdote would be uninteresting in itself if it were not perfectly consistent with the logic of the discourse of the MAN activists. In effect, when the editors of a journal have a platform that gives them the possibility (and duty) to respond to criticism that they consider unjustified, but they refuse to publish an article that they themselves have requested (whereas a short note would have sufficed to indicate that the views were the author's responsibility alone), we have to admit that they demonstrate having an unusually open mind. If, moreover, the journal is the mouthpiece of a nonviolent movement, we have the right to ask what meaning they give to the words "violence" and "nonviolence."

However, since at the roundtable in question it was clear that the MAN activists defined nonviolence as all means of fighting and exerting pressure without resorting to open violence, it immediately follows that refusing to give an adversary the right to speak by preventing him from having access to means of expressing himself publicly is a form of nonviolent action that works in the political realm.

The MAN activists' consistency was just as admirable as it was regrettable. Indeed, this was neither a case of nonviolence nor of political action. The MAN activists refused to allow the dispute the only thing that could give it political meaning: the fact of occurring in a public space where it would be made available to the criticism and, in the end, judgment of others, the judgment of those not immediately involved in the conflict. This alone could have prevented the mimetic mechanisms of rivalry from being brought into action and permitted the clash to be resolved in a manner other than by making might right.

I am grateful to *Esprit* for having agreed to publish this article, and thus for allowing the debate to exist. My analysis of nonviolence remains essentially the same as it was in the original text, and my criticism of Girard has been expanded to show why he also fails to take into account the dimension specific to politics.

Violence Rooted in Objects?

If the fundamental reason for violence were in objects, then good social, economic, and political organization of the world would suffice to eliminate violence: as soon as you say that the true reason is not in objects, that they are merely pretexts, does it not make us despair a little? Does it not mean that violence can never be eliminated, that it is inscribed so deeply in human relationships that we can never go beyond it?[3]

This question, which was asked by Christian Mellon, can be used as a thread that reveals the meaning and goal of the ANV activists' shared undertaking. The question is in fact twofold. On the one hand, what is the origin of violence? Is it rooted in objects or in human relationships? On the other hand, can violence be eliminated? The ANV activists' answer can inform us about the "effective nonviolent action in the political sphere" to which they have devoted themselves.

Yet their convictions are not expressed very openly; they are generally formulated as questions and hypotheses. "If the fundamental reason for violence is related to objects (CM), could conflict not also come from the absence of objects (JS)? Many think that violence results from lack (CM), but we do not agree about the deep void of all conflicts at their point of departure, when they are centered on an object that is of unequal vital importance to both parties (JS)." Or, as F. X. Verschave says, "Non-violence accepts conflict. It agrees to enter into it, because in this violent world the question of how things should be shared has not been resolved."[4]

For the MAN activists, thus, violence is rooted in objects, in the problems that arise concerning the distribution of objects. This objective violence justifies and legitimates the entrance of nonviolence into the conflict—in other words, effective nonviolent action into the political sphere. However, it has to be clearly noted that, strictly speaking, this position is the exact contrary of Girard's. Mimetism is not something that occurs only when conflicts become worse; the mimesis of desire is prior to conflict: it is the cause. As Girard says, the absence of any object is indeed derived; it is the necessary illusion of the one who desires what the other possesses. The desire to remain focused on the object is not specific to MAN activists. Every adversary is convinced of the "objectivity" of the conflict, of the fact that he or she is in the right. All believe that they are in conflict with others for excellent reasons; all think that they are always focused on the object that seems to them to be the unique cause of the clash.

Violent Conflict, Nonviolent Clash

This said, since the nonviolent activists accept conflict, consent to take part in rivalries, they have to define a form of nonviolent conflict that is different from violent conflict, despite the surprising fact that it is the objective violence of the world that legitimizes their entrance into rivalry.

Jacques Sémelin's attempt to distinguish violent conflict from nonviolent clashes seems to be a little utopic: "In non-violent conflict, even if a partner, the persecutor, wants to resolve the conflict in a sacrificial manner by engaging in mimetic violence, the other rejects from the beginning any mimetic evolution of the conflict, and announces this rejection, which is very important."[5] However, no one ever *wants* to resolve a conflict in a sacrificial manner. To want to do so would suppose awareness of mimetic mechanisms, which would undermine their effectiveness. Sacrificial resolution of mimetic crises escapes the participants' will because such resolution is based on misapprehension of the mechanisms. Likewise, no one ever *wants* to engage in mimetic violence. The mimetic nature of violence is never the object of a clear decision on the part of either adversary; much to the contrary. The mimetic nature of the violence is the growing identicalness of the rivals as it appears to an observer who is outside the conflict, and it remains invisible to those who are caught inside the rivalry, those whom Girard calls doubles. The antagonists constantly seek to distinguish themselves, to differentiate themselves. Each tries to show that he or she is not like the other. In this symmetrical clash of wills, the mimetic nature of violence is refined. In *L'enfer des choses*, Jean-Pierre Dupuy very clearly described the forms of this negative mimetism.[6] Rejecting any mimetic development of the conflict and announcing this rejection do not in any way distinguish violent conflict from nonviolent conflict because the mimetic development of conflict is how conflict develops, period. I know of no rivalry in which each does not cast onto the other the entire responsibility for making the dispute worse.

Even supposing that the nonviolent activists' determination to reject all violence within disputes constrains their adversary to also abstain from open violence—in other words, supposing that the mimetic development of the conflict occurs through dissimulated violence, nothing has been won. In *L'enfer des choses*, we showed that the economic order of the modern world, which the nonviolent activists consider to be the origin of conflicts (the problem of the distribution of objects), is based on a mechanism of this type. It would be false to say that this order is without violence.

Techniques and "dispute management" methods that are determined by tactical and strategic considerations and enter into the preparation of action are, they claim, "neither moral nor religious" but stem from the fact that the adversaries are the ones who have all the guns. However, I find it hard to conceive that they define nonviolence. To abstain from the use of weapons because one does not have any is to do what all antagonists do: situate the conflict where they have the least chances of losing. However, this strategy remains outside the meaning of the action. The violent also make the best of a bad situation; vengeance is patient.

Nonviolent Strategy and Forgotten Ethics

The importance placed on strategy and techniques bothers me, not in itself, but because it is paired with clear reticence to talk about the moral and religious content of nonviolent action, especially when the fact that this content exists has been recognized. Indeed, if I have understood what Christian Mellon said, the restraint, and the insistence on methods are themselves tactical, provisional and temporary: within twenty to thirty years, it is possible that they will weaken. Does not the tactical restraint consist in sacrificing the meaning of the present action out of concern for effectiveness—in other words, out of a desire to win?

Thus, the roundtable ended with a test case: imagine two nonviolent activists oppose each other and go on unlimited hunger strikes. Let us specify the case: I am young, in good health, in perfect physical condition, and some dispute places me in conflict with my father, who is already old and sick but, like me, a nonviolent activist. We both go on hunger strikes. Believe me, I will beat the old man; he will not be able to take it. There are a thousand and one ways to kill people. More clearly, techniques in no way guarantee the meaning of the action. If, even by mistake, nonviolent activists espouse an unjust cause and win, what should we call their action? Violent or nonviolent? What if they did it on purpose? It is true that my hypotheses are absurd, unlikely, borderline cases, and that they are grotesque and cynical. So what? They are possible, and that pure possibility clearly shows that techniques, strategies, and "conflict management" guarantee nothing about the meaning of the action.

It is true that I am not taking into account the intentions and repeated declarations of the MAN activists. Those who are nonviolent take the side of the "real victims," "put themselves in the shoes of the real victims," "identify with the real victims" (JS and HO). Who would claim otherwise? The protagonists of all clashes, whether violent or nonviolent, think the same.

Each always believes that the victims with whom he or she identifies are "real victims" and that those supported by the people on the other side are "persecutors." The ANV activists also say: "Neither the choice of victim nor the object of the conflict are [*sic*] abandoned to the arbitrariness of mimetic violence," but since mimetic violence is what they are not engaging in (or what nonviolent activists believe they are not engaging in), this sentence has to be understood as follows: neither the choice of victim nor the object of the conflict is abandoned to the adversary. This underlying identification of mimetic violence with their opponents always occurs with the nonviolent activists insofar as they seem to conceive of mimetism as the conscious process by which a "persecutor" wants to make his or her "victim" guilty, not only injure the victim, but shift the entire responsibility for the conflict onto him or her.

However, since all antagonists in all antagonisms always think that the victims with whom they identify are "real victims," objective victims, all always seek to show that their opponents are "persecutors"—in other words, they seek to shift the responsibility for the conflict onto them. This is what the nonviolent activists do when they identify their opponents with mimetic violence. So long as the conflict remains open, no one ever wants to abandon to the adversary the choice of victim or the object of the conflict, and it is the logic of mimetic violence that is at work in each one's symmetrical opposing desire to designate the real victims. Yet no matter what they think, if the sacrificial resolution of the conflict is achieved, the victim will have been chosen by neither adversary but by the arbitrariness of mimetic mechanisms.

This is why nonviolent action, as it was portrayed by the MAN activists at the roundtable, does not seem to me, contrary to what F. X. Verschave thinks, likely to invent "mimetic decontamination rituals," but is instead pregnant with new forms of sacralization. Here is an example:

Hervé Ott says of nonviolent activists who identify with a "real victim" that "it is because they manage to make it known that they are not guilty that they succeed in exposing the fact of the innocence of the real victim."[7] Yet since, according to the MAN activists themselves, designating the "real victim" is what is at stake in the debate, this strategy is pointless. Unless one has abandoned all logic, it should be obvious that the nonguilt of the nonviolent activists tells me nothing about the innocence of the people with whom they identify.

The point of this criticism is simple. If we define nonviolence only in terms of techniques and strategies, we define nothing at all because we are rapidly led to define nonviolence as the set of pressure and combative tactics that do not involve open violence. If we change only one word in this definition, we immediately see the degree to which it is fallacious—for example, nonviolence is the set of pressure and oppression tactics that do not involve open violence. This set exists, and everyone agrees, especially nonviolent activists, that it is not nonviolence. Of course, the nonviolent define themselves by the fact that they do not engage in oppression—in other words, by the fact that they take the side of "real victims." In a world where, according to both Girard and the MAN activists, violence has the special aspect that "we now persecute only those who have already been shown to be persecutors," and where "persecution is pursued in the name of anti-persecution," this definition of nonviolence by identification with "real victims" cannot be distinguished from the usual definition of violence, and it is, in fact, difficult to imagine a more sacrificial form of violence.

To reduce nonviolence to a set of tactics and strategies is to transform the ethical and political issue of violence into a technical problem. But to what end? Christian Mellon's question, which I quoted at the beginning of this essay, provides an answer to this. It says that it is rather disheartening to think that violence is rooted in human relationships because then violence cannot be eliminated or escaped, whereas if its source is the problem of how to share objects, "then good social, economic and political organization of the world would suffice to eliminate violence." Transforming the ethical and political question of violence into a technical problem is, it seems, a way of giving us the means to a final solution. However, as we have seen, and as we will see again, this final solution is indistinguishable from violence and, by sacrificing at this point the meaning of the action to the desire to win, what we are dispensing with is personal responsibility.

It is important to note that in Girard there are no "real victims." More precisely, and this amounts to the same thing, there is only one: Christ. This is because he alone never participated in violence. This does not mean that victims are guilty. They are neither gods nor devils, angels nor beasts, innocent nor guilty; everyone takes part in the violence, but reconciliation is achieved against one only. Thus, the arbitrariness, but neither the innocence nor the guilt, of the victim. We are moving away from the sacrificial, from the infantilism that divides the world into "real victims" and "persecutors." This is so rare that we have to give Girard credit and temper any criticisms we may make of him for other reasons.

The criticism of nonviolence based on Girardian theses nonetheless has unpleasant consequences. This is because the reason why nonviolent strategies prove in the end to be indistinguishable from violence is that the nonviolent activists accept to enter into the conflict because they take the side of one of the opponents. As focused as they are on victory, rationalizing their discourse and actions with a view to that end only, they reduce nonviolence to a series of strategies, methods, and tactics that the logic of conflict—in other words, violence—controls and commands.

The Origin of Violence

Yet can we renounce all conflict? Is political action necessarily condemned to violence, injustice, and arbitrariness? Girard seems to think so. It seems that his method of analysis inevitably leads us to this conclusion. Should we not reject this thought, which confines us to inaction and teaches that all political will and initiative bring us back to the mortal violence that they seek to escape?

The analysis is good, but the conclusion is incorrect because we have not made a rigorous distinction between what we know and what we can hope. The nonviolent activists confuse the domain specific to politics with the pure and simple exercise of rivalry. Girard helps us to understand how this confusion is harmful and how it erases any distinction between politics and violence. However, he in turn fails to understand the special aspect of politics, which is not the Kingdom of God—far from it. Of course, Girard will respond that he has not written a book on politics, but unfortunately, insofar as he claims that his recommendations and warnings have clear historical implications, insofar as they order us to take action, or rather to engage in inaction, we are indeed talking about politics. The misfortune is double because the very meaning of Girard's promise to us is lost in this way.

How does Girard respond to Christian Mellon's double question of what is the origin of violence and can we escape it? He responds in a complex, ambiguous way, in a double way. On the one hand, he says that violence is neither in the subject nor in the object, but in "subjects' mimetic relationship to an object."[8] In this sense, and insofar as he says he begins with "two individuals who are rivals for the same object," it is indeed human relationships that are first. Violence springs from our mimetic relationships; objects are innocent in the conflicts for which they serve as pretexts. The fundamental reason for violence does not lie in objects but in human relationships, in our conflicting relationships.

The whole question of responsibility, a constant appeal to people to recognize their complete and entire responsibility for violence, is connected to Girard's first response. From there comes the reference to the individual, the reference to individual conversion as the unique means of going beyond violence. From there also comes his rejection of sacrificial theology that discharges people from their responsibility by projecting onto God a demand for violence.

Girard's second response initially looks almost the same as the first, but if we examine it a little closer, it is profoundly different. In addition, thus, Girard responds that violence is rooted in mimetism, "which is not even exclusively human, for it is present in animals."[9] We know that increased mimetism in anthropoids is the driving force behind hominization. Thus, the source of violence lies in a biological characteristic of the species (shared by all higher mammals), which comes from before the time our relationships could be called "human" and which makes us both human and violent at the same time. We are no more responsible for this than we are for the color of our eyes.

The origin of violence is thus not in human relationships but in an object defined by a scientific theory, a biological feature of the species. This paradoxical object is the cause of all conflicts but the object of none.

Can these two responses be reconciled? Is it possible to arrange them together in a satisfactory manner? Or are we dealing with only one response, the latter? If this is the case, then why the appeal to responsibility? If mimetism makes us human, if it explains our conflicts without the need to specify an object, if it makes rivals identical doubles of each other, if mimetism is what history is really about, then nowhere do I find any trace of the responsibility for violence that is said to be mine and that I am asked to shoulder. If I cannot see the power of human freedom anywhere, if I cannot grasp its presence within the mimetic straitjacket that binds me, then it is vain and simply a cruel joke to speak to me of responsibility.

The ambiguity in question is everywhere in Girard's work; it is not specific to a few hasty declarations made in the heat of debate. In *Violence and the Sacred*, there is a long passage concerning the death instinct in Freud:

> The notion of an instinct (or, if one prefers, an impulse) that propels men toward violence or death—Freud's famous "death wish"—is no more than a last surrender to mythological thinking, a final manifestation of that ancient belief that human violence can be attributed to some outside influence—to gods, to Fate, to some force men can hardly be expected to control. Once again, it is a mode of thought that refuses to confront human conflicts squarely. It is an act of evasion, an attempt to "pass the buck" and find an alternate sacrificial solution in a situation which makes such a solution increasingly difficult.[10]

This text can be read in conjunction with certain passages from *Things Hidden* in order to show the links between the issue of responsibility and the Girardian interpretation of the Gospels. Thus: "We must realize that the apocalyptic violence predicted by the Gospels is not divine in origin. In the Gospels, this violence is always brought home to men, and not to God."[11] "The really important apocalyptic writings say nothing except that man is responsible for his history."[12] "If what threatens us is the result of an instinct, and if every embodiment of our history is simply a particular aspect of an inexorable scientific law, then there is nothing to do but abandon ourselves to the movement that carries us along with it; we are caught up in a destiny that we have no hope of mastering."[13]

In order to find the other side, the other face of the ambiguity, we need only remember other texts, also taken from *Things Hidden*: "If desire is the same for all of us, and if it is the key to the system of relationships, there is no reason not to make it the real 'subject' of the structure—a subject that comes back to mimesis in the end."[14] "In effect, desire is responsible for its own evolution. Desire tends to become a caricature of itself or, to put it another way, to cause all the symptoms to become more and more aggravated."[15] "The intensification of mimetic rivalry, which is already very much in evidence at the level of primates, destroyed dominance patterns and gave rise to progressively more elaborate and humanized forms of culture through the intermediary of the surrogate victim."[16]

It is sad to say, but readers generally have some difficulty distinguishing biological characteristics of the species from instincts and impulses.

If mimesis is the real subject of the structure and history, it is hard to see how we can hold humans absolutely responsible in history and simultaneously agree that mimetic desire is responsible for human evolution—in other words, human history. Can we say both that violence is rooted in human relations and thus that we are responsible for it, and that the humanness of our relations is rooted in violence and thus that violence is responsible for our relations?

Though they are always interwoven in his discourse, there are thus two different responses that Girard brings to the question of the origin of violence, two contradictory responses that he uses as foundations to solve a second problem: can we escape violence, and how? In fact, the solution that he proposes, the Rule of the Kingdom of God, love your neighbor, clearly flows from the first response, from our responsibility for violence, but Girard himself seems unable to believe in it except insofar as the necessary evolution of mimetism leads to a situation conducive to obedience to this rule—in other words, increasingly toward the impossibility of violence.

Obeying the Rule of the Kingdom of God means renouncing violence. Yet such renunciation seems extremely uncertain and unlikely, and if we grant that violence comes from mimetism, from a biological characteristic of the species, it seems frankly impossible. Girard deals with this in an elegant manner that reveals the mechanistic turn of his mind.

Toward a Nonviolent Society

As improbable as renunciation of violence may be, it will become increasingly necessary. History will, and already does, force us to renounce violence, to abstain from any form of retaliation. Two things support this. One, by destroying the effectiveness of sacrificial defense mechanisms against violence, Christian Revelation gradually deprives humanity of any way out, of any way to sidestep and escape the consequences of violence without necessarily renouncing it. It destroys the positivity of violence, its capacity at the peak of the crisis to transform into stable, peaceful order. Two, the increase in means of destruction, nuclear weapons, makes it entirely possible that humanity could annihilate itself. Renouncing violence becomes our only chance of survival; it thus ceases to be a dreamer's utopian wish and becomes a terrible reality. Twenty-five years of balanced terror have already gone by, and this shows that we have begun to employ this approach: we stockpile weapons to avoid using them. It is this weight of necessity that makes renunciation of violence plausible. We have to believe that the hard school of the inevitable will transform this simple concern for survival into love for our neighbors.

Yet this brings us back to uncontrollable destiny, and responsibility is transformed into the impossibility of violence. A short passage from *Things Hidden* confirms this conclusion:

> The failure of the Kingdom, from the viewpoint of the Gospels, does not amount to the failure of the mission Jesus undertakes; but it does amount to the inevitable abandonment of the direct and easy way, *which would be for all to accept the principles of conduct that he has stated.*[17] It is now necessary to turn to the indirect way, the one that has to bypass the consent of all mankind and instead pass through the Crucifixion and the Apocalypse. To sum up: the revelation is not impeded by the obstinate attachment to violence that the majority of men demonstrate *since from now on this violence has become its own enemy and will end by destroying itself.*[18]

We now see that, for Girard, there is no such thing as nonviolent action, that there can be no nonviolent activism. This is because nonviolence is not an action, but the impossibility of action, and renunciation of violence is the impossibility of violence. The establishment of a nonviolent society does not suppose so much that we take action and do something, but that we abandon ourselves to the necessary, implacable flow of a history full of meaning and hope, until the crucial day of the absolute alternative between the Kingdom of God and total destruction. History is reduced to this final choice, which will end human history with death or universal reconciliation.

This solution is elegant, but nonetheless contradictory. On the one hand, violence's return against itself is the definition par excellence of the surrogate victim mechanism as a self-regulating mechanism.[19] On the other hand, this return introduces into the action, between the means employed and the end obtained, an unfortunate disjunction that diverts actions from their present consequences, but gives them meaning and value on the final day of reconciliation that they will have produced against their will.

In *Things Hidden*, we find a sentence that is extremely significant in relation to this: "We have carved out such a strange destiny for ourselves so that we can bring to light both what has always determined human culture and what is now the only path open to us—the one that reconciles without excluding anyone and no longer has any dealings with violence."[20] The very structure of this sentence is in fact more revealing than its content: "so that we can bring to light . . ." The meaning of our destiny is not that destiny itself, but some other purpose for which it is the means. At the roundtable with the MAN activists, faced with their insistence on methods and strategy, Girard said: "The word 'instrumental' bothers me." Surprisingly, he does not seem to notice that his own thought gives all of human history a purely instrumental meaning!

Defining a nonviolent society as the Kingdom of God is certainly to define it in the most rigorous way possible, but, at risk of sinking into absurdity, the coming of that kingdom can never be the object of knowledge or the goal or purpose of political action. Why? Because the Kingdom of God is the promise of universal reconciliation, and this promise has meaning only in the truth of its universality—in other words, only if it includes all people, all peoples, and all times. It requires believing, in the literal sense, in the resurrection of the dead. This is something that can be neither the object of knowledge nor the result of political action because it is clearly not within our power. It is God's promise to us; it is an article of faith. We may believe in it or not, but all we can do is believe. It is not something we can know, but something for which we can hope.

Does this seem irrational, impossible to believe? No. This belief is in no way irrational because it is only if we understand it in all its universality that the promise of reconciliation makes sense. That it may be difficult to believe is another matter! What is irrational, in contrast, is to reduce the Kingdom of God to something less, to believe that it can come into the present of our history but not be the coming into the present of all of human history. If it is an object of knowledge or political action, then the promise of reconciliation crumbles when faced with the criticism of classical philosophy of history.

All of the world's generations would have been sacrificed to build a house in which only the last would live. The people of the past and the present would thus be reduced to pure means to an end that they would never experience. Their present lives would have only the meaning, to them unknown, that tomorrow would give them. If the meaning of history diverts actions from their present consequences, it frees people from their responsibilities in the time in which they live. It opens the door to all forms of nonsense, and allows each to see the workings of the final good in the unfolding of today's misfortunes.

Political—in other words, rational—action supposes precisely that we renounce the incredible conceit that we want to save humanity. We thus give future generations the freedom that we accord ourselves: the freedom to be lost or saved, not in the sense of eternal salvation, but in the history that we create in the century in which we live.

The impossibility of violence is never anything but the impossibility of a specific form of violence. It is not a political action in itself because greater violence suffices to bring it about. This is shown very clearly both in the analysis of the surrogate victim mechanism and in the analysis of the nuclear standoff; it is not the reign of freedom but of terror. This short criticism leads us to an interesting conclusion. If Girard's analyses condemn us to inaction, it is not, as one might think, because he counts on personal responsibility, but because in the end he does not appeal to it. Why not? Because, like the MAN activists, he seeks a final solution to violence.

If violence is rooted in human relationships that engage people's responsibility, then there is no abstract, intellectual, definitive response to the problem of how to rise above it. The problem has only practical, concrete, circumstantial responses: yes, we can escape violence here, now, as we do it, when we do it. That is all. It is not much. We should not expect more.

Yet it is generally for this reason that we conclude that violence is ineradicable. Since there are only contingent, temporary, piecemeal responses, only unknown responses subject to the fancies of the time and the caprices of individuals, violence can never be eliminated. Sooner or later we will sink back into it. There is no means of getting away from it once and for all; there is no escape. The circumstantial, temporary concrete points at which we rise above violence do not rise above anything at all. Being subject to violence does not mean living in a constant state of pure violence: it means always being more or less rapidly led to its brutal exercise. There are no final solutions. There are only practical, in-the-moment responses: political answers.

Differences and Paradoxes

Reflections on Love and Violence in Girard's Work

"Like violence, love abolishes differences," says René Girard in *Things Hidden since the Foundation of the World*.[1] Yet, clearly, if both love and violence abolish differences, love does not do so *in the same way as* violence. Girard says that "love makes no distinctions between beings."[2] In contrast, violence and mimetic desire not only mark and seek to mark differences, but re-mark differences even where there are none. Moreover, there is at least one difference that love does not abolish: the difference between love and violence. At least we have to claim this under the threat of no longer being able to distinguish the Kingdom of God from the reign of violence. At one point, Girard speaks of the radical incompatibility of these two realms, which no formal reading will ever be able to detect. Yet if love does not abolish the difference between love and violence, then we have to admit that it does not mark that difference either because we are told: love your enemies.

In short, in Girard's work, the word "difference" is far from clear: it has different meanings. In fact, there are at least three different meanings of the word "difference," three explicit meanings, organized by themes, which refer to three different differences. Girard does not always take the trouble to distinguish the three meanings when he writes, but he nonetheless never confuses them.

Indeed, when Girard says "Like violence, love abolishes differences," what differences is he talking about? All of them? Only one? Two of the three? Do love and violence abolish the same differences? Thus, let us begin with violence: what differences does it eliminate?

The first meaning of the word "difference" is the illusion of difference. The illusion of difference is the advantage that the disciple gives to the master, the subject to the model. It is the difference between the other and me, which my desire seeks to acquire. It is the difference between Don Quixote and Amadis de Gaul that transforms the shaving dish into the Golden Helmet of Mambrino. The illusion of difference is the difference that feeds mimetic rivalry, maintains it, causes it to escalate. Indeed, we should keep in mind that in Girard's theory, while desire is mimetic, it "never aspires to something that resembles it; it is always searching for something that it imagines to be most irreducibly *other*."[3] The illusion of difference is the difference that there is between adversaries; in other words, it is the difference that adversaries perceive between themselves, and that perpetuates their conflict. The reason people keep fighting is because they do not manage to see that they are the same. Girard says this very clearly in *Violence and the Sacred*, when he speaks of the monstrous double who "gives the antagonists, incapable of perceiving that nothing actually stands between them (*or their reconciliation*), precisely what they need to arrive at the compromise that involves unanimity minus the victim of the generative expulsion."[4]

Yet if violence abolishes differences, surely it does not eliminate the illusion of difference on which it is based. On the contrary: the more intense the rivalry, the more each believes himself or herself to be different, foreign to the other, and the more each will try to distance himself or herself from the other. Indeed, the reason the climax of the crisis takes place in an atmosphere of hallucination is because, for doubles, the illusion of difference becomes more and more real: it has swept away the reality that they are identical, and, insofar as all the differences spin out of control, it has swept identity away from reality. For doubles, violence does not destroy the illusion of difference; it does not abolish it, but confirms it. If violence destroyed the illusion of difference, there would be reconciliation without expulsion. The scapegoat mechanism works because it satisfies this illusion, because it confirms each in his or her illusion of the difference between himself or herself and the other, between me and the victim. This preserved illusion is the misrecognition characteristic of the crisis resolution mechanism: the community's incapacity to see the sacrificial victim as victim of a blind, arbitrary mechanism, rather than as both guilty and a god.

While violence abolishes differences, it does not abolish the illusion of difference that drives it. Thus, let us move on to the second meaning of the word "difference," to illusory differences.

It is the illusion of difference consecrated, in the proper sense, by the scapegoat mechanism that is the principle of the illusory differences characteristic of the cultural order after the crisis. Illusory differences include culture, social differentiation, and the whole system of cultural differences that in the end, according to Girard, are based on the scapegoat mechanism.

Why are these differences illusory? Because they flow from the illusion of difference and are rooted in the arbitrary nature of the mechanism. It is because they legitimize the arbitrary and establish among people differences that do not exist.

Since illusory differences come from the illusion of difference, we may wonder whether they should be distinguished in greater detail than Girard does. I think so, and here is why.

According to Girard, these illusory differences play—or, more precisely, played before their arbitrariness became clear—a very special role in human communities: they protect them from violence. The religious, the sacred, and the sacrificial prevent the escalation of violence. While social differentiation has never had moral legitimacy, it at least used to have a certain degree of functional legitimacy.

The reason they have to be distinguished from the illusion of difference is because they react to violence in the opposite way. Not only does the illusion of difference act as a driving force behind conflict, whereas illusory differences act as brakes, but illusory differences evolve in the opposite direction. Girard often notes this idea, which was already present in Tocqueville: the more we eliminate concrete differences among people, the more bitter and violent struggles for equality become; as the system of illusory differences that protects us becomes weaker, the illusion of difference proliferates.

Does violence destroy illusory differences? Yes. Girard's response is unambiguous. The mimetic crisis is the gradual loss of all cultural differences, and it is precisely this loss of differences that defines the modern world as a slow-motion sacrificial crisis. Violence is gradually undermining the differences that structure the community.

Yet as we have seen, violence is the exercise of the illusion of difference: it both confirms the illusion and flows from it. Since the illusion of difference is moreover the principle of illusory differences, violence abolishes differences in a contradictory way: to prolong them. While it erases illusory differences, it maintains the illusion of such differences. The differences that it destroys are accidents of history, and the illusion that it asserts is its necessity. This is the special feature of the differences that are lost in the very movement by which the illusion that underlies them is universally asserted.

In consequence, the climax of the crisis, the moment of its resolution, and the founding expulsion can be construed as the perfect coincidence of the illusion of difference and illusory differences, and the crisis itself can be seen as the gradual disconnection of the illusion of difference from illusory differences.

There remains a third difference, a real difference, the absolute difference between love and violence. Does violence abolish this difference? It is easy to destroy an illusion or an illusory difference: it suffices to look at things differently and to begin to see correctly, to blink one's eyes for the fantasy to fade away. However, to abolish a real difference is to truly erase it. Must we believe that violence does in fact destroy the difference between love and violence? Then love and violence would become indistinguishable, and the absolute difference by which we try to separate them would be revealed to be relative, illusory. Love would return to the common grave, and join the other forms engendered by the scapegoat mechanism. Thus, by definition, violence does not abolish the difference between love and violence. By saying that this difference is true, Girard means nothing other than the fact that it escapes the cycle of construction and destruction of the crisis and its resolution.

Yet this answer is incomplete and unsatisfactory because violence abolishes the difference between love and violence in the sense that violence makes those who are violent incapable of distinguishing between love and violence, unable to recognize disinterested actions for what they are, without giving their authors insidious, secretly evil intentions. It also abolishes the difference in the sense that violence uses to its own advantage all that we do to stop it, in the sense that the crisis accelerates irresistibly and comes to encompass the whole community. Contact with the crisis causes the goodness of those who resist it to decline, and the actions that they take to counter it become, through its operation, violent. Violence truly does destroy the difference between love and violence: it dissimulates the difference from those who are violent, and finally from all people.

We can now refine our question by asking for whom violence abolishes differences. In effect, in Girard's work, point of view is very important, and his explanatory method is based on a constant shift between the antagonists' point of view and that of external observers—in other words, those who are not involved in the conflict. The latter point of view is considered superior because it can account for the antagonists' perceptions, whereas the inverse is not true.

Does violence destroy the illusion of difference for the antagonists? We have already answered that it does not; on the contrary, it confirms it. What about for us, as external observers? Yes. Violence destroys the illusion of difference: the development of the conflict reveals that the doubles are identical. However, since being external is relative, this knowledge is relative also. In other words, it concerns only others; it is almost impossible for us to apply it to ourselves. When it comes to our own conflicts, the identical nature of the doubles remains hidden to us.

What about illusory differences? They are destroyed for all, both antagonists and external observers, because in a sense it is no longer possible to be outside, and their collapse means that violence invades the entire community. It is no longer possible to contain the conflict. Yet the disappearance of illusory differences does not reveal that the doubles are identical because that flows from the illusion of difference.

We have to think that the real difference between love and violence is preserved for all, despite everything, but also that it is destroyed for the antagonists, and then, as the conflict spreads, for all.

However, this formulation is contradictory and relatively difficult to understand: violence both abolishes and maintains the difference between love and violence. Things become clearer as soon as we see the paradoxical nature of violence. Girard says that violence is undifferentiation, but this loss of differences results from the antagonists' very efforts to distinguish themselves from each other. If we leave aside for the moment the question of whether these differences have to be called real or illusory, we obtain as the pure paradoxical form of violence that violence is the assertion of a relation of identity—namely, that of doubles—through its negation, the assertion of their difference. By considering the intention motivating the violence—asserting one's difference, in the first sense defined above—to be on the same level as its result—the negation of illusory differences—we obtain the paradoxical definition of violence as the negation of itself. This makes it easier to understand the "true" difference between love and violence. It is the backlash of the destruction of illusory differences on the illusion of difference. Girard constantly asserts this backlash, but our earlier analysis obscured it. The growth and escalation of violence are linked to the loss of differences, to the fact that the doubles are becoming more alike, and violence increases so as to deny the identity as it is affirmed more and more strongly.

The real difference between love and violence can thus be seen as the capacity to perceive, from inside the conflict, the identity of the doubles. This difference is both abolished and maintained by violence, as the stable result of the incessant oscillation between affirmation and denial.[5] We can also see why this difference is true in Girard's sense—in other words, why it escapes the cycle of destruction and construction of differences that is accomplished by the crisis and its resolution—in other words, by violence.

Now, let us see how and which differences love abolishes, and how it is different from violence.

The first difference is thus the illusion of difference. Love abolishes the illusion of difference, but from the inside. It puts an end to antagonism because it reveals its falsehood, its vanity, the fact that no difference lies behind the dispute. It is important to see that it is from the inside that love reveals the identity of doubles, and thus that it does indeed destroy the illusion of difference. Love abolishes the illusion of difference for all since it consists in establishing the point of view of the exterior in the interior of the conflict. It is globalization of the external point of view. This is how it is the opposite of the resolution of the crisis, which is globalization of the internal point of view, the transfer of all of the doubles' illusions onto a single one among them.

What about illusory differences? Does love destroy them? This time we will again find relativity of points of view. One who loves in the Girardian sense sees illusory differences as what they are: illusory differences. Love abolishes them for him or her, but not for others, not for those who remain fascinated by such differences. Since violence is the exercise of the illusion of difference that eliminates illusory differences, the love that escapes from this illusion is limited to not paying attention to illusory differences; it does not seek to destroy them. Love arbitrates between the moral illegitimacy and functional legitimacy of illusory differences.

There remains the real difference between love and violence: does love abolish this difference? The question may seem strange: no, clearly love asserts this difference. Yet here we find the same ambiguity that we saw above when we said that violence both abolishes and maintains the real difference between love and violence. Love consists in perceiving the identicalness of doubles from the inside. If this revelation affects only one of the protagonists, love abolishes the difference between love and violence by affirming it. Indeed, he or she who recognizes the fact that the doubles are identical introduces a real difference into the relationship, a difference that negates their identity. We thus find within the relationship the assertion of a real difference, the difference between love and violence, through the assertion of its negation, the assertion that the doubles are identical.

In contrast, if we suppose that he or she who asserts the identity of doubles recognizes the difference that he or she thereby introduces into the relationship and asserts that difference, then he or she asserts what the other asserts, namely, the difference between myself and the other. We thus obtain the assertion of a true identity, that of the doubles, through its negation: assertion of their difference.

Love and violence thus have the same paradoxical form, in which self-affirmation is based on self-negation. By denying that there are any differences, love introduces a real difference into the relationship, and by denying that there is any identity, violence establishes true identity. We are thus led to imagine a certain proximity, a kinship between love and violence, an identity that seems to flow from the fact that neither can be reflexive. Indeed, neither love nor violence can have self-knowledge without being destroyed. What violence refuses, what it rejects and expels, what it denies through words and actions, is its identity with the other. What violence can never know is itself as an undifferentiation process because its goal is for each to be differentiated. This knowledge is its downfall and failure. The same goes for love, which cannot have self-knowledge without destroying itself, without transforming into pride, for goodness that cannot appear to itself without vanishing.

There is something strange here because reflexiveness has always been linked to paradox, and here it is from their paradoxical forms that the nonreflexiveness of love and violence seems to flow. However, in order to solve the paradox of the formal identity of love and violence, it suffices to introduce time into our analysis, though doing so does not eliminate or reduce the paradoxical form of love and violence. On the contrary.

Hegelianism defines freedom and consciousness as reflexiveness, as a being that is both subject and object—in other words, which is what it is not, and is not what it is. It is easy to agree that this is a pretty good definition of paradox; for example, consider the Liar's Paradox: "I am lying" or "This statement is false." If these statements are true, they are false; if they are false, they are true. The identity of these beings consists in being what they are not and not being what they are. The detour through Hegelian thought has the advantage of showing clearly what is the opposite of reflexiveness: a being that is what it is and is not what it is not—in other words, a being whose identity is immediate with itself.

Now, let us go back to the love-pride paradox, which is the paradox of violence as we framed it above: "if we suppose that he or she who asserts the identity of doubles recognizes the difference that he or she thereby introduces into the relationship and asserts that difference, then he or she asserts what the other asserts, namely, the difference between myself and the other. We thus obtain the assertion of a true identity, that of the doubles, through its negation: assertion of their difference." This is the crux: what is being done by a person who asserts the difference that he or she has introduced into the relationship by asserting that the doubles are identical? That person is denying time, wants to be the being that he or she is here and now, and is seeking immediate identity with himself or herself. He or she is denying the paradox and denying reflexiveness. The case of pride is paradigmatic insofar as it reveals clearly what is in question. However, negation of time and seeking immediate identity with oneself are true of all violence, and Girard's analysis of doubles show this clearly.

The reason doubles do not see that they are identical is because, at every point, victory and defeat are in the scales, which tip to one side and then to the other, and equilibrium is distributed over all of the moves. Since each adversary pays attention only to the latest move, neither sees the identity.

When one of the adversaries recognizes the identity of the doubles, he or she takes into consideration the whole set of moves, and thus time. If he or she then refuses to assert the difference which he or she thereby introduces into the relationship, it is simply because he or she continues to take time into account and does not seek immediate identity with himself or herself; it is not that this difference escapes him or her. He or she asserts time, mediate identity with himself or herself, and the paradox. He or she is that reflexiveness that violence denies.

Creation and Conversion
in Girard

T he question of creation and its relationship with mimesis in René
Girard can be approached first through literary creation. Such an
approach has a twofold advantage. First, it is faithful to Girard's
intellectual evolution, since he began his work with reflection on the relationships between mimetic desire and literary creation, specifically the novel,
before turning toward anthropology and the question of cultural creation, in
particular, religious creation. The second advantage, which is hidden in the
first, is that it allows us to follow, at least a little, the evolution of the Girardian conception of mimesis.

Indeed, in his first book, *Deceit, Desire and the Novel* (published in
French in 1961, in English in 1966), as in his second, *Resurrection from the
Underground: Feodor Dostoevsky* (published in French in 1963, in English in
1997), Girard does not yet speak of mimesis, and if I am not mistaken even
the expression "mimetic desire" never appears. We have to wait until *Violence and the Sacred* (published in French in 1972, in English in 1977) for the
expression to take hold, and finally until *Things Hidden since the Foundation
of the World* (published in French in 1978, in English in 1987) for the word
"mimesis" to come to designate what Girard considers to be his fundamental
discovery and a central aspect of human relationships, the essential role of

which generally goes unseen in the modern world except, precisely, in the work of great writers.

In his first two books and his articles at the time, all of which were works of literary criticism, Girard speaks of "triangular desire" and "desire according to Another." He also employs the terms "imitation" and "model," but the word "mimesis" and the derived adjective do not appear. In fact, none of the texts published between 1954 and 1978, inclusive, that are contained in the recent collection of Girard's articles edited by Robert Doran uses the terms "mimesis," "mimetic desire," "mimetic rivalry," or "mimetic contagion."[1] Even more surprising, "Narcissism: The Freudian Myth Demythified by Proust," which dates from 1978, contains neither the expression "triangular desire" nor "desire according to Another."[2] It is as if neither of these terms was indispensable to what Girard wants to do. In "Narcissism," Girard confines himself, clearly voluntarily, to using Freudian and psychoanalytic vocabulary to show that we can find in Proust's novels an analysis and understanding of narcissism that is superior to that of Freud, superior because it is less essentialist: instead of conceiving of narcissism as a characteristic of certain persons, Proust presents it as a relational feature of interactions among persons. This text provides a paradigmatic illustration of a central Girardian thesis, namely, that some literary works show better knowledge of human relations than what we find in human and social sciences or in the philosophical theories we use to try to analyze literary texts. In contrast, Girard proposes to analyze Freud using Proust, to show that the writer demystifies the theoretician, and that the conceptual wealth of the literary work is much greater than that pretended by the theoretical reflection. However, and this is also an important aspect of Girard's position, when Proust ventures to talk about desire in a theoretical manner, he shows himself to be by far more boring, more conventional, and less interesting than Freud. The thesis that Girard defends is thus not only about the cognitive superiority of Proust over Freud concerning desire but also about the cognitive value of literary creation.

According to Girard, some literary works contain knowledge about human relationships that is richer and more accurate than what is often found in philosophy and the human sciences. However, his position is not dogmatic with respect to individual authors: a sociologist such as Tocqueville or a philosopher such as Kierkegaard is much more knowledgeable about mimesis than many writers. In the end, the goal is not to distribute good or bad grades, but to understand certain fundamental aspects of our reciprocal relations. There is, however, one point on which Girard remains intransigent (and sometimes provocative), and it is that the literary form of works, be they novels or plays, is not an obstacle but, much to the contrary, the tool par excellence for gaining access to a type of knowledge that most often escapes those who want to be more "scientific" and who seek to confine works of art to the noncognitive world. As he writes concerning Dostoyevsky: "Dostoyevsky is not a philosopher but a novelist: he does not create the character Stavrogin because he had formulated intellectually the unity of all underground phenomena. On the contrary, he comes to this unity because he has created the character Stavrogin."[3] According to Girard, literary creation is an essential form of knowledge, and its cognitive worth is neither external nor foreign to its aesthetic value.

In fact, we have to consider this thesis on the cognitive nature of literary works as the point of departure for Girard. At the beginning of his reflection, there is the discovery (the intuition) that great novels and theater, such as plays by Racine and Shakespeare, contain knowledge about human relationships, more specifically about desire, and that this knowledge can be found nowhere else. What is this knowledge? According to Girard, it concerns the nature of desire. It is what he initially calls triangular desire or desire according to Another. The central idea as it was framed at the time is that we imitate one another in our desires. This thesis has in fact a metaphysical foundation, and Girard also sometimes talks about "metaphysical desire." As he enjoys repeating, as soon as our natural needs are met, we do not know what to desire, and we turn to one another to find it out. This is because what we really desire is *being*, what we desire is to be. We think we see in the other the metaphysical autonomy, certitude, self-confidence that characterize the full, entire existence that we are lacking, but obviously this is an illusion. The heart of Girard's discovery is that we imitate one another in our desires, and that the driving force behind this imitation is the desire to be the other, the desire for the being of the other, and that this desire itself is not a desire for a specific object, it is not even desire for the "other," but a desire to be. Except in chapter 2 of *Deceit, Desire and the Novel*, Girard never really spends a lot of time on the metaphysical nature of desire, though it is essential to his theory. This is in contrast with other authors—for example, Levinas—who place the metaphysical dimension of desire at the center of their thought.

Rather than on the metaphysical dimension of desire, which in the end probably does not interest him very much, Girard ends up focusing his attention on the forms of desire according to Another and on the cultural consequences of this. As he says at the beginning of chapter 2 of *Deceit, Desire and the Novel*, "There is only one metaphysical desire but the particular desires which instantiate this primordial desire are of infinite variety."[4] The analysis of these specific desires is the topic of most of this first work. Its first chapter is entitled "'Triangular' Desire." It is simultaneously an introduction to the book's general theme and a summary of the central thesis, about literary conversion, which I explain more fully in this essay's conclusion. Desire is presented as "triangular" because it is according to Another, because one individual's desire imitates the desire of another, and the simplest shape that this imitation can take is that of a triangle: two hands, one belonging to the subject and the other to his or her model, both reaching for the same object. The image of a triangle also has another fundamental pedagogical advantage, which is that it shows very clearly the spontaneously conflictual nature of desire according to Another. This is the aspect of mimetic desire that Girard thinks provides the most important contribution to our understanding of imitation. The triangle reveals the "spontaneously conflictual" nature of desire according to Another because it shows how a conflict can emerge out of imitation even if the people involved do not directly aim for it, without conflict being at any time the intention of either of those who will become adversaries, and it shows why, in consequence, it so often appears to each adversary that he or she did not want the conflict and that it is the result of the unprovoked nastiness of the other. The stupid, mechanical, involuntary, unconscious nature of conflict later comes to play a central role in the development of Girard's thought, as does the direct link between imitation and conflict, which is established from the beginning of his research.

However, the triangle soon fades and gives way to the various shapes that desire according to Another can take. The reason the triangle fades is first because, according to Girard, when the model or mediator of desire gets close and the conflict intensifies, the object itself tends to become less interesting and the direct clash between the rivals more interesting. The object disappears in the sense that the adversaries tend to lose interest in it and no longer focus on anything but the conflict that opposes them. As soon as the object has disappeared, there is no longer really a triangle; all that remains is the desire according to Another. The analyses of the "metamorphoses of desire" in the first works lead to a fundamental finding, which is that imitation of desire can give birth to forms of behavior that have very little to do with imitation. There are a number of reasons for this that should be elucidated, but before we do so, we need to provide some explanation of this paradoxical statement that "imitation of desire can give birth to forms of behavior that have very little to do with imitation" because this phenomenon is one of the major obstacles to understanding Girard's approach and what should be understood by mimesis.

The first chapter of *Deceit, Desire and the Novel* focuses, partially for pedagogical reasons, on examples in which imitation of desire is generally visible at the level of superficial observation. For example, in Stendhal's *The Red and the Black*, Monsieur de Rênal desires Julien Sorel as a tutor for his children. Valenod, his rival, also desires Sorel. Don Quixote sees a shaving basin as the helmet of Mambrino, windmills as giants, and from the beginning of the novel declares loud and clear his intention to imitate Amadis de Gaul. It is obvious that his desire to emulate the exploits of his hero metamorphoses ordinary objects into precious helmets and furious enemies. The imitation is clear and easy to identify. However, things are not always so simple. Here is an example:

> Anselmo has just married the pretty young Camilla. The marriage was arranged with the help of Lothario, a very dear friend of the happy husband. Some time after the wedding Anselmo makes a curious request to Lothario. He begs him to pay court to Camilla, claiming that he wishes "to test" her faithfulness. Lothario refuses indignantly but Anselmo does not give up. He entreats his friend in a thousand different ways and in all his suggestions reveals the obsessive nature of his request. For a long time Lothario manages to put him off and finally pretends to accept to put him at his ease. Anselmo arranges for the two young people to be alone together.... In short his behavior is so mad that he finally drives Lothario and Camilla into each other's arms. Learning that he has been betrayed, Anselmo kills himself in despair.[5]

Where is the imitation? The text cited is a partial summary of a tale by Cervantes, "The Curious Impertinent," which Girard analyzes in parallel with *The Eternal Husband*, a short novel by Dostoyevsky. In both cases, there is a man who introduces to another man, in an insistent and ambiguous manner, the woman whom he has married (or will marry). Inevitably, the story ends badly, and Girard shows that the unhappy protagonist was in fact trying to get the other, his rival, to desire the woman who is intended for him because only the prestige of the model, only imitated desire, could make the woman desirable. In this example, at first sight we can at best say that the husband wants the other to imitate him in his relationship to his wife. However, this hypothesis is false and sterile on the interpretive level. In truth, Anselmo and the eternal husband want to arouse their rival's desire in order to imitate and triumph over them. Yet this "imitation," which remains hidden from the eyes of both the imitator and the model, has nothing obvious about it, and the characters' apparent behavior does not clearly fall into the category of imitation. In order to make visible the desire according to Another that is hidden under the incongruous behavior, we require all of the literary genius of Cervantes and Dostoyevsky, and all of the subtlety of Girard's analyses. Speaking of imitation in this context requires a huge stretch in the meaning of the word, but it is very clear that here we are dealing with reciprocal dependency of one person's desire on the desire of another, a dependency that gives rise to unexpected behavior that no longer has much to do with what we usually understand by imitation.

The fundamental reasons why this happens are relatively easy to understand. First, imitation of the desire of the other is not, aside from in a few especially simple cases, imitation of specific behavior but of an abstract relationship between an individual and an object (in the sense of the object of one's desire), an abstract relationship that can be made real by a number of different specific forms of behavior. Thus, imitating the desire of the other does not generally mean imitating the other's concrete behavior. Second, owing to the close link between imitation of desire and rivalry, the stakeholders are generally motivated to dissimulate their imitation. This is why imitating another man's desire for a woman generally involves acting in a way that is quite different from the other so as to appear in her eyes as very different from him. However, and for Girard this is an essential characteristic of desire according to Another, the symmetry that inevitably exists at a certain level between those who imitate one another will inevitably end up appearing, despite the doubles' duplicity—in other words, despite the efforts they make to dissimulate their imitation from themselves and others. The art of a great writer is to reveal these doubles who seek to hide from others and from themselves that they are the same.

Here, we can see a first manifestation of an aspect of mimesis that will later play a fundamental role in Girard's work on the origin of culture. What Cervantes and Dostoyevsky show us is the creative aspect of imitation. What imitation of desire produces is not pale conformity, monotonous repetition of the same, but unexpected behavior. Imitation produces different things, but it also produces things that are the same, though they remain hidden, or when they do appear they do so in a mystifying form and so remain incomprehensible to us.

This brings us back to literary creation and to mimesis, but in a sense different from that of Girard: more or less in Erich Auerbach's sense—namely, mimesis as a representation of reality. Girard's thesis is that the representation of reality in a literary work, a representation that, like Auerbach, he conceives of as always relying on moral concepts and judgments, is a special means of discovering and revealing phenomena of behavioral symmetry and doubles resulting from reciprocal imitation of desire or, if one prefers, from desire according to Another. However, literature alone does not suffice: on their own, the arts of mimesis are no guarantee. What is also required is that the author, the writer, experience a certain "conversion." In the Western, Christian world, the term "conversion" is associated essentially with a religious experience such as the discovery or rediscovery of faith. Conversion corresponds to a change in religion or a return to a practice that one had abandoned. Girard uses this term very consciously, not in order to argue that "literary conversion" is a form of religious conversion, though it can be the case that for some authors the two things go hand in hand, but because, according to him, the two experiences deeply resemble each other, to the point that even authors who explicitly reject any religious interpretation of their work are nonetheless tempted to use the imagery of religious conversion to describe the event. According to Girard, the heart of this similarity lies in the fact that in both cases the experience is of a deep, often sudden, transformation of the way that the subject perceives his or her relationship to the world and particularly to others.

While literary conversion is an event in the life of an author, it is also a literary element that can play a role within a work. It operates either directly, in the form of an experience of one of the characters, generally the narrator, or indirectly, in which case it can be seen in the difference between an author's first works and his or her later works, sometimes only in the last work. This conversion is an awareness of the role of desire according to Another and of the fact that the author in his or her life and earlier works succumbed to the illusion of the autonomy of desire and remained fascinated by his or her model. There is thus, in the first stage of Girard's work, a complex relationship between mimesis and literary creation. On the one hand, mimesis in Auerbach's sense—literature—is a special tool for revealing the role of desire according to Another—in other words, mimesis in Girard's sense. It is what gives literary creation its fundamental cognitive value. On the other hand, this is possible only insofar as the author succeeds in taking some distance, in breaking away, at least partially, from mimesis in the sense of desire according to Another. Mimesis is thus at the foundation of literary creation, but the latter, at least in the case of great works of literature, requires that the author have a very special relationship to mimesis.

However, we also already find a history of desire in *Deceit, Desire and the Novel*. Indeed, according to Girard, there is an evolution of desire according to Another toward forms of desire that are always more intense, conflictual, negative relationships with others, and this evolution is linked to the political and social transformations of the modern world. In particular, the development of equality is, according to him, inseparable from the generalization of internal mediation in contrast with the external mediation that was characteristic of more hierarchical societies. At the time, it was not yet entirely clear whether these social transformations were an independent element that affected the evolution of desire according to Another from the outside—in fact, in *Pour une sociologie du roman*, this is how Lucien Goldmann interpreted Girard's first book, to which he gave an enthusiastic welcome[6]—or whether, on the contrary, it is desire according to Another that is itself at work in these social and political transformations, and thus whether it is what is, as Girard later asserts in *Things Hidden*, the "real subject of history." Writers attest to this evolution, but each in his or her own way. In particular, and this is the meaning of Girard's distinction between romantic literature and the novel, some writers, the greatest according to Girard, reveal the escalation of desire according to Another: they stage it and reveal it, while in contrast other writers simply reflect an evolution of which they themselves are victims.

There is thus, and Girard insists strongly on this point, a fundamental unity of inspiration among those who write novels. All great writers—Cervantes, Shakespeare, Racine, Stendhal, Flaubert, Dostoyevsky, Proust—talk about the same thing: desire according to Another. However, this unity does not destroy the differences between the works. On the contrary, it lives alongside the immense diversity of literary creation, with everything that separates Proust from Cervantes, Stendhal from Dostoyevsky.

◆   ◆   ◆

Beginning in *Violence and the Sacred*, the introduction of "mimetic desire" and "mimesis" to replace triangular desire and desire according to Another corresponds, I think, to the discovery that desire does not come first, that imitation precedes and encompasses it. At the beginning of his career, Girard thought that the great writers had discovered a fundamental phenomenon, namely, imitation of desire, the fact that human beings imitate one another's desires. The introduction of the term "mimesis" corresponds to the point when Girard becomes aware that imitation phenomena extend far beyond desire, which in this sense is only a specific, historically and culturally limited example of the mimetic phenomenon. This reversal can be interpreted as a renunciation of the metaphysical thesis about desire that we find in *Deceit, Desire and the Novel*, but I do not think that this conclusion is inevitable. In *Violence and the Sacred*, at the beginning of the chapter entitled "From Mimetic Desire to the Monstrous Double," Girard says that rivalry does not arise out of the fact that two individuals desire the same thing. Instead, they desire the same thing because they are rivals. Desire, even when it is mimetic, is not first. It is rooted in rivalry, and rivalry itself flows from imitation.

In fact, the central discovery in *Violence and the Sacred* is of the mimetic, contagious dimension of violence. Violence, like any form of rivalry, is mimetic because when two (or more) individuals are in conflict, there is always a true description of their relationship such that they are doing the same thing. Each seeks to vanquish, to surpass the other. The symmetry that characterizes their actions in such cases is an effect of the system. It does not suppose any specific force that leads them to imitate each other; the symmetry and similarity of their actions flow directly from the nature of their relationship. Consequently, it is refined and becomes more obvious as the conflict becomes more intense. However, violence is also contagious in the sense that violence gives rise to violence. It solicits violence even among those whom it does not directly threaten. In this case, this is not an effect of the system: the contagion of violence, when it extends to others than whom it affects directly, supposes a power, a tendency that makes the forms of behavior converge. "Mimesis" is the term Girard uses to designate both forms of convergence of agents' behavior.

We can wonder whether this amalgamation is legitimate in analytical terms. Would there not be an advantage in distinguishing between these two types of "imitation"? For example, in order to explain the similarity and convergence of the behavior of two people sitting in the same boat, rowing, it is not necessary to employ a real relationship of imitation to explain the convergence: the symmetry of the behavior emerges directly from the situation that they share. In contrast, the fact that in a group if one person yawns or crosses his or her legs, the probability that another person will yawn or cross his or her legs within a minute increases, supposes the existence of a force or tendency that leads us to reproduce the behavior that we witness. Is not the etiology, the underlying causal mechanisms, sufficiently different for us to, in opposition to what Girard does, distinguish clearly between these two types of behavioral convergence, rather than conflating them within a single term: "mimesis"?

Although Girard never asks the question directly, I think that we can find in his work the components of a consistent response. If, according to him, it is legitimate to treat as one and the same phenomena that in certain aspects seem so different, it is because they interact and create a system among themselves. It is because, in a description of a conflict, for example, the two forms of convergence prove to be closely linked and function together toward the final result. The reason it is possible to speak of *the* mimesis, even though the term refers to phenomena based on different proximal mechanisms, is because at the social level their consequences interweave to create a coherent whole. This is especially obvious in the case of contagious violence, which spontaneously extends to others whom it does not directly concern, and contagion itself establishes a situation in which agents' behavior will necessarily converge. We are thus dealing, in this specific case, with a dynamic system in which two processes of behavioral convergence support each other to create ever more perfect symmetry and similarity between the agents.

Yet this specific case will, through a tremendous turn of events, prove to be perfectly general, of a generality that is the direct consequence of the process of nondifferentiation—in other words, imitation—that defines it. According to Girard, the essential feature of violence is that it abolishes, destroys differences. First, it erases the differences between agents, whom it transforms into twins of violence, doubles with nothing that distinguishes one from the other. However, it is also the fact that it renders all cultural, moral, social, and political differences null and void insofar as they count for increasingly less as a conflict becomes increasingly violent. Here there is more than a simple metaphor or image. This nondifferentiating aspect of violence corresponds to a spontaneous judgment that we all make. Even when we condemn it, we consider that violence that is restricted to enemy combatants—in other words, that takes aim only at military installations and attempts to avoid harming civilians—is a more limited, reasonable form of violence than that which rains down indiscriminately on all: men, women, and children, civilians and military personnel alike. As it is so well put, the more violence is blind, the less it sees the differences between combatants and the civilian population, military bases and hospitals, and the more extreme, enormous, excessive we consider it. According to this spontaneous judgment, the greater the violence, the less it takes differences into account. However, violence's failure to recognize differences is more than a simple intellectual error or false belief; it is a real process that changes the world, that leads to the de facto destruction of differences. Here we have a form of imitation that truly reduces everything to the dismal repetition of the same.

However, the driving force behind this leveling of differences is paradoxically the combatants' efforts to differentiate themselves, the attempt to take possession of the only difference that counts: the definitive victory that will finally bring peace. This difference is both absolute and illusory. It is absolute because, between generalized violence and rediscovered peace, the difference is total. It is illusory because the more the rivals rival each other, the more they look alike and become indistinguishable. According to Girard, it is at the point when violence is most intense, when it is shared by the whole community, all differences have disappeared, all have become doubles, all have become twins of violence, that the difference can finally reappear and stabilize. At the point when there is no longer anything to distinguish the adversaries from one another, all can, by mimetism, converge against a unique adversary who becomes their common victim. This convergence of all against one brings peace back because all are intimately convinced that they have destroyed the one who was their enemy par excellence, and the rediscovered peace confirms everyone's belief that the victim was indeed the person responsible for the violence. There is thus an absolute difference linked with the one who is no longer and by whom peace has been brought back.

Note that no necessity is involved in this, and Girard does not say that this convergence always takes place, simply that, given what mimetism is and the dynamic deployment of the system up to that point, *it can happen.* In fact, Girard thinks that a number of human groups must have destroyed themselves completely, but that our ancestors were groups in which this self-regulating mechanism of violence worked. The other groups simply disappeared; they did not succeed in reproducing as groups. Mimetism does not explain everything: a form of natural selection also plays a role. What leads us to believe that things happened this way is that we find in myths and rituals traces of this founding event. It is important to note also that this origin is a mechanism, rather than a unique event. It is thus a recurring phenomenon that must have been produced many times, independently, in groups that were isolated from one another.

This first difference, this absolute difference, is, according to Girard, the source of all cultural differences. It is above all a difference of a very special type. In the conflict, each tried to seize the difference that would distinguish him or her from his or her adversaries, but peace was returned when each was dispossessed of that difference. No one can have or incarnate this difference. According to Girard, this difference is the first nonnatural signification of which the dead victim is the sign.[7] The first signification is thus both the crisis itself and its resolution, a complex event. Girard thinks that all of the effort that will follow is an attempt to avoid the return of the crisis, the functioning of which is only very imperfectly understood. It will lead to the invention of rituals and prohibitions, and to the creation of myths that tell the story of what happened. In all of these cultural phenomena, mimesis in all its forms plays a fundamental role. The point of rituals is to replay the events that led to the end of the crisis in the hope that this will reactivate the beneficial effects. The purpose of taboos and prohibitions is, on the contrary, to avoid reproducing the actions that triggered the crisis. A form of negative mimetism is thus involved. Finally, myths portray the crisis and its ending, including the birth of the cultural differences that characterize the group.

In all of these phenomena of cultural creation, mimetism is indispensable but always works on material that is provided from outside: basic forms of behavior, such as hunger, fear, and sexuality (and, perhaps even aggressiveness); different physical environments; special features; and chance events. These lead to the way the crisis unfolds in a given group at a given time or level of cultural development. Mimetism works on "matter" that is given, and the final result is the fruit of chance and necessity.

Mimetic Theory

Concepts and Models

René Girard is generally considered a writer with a doctrine, an author with sweeping theses of fundamental importance, such as, to name only a few, his theses on the origin and social function of violence, on the founding mechanism of human institutions, on the nature of the sacred, on the historical role of Christianity, and, finally, on the essence of human desire. This reading is not entirely incorrect, but I think it is incomplete. This is because these highly ambitious theses rest on a new conceptual apparatus that is, I believe, actually Girard's major contribution to the human sciences. Yet this conceptual contribution is often overlooked both by those who agree with Girard's theory and by those who reject it. The former do so because their adherence to the substantial positions that it contains minimizes in their eyes this aspect, since it is much more methodological and epistemological. The latter sometimes get a better feeling of the challenge to existing approaches that is implied by Girard's work, but they do not see its conceptual consequences, and, on the contrary, consider his new method to be a violation of accepted research canons. Girard's abandonment of the best-established methods seems to these critics to explain the sweeping theses about the history of humanity, theses that, according to them, are undermined by the totalizing pretensions that they contain.

In what follows, my goal is to shed light on this new conceptual apparatus. I will try to defend three points. First, I argue that the Girardian approach is not in contradiction with our best scientific criteria. However, it is much more closely related to methods that are employed in the natural sciences than to those now dominant in the human sciences. In fact, I think this is a major advantage that has to be recognized. Second, the Girardian theory makes it possible to better define our reflections on culture and society in relation to the biology of the human species, though without reducing the social to the biological. This is because it proposes a model that helps to explain how social phenomena acquire relative independence in relation to their underlying biological foundations, though without supposing a radical rupture between the two. This advantage is bought at a price that some could find exorbitant at a time when cognitive psychology is undergoing extraordinary development: the abandonment of commonsense psychology. Yet this "cost" seems to me to constitute fundamental progress, and this is the third point that I try to defend. Nonetheless, the exercise I am proposing is not purely methodological. Indeed, better understanding of the theoretical architecture of Girard's work changes the way we see the Girardian theory and how we react to it. It makes it possible to find a different approach to a line of thought that sometimes seems to be a set of final answers or a doctrine that can be interpreted in only one way. I would like to show that Girard's work, rather than constituting a complete closed system,[1] is essentially unfinished and opens perspectives for new research. This said, while disinterest in Girard's properly conceptual contribution has been frequent, it has not been total.[2]

•   •   •

In chapter 1 of *Kings of Disaster*, a study on sacred kingships in southeastern Sudan, Simon Simonse points out that the scapegoat mechanism theory developed by Girard is too abstract. More precisely, he says it is too general to be directly applicable to anthropological data.[3] Simonse consequently develops three intermediary scenarios that make it possible to relate the conceptual model to reality. I will not go into the details of these scenarios, but it seems fundamental that a field anthropologist would feel the need to specify the scapegoat model before using it to understand empirical data. In effect, the scapegoat theory is a general, abstract model, and, like a model of an object sliding down a frictionless inclined plane, it provides neither a direct description of an existing empirical reality nor even, in a sense, of a real situation. It is an ideal model intended to explain a class of events, in this case, collective violence, that it posits as producing social order, or at least a certain type of social order. The model specifies the events in question and the circumstances in which they produce the predicted results. However, it does not say whether somewhere in nature there is a situation in which the set of circumstances that it specifies occur, or whether there is a natural situation in which the circumstances that the theory identifies as active in producing the phenomenon to be explained are the only ones present.[4] What it says is that in nature there are analogous situations that are sufficiently similar to produce the events that the model predicts. In this sense, the model describes an ideal, unreal situation, and uses the description to explain real events that constitute the scope in which the theory applies. Sometimes we can create artificial situations that embody as closely as possible the ideal circumstances postulated by a theory, and this allows us (though it is not the only means) to assess the theory and evaluate its implications. This is an aspect of what we call experimentation. In experimentation we create an artificial, prepared milieu, thus a real milieu rather than one that is purely ideal, but in which there are essentially only the components that the theory identifies as producing the phenomenon. Sometimes, if we are lucky, we can even vary an aspect of the prepared milieu (for example, the degree of friction on the inclined plane) and see how the theory's predictions fare. It is then possible to integrate this aspect of the real milieu into the ideal theory. There is nonetheless a limit to how much reality the ideal can absorb. The model always employs ideal components and is not a direct description of a specific real situation. This is what Simon Simonse clearly felt about the scapegoat crisis resolution mechanism, and it explains the need for intermediary scenarios to play the role of what Hempel called "bridge laws."[5] They make it possible to go from the model to reality and to explain why in this specific case the resulting institutions tend toward one type, a dual organization, or another, for example, sacred kingship, or, more specifically, why in southern Sudan, contrary to the predictions of the leading anthropological theory, sacred kingship systems do not exclude dual segmentary social organization.

However, can we say that the Girardian explanation of the mimetic crisis, its evolution, and the resolution through a scapegoat victim is a model in this sense? It is true that this is not always clear when we limit ourselves to *Violence and the Sacred*, in which most descriptions of the crisis refer to specific examples—for example, the description of the crisis in chapter 3 on Oedipus and that in chapter 5 on Dionysus and Euripides's tragedy *The Bacchantes*. It is not until the last chapter of the book that the theory truly appears with its entire scope, but readers have to reconstruct the underlying theory on their own, by cross-referencing preceding descriptions. In contrast, the description of the crisis and its resolution on pages 26–28 of *Things Hidden since the Foundation of the World* is much more succinct and abstract, and clearly constitutes the introduction of a theoretical model. The following is a key passage:

> Acquisitive mimesis is contagious, and if the number of individuals polarized around a single object increases, other members of the community, as yet not implicated, will tend to follow the example of those who are; conflictual mimesis necessarily follows the same course because the same force is involved. Once the object has disappeared and the mimetic frenzy has reached a high level of intensity, one can expect conflictual mimesis to take over and snowball in its effects. Since the power of mimetic attraction multiplies with the number of those polarized, it is inevitable that at one moment the entire community will find itself unified against a single individual. Conflictual mimesis therefore creates a *de facto* allegiance against a common enemy, such that the conclusion of the crisis is nothing other than the reconciliation of the community.[6]

It seems to me that the most striking feature of this presentation is what it omits: the concrete and the specific. Individuals, community, crisis, and reconciliation are all mentioned, but these are all terms that refer to classes of objects and events. The model concerns sets of phenomena insofar as they fall under a certain description, but it is not a description of any specific one of them. This is why it has to be specified in order to be applicable to a given case. The model also mentions acquisitive mimesis and conflictual mimesis, which are likened to forces. Without, for now, exploring the question of mimesis's exact status—is it really a force or simply a term that refers to a certain type of symmetrical behavior?—whether we decide to interpret mimesis in terms of acquisition or conflict, it does not correspond to any specific form of behavior. Between these abstract elements, the theory introduces a simple rule governing their relations: the more individuals infected by mimetic contagion, the more contagious it becomes. Finally, the switch in the effects of mimesis, from initial division to later unity, is caused by what is imitated, namely, violence against an individual or desire for an object. However, the passage from imitation of desire to imitation of violence is no chance occurrence and does not result from an event exterior to the model; it is the normal consequence of intensification of mimetic rivalry. In this respect, we can criticize Girard for having introduced two separate denominations, acquisitive mimesis and conflictual mimesis, which suggests that we are dealing with two different phenomena, a suggestion that Girard himself immediately feels the need to reject by adding that what is in question is the same "force." The complete model is of a self-regulatory mechanism for violence. It predicts how the process by which violence and conflicts multiply within the community can, by itself, without the intervention of any outside element, bring back peace. This model is ideal because all of the elements that come into play are abstract, not specific existing events and objects, and it describes an ideal situation in which only the elements mentioned are taken into account. Of course, in any real situation that is an embodiment of the model, there are also many other components that influence the course of events. The model says nothing about them even though, as we will see below, given the type of theory involved, they sometimes have a substantial role to play.

The major advantage of such a model is its simplifying power, which is partly due to what it does not say, what it does not speak about. It is also partly due to the fact that the theory is abstract, that it concerns sets of phenomena under a certain description. The more abstract and general the description, the more sets of phenomena to which it is likely to apply. However, at the same time and at first sight paradoxically, the more abstract the model is, the more difficult it is to find real phenomena to which it can apply. This is paradoxical because if there are more such sets of phenomena, it should be easier to discover them. However, the paradox is only apparent because the difficulty lies essentially in identifying the phenomena in question. This difficulty also has two closely linked sources. First, the more abstract the theoretical model is, the more its fundamental concepts diverge from the ordinary cultural categories that we spontaneously use to structure day-to-day experience. It is then difficult to see embodiments of the model in that experience. Second, applying the model requires sorting the elements that are empirically present, and this corresponds to a hypothesis about the fundamental role of some of them. Yet the more abstract the model (the more distant it is from our everyday categories), the more it is likely that the hypothesis that it contains will be distant from our spontaneous cognitive anticipations. As philosophers as different as Quine and Popper have argued, those anticipations are hypotheses about reality that are challenged by our scientific conjectures.[7] This is why, as Thomas Kuhn saw so clearly many years ago, in order to use a theoretical model, we have to learn to see sets of phenomena as similar to the problem solved by the model.[8]

In compensation for this application problem, the model has great heuristic power. The two things are clearly linked. Applying the model consists in seeing as similar things that, at first sight, are not, which is something I recently tried to do by analyzing bullying in Japanese schools in terms of the scapegoat mechanism.[9] Every application thus reveals regularities where we used to see only differences, and the model's value stems primarily from its fruitfulness. However, as can easily be seen, the more abstract and general the model, the more the phenomena that it groups together risk appearing at first to be distinct and separate, unrelated to one another from the point of view of our usual way of dividing up the world. In other words, the more fruitful a model is, the less plausible it will seem at first sight; in classical epistemological terms, the more informative a hypothesis is, the less probable it will be a priori. The explanatory claims of the Girardian theory thus go hand in hand with a challenge to our everyday classification of social objects, and also to our scientific categories. The reason for this is that our scientific categories, at least in the area we are interested in, look essentially like refinements or criticisms of our everyday classifications. Thus, today's anthropologists tend to reject the way their predecessors used terms like "sacrifice" and "totemism." They argue, for example, in the case of totemism, that the institution does not exist and that it is, properly speaking, a mistake made by anthropologists of past generations, who placed very different social and cultural realities in the same category.[10] In the case of sacrifice, they argue that the institution does indeed exist, but that, as an anthropological category, it is a specific object limited to a well-defined sociocultural state (for example, there is no sacrifice among hunter-gatherers), contrary to what we are led to believe by the usual way the term is employed, an ordinary usage that anthropologists too often adopt uncritically.[11] In its most extreme form—for example, that of

Rodney Needham—this criticism consists in saying that human institutions do not form sets of homogenous objects sharing characteristic common features.[12] This entails that medieval empires, sacred royalty in southern Sudan, ancient Greek kingships, and the other examples of monarchies that can be found in various cultures have no features that are universally shared by all members of the class of institutions we call royalty. The same would go for all major human cultural institutions—for example, kinship systems, the sacred, sacrifice, and the gift. In contrast, what there would be, and what explains our tendency to classify these objects under the same heading, are family resemblances. In other words, while there may be no one feature that is shared by all institutions of a given type, there are nonetheless partial intersections of features that are shared by many if not the majority of the members of a class. This hypothesis has a major advantage over the preceding criticisms in that it explains both our spontaneous tendency to call these institutions by the same name and anthropologists' need to break the groups up into smaller categories. However, it also risks justifying a search for ever finer distinctions, until we end up with a perfectly useless classification in which there are as many categories as objects. This danger arises because Needham takes as a brute fact what we actually have to explain: how is it that human institutions, unlike minerals and atomic elements, but like animal species and terms for basic colors, form sets of polythetic objects?[13]

    We have to take the investigation, and the criticism, further. Girard, like Maurice Hocart long before him, thinks that not only do the various human institutions form polythetic classes of objects, but that between the institutions themselves, between sacrifice, royalty, ritual, myth, kinship, and animal husbandry systems, there are family resemblances.[14] Hocart, a specialist of India but above all of comparative anthropology, noted these similarities between the various institutions and examples of the same institution in different cultures. He patiently documented them and drew up a diffusionist hypothesis. Unfortunately, he was unable to explain the mechanism responsible for diffusion or to prove directly that it really exists. He could only prove its possibility indirectly using the very similarities that he hoped the mechanism would explain. However, rejection of this diffusionist thesis, which is rightly considered ad hoc, should not be confused with falsification of Hocart's comparativist investigation.[15] The problem raised by the similarities remains, and Needham's skepticism is not much help in solving it.

However, Girard's hypothesis can be useful in this, at least for those who are ready to abandon the prevailing prejudice in favor of ever finer classification of institutions.

As Jean-Pierre Dupuy pointed out long ago, Girard's theory is morphogenetic.[16] The aim of the scapegoat crisis resolution theory is not only to explain a class of specific phenomena—namely, fundamental violence and how it is resolved—but also to account for the different types of phenomenologies that can be generated following specific historical trajectories on the basis of various "lineage" processes flowing from the founding event of the killing of the scapegoat victim. This makes it a special type of model. It is not limited to deploying a set of potentials that we could, in a sense, consider as already contained in the theory from the beginning. On the contrary, in a morphogenetic theory, the model is a dynamic process that can encompass events that are external, and thus random with respect to it. These random events correspond to points of bifurcation in the dynamic process described by the model, and they explain the evolution of the dynamic process in such and such a direction. This type of theory has the advantage of being able to explain historical phenomena properly speaking—in other words, temporal successions of events that contain new elements—in the sense of events that were not contained in the initial model and that it could not predict.[17] This is contrary to what we find, for example, in models of classical physics.[18]

This historical dimension of the model consists in showing how various institutional developments can be brought back to the scapegoat mechanism, how they are expanded, more complicated embodiments of the model. This morphogenetic dimension of Girard's theory is based on the key concept of misapprehension, which will allow us to immediately discuss the issue of Girard's theory's relationship to commonsense psychology. In the model, the stakeholders are unaware of the exact functioning of the scapegoat mechanism that their actions determine. The real meaning of the shift presupposed by the passage from acquisitive mimesis to imitation of the antagonist escapes them, and the imitative processes themselves are, for the most part, unconscious.[19] Moreover, misapprehension of the substitution process by which players finally converge on a single antagonist is, in the model, so inseparable from the convergence itself that one cannot occur without the other. Thus, if the observable phenomenon of convergence takes place, we have to suppose that the unobservable psychological condition has been satisfied. However, it is important not to think of this psychological condition in the framework of individualist psychology, which Girard rejects as incompatible with mimetic analysis. We therefore must not think of misapprehension primarily as a false belief that agents have about who is responsible for the violence that has struck the community. Such misapprehension does indeed sometimes exist, but it occurs only later, once the crisis has been resolved, when agents try to make sense of the extraordinary events that they have experienced. It is based on an older misapprehension, one that we might call more archaic and fundamental, and that is simply one with the mimetic illusion, one with the prestige given to the mediator. In order to illustrate this fragile bridge, we can employ a slightly modified form of the distinction between *constitutive* concepts and *theoretical* concepts that Hayek introduced into analysis of social phenomena.[20]

As their name indicates, the former are cognitive components of actions by which agents constitute social reality. The latter are notions that they employ to understand this reality once it has been constituted. Constitutive elements thus refer to cognitive (intentional?) elements present in action, and theoretical concepts are the explanations that agents or social observers give for actions or the social phenomena that flow from them, even though, very often, neither agents nor observers immediately recognize that the phenomena that they are trying to explain depend on the agents' actions, but believe, on the contrary, that they are imposed on them from the outside. Thus, in mimetic rivalry, according to Girard, what motivates agents is the fascination that the rivals have for each other. The fascination develops during the oppositions that mark the first beginnings of the rivalry, and it feeds the rivalry, little by little. Clearly, this fascination has an affective dimension. It facilitates or provides an obstacle to certain emotions. It also tends to have a "valuating" effect. It situates the "fascinating" Other or the object of rivalry on the scale of what is desirable, attractive, or repulsive. Finally, it has a cognitive dimension or scope, which does not necessarily have to be understood as propositional content concerning the Other. This cognitive aspect of fascination may be nothing more than a stronger or weaker propensity to accept as true one statement rather than another about whatever fascinates us, or the general influence that fascination has on the rules that determine beliefs. Once the crisis has come to an end, the surviving antagonists, who are still fascinated, see with incomprehension that the death of a single one has brought peace back among them. They fail to understand how this state could have resulted from their actions alone. Yet this result, and Girard often insists on this, convinces them that they have indeed chosen the right victim, so to speak. The agents' explicit beliefs about the victim's role in the violence and the following peace spring from the new situation of suddenly rediscovered calm, the memory of their past conflicts, and the sudden elimination of those conflicts. These beliefs are thus already constructions, explanatory scaffolding about the agents' past actions and their consequences. As such, they correspond to what Hayek calls theoretical concepts. In this sense, we can consider the various forms of the sacred that spring from the scapegoat mechanism as so many theories about the crisis and its resolution. Yet before they are explicit beliefs about the victim, these "theories" are sequences of actions that the agents recognize as efficient, though the reason for the efficiency escapes them. The efficiency consists in calming tensions, facilitating the return to harmony. Girard postulates that this is why agents tend to reproduce these sequences of events and use them in all circumstances where the need for their mysterious efficiency is felt. Girard argues that the various human institutions, beginning with rituals, spring from this repeated reproduction and the variations that such reproduction always introduces into events. Girard thus reduces to a minimum the hypotheses about agents' beliefs. Even the idea that humans have a tendency to repeat actions that delivered satisfactory results in the past does not have to be conceived of as a properly psychological hypothesis.[21] It is entirely possible to see it only as a behavioral regularity that was selected long ago for obvious biological reasons, without making any hypothesis about the proximal mechanism through which it occurs. It would thus be a behavioral disposition that has origins far back in the phylogenetic tree, that is much older than mimetic crisis phenomena, and its co-option in reproducing events typical of the crisis and its resolution. Moreover, perhaps this ritual reproduction itself, before any explicit reflection on the crisis and its resolution, constitutes the scapegoat phenomenon as a theoretical object available to agents' cognitive activity. Indeed, the simple fact of repetition transforms what was a unique sequence of specific events into a class of typical, temporally organized phenomena.

Agents' explicit beliefs thus initially have virtually no role; they come into play late and are essentially false. Yet they rapidly become fundamental because it is through them that the ritual becomes more complex, diversifies, and a theory is formed. We are very far from commonsense psychology. Agents' beliefs and desires do not form an autonomous level that determines their actions on the basis of preferences and adequate knowledge of the social world. On the contrary, they are phenomena dependent on motivations that have to be understood as more fundamentally biological, but that nonetheless react with desires and beliefs so as to change and reorient them. In fact, agents' explicit beliefs about the sacred, about what is prescribed and forbidden, are essential components of the apparatus by which cultures tame mimetism and limit the number and scale of the conflicts that it causes. This is to say that, according to Girard, the human psyche is historically constructed through the interaction of several levels of phenomena, including the original mimetic processes, which are transformed in the historical process in which agents' explicit beliefs are also changed.

◆ ◆ ◆

The mimetism of the first humans, before it was picked up and changed by culture, was only a biological feature of the species, a tendency toward reciprocal imitation that is stronger among humans than among most other animal species, and above all more open.[22] The disposition toward imitation is first a learning mechanism. This is its biological utility and probably the reason why it has been kept in the phylogenetic line. However, as Girard points out, there is in principle no reason to suppose that acquisition phenomena escape the influence of mimetism. On the contrary, there are many reasons to think that they have to be subject to it because such phenomena play a fundamental role in learning forms of behavior that are essential to survival. However, acquisitive mimesis will inevitably give rise to conflict, and in a social species, the stronger mimetism is, the more likely the conflict will spread throughout the whole group. Of course, all animal species have brakes that limit the scope and extent of intraspecific conflicts. The brakes control not only the frequency, seriousness, and distribution of conflicts within the group, they also have indirect influence on the maximum size of the group. Beyond a certain threshold of population, the growth in the number and seriousness of conflicts leads to division of the group, or forces some members into exile. Since smaller groups and isolated individuals are more fragile and threatened with extinction, intraspecific conflicts thus act as a form of selective pressure.[23] Violence among members of the species both limits the size of groups and is a form of selection that acts directly on individuals. Biologically, Girard's thesis takes as an initial hypothesis that, owing to our stronger mimetism, which is inseparable from our superior cognitive abilities, conflicts among us escape the control of the usual mechanisms that protect against violence among members of the same species. Under such conditions, it is not necessary to think that the species would have been condemned to disappear if new protective mechanisms had not been invented, but it would quite certainly have been very different from what we know it to be today. We would be able to live only in extremely small groups, under the constant threat of mortal conflict. From a biological point of view, the scapegoat mechanism thus looks like an adaptation. It is a group adaptation in a sense, but based on a variation of individual mimetism. In effect, the success of the scapegoat mechanism in some groups seems to come from a minimal variation in the individual disposition to imitation. This variation gives rise to the auto-regulatory mechanism of violence, which is a social mechanism. Groups in which such individuals are sufficiently numerous for the mechanism to operate will thus become more dominant, both because of the reduction in the number of conflicts within the group and because the mechanism makes it possible to have a larger group. There is no need to think that they will win in conflicts with other groups, but rather that they will be better able to manage their relationship with their environment in general. It is true that this is a case of group selection, a phenomenon the existence of which was challenged in evolutionary biology for a time; however, a few recent works have shown its importance in a very large number of animal populations.[24]

However, this initial, typically biological evolution will be rapidly followed or will take place in parallel with another phenomenon. Ritual reproduction of the crisis and its resolution will give rise in the various groups to institutions that are more or less different, depending on local circumstances, and those circumstances will result in different cultural lineages. For this, it suffices to imagine that the groups remain isolated from one another long enough. It is not necessary to think that the lines will be in competition with one another or that such competition, if it exists, will play an important role in the evolution of the lines. In any case, since by hypothesis these lines all come from the same generating mechanism, we should expect that the institutions that they contain have both some family resemblances and certain differences. This is, properly speaking, a prediction of the model. However, this prediction is not a complete explanation of the institutions that we find in a given cultural line. Such an explanation can come only from many case studies, and we should expect them to lead to modifications of the model.

At the same time, as was said above, this process is inseparable from a transformation in the agents' psyches. The general direction of this transformation seems to be toward greater importance of agents' explicit beliefs. The final picture that we obtain of the human mind and culture is of a complete but nonreductionist naturalization. However, one of the consequences of this naturalization is to withdraw the privileges generally given to commonsense psychology. In a mimetic explanation, agents' explicit beliefs and desires no longer explain their actions. It is rather their mimetic behavior that, in the last resort, explains why they have the beliefs they have, and the state of the culture produced by that mimetic behavior determines whether they have access to a true theory about their actions. I think that there are at least two advantages here in comparison with theories that take as given the present state of commonsense psychology.[25] First, by pushing back into a far-away past, such as the ancient Paleolithic, the time when our cognitive apparatus attained its present form, such theories remove all possible access to a history other than the perfectly speculative story of selective pressures that could have led to the establishment of our cognitive capacities. Second, such theories pass over culture in complete silence. Not only can they be criticized for the fact that they posit that commonsense psychology was established in the ancient Paleolithic but is more or less that of the average contemporary North American, which seems a little unlikely, but especially for the fact that they seem to completely fail to understand the human mind in a context in which culture plays a fundamental biological role. What Girard's theory offers us is precisely an approach in which it is possible to understand the link between the biological and psychological aspects of cultural activity.

An epistemological analysis of a theory such as the one I have just made concerning the Girardian hypothesis is not intended to and cannot show that a theory is true. However, it can show whether the theory in question has certain features that we seek in or even require of our scientific hypotheses. If what we want is a naturalist theory of culture and the psyche that makes it possible to understand the relationship between the cultural and biological worlds, though without reducing one to the other, Girard's theory satisfies the epistemological requirements. The question of whether it is true or false can be answered only in another context and using different methods, such as through case studies; through the discovery of counterexamples or phenomena that show, for example, that the theory has only local, limited value; or through new hypotheses.

"De la *méconnaissance*"

The idea of *méconnaissance* plays a major role in the work of René Girard. It is one of the central concepts of his mimetic theory. *Méconnaissance* is at the heart of the mechanism that brings about the resolution to the mimetic crisis, and it is, according to him, a necessary condition for the success of this resolution. Because this self-regulating mechanism of violence is at the origin of human institutions, *méconnaissance* remains present as a fundamental dimension of culture. There are, however, among those who are interested in mimetic theory numerous debates and disagreements concerning *méconnaissance*: What is it? What precisely is its role in human culture? What is its value? Further, Girard argues that Christian Revelation lifts the veil of *méconnaissance* concerning the innocence of the victims of the scapegoating process that protects us from our own violence. As a result, this revelation reduces the efficiency of that mechanism and of the institutions that flow from it, and progressively brings about the demise of all that was built upon "the founding murder." Is culture as we know it then doomed to disappear as a result of the revelation of its violent origin? Alternatively, is a perfectly transparent culture, one from which all *méconnaissance* has disappeared, possible, even simply conceivable? Given that what is disappearing with the revelation of the fundamental *méconnaissance* that is at the heart of human culture is the mechanism that historically, more or less successfully, protected us against our own violence, it seems that we are now left with the stark, and probably impossible, choice between abandoning all violence and total destruction. Therefore some authors have been wondering if it is possible to "cheat," so to speak, with the knowledge of violence that we have gained, and to devise institutions that incorporate it—institutions that can take advantage of what we have learned, while retaining a form of opacity that is indispensable to their stability.

How Is *Méconnaissance* Possible?

Before attempting to answer these fundamental, urgent, and dramatic questions, it might be useful to ask more simply, what is *méconnaissance*? What exactly does the word refer to? Is *méconnaissance* to be understood as a mistake, as false information, as an illusion, or as a form of delusion? Until now, I have retained (and I will continue to do so) the French word *méconnaissance* and avoided translating it into English. In fact, different translations of *méconnaissance* have been used in English translations of Girard or in his own English-language writings. The most common perhaps are "misrecognition" or "miscognition." However, many French readers argue that there is no single translation of *méconnaissance* that adequately captures all of the term's connotations and nuances. There is more here, I think, than just another expression of French chauvinism. What is involved, I argue, is a different understanding of knowledge.

Interestingly, bilingual dictionaries give as the English equivalent of *méconnaissance* first "ignorance" and second "misreading." French dictionaries define *méconnaissance* as, "le fait de méconnaître, de ne pas apprécier, de ne pas reconnaître la valeur de . . ." That is to say: "the fact of ignoring, of not appreciating, of not recognising the value of . . ." *Méconnaître*, then, is to ignore, it is to fail to appreciate or to recognize the value of someone or something. It is ignorance in the sense of the verb "to ignore," which, in English, does not simply mean a failure to know, but also willfully disregarding something or someone. Thus, there is a dimension of action in *méconnaissance*. The heart of the concept is not so much the idea of a false or mistaken belief, of inappropriate "propositional content," as that of a particular relation to knowledge. That is why I said that the difficulties of adequately translating *méconnaissance* into English point toward a different conception of knowledge.

In the English-speaking world there is a long philosophical tradition of understanding knowledge as "true, justified belief." In that particular tradition anything that qualifies as knowledge is by definition true; the agent's mental attitude to the propositional content, to what he or she knows, is one of belief and that belief is justified. Therefore if what you believe is not true, it is not knowledge; if your belief is not justified, it is not knowledge; or if your attitude toward the propositional content is not one of belief, but, for example, one of irony, doubt, or willful disregard, again it is not knowledge. However, the two components of *mé-connaissance*, *mé* as in *mé-prendre* (to mistake), *mé-dire* (to speak ill), or *mé-content* (unhappy), and *connaissance* (knowledge), clearly suggest that the meaning of the term can only be "false knowledge" or "bad knowledge," literally "misknowledge." Thus, the verb *méconaître* should mean "misknowing." However, that is something that is impossible in the dominant philosophical tradition in the English-speaking world. When knowledge is construed as true justified belief, "misknowing" is more than a mere oxymoron; it is a self-contradiction.

Should we conclude then that *méconnaissance* is an inconsistent idea, a meaningless concept, a mere sound? I don't think so, but we need a different conception of knowledge to make sense of this "misknowledge," of this "false," "bad," "wrong," or "ill" knowledge. Many years ago, Karl Popper put forward the idea of objective knowledge.[1] Knowledge, he argued, should not be reduced to beliefs, that is to say, to the thought content of individual agents, to propositions and ideas imprisoned in peoples' heads. Rather, it should be considered as a kind of exosomatic artifact. Knowledge is objective, according to Popper, in the sense that it is something in the world that various agents can grasp and use, each one in his or her own particular way, rather than in the sense of private thought content that is identically repeated over and over again in myriads of individual subjects. Knowledge is like a tool that we can use to do things, to change the world that surrounds us. In the context of such a conception of knowledge, it becomes possible to make sense of "misknowledge" in two rather straightforward ways.

First, there are better and worse tools to do the same thing, and there are better and worse families of tools as well as better and worse tokens of the same type of tool. For example, it is better to use a screwdriver than a hammer to drive a screw; some types of screwdrivers are better than others types; and some individual screwdrivers are better than others of the same type. Second, there are better and worse ways to use the same tool to do either the same or different tasks; carpenters are more or less gifted as carpenters. *Méconnaissance*, I believe, corresponds to both types of failings. Our knowledge can be more or less adequate for the task at hand, and here *méconnaissance* refers primarily to the content of knowledge, to its truth. We can also use our knowledge more or less successfully, and here *méconnaissance* primarily refers to the ability and attitudes of the tool-wielding animal. In order to make sense of *méconnaissance* in this way, it is not necessary to adopt all or even much of Popper's philosophy of knowledge; all we need to accept is that a statement about the world can be more or less exact or true and still constitute a form of knowledge, and that agents can have different attitudes toward this knowledge. It then becomes possible to say, as Girard sometimes does, that misknowledge augments as knowledge grows, "la méconnaissance croît au fur et à mesure que la connaissance augmente." In other words, one can have "perfect knowledge" about something, in the sense of true and justified belief, and yet still be in complete *méconnaissance*.

The Origin of *Méconnaissance*

The *méconnaissance* that interests Girard is not just any kind of inadequate knowledge or of inappropriate relation to what we know. In fact, it could be argued that, according to him, *méconnaissance* precedes *connaissance*, that "misknowledge" comes before "knowledge," which is a way of saying that knowledge always constitutes a gain over an original ignorance, an ignorance that is not only a passive failure to know but also an active form of "not-knowing." This original ignorance, unlike what is the case in Rawls, is not a veil that prudishly protects the subject from those elements of knowledge that may subvert the pure exercise of his or her rationality, but a mist in which nothing appears clearly. It will be objected perhaps that this priority of *méconnaissance* is impossible. There cannot be "false-knowledge" or "bad-knowledge," it will be argued, before there is knowledge. "Bad-knowledge" necessarily implies the prior existing knowledge. It is true that there cannot be a bad tool before there are any tools, but clearly there does not need to be any good tool before there can be bad tools, though we may of course have a hard time recognizing a bad tool as such before we have a better one at hand. That, I think, is precisely Girard's point.

The objection that there cannot be "false-knowledge" before there is some form of knowledge supposes that among all that we "know" there are some elements of "true" or "real" knowledge that can in principle be distinguished from the rest, and that knowledge grows, or becomes more adequate, as the number of these elements of "knowledge" augments. This, however, brings us back to the previous conception, where knowledge is always by definition true. Girard, to the contrary, repeatedly argues that what is true and what is false cannot be separated as if they constituted discrete elements, some of which correspond to knowledge and others to falsehood. The reduction of *méconnaissance*, cognitive progress, therefore corresponds more to the reorganization of our knowledge than to the addition of new elements. That is why Girard often compares this experience to a religious conversion: a conversion that does not consist so much in discovering new knowledge as of suddenly seeing everything in a new light or from a different point. According to him, it is precisely those shifts in our outlook on the world that allow our knowledge to expand and that make us able to progress into new domains of inquiry.

The *méconnaissance* that interests Girard concerns our relation to others, and that is why it affects and colors all that we know. Not only because most of what we know we learn from others, or because we mostly only know what others know, but mainly because we do not realize or want to recognize the role others play in the determination of our "true and justified beliefs."[2] *Méconnaissance* primarily concerns others and our relations to them. What we ignore is the extent to which others, by their mere presence, act upon us, determine our beliefs, our desires, our choices, and our preferences. The point of *méconnaissance* is precisely that we *ignore* it, not necessarily that we do not *know* it. So *méconnaissance*, like *mauvaise foi* (bad faith) according to Sartre, who clearly influenced Girard on this, implies a kind of "lying to oneself."

It is true that lying to oneself as opposed to lying to others is often considered extremely difficult to understand. In order to successfully lie to oneself, it is argued, an individual would have to know that X is true, because if one does not know that X is true, one is not lying when one asserts that X is not true, and one would have to simultaneously believe that X is not true, because if he or she does not believe that X is not true, he or she has not been lied to and has not lied to himself or herself. This seems like an extremely difficult thing to do, as it would require one to simultaneously believe and not believe that X is true and justified. Furthermore, the common solution that divides the individual into an unconscious that "knows" that X is true and a consciousness that falsely believes that X is not true is unavailable here. For when such is the case, it can be argued that it is not the individual that lied to himself or herself, but part A of individual "I" that lied to part B of individual "I."

There is, however, another way of understanding "lying to oneself," or, if you prefer there, is also another form of "lying to oneself"[3] that implies an altogether different intention of action than does "lying to others." Start with the following example: suppose you and I are both interested in the same woman. She and I are both at the library where I am peacefully enjoying her presence, and she has just gotten up looking for a book, or perhaps she is gone to the washroom. At that moment you, my archrival, arrive and ask me, "Is Julia there?" and I, since I would rather you do not meet her, lie to you and respond, "I'm not sure, I think she went back home," while I know perfectly well that she is still here and will be coming back to her seat at any moment. If, however, unbeknownst to me, Julia has suddenly decided to return home and you, acting on the false information I gave you, meet her there, my plan will have failed miserably. This example indicates that when we lie to others, we seek to manipulate the information they have about the world, but we want the world to remain as it is. When I tell you that Julia has gone back home I do not wish her to have returned there, where I am now sending you. When lying to others (at least in this way)[4] we do not aim at changing the world, in the sense of making it adequate to the propositional content of the lie; to the contrary, a lie is only successful, both as an illocutionary act and in regard of the intention that animates the liar, if the world remains different from what the lie says that it is. Of course the world may and often does change as a consequence of the lie, and many times bringing about that transformation was part of our objective when we lied. However, what we do not wish is for the lie itself to be true. Lying to others does not aim at changing the world in the sense that it does not aim at realizing its propositional content in the world. In that sense, a lie is anything but a performative.

When one lies to oneself, however, the intention and the conditions for the lie to be successful are often quite different. Suppose that I am finding more and more indications that my wife is having an affair. Yet I do not want to recognize that this can be the case, and I deny flatly the relevance of the growing evidence. My friends and others observing my behavior may say that I am lying to myself, that I know, but that I refuse to believe what I know. Note, however, that when I say that my wife is not having an affair, I want this statement to be true. *I want the world to be as I say that it is*, unlike that which is the case when I lie to others, where I want the world *not to be* as I say that it is. This difference, I believe, is crucial; lying to oneself is guided by a different intention than lying to others. This fundamental intention is to change the world; it is to make the world *as we say that it is*. Of course it may be argued that this intention is doomed to failure. In this case this is certainly true, if my wife is having an affair my not wanting it to be the case will not change anything. But, as we all know, our intention to change the world is not always doomed to failure. This fundamental intention, this desire to make the world as we say it is, is the reason for the close relationship between violence and lying to oneself, for violence also aims at changing the world.[5]

Méconnaissance constitutes a form of lying to oneself. In knowledge classically understood with truth as its regulative ideal, we try to adapt or adjust our statements and our beliefs to the world. We seek to make what we say and believe adequate, "similar" to how the world is made. Our knowledge aims at "representing" the world as it is. In *méconnaissance*, on the contrary, we want the world to conform to what we say or believe. The goal of an adequate representation or fit between the world and what we believe is the same in both cases, but the direction of fittingness or of adaptation is opposite. *Méconnaissance* is "misknowledge" not because the desire to change the world is irrational or unacceptable, but because of where this intention intervenes here: within knowledge itself. It inverts the direction of adaptation within the exercise of cognition itself.

Nonetheless, it may in fact be argued that the desire to know the world is inseparable from the desire to change it, that our ability to change the world requires knowledge and that this capacity augments as our knowledge grows.

That is certainly the case, and it is why *connaissance* and *méconnaissance* are inseparable and why the growth of our knowledge rests on successfully articulating to each other these two "contradictory" intentions and strategies in our relation the world. Understood in this way, *méconnaissance* can never be entirely expelled out of *connaissance* or excluded from our knowledge of the world.

Méconnaissance in Culture

There is also in Girard a more cultural and less individual use of the term *méconnaissance*. Here *méconnaissance* refers to an absence of knowledge concerning the violent origin of culture and more particularly to the fundamental role of the scapegoating mechanism. These two meanings of *méconnaissance*, the individual and the cultural, are closely related for at least two reasons. First, because the ignorance that cultures manifest concerning their violent origin is usually not conceived by Girard as a mere absence of knowledge, but as the result of a kind of "shying away" or of refusing to probe further a body of knowledge that, if questioned properly, would reveal the truth about the origin. Hence *méconnaissance* in culture is also *méconnaissance* in the sense of not wanting the world "to be like that," of not wanting the culture we love and cherish to have sprung from the blood of victims. There is a second reason, which is that cultural *méconnaissance* ultimately finds its ground and origin in individual "méconnaissance." The shared collective cultural *méconnaissance* proceeds from the individual *méconnaissance* of all and may be viewed as a kind of "unanimous misunderstanding." Girard describes the violent scapegoating that puts an end to the sacrificial crisis as a self-organizing mechanism of violence. As violence intensifies and includes more and more members of the community, individuals become doubles of each other. This loss of differences facilitates rallying against a unique antagonist on whom all others can simultaneously discharge their violence. This unanimity-minus-one brings back peace, and the victim, who was randomly designated through the blind substitution of antagonists, retroactively appears as having been singly responsible for both the violence and its end. Such, according to Girard, is the violent origin of the sacred. Cultural *méconnaissance* is precisely the transcendent prestige this self-regulating mechanism of violence confers on its victim as it transforms a dead body into a deity. What this *méconnaissance* hides is the radically human and violent origin of culture and of the sacred. All of human culture, argues Girard, stems from this mechanism and consequently plays a role in protecting us against violence in its various and sundry forms. However, given the self-regulating nature of this mechanism, in every case it ultimately always is violence that protects us against violence, or to put it another way, culture protects us violently against violence, though this violence that culture contains, Girard argues, diminishes as distance from the origin grows and as the traces of the founding scapegoating are slowly erased.

Christianity, according to Girard, reveals the purely human origin of this foundation and as well as the arbitrary designation of the victim. In consequence it ruins, he argues, the efficacy of this self-organizing mechanism. It progressively reduces its ability to protect us from violence. It destroys the paradoxical capacity of violence being used against violence in order to reduce violence. What exactly does this mean? How does this revelation function? At one level it simply means that if the agents do not all "believe" that the victim, against whom they simultaneously discharge their violence, is guilty—in other words, if they do not believe that he or she deserves the violence he or she suffers—the transfer will not take place. The operation will not succeed; the victim's death will not bring peace back. I wrote "believe" (with quotation marks) because there is a sense in which all believe that the victim is guilty because they all simultaneously discharge their violence against him or her and because the victim's death brings back peace. This "belief" as all forms of *méconnaissance* is thus inseparable from an action. Therefore the revelation that is necessary in order to make unanimous victimage impossible is something that will help dissolve individual *méconnaissance*, something that will make less likely both the actions and representations that come with it. This, as I argued elsewhere, is not so much the revelation of the innocence of the victim as the revelation of the innocence of the other, which is not so much the revelation of the "sanctity" of the other as the revelation of his or her radical and fragile humanity. What destroys this *méconnaissance* is not a belief, a propositional content, but new attitudes like forgiveness and charity extended to all.[6] It is not therefore only *connaissance*, knowledge in a classical sense, that is involved in this revelation; it is also the *mé* of *méconnaissance* that is transformed and weakened. That is why this "revelation" makes the unanimity against the victim more fragile and short-lived. This fracture of unanimity, according to Girard, slowly consumes cultures from the inside.

It is in fact the fracture of the unanimity, rather than the revelation itself, that transforms our cultures. It is true that this fracture is the result of the revelation, but not alone; it is also the result of the fact that *méconnaissance* persists. Individual *méconnaissance* does not disappear, but it tends to become, so to speak, "discontinuous." It is in fact the interplay between revelation and *méconnaissance* that drives the system, or, if you prefer, it is the interplay between *mé-connaissance* and *connaissance*. In the last sections of this essay I illustrate this thesis with the help of two at first sight rather different cultural objects: Ernesto De Martino's analysis of tarantism in *La terra del rimorso*[7] and John Rawls's theory of justice.

Veiled Knowledge

De Martino's fieldwork on tarantism in the south of Italy is presented as an inquiry whose primary objective is to determine whether tarantism is a disease, either a medical condition caused by the bite of a spider or another animal, or a form of mental illness, or if it constitutes a particular cultural formation, a minor form of religion, as De Martino concludes at the end of his inquiry. In fact, that debate, or perhaps a slightly different one, had been going on for centuries. From the age of the Counter-Reformation at least, "educated" persons have been asking: what is behind this strange "superstition" according to which those who have been bitten by a spider not only can be "cured" by dancing, but are actually forced to dance, for days without end, when they hear the right music? Beginning in the seventeenth century, people started asking: are the symptoms of tarantism the result of a real spider's bite, the expression of a particular form of mental derangement, or perhaps, even, a sign of possession by the devil? Apart from the disappearance of this last alternative, possession by the devil, the debate had not changed very much by the time De Martino arrived in Puglia in the late 1950s.

In fact, De Martino and his research team rapidly ruled out the first two alternatives, either a reaction to animal venom or mental illness, and the book is essentially dedicated to the description and analysis of tarantism as a cultural formation. It is nonetheless interesting that these two ways of mis-understanding tarantism remained common for such a long time. Consider first the animal venom hypothesis. According to its victims, tarantism can be "caused" by many different types of animals, either a spider, but any one of a number of different types of spider, or a scorpion, or a snake. In fact, a bite is not always necessary—for example, one can become a *tarantata* (a victim of tarantism) by seeing a snake killed. One can also become a *tarantata* as a result of showing disrespect to St. Paul, the patron saint who protects people from tarantism and who can cure the disease. Further, most victims of tarantism usually experience their symptoms again every year, at about the same date as when the first crisis happened, and this yearly recurrence of symptoms can continue for forty or fifty years! No known animal venom can cause such a phenomenon. Of course it may be argued that tarantism is a cultural formation that is "grafted" upon a real medical condition. Perhaps, but observe. Tarantism is not only subject to a particular temporal rhythm but also to strange variations in space. Outside of a well-circumscribed area around Lecce and Galatina, spiders do not cause tarantism, and even in that area there are sanctuaries protected by particular saints where the "disease" is unknown. Add to this a few more recent observations. Spiders usually bite men who work in the fields, but tarantism predominantly strikes women to a proportion of about three to one. Most people who seek medical help for bites from venomous animals do not show any symptoms of tarantism, and *tarantati* do not seek medical help. Finally, the area of Italy where tarantism is rife is known to have fewer spiders than adjacent areas where tarantism is not found! Of course, as De Martino recognizes, it may be the case that some *tarantati* have been bitten by spiders or other venomous animals, but clearly this accident that happened to some individuals cannot explain the social phenomenon of tarantism.

The situation concerning mental illness is a bit different. *Tarantati* do manifest abnormal behavior and some signs of psychic disorders, at least when they are in crisis, and some individuals also do at other times, but these symptoms are relatively mild; they do not correspond to any particular mental disease; and they vary extensively from one *tarantata* to the next. In other words, persons who suffer from tarantism have usually experienced some form of trauma or of unresolved conflict, but their symptoms do not indicate any particular pathological condition.

Therefore the question arises why did these manifestly false interpretations of tarantism (especially the first one) persist for so long? (In fact, they
remain popular even today.)[8] De Martino in his interviews of *tarantati*, of
their families and friends, found that in every case the first episode of tarantism, which usually strikes teenagers and young adults, happens at a time
when the person experiences strong social and psychic conflicts or trauma,
like a forced wedding, an impossible love, loss of one's employment, death of
a loved one, and so forth. Tarantism, argues De Martino, allows a person to
express through his or her symptoms, and through the burden they impose
on others, his or her rejection of an impossible social situation, which for
various cultural reasons cannot be addressed directly. It also gives him or her
a day or two of glory when he or she is at the center of the community's
attention. Finally, sometimes only after many years, it allows the person to
come to terms with the difficulty. De Martino also shows that tarantism,
both the "disease" and the musical and choreuthic cure, constitutes a well-
established ritual in which the *tarantata*, the musicians, and the audience all
have their properly defined roles. As mentioned earlier, De Martino defines
tarantism as a minor form of religion, and this religious ritual, according to
him, functions as a way of alleviating conflicts within the community and
of reconciling agents with a life that is a constant source of frustration and
tensions. These tensions, frustrations, and unresolved conflicts form the
background of "remorse," which he defines as a relation to a past that cannot
be changed and that could not have been different. Tarantism is, says De
Martino, a means of coming to terms with remorse. Hence this "minor religious formation" fulfills the normal role of religion and of the sacred, according to Girard. It is not the "opium of the people," but a means of protecting
families and communities from tensions and conflicts that threaten them,
offering them a minor catharsis through the actions of the *tarantata*, who is
halfway between a scapegoat and a sacred being. Of course this is not the way
De Martino presents his finding, but this Girardian reading very naturally
comes to mind.

From this point of view, one interesting aspect of *La terra del rimorso* is
how much all participants in this ritual—the *tarantati*, their families, and
neighbors—are close to knowing the whole truth about tarantism. They are
well aware of the fact that those who are struck by tarantism are often living
in difficult times or caught in irresolvable conflicts. They even point this

out to the anthropologist. In fact, they know a lot more about tarantism, about its function and purpose, than "scientists" who try to reduce it to a disease, either physical or mental. What allows them to have this greater knowledge, I suspect, is the fact that they "believe" in spiders that make you dance and who dance with you to the rhythm of a specific type of music, different spiders reacting to different music, and in spiders that prefer different colors and that will die of exhaustion after dancing with you for three days. Nonetheless, they "believe" that these spiders can pass on their venom, and their victims, to their daughters, their sisters, or even their granddaughters. They, in turn, will make you sick and dance with you until they also die. *Tarantati*, their friends, and their families all "believe" this. They believe it in the sense that they are ready to spend a large part of their savings, or even to borrow money, in order to pay for musicians who will provide a cure by making you dance, and to feed them as well as at least part of the audience for two or three days, as long as it takes! They also go through the trouble of decorating the patient's room with tissues and scarves of the particular color that suits the spider and hang from the ceiling strings that look like a web so that the spider can feel at home and comfortable. Finally, they take a yearly pilgrimage to St. Paul's chapel in Galatina. These "beliefs," this *méconnaissance*, is probably what allows them to know so much, because this *méconnaissance*, the actions that make it up, are precisely what prevents the conflicts, tensions, and rivalries that lurk behind tarantism from destroying families and communities.

When Ernesto De Martino conducted his fieldwork in the south of Italy in 1959, he concluded that tarantism was a dying tradition. He judged that his observation in the field corresponded to the scattered remains of what had been a much richer cultural formation whose traces he found in ancient writings and other cultural artifacts from the past. He partially blamed the Catholic Church and partially the modern state for the demise of tarantism. He was probably right on both counts. However, the fact that he conducted his inquiry within the ruins of a cultural edifice that for the most part had already disappeared raises important questions to which it is difficult to bring any clear answers. Did the extensive knowledge that participants had of the inner workings of the phenomena correspond to the normal functioning of the tradition? Was the extensive knowledge a sign of the advanced state of dissolution of the tradition? Was it the cause of the tradition's disappearance?

A Land without Remorse

John Rawls, in his *Theory of Justice*,[9] introduces a new type of device in moral
and political philosophy: the veil of ignorance. This is a two-step procedure.
First, we are asked to imagine individuals who are called upon to choose the
best theory of justice to regulate their common existence. It is therefore not
us who are choosing the best theory of justice, but the individuals whom we
are asked to imagine. That is the first step. Then we are asked to imagine that
they are placed behind a "veil of ignorance" that filters the type of information that they can access. Behind that veil of ignorance agents cannot know
anything of what concerns them personally. They do know who they are.
They do not know if they are rich or poor, to which social class they belong,
what their profession is, whether they are risk adverse or not, and so on. The
veil of ignorance makes them, so to speak, anonymous in their own eyes.
However, it allows the passage of all general information concerning society
and people. Thus, they can know our best theories about society, economics,
or psychology, as well as the results of natural science that are relevant to the
understanding of social life. The goal of the device is to prevent them from
being biased in their own favor when they are asked to choose a theory of
justice. They have access to all knowledge that can be relevant to their decision and are "protected" from the irrelevant information that could prevent
them from reaching the right conclusion.

In view of the nature of the above argument, we can conclude that it
is hoped that we will learn something about justice by seeing how "they"
will choose in this ideal situation, where "they" are not distracted by the
advantage that each one "naturally" gives to himself or herself. The goal of
the veil of ignorance is to render our vision clearer, as it protects us from the
passions and biases that blind us. Of course we who are reading John Rawls's
Theory of Justice have the knowledge of who we are and of our situation in
society. We also have interests of which we are well aware, and know which
social arrangement would serve them best, but we are asked to ignore all this.
Understood in this way, the veil of ignorance constitutes a willful form of
ignorance, a conscious *méconnaissance* from which it is hoped that moral
knowledge will emerge.

Given its structure, once the veil of ignorance is lifted, and agents discover who they are, their weakness and advantages, they should have no

regrets concerning the decision they previously reached. No matter what it is, this decision was reached in ideal conditions. No one can object to it; its rationality and fairness are unimpeachable. In that sense, a just society is a land without remorse. More precisely, it is a land where remorse may have a cause, but where it cannot have a reason. It is a land where remorse is illegitimate. Given the place of the veil of ignorance in the conceptual economy of Rawls's theory, if you regret the decision that you took under the veil of ignorance, now that you know what was previously hidden from you, your desire to change what happened cannot be justified.

Méconnaissance the unfounded beliefs that associate spiders, dance, music, and colors, according to De Martino, is what makes remorse possible, in the sense that it allows agents to come to terms with a past they regret. Here, to the contrary, *méconnaissance* makes remorse impossible, in the sense that it deprives agents of all means of dealing with a past they regret. Of course it may be answered that in this case the past does not exist, the original position is a logical fiction that by definition takes place in the eternal present. True enough, but it can also be argued that what this *méconnaissance* willfully hides, by excluding all knowledge of the relations that we have with each other, are the sources of frustration and tensions that lead to regret and remorse. Educated persons who reject tarantism as a meaningless superstition know nothing of the specifics of the conflicts and tension that exist in the society that cultivates the musical cure. More precisely, they believe that these conflicts and tensions have their origin in poverty and in the cultural and technological backwardness that is responsible for it. Of this general backwardness, tarantism constitutes, in their eyes, an evident symptom.

There are many forms of *méconnaissance*, and none of them, I believe, is an endangered species. However, the *méconnaissance* that completely misreads the role of *méconnaissance*, threatens the stability of our societies much more than does the knowledge of its violent origin.

PART 3

On Violence and Politics in Modern Societies

Hobbes

The Sovereignty Race

Well, the law is costly, and I am for an accommodation: that M. Thomas Hobbes should have the sole privilege of setting up his form of government in America, as being calculated and fitted for that Meridian. . . . And if it prosper there, then have the liberty to transplant it hither; who knoweth (if there could but be some means devised to make them understand his language) whether the Americans might not choose him for their Sovereign? But the fear is that if he should put his principles into practice as magesterially as he doth dictate them, his supposed subjects might chance to tear their Mortal God to pieces with their teeth and entomb his sovereignty in their bowels.

—John Bramhall, *Catching of the Leviathan* (1658).

Bishop Bramhall suspected that a sordid story of murder lay upon the threshold of the Hobbesian contract. Whether this was rhetoric or intuition, Hobbes is certainly the social contract thinker closest to Girard. He is one of the rare philosophers who does not underestimate the role of violence in human affairs. He made society spring from a state of nature that is a state of war of all against all, and that state of war, insofar as it is revealing of certain features of human nature, determines the kind, form, and extent of political government. In Hobbes, there is no civil society prior to political government. Violence is first, and the institution of sovereignty, which is supposed to solve the problem of violence, is the founder of civil association. Moreover, Hobbes knows that people find peace only in the shadow of their own violence made sacred; the Sovereign, he says, is a mortal god. We are protected from the most extreme violence by a power that is "as great as possibly men can be imagined to make it."[1]

This said, Hobbes is not imagining people drunk on death and fury finding reconciliation around a common victim. The contract does not take place in an atmosphere of collective hallucination. On the contrary, it results from the calm solitary reasoning of rational agents, individuals wishing to promote their own self-interest, which in this case is limited to their security. Hobbes wants people to consent to the Sovereign and the state of society in their own best interest, voluntarily, with full awareness of why. In his work, no original misapprehension is thus necessary for reconciliation, or at least there should not be any. People choose peace. As soon as they become aware of the causes of the state of war, it becomes possible for them to escape it; they no longer experience the state of nature as an unavoidable destiny. As soon as they imagine the artifice of the contract and the Sovereign, they can indeed escape. It becomes rational for each, in terms of self-interest, to opt for the state of society. People are not evil. They are simply ignorant and lack imagination.

The rationality of the passage from the state of nature to the state of society is important. The contract is not the sudden discovery by a horde of bloodthirsty barbarians of the beneficial virtues of rationality. Instead, it flows from thinking about the conditions of possibility and operation of the state of nature. People thus become of the opinion that the state of nature is simply the unintentional result of their rational behavior in a situation in which there is equality but insecurity. The equality and insecurity are the results of their own activity. However, the adjective "unintentional" could cause problems here because so long as no one has imagined the artifice of the contract, it remains rational for each to persevere in behavior characteristic of the state of nature. The result is thus the war of all against all, and it is intentional, even if all hate it. Yet inventing the contract does the trick: it provides a rational way out.

Nonetheless, there is still a problem: of all the people who will soon come together in society, which one will be the Sovereign? Who will sit on the throne, hold the power and the glory? Here is finally an attractive position, a worthy prize for which all the envious and proud will happily tear each other apart. This is finally a reason for conflict that is worthwhile. But I am forgetting: they are rational, they are renouncing war for security. Will they be able to come to a rational agreement on a Sovereign? To whom will they all abandon their rights? How will they abandon them if they do not know to whom and if they cannot come to an agreement on this? Does the contract have any meaning if it is impossible to choose the Sovereign rationally? Whom will it be?[2]

Hobbes is strangely laconic on this topic. He hints that the choice of Sovereign is arbitrary. Since people are naturally equal, it does not matter who becomes the Sovereign, so long as there is a Sovereign. Anybody or the worst of all would be just as suitable. What is important is that there be a Sovereign.

In a way, we can accuse Hobbes of obscuring the issue, of acting as if it did not arise; of making it a question without meaning or interest for rational, naturally equal people; of pretending it is an issue that should not be problematic.

It is a good idea to look at the reasons why Hobbes refuses to discuss the question of who the Sovereign should be. They stem from two fundamental articles of his political doctrine. The first is related to the goal of universality. Hobbes is not writing a collection of pieces of advice and precepts for a prince; he is establishing political science as universal knowledge. It is thus out of the question to require the Sovereign to have specific moral, intellectual, or human qualities, to link universal knowledge with the Sovereign's person and thus subject its validity to contingent historical events.

The second reason is related to Hobbes's absolutism, to the absolute, unlimited, and uncontrolled nature of sovereignty as he sees it. In *The Open Society and Its Enemies*, Popper says that those who think that the question "'Who should rule?' is fundamental" "tacitly assume that political power is 'essentially' unchecked. . . . They assume that political power is, essentially, sovereign. If this assumption is made, then, indeed, the question of 'Who is to be the sovereign?' is the only important question left."[3]

In contrast, Hobbes knows that the question of who the Sovereign will be does not arise for those who have a truly absolute, unlimited conception of political power. Asking "Who will be the Sovereign?" or "Who should reign?" means already subjecting political power to the nit-picking censure of philosophers. Above all, it is to quickly abandon the question of the Sovereign's legitimacy to each individual's changing opinion, for asking "Who should reign?" is of course to ask whether the person who is reigning is indeed the right one, and any power subject to such a question is not absolute and cannot be so. A consistent conception of absolute sovereignty excludes any questions about the legitimacy of the *holder* of political power while at the same time takes responsibility for demonstrating the legitimacy of the power itself, at least when one thinks, like Hobbes, that political authority "exists only through the consent of those subject to it."[4]

These two concerns—namely, universality of the discourse and absoluteness of sovereignty—explain the status of the contract and the state of nature in Hobbes. They are not historical events inaugurating transmissible legitimacy, but logical fictions designed to persuade people that it is always rational to be in favor of sovereignty and against any form of challenge to it—in other words, to adopt a Sovereign, no matter whom. Hobbes targets consent to the fact of sovereignty, a consent that has to be independent of the question of the choice of Sovereign.

The question "Who will be the Sovereign?" is thus never really discussed because history has always already answered it. Even several centuries later, Hobbes's readers generally know who their Sovereign is. The rational decision in favor of the fact of sovereignty should be sufficient.

Unfortunately, in the land of philosophers' dreams, rational actors in the state of nature do not find this so easy. It is difficult to see how they can abandon their rights if they do not know to whom or how they can choose sovereignty rationally if they fail to find a rational way of selecting the person who will be the Sovereign. Insofar as logical fictions are designed to persuade rationally, they are subject to some consistency requirements. People in the state of nature have to choose or continue warring.

Supposing we can answer the question "Who shall be the Sovereign?" The answer will be truly Hobbesian only if it proves to be consistent with the twofold requirement of universality and absolutism, only if readers of Hobbes wondering about the rationality of the choice of Sovereign come to an answer that can accommodate all existing Sovereigns and all historically possible Sovereigns.

How can this question be answered? How can we succeed in our inquiry? We want to know who among Hobbesian individuals will be rationally chosen by them as the Sovereign when they consent to the state of society. It is thus important to fully understand how and why individuals in the state of nature renounce the war of all against all. What reasons lead them to agree to become associates?

Since Hobbes claims that what is in question is a decision by rational individuals seeking to promote their self-interest in a specific situation, the first thing to do seems to be to analyze the situation in which they find themselves, namely, the war of all against all.

The decision's rationality requires that we provide a description of the state of nature in terms of pure rational behavior of rational actors. In other words, we have to show that in the course of the war of all against all, the behavior of all is rational. It does not matter whether it is a perverse effect or an unintentional result of rational individual initiatives: in its warlike madness, the state of nature has to be able to be reduced to a model of rational behavior in accordance with Hobbes's text. Otherwise we will not be dealing with a decision but with a change in the individuals involved: they may have been envious and proud before, but reason has now befallen them. They abandon war.

Moreover, the model has to be of a rather special type. It has to be the model of what I call a rational order: a system of human behavior such that it neither excludes nor requires that the individuals who are part of it be aware of its conditions of possibility and operation. Such knowledge is simply irrelevant. It is easier to fully understand what a rational order is if we compare it with two extreme situations between which it is located.

On the one hand, there are irrational orders—in other words, systems of human behavior in which it is impossible for those who make them work to know the conditions of possibility and operation of the system. The most perfect example that we can give of an irrational order is the sacrificial system in René Girard.

The scapegoat mechanism is based on a form of misapprehension. It can operate and produce its effects only if those who make it work are unaware of how it functions. The sacrificial system emerges from the scapegoat mechanism and is structured by this misapprehension. Revelation that the god is in fact simply an arbitrarily chosen victim with no special powers suffices to destroy the system. This order is irrational because, clearly, it exists only as long as people do not know what they are doing.

On the other hand, there are reasoned orders: systems of human behavior that require that those who make them work be aware of their conditions of possibility and operation. The state of society in Hobbes is an order of this type. Civil peace can exist only if citizens know that they have to abandon all of their rights to the Sovereign and that the Sovereign's power has to be absolute. The Sovereign's sword can persuade no one of this. On the contrary, if people are not convinced of the well-foundedness of the Sovereign's essential rights, then the Sovereign has no sword.[5]

Rational orders are halfway between irrational and reasoned orders. They are not sensitive to whether or not those who make them work know about their conditions of possibility and operation. Such knowledge is neither required nor precluded by the system's operation.

Irrational and rational orders are both spontaneous. Establishing a reasoned order requires, on the contrary, a conscious decision by those who operate it. However, while rational orders do not disintegrate when society members become aware of their conditions of possibility and operation, it does not follow that such awareness has no consequences, that it does not open new perspectives to society members and the system.[6]

We have to suppose that the state of nature is a rational order because in Hobbes the state of society is a reasoned order. If the state of nature were irrational, there would be no conscious decision in favor of the state of society: in the absence of an alternative to the state of war other than absolute sovereignty, emergence of awareness of the mechanisms of how the state of war functions suffices, without requiring a voluntary decision by the actors.

It does not matter how people become aware of the mechanisms of operation of the state of nature. It does not matter whether they do so by reflecting on their sad condition or through divine intervention that reveals it to them. If the state of war is an irrational order, then the decision to abandon it is no longer theirs because it is one thing to understand, discover, or receive an explanation of the causes and consequences of a given form of behavior; it is something quite different to decide to change one's behavior. (Despite what some may think, we cannot make the same argument with respect to the passage from the sacrificial system to Christianity as defined by Girard, and believe that God traps people by depriving them of all defense mechanisms against violence. While the sacrificial system may be an irrational order and Christianity a reasoned order, it is incorrect to believe that there is no alternative to the sacrificial system aside from Christianity. There is at least that within which we live.)

However, we are not generally accustomed to thinking of the Hobbesian state of nature as an order, but rather as a form of human disorder, as relational chaos. We also do not think of the war of all against all as a system of actions, but as the absence of society. We thus have to begin by showing that this human disorder is logically an order, a set of clearly determined relations, that this absence of society is a system of actions. It is a stable system, unable to evolve "naturally" toward something other than itself, toward something other than the war of all against all. To evolve "naturally" is, for example, to change through the simple temporal deployment of the system without there having to be a voluntary decision by society members.

The primary feature of the state of nature in Hobbes is equality among individuals. This has two sides: physical and intellectual. They are distinct and yet complementary. However, when we examine it more closely, this equality seems strange. It does not correspond to a real quantity or substantial quality; it is not the case that, when measured, the intellectual and physical capacities of different individuals are always identical. On the contrary, equality refers to a situation in which relations among individuals eliminates the real differences that there may be between their capacities.

> Nature hath made men so equal in the faculties of body and mind as that, though there be found one man sometimes manifestly stronger in body or of quicker mind than another, yet when all is reckoned together the difference between man and man is not so considerable as that one man can thereupon claim to himself any benefit to which another may not pretend as well as he. For as to the strength of body, the weakest has strength enough to kill the strongest, either by secret machination or by confederacy with others that are in the same danger with himself.[7]

Our physical equality is ensured by mortality, but equal capacity to destroy is physical only because it is seen against the background of the body's ultimate fragility. The mortal rivalry that reveals it requires that an individual employ all physical and intellectual powers, in the form of secret machinations, alliances, cunning, and communication with others. Physical equality is simply the revelation that the possibility of a fight to the death suffices to eliminate differences among people, or at least to make them uncertain.

Hobbes begins by presupposing intellectual equality: "For prudence is but experience, which equal time equally bestows on all men in those things they equally apply themselves unto."[8] If prudence is bestowed equally in equal time to all people with respect to the things that they attend to equally, it is of course because their abilities are equal from the beginning. Next, he deduces intellectual equality from each individual's claim to intellectual superiority: "That which may perhaps make such equality incredible is but a vain conceit of one's own wisdom."[9] Hobbes interprets this claim as each individual's expression of satisfaction with the share of intelligence he or she has received, and concludes "there is not ordinarily a greater sign of the equal distribution of anything than that every man is contented with his share."[10]

Hobbes seems to deduce intellectual equality from the clash of claims. It is again against a backdrop of rivalry that equality emerges. However, his obvious sarcasm leads us to think that we should not conclude that intellectual capacities are in fact equal, but that only such claims are.

What gives rise to conflict and rivalry is neither the content of the claim—individual superiority—nor the fact of its universality—it is claimed by all—but, in the absence of any criterion, the impossibility of determining the legitimacy of such a claim. While not all such claims may be true, it is not necessary that they all be false. Hobbes's sarcasm suggests that they are not.

If conflict erases differences among people, if in a fight to the death the difference between the weakest and the strongest fades given the weakest's ability to kill the strongest, in the absence of differences among people, only conflict can decide among clashing claims. In the absence of any criterion, only combat can determine differences among people.

The possibility of fighting, the possibility of rivalry, reveals how people are equal. Conflict comes from the possible equality manifested by the sameness of claims and the absence of a criterion allowing us to distinguish between them. Hobbes deduces equality from possible rivalry, and possible equality from rivalry. Rivalry is the stable state of equality, and equality is the stable state of rivalry.

The state of nature is a strange situation marked by uncertainty. If two people come to desire the same thing, then the equality of their rights—in other words, the uncertainty related to defining their reciprocal rights—leads them toward combat. The uncertainty of combat, the fact that the weakest can kill the strongest, affirms the equality of the adversaries, eliminates the differences between them. In order to put an end to this uncertainty, nothing remains but to go from possible combat to a real clash, to allow combat to decide between opposing claims.

Hobbes now deploys this short, circular structure, a structure curled upon itself, in which equality presupposes rivalry and rivalry equality, while showing the causes of the war of all against all in the state of nature, a state of equality, insecurity, and uncertainty.

> From this equality of ability ariseth equality of hope in the attaining of our ends. And therefore if any two men desire the same thing, which neverthe-less they cannot both enjoy, they become enemies. . . . And from hence it comes to pass that where an invader hath no more to fear than another man's single power, if one plant, sow, build, or possess a convenient seat, others may probably be expected to come prepared with forces united to dispossess and deprive him, not only of the fruit of his labour, but also of his life or liberty. And the invader again is in the like danger of another.[11]

It is useful to note the uncertainty of the beginning of the state of nature. Unlike Girard, Hobbes does not have an operator that necessarily makes desires converge on a single object. The indication is fuzzy: "if"—in other words, it is possible to imagine that this need not occur very often or regularly, but it is possible; it can happen. Later we find "others may probably be expected to come prepared": it is reasonably possible, not certain, that this could happen, that there is a strong risk that this could happen at least once. The edifice is uncertain. Hobbes does not need anything more. In fact, we can suppose that none of that has yet happened because conflicts do not need to have had occurred in order to appear now. Fear flows from uncertainty, and uncertainty is sufficient for rational fear.

There is nothing more reasonable than to protect oneself from this fear than by anticipating it—in other words, "by force, or wiles, to master the persons of all men he can so long till he see no other power great enough to endanger him."[12] This is a reasonable decision for a Hobbesian individual who seeks only to promote his or her self-interest, which is, in this case, the minimal form of self-interest: survival. However, the result of dealing with this uncertainty in a rational manner is to make certain what was only probable—that is to say, the probability of being invaded rationally motivates agents to invade each other. The end result is that reciprocal invasion that was just a possibility and which they feared now becomes real and the rule.

This is a paradoxical result that ensures that the conditions of the conflict's uncertainty will be met. It is a contradictory result despite its individual rationality because it is specifically through their rational behavior that individuals drive others to do the very actions that each fears most and seeks to prevent. Finally, the result is circular since, by acting rationally, each initiates the conditions that motivate his or her action.

The most fearful may very well be the one who unleashes the state of war. It follows that there is an initial equivalency between an envious person and a person who is reasonably fearful, between a person who invades another to dispossess and one who invades another preemptively. This equivalency is nothing other than a way of expressing the equality and uncertainty characteristic of the state of nature.

It seems that preventive conquests may gradually pacify the state of nature and make it possible for dominions to emerge that are large enough for people to no longer see themselves as threatened by any other power. Hobbes now destroys this possibility because some take "pleasure in contemplating their own power in the acts of conquest, which they pursue farther than their security requires."[13] Others, who would have been satisfied to live at ease within modest limits, must increase their power if they wish to survive. They must thus be given the right to engage in conquest.

The result of this unbridled mechanism is that the domains sketched out here have no definite borders. All possible fragile truces depend on a balance of power that reproduces on a larger scale the fundamental equality of the state of nature. Any step away from the balance leads to a resumption of the fighting destined to reestablish the balance—in other words, destined to reestablish the conditions that ensure that any deviation from the balance leads to a return to fighting. Through war, the state of war returns only to equality, the condition for war.

Rational Hobbesian actors determine this mechanism once again. For each, it is rational to maintain through war the uncertain balance of power, and each is led rationally to imitate the vain who take "pleasure in contemplating their own power in the acts of conquest."[14] The second way that the vain and the reasonably fearful person are equivalent is also based on the uncertainty characteristic of the state of nature. In it, each person is the sole judge of what is required for his or her security. What one calls cruelty the other calls justice, and it becomes impossible to distinguish between a person who takes acts of conquest further than his or her security requires from one who has reasonable fears about the excessive growth of his or her enemy's dominion.

Armed with this second equivalency, we can see how the state of nature returns back to the beginning. Initially, people divided by fear mutually invade one another, and then this same fear tends to associate them into groups that control greater realms. Hobbes will now show why, if there is no Sovereign power, such associations cannot hold, why people must necessarily return to their original conflictual solitude.

> For every man looketh that his companion should value him at the same rate he sets upon himself, and upon all signs of contempt or undervaluing naturally endeavours, as far as he dares (which amongst them that have no common power to keep them in quiet is far enough to make them destroy each other), to extort a greater value from his contemners, by damage; and from others, by the example.[15]

Because they care about what they call their honor, people are sent back to their original solitude. The pride that leads people to resort to violence "for trifles, as a word, a smile, a different opinion"[16] is certainly insensitive to fear of death. Vanity dissociates what rational fear tends to associate. However, in the absence of a Sovereign power, does not a Hobbesian calculator who fails to demand compensation for a trifle today expose himself or herself to greater threats tomorrow?

The state of nature is a stable chaos, a well-structured disorder, with mechanisms that maintain its stability. Human discord is a spontaneous order, a self-organized system, that is circular and looped, and never evolves into anything other than itself: the war of all against all.

The state of nature may be a spontaneous order, but is it rational? Will the state of nature continue to function as a state of war of all against all if all those involved in it know that all are acting as rational individuals in a situation of equality and insecurity? In other words, will it continue to function if they know that all of them are neither envious nor vain, since we already know that there are rational actors among them. The circumstances of equality and insecurity, uncertainty, are taken as known.

Hobbes could answer this question in two ways that are at first sight contradictory. However, in the final analysis, his two answers are one and the same. Everything hangs on the meaning we give to the expression: the circumstances of equality and uncertainty are taken as known. The first answer is yes. Yes, even if all the actors in the state of nature are rational Hobbesian actors who know that all the others are also self-aware rational Hobbesian actors, this state will continue to function as a state of war of all against all. Why?

What does Hobbesian rationality mean when applied to actors' behavior? It flows from the principle that in a given situation, each acts appropriately in function of something that is good for himself or herself, and on the basis of the information that he or she has, or, if one prefers, according to his or her own assessment of the situation. Of that assessment of the situation, he or she is, by definition, the sole judge.[17] For epistemological reasons internal to Hobbes's work, it is relatively difficult to define what is good for someone or what is his or her scale of preferences. Nonetheless, we can assert without risk of error that for every Hobbesian calculator, both survival and security are good, and that he or she prefers survival to security. Thus, each is rationally forced, in every situation, to behave in a manner that is at least adequate to preserve his or her life.

This provides us with a criterion that makes it possible, in principle, to distinguish rational actions from those that are not. It is true that this criterion is very weak, since in a given situation a wide range of forms of behavior can be considered rational. However, it is not completely useless because it nonetheless makes it possible to exclude certain forms of behavior.[18]

In the state of nature, a rational actor targeting a good for himself or herself thus cannot accept a change in power relations that is to his or her disadvantage. Rational actors have as a categorical imperative the obligation to maintain equality, but it is not irrational for them to seek to transform power relations in their favor. Insofar as a situation of equality and insecurity means that any change in power relations could be to my disadvantage, it seems that I am rationally constrained to never initiate any attempt to change power relations. Yet insofar as a situation of equality and insecurity means that changes or attempts to change power relations can occur at any time, it is obvious that this constraint does not hold. It is entirely rational for me to take the initiative, as Hobbes says, if I can gain some advantage from doing so or thereby avoid a possible defeat. In this sense, the same actions that vain and envious people do through ignorance or misunderstanding of the situation of equality and insecurity may be performed by rational actors because they know that they are in a situation of equality and insecurity.

If all actors are rational and know that they are, what will happen in the state of nature? Hobbesian rationality says that each is entirely free to choose which actions are indispensable to his or her survival. The problem is that nothing guarantees that what I consider indispensable to my survival will not be perceived by another as dangerous to his or her survival. The fact that he or she knows that I have no evil intentions changes nothing. He or she can very well consider that my action is dangerous, and that is sufficient for him or her to be rationally constrained to take action. Once again, this means that the state of nature is a state of uncertainty. We can interpret this uncertainty as an information deficit, though the deficit is not with respect to the intentions of others: I know that they are neither vain nor envious. Instead, it is with respect to other people's interpretation of my behavior. I cannot know whether the actions that I perform will be interpreted by others as dangerous to them, and thus whether or not they will attack me.

We are coming to the foundation of the equivalence between vain and rational people. Hobbes deduces intellectual equality from the equal claim to intellectual superiority. This claim can be interpreted as an expression of vanity. However, the universal intellectual claim means simply that each prefers his or her own interpretation and assessment of the situation to that of anyone else, and rightly so according to Hobbes.

It follows that it is neither rational for me to renounce my assessment of the situation according to which a given action is indispensable to my survival, nor rational for the other to give up his or her interpretation of my action as dangerous to him or her. How can we avoid fighting?

This amounts to saying, in a sense, that in the state of nature we cannot know whether or not some people are vain. The question is undecidable. This is why there are two answers to the question asked above.

Even if no one is vain in the state of nature, that state will function like the war of all against all. If saying that there are no vain people is to remove uncertainty, then there will no longer be a war of all against all. However, we would no longer be in a Hobbesian state of nature, and these are not the conditions of possibility and functioning of the state familiar to members of society because the conditions of that state are equality and insecurity.

Given the determining role of uncertainty in the functioning of the state of nature, we can reformulate our question in the following way: is knowledge of equality sufficient to eliminate uncertainty? If equality is conceived of as each person having equal rights over various objects, or as each having an equal claim to his or her own interpretation of the situation, then the whole problem is to know whether or not it is rational to abandon the decision to a random event, such as "first come, first served" or drawing straws, so as to avoid fighting. Even if this approach is adopted, it is formally indistinguishable from recourse to the uncertain undertaking of a fight. In principle, despite this formal equivalency, Hobbesian rationality makes it possible to distinguish between occasions when it is rational to resort to fighting. If my life is not threatened by the dispute, given the object in question and the adversary's strategy, it is forbidden for me to place my life in danger by choosing a clash instead of the arbitrary decision of fate. However, since identifying what is dangerous is left entirely up to each individual, it is impossible for me to know with certainty what others consider dangerous. Recourse to fighting is always legitimate.

Here we come to a relatively sensitive point. In what way does this uncertainty, this deficit of information about the other's interpretation, differ from misapprehension, in the sense in which Girard speaks of misapprehension with respect to the scapegoat mechanism? It seems to me that the idea of misapprehension includes that of mistake and error in the proper sense and in the most commonly used sense. I thought that the table was at the back of the room, to the left, near the window, but it is at the front, to the right, near the door. Doubles think that the victim/god is entirely responsible for all their woes. They are mistaken; that is not the case.

Hobbesian actors in the state of nature are in an entirely different situation. They are in a situation of equality and uncertainty that they are aware of. The preference that they give to their own definition of the situation is not a mistake. They know the rational mechanisms of the war of all against all. They have no illusions about the role of their own rational behavior in perpetuating the state of war that they detest. However, so long as uncertainty has not been lifted, it is rational for each of them to continue warring.

The state of nature is a rational order. It does not require those who create it to know the mechanisms of how it functions. It can include a large number of vain and envious people. However, if all participants discover that they are all rational actors in a situation of equality and insecurity, the system nonetheless does not crumble. It still operates as the war of all against all.

Yet such awareness does have some effects. It gives participants in the state of war the possibility of becoming members of a pacified society. For this, they need only lift the uncertainty that traps them. Indeed, for actors in a state of nature, any state would be "more" rational if it offered them security in addition to survival. This is the purpose of the contract. How does it work?

In Hobbes's work, there are two contracts: a social or instituting contract, and a contract that can be called natural, insofar as Hobbes says that it corresponds to the acquisition of sovereignty by natural force, such as when a father forces his children to submit to his rule, or a conqueror the conquered. In contrast, the other contract is artificial: it is an artifice of reason used to escape the state of war.

The natural contract seems to raise a problem for our thesis. As a pact between a conqueror and the conquered resulting from the exercise of natural force, it seems to go against our description of the stability of the state of nature, which highlighted mechanisms for preventing the natural emergence of an individual stronger than the others, thus for maintaining equality and therefore war. These mechanisms are supposed to persuade people that they should choose sovereignty because violence leads only to itself, but now we are hearing about sovereignty through natural force!

However, the natural contract is also a contract. It supposes that the contracting parties have the same rational commitment as they do with respect to the social contract. Even natural sovereignty requires the artifice of a contract: the strongest never emerges entirely "naturally."

Leviathan gives two versions of the social contract. Here is the first one:

> This is more than consent, or concord; it is a real unity of them all in one and the same person, made by covenant of every man with every man, in such manner as if every man should say to every man: *I authorise and give up my right of governing myself, to this man, or to this assembly of men, on this condition; that thou give up, thy right to him, and authorise all his actions in like manner.*[19]

Now, since under the terms of the contract I give up my rights to *this* man on the condition that you give up your rights to *him* in the same way, it seems that the future Sovereign has to be known already. Given that the contract is between all individuals with all individuals, if we are to be rigorous, it has to be universal, or at least there has to be unanimity minus one: the Sovereign, who remains external to the whole thing. People have to know who the Sovereign is, and they agree to give *him* or *her* their rights.

The second version of the social contract is slightly different:

> A commonwealth is said to be instituted when a multitude of men do agree, and covenant, every one with every one, that to whatsoever man, or assembly of men, shall be given by the major part the right to present the person of them all, that is to say, to be their representative; every one, as well he that voted for it as he that voted against it, shall authorize.[20]

Here we are thus dealing with a second version in which people no longer agree unanimously minus one, but by simple majority. The second contract also seems to involve two stages: a first stage in which people agree to agree—in other words, agree to abandon their rights to the one who will be chosen by the majority—and a second stage in which the Sovereign is chosen.[21] However, a little later in the same chapter 18 of *Leviathan* we find another text that both supports and transforms this interpretation:

> because the major part hath by consenting voices declared a sovereign, he that dissented must now consent with the rest; that is, be contented to

avow all the actions he [the Sovereign] shall do, or else justly be destroyed by the rest. For if he voluntarily entered into the congregation of them that were assembled, he sufficiently declared thereby his will, and therefore tacitly covenanted, to stand to what the major part should ordain: and therefore if he refuse to stand thereto, or make protestation against any of their decrees, he does contrary to his covenant, and therefore unjustly. And whether he be of the congregation or not, and whether his consent be asked or not, he must either submit to their decrees or be left in the condition of war he was in before; wherein he might without injustice be destroyed by any man whatsoever.[22]

It seems this time that the logical structure of the contract is unanimity among those whom Hobbes now calls the majority. The members of the minority, whether or not they tacitly agreed, expose themselves to being exterminated or conquered—in other words, to signing the natural contract. The true social contract or institution is the one that occurs unanimously among the members of the so-called majority.

Now, what is required for the contract to take place and the decision to be rational? I think that it suffices for one of the actors in the state of nature to have the idea of a contract and to suggest it to the others. The idea of a contract is rational for each of them. They all consent to give up their rights to the Sovereign so that the latter can ensure their security, and their abandonment of all their rights ensures that the Sovereign has sufficient power to ensure compliance with the terms of the contract. Moreover, since the Sovereign has complete authority over what defines insecurity, the uncertainty characteristic of the state of nature is removed. The contract provides them with survival and security, whereas the state of nature offers them only survival with no security. The contract is thus grosso modo rational.

This said, these are rational actors who make decisions individually in the isolation of their rationality. How do they do this? The only danger and only possible objection to the rationality of the contract comes, it seems, from the Sovereign's absolute power. They are neither envious nor vain. They are naturally equal and know that they cannot all be the Sovereign. (Monarchy is assumed.) They thus ask themselves the following question: is it more advantageous to me for another to be the Sovereign or to remain in the state of nature? In the state of nature, each is responsible, at his or her own risk, for his or her own security. It is advantageous to place this responsibility on someone else. What dangers come from the Sovereign? He or she is a rational actor who does not have bad intentions with respect to me; all the evil comes from the uncertainty related to the way situations are defined as insecure. Since the Sovereign will remove this uncertainty, it is thus advantageous to choose sovereignty.

However, while each actor makes up his or her mind alone, he or she also knows that the others are making decisions. He or she thus has to wonder whether his or her decision is rational, given the others' decisions. The contract has the logical structure of unanimity, but it can in fact work like a simple majority. Let us simplify things. Each will employ the following calculation: If I vote in favor, if I say yes to the contract, and if the others are mainly in favor, then we get out of the state of nature, we end the state of war of all against all: +1. If the others mainly vote no, we remain in the state of nature as before: 0. If I vote against, if I say no, and if the others mainly say no, we will remain in the state of war, 0; but if they vote yes, then I will remain in the state of war, the enemy of all the others united—in other words, anyone at all will be able to kill me without injustice: -1. Therefore I vote yes. It is the most rational choice: it yields the highest absolute value and is the best strategy.

Since all the others reason in the same way, and all know that all do so, they are forced to vote yes. The contract will be made. This is why it suffices that someone suggest the idea of the contract to rational actors in the state of nature for it to necessarily take place.

As soon as everyone comes to the conclusion that it is preferable for someone else to be the Sovereign rather than remain in the state of nature, as soon as they see that saying "no" is an irrational strategy, then it seems that the problem of knowing who will become the Sovereign is indeed unimportant, as Hobbes's silence leads us to think. Each decides in favor of the contract based on reasoning in which he or she supposes by hypothesis that he or she will not be the Sovereign. It is difficult to see why there would be a problem with this. No one has any objection to someone else being the Sovereign. Why not choose the Sovereign by giving each an equal chance and simply pulling straws?

This is something that rational Hobbesian actors will not do because they are prudent. Recourse to chance is not in contradiction with their conception of rationality; but in this case it is dangerous. Here is why.

The answer to the question "Is it better for someone other than me to be the Sovereign or to remain in the state of nature?" involves a certain degree of comparison. Each wonders whether the fact that someone else is the Sovereign will entail that someone could acquire a special advantage against him or her. The answer is no, since all abandon their rights in the same way: no one has the right to accept a change in power relations that is to his or her disadvantage. Of course, the Sovereign will acquire power that is superior to that of anyone else, but this change is to the disadvantage of no actor in particular in the state of nature. On the contrary, it is to the advantage of all. It leaves unchanged the existing power relations among the contracting parties. They all consent equally.

Yet as soon as they understand that yes is not only the best response but also the best strategy, they know that the contract will take place, and they have to vote yes. They are then the victims of a strange trap.

While it may be in my interest for someone other than me to be the Sovereign, it does not follow that it is in my interest for anyone at all to be the Sovereign. More specifically, in the state of nature there is a category of people such that it is to my advantage to remain in the state of nature rather than to allow them to become the Sovereign. How is this possible? Who are they?

How can it be that each can both say that he or she prefers that someone else be the Sovereign rather than remain in the state of nature, but also say that he or she would prefer to stay in the state of nature rather than let certain others become the Sovereign? Is this not a contradiction that undermines the whole edifice? The problem raises no special difficulties. The reasoning through which each came to the conclusion that he or she preferred that someone else become the Sovereign rather than remain in the state of nature has the logical form of "there is an X such that" and not the form "for all Xs." The quantifier is existential, not universal. It suffices for each that there be an X such that I prefer him or her to be the Sovereign rather than to remain in the state of nature for the contract to be formally possible. It is not necessary that this be true of all Xs. There is no contradiction if there is an X or even several Xs such that I would prefer to remain in the state of nature rather than to allow them to become Sovereign.

The state of nature is a state of war of all against all defined by conditions of equality and insecurity. Even though the state of war is of all against all, it nonetheless does not follow that I am in open conflict with all others. As Hobbes says, "war consisteth not in battle only, or the act of fighting, but in a tract of time, wherein the will to contend by battle is sufficiently known," and "the nature of war consisteth not in actual fighting, but in the known disposition thereto during all the time there is no assurance to the contrary."[23]

It is thus possible to identify for each individual those with respect to whom he or she would prefer to remain in the state of nature rather than see them become the Sovereign: they form the set of people with whom he or she is in open conflict. The reason for this is simple. While it may be advantageous for me to abandon to another the responsibility for my security and to let that person define the danger contained in situations for all individuals, this is true only if that other is not one of my present enemies. If the potential Sovereign is my current enemy, it is more dangerous for me to accept his or her sovereignty than to remain in the state of nature. The uncertainty of victory over an enemy of equal strength is preferable to the certainty of defeat at the hands of an absolute Sovereign. No one can agree to a change in power relations that is to his or her disadvantage.

However, why we should limit the set of people who are unacceptable to me to those with whom I am in open conflict? Why is this limitation legitimate? Why not extend the set to all of those with whom I have been in conflict in the past, or even to all the other people in the state of nature, since it is a state of war of all against all? That would make the contract impossible.

I think that the set of unacceptable persons should indeed be extended to include those with whom I have been in open conflict in the past. Why? We know that Hobbesian rational actors are neither envious nor vain, but we do not know whether they hold grudges, or rather we know that in a sense they do. Hobbesian rationality reasons based on the past: "prudence is a presumption of the future, contracted from the experience of time past."[24]

Why not extend it to all other actors in the state of nature? We can approach this question obliquely by asking: What happens if, at the time of the contract, for all the actors in the state of nature the set of those with whom one is or has been in open conflict is empty? What if no one has been or is in open conflict with any one at all? We know that this is impossible owing to the first equivalency between envy and rational fear, which shows that in the state of nature it suffices that conflicts be possible for them to become real. However, nothing prevents us from analyzing this imaginary case. If no one is or has been in open conflict with anyone else, the contract will not take place for the excellent reason that the probability that I will come into conflict with one of the actors in the state of nature is no greater than the probability that I will come into conflict with the Sovereign (who is one of those in the state of nature). Since entering into conflict with the Sovereign certainly means losing and entering into conflict with someone in the state of nature means perhaps winning, I must not consent to the contract.

Yet we should not imagine that in a situation in which the actors maintain relations of open conflict with certain other people, they opt for the contract because they think they have fewer chances of coming into conflict with those with whom they are not yet in conflict than with those with whom they are fighting. This is a form of reasoning used tacitly by those who criticize the contract for the fact that it has little psychological verisimilitude. Why would the Sovereign be better than the others? Why would the Mortal God not be a wolf with respect to others? Why exchange one's enemies, who might be numerous but who are scattered and weak, for an enemy who is unique but all powerful?

Indeed, why? The rational actors in the state of nature reason in another manner. To say that there is not and has not been open conflict in the state of nature is to make a hypothesis about the relationship between the uncertainty related to the definition of situations in which there is insecurity and the number of conflicts. If there are not and have not been open conflicts, then this influence is more or less zero. However, in the Hobbesian state of nature, the opposite of this hypothesis is a given on the basis of which each actor thinks. Each knows that the number of conflicts is in direct relation to the uncertainty flowing from the definition of situations of insecurity. The purpose of the Sovereign is to remove that uncertainty. They are thus entirely right to think that the probability of entering into conflict with the Sovereign is less than the probability of entering into conflict with any actor in the state of nature, including those with whom they are not now in conflict. If they limit the set of potential acceptable Sovereigns to only the latter, it is because they cannot do otherwise without shifting to the probability that they will be in conflict with the Sovereign. There is no reason to extend the set of unacceptable Sovereigns to all other people in the state of nature.

Rationally obliged to contract, rationally obliged to consent, the actors in the state of nature are just as obliged to exclude a certain number of people from the list of candidates eligible to be the Sovereign. Since all have an equal right to everything, including the right to be the Sovereign, they are all on that list. They are also held to an equality clause according to which no one has the right to accept a change in power relations that would be to his or her disadvantage. No one has any objection to being removed from the list because everyone has chosen in favor of a state of society on the basis of an argument in which they have by hypothesis excluded themselves from sovereignty. However, while they have agreed to be excluded from the list, no one will renounce his or her right to exclude others.

We thus have to suppose that they all receive a veto that they use to eliminate from the sovereignty race those with whom they are or have been in open conflict. They come to an agreement by eliminating those who are unacceptable to them.

We can imagine two situations. First, all have been in at least one open conflict. Second, some have not been in and are not in any open conflicts. Let us begin with the latter. What interest would the contract hold for those who have not been in open conflict with anyone? Does each of them have interest in having someone other than himself or herself be the Sovereign? No. For each of them, it is not more likely that they will enter into conflict with any other actor in the state of nature than with the Sovereign. They will not take part in the contract, and we will end up in the first situation. The other possibility is that they have an interest in the contract in virtue of the strategic reasoning according to which they would otherwise remain alone against all, exposed to the violence of the assembled multitude. In this case, they will enter into conflict over sovereignty. Of course, this means that they will go from possible conflicts to real conflicts, but if they do not do so, they will remain alone in the state of nature, which is worse. Once again, we end up in the first situation.

They are all in at least one relationship of open conflict. They all have a veto that allows them to eliminate those who are unacceptable to them. Whom will they choose? Since the conflict relations are reciprocal, it is clear that no one can be placed on the list of candidates for sovereignty; all are eliminated. We could of course imagine counting the number of vetoes received by each candidate in order to identify the least unacceptable to all, but the equality clause that links them makes this solution impossible. No one can accept a change in power relations that is to his or her disadvantage. This is what would happen to those who reject the candidate who has been vetoed the least.

It seems to me that the problem has only one solution. Since they have to consent to the contract and choose a Sovereign, the only possible candidate, the only one in accordance with the equality clause, is the unique candidate who appears on all lists of unacceptable candidates, the only one who is in open conflict with all: the enemy of all.

Is this candidate really Hobbesian? Is it true that, historically, people thinking about the rational choice of actors in the state of nature find no fault in their present Sovereign? Is it accurate to say that if the only legitimate Sovereign is the enemy of all, people will not challenge the one who they end up sharing? Is it the case that the definition of the Sovereign as the enemy of all fits all possible Sovereigns in history? Or is Hobbesian political science wrong?

Yet it will be objected that this Sovereign does not exist. If conflictual relations are reciprocal and the Sovereign is the enemy of all, if he or she is on all the lists of those who must be eliminated from the sovereignty race, all will be on his or her list. He or she can find no other one whose sovereignty will be preferred to the state of nature. That person will not take part in the contract. Is this a problem? Hobbes always said that the Sovereign did not take part in the contract, that he or she was not one of the contracting parties.

Commentators often claim that once the contract is made, the Sovereign remains alone in the state of nature. I do not think that Hobbes ever thought this because he says that he or she who remains alone in the state of nature can be killed by anyone, with no injustice. He never writes that anyone can kill the Sovereign without injustice.

The Sovereign is not in the state of nature, and he or she is not among the contracting parties: he or she is absent, the enemy of all and a mortal god. "But the fear is that . . . his supposed subjects might chance to tear their Mortal God to pieces with their teeth and entomb his sovereignty in their bowels."[25]

Ijime

In Japan, in particular in junior and senior high school, there is a violent
phenomenon known in Japanese as *ijime*, a term that could be translated
as "bullying." While the word may be culturally marked, the phenomenon it refers to is certainly universal. Bullying is a process through which a
child becomes the victim of one or more of his or her classmates. A bully is
a little brute, a person who pushes with his or her elbows, steps in front of
others, and, generally, brutalizes his or her comrades for no reason, it seems,
except because he or she can. A bully is a torturer, and "bullying" refers to the
set of actions involving torment, molestation, persecution, teasing, harassment—in short, the set of cruelties and vexations inflicted on the victim.
This is something that exists at every latitude, but in Japan it sometimes
takes on disturbing proportions, both in terms of number and seriousness
of incidents. Between January and April 1995, it was possible to identify four
suicides that clearly resulted from bullying—in other words, where notes
(generally called "testaments") left by the suicide victims explicitly stated
that the cruelty of which they were the victim was the reason for their suicide. Four suicides between January and April—in other words, an average of
one per month. This is enough to raise a few questions.[1]

Japanese educators, sociologists, and journalists often wonder, especially during bad years like 1995, what could be the cause, origin, or reasons for the *ijime* phenomenon. In general they blame the greater individualism characteristic of the period since World War II, the excessive competition typical of both Japanese society and schools, the father's reduced role in family discipline, or the fact that children in today's society of abundance are too weak and spoiled. In short, the phenomena invoked are all related to the modernization of Japan, even to its recent modernization, that which took place since the end of the war. I tend to believe that *ijime* is not linked so much to the modern world, to anomy, individualism, excessive competition, as it is to the immemorial origin of society (and not just that of Japanese society, of course). Likewise, I tend to believe that incidents of bullying are not accidents, that they are not malfunctions, ruptures within the Japanese education system, but to the contrary a virtual institution, events that until very recently were relatively normal. It is not that I believe such persecution is the result of an open policy; much to the contrary: the phenomenon is much more fundamental than that. The high number of incidents of bullying that are reported now, and which are found in all sociological studies and research, do not indicate so much that the phenomenon is more frequent than before as they do that it is working less well, that it is beginning to crumble, and that it is possible to talk about it and see it. Allow me to explain.

Numerous studies on Japan[2] provide certain reasons for thinking that the phenomenon of *ijime* among secondary school students is not recent, that it can be traced to the prewar period and perhaps even farther back. (I do not know if this phenomenon was present in the period preceding the Meiji era. It would be interesting to see if phenomena of the same sort already existed in the temple schools that were responsible for most education during the Edo period.) The little information I have on this subject during the Meiji period seems to indicate that the victim perished more often at the hands of his or her torturers than he or she did by his or her own hands. However, this is nothing but an assertion. We will see below why it is unlikely that we will find easy access to information on *ijime* in ancient Japan.[3]

It is true that Japanese elementary and secondary schools are very restrictive for students, but they are so in their own way, which is not ours and which is inseparable from the special role school in Japan plays in the socialization of children. Indeed, above and beyond purely academic activities, school is a place of many sports and cultural activities in which children are strongly encouraged to participate. As well as requiring uniforms, schools regulate the appearance of students even outside of school. For instance, they stipulate the length of students' hair, and the places students can go alone or in the company of their parents or other adults. In other words, the school's authority has precedence over that of parents. The school, not parents, has the final word on what children may or may not do outside of school hours, on holidays, and even during vacations. Very often if the parents wish to take their children on a long trip during the annual vacation, they must inform the school. In consequence, one might think, as it is generally believed, that Japanese secondary schools are very strict and that they have a semimilitary discipline. This impression is not entirely false, but, if I am to believe my colleague Richard Rubinger, a specialist on education in Japan whose three daughters, ages eleven to fourteen, spent a year in Japanese schools, it is certainly misleading.

Anyone who enters a Japanese secondary school will be struck by the disorder and chaos reigning there. There is running and chasing in the hallways. In one class there is a fight; in another, students are jumping on the desks. What are the teachers doing? Why, they are not there. They are all in the staff room waiting for the bell to call them to the next class. In the meantime the students are under no supervision whatsoever. Thus, when there is a case of suicide or especially serious *ijime* and teachers claim that they knew nothing about it, that they were not aware, they are not always in bad faith. With the teachers, discipline, or at least a certain form of it, returns. The notion of leaving groups of adolescents unsupervised for a certain time comes, perhaps, from the desire to let them breathe a little, to compensate for the usual rigors of discipline. Yet it is in continuity with the attitude of parents of young children I know, and it is not without consequences. Japanese parents of children between two and four years old, the ages of my sons Étienne and Mathieu at the time I was in Japan, discipline their children very little and almost never intervene in their conflicts. It is as if they consider that resolving their conflicts on their own is not part of the training they must be given, but to the contrary that it is something obvious, or that can be learned without the help of an adult. The main consequence of such an attitude is that it recognizes as legitimate the relation of strength, whatever form it takes, which is established following a confrontation between children.[4]

When the teachers return to class a certain discipline is restored. In Japan there is a high number of reports of incidents of violence by students against their teachers. Moreover, in Japan corporal punishment is widely accepted, and it can sometimes have very serious consequences. Some students have died or committed suicide after having been too severely punished by their teacher. In the cases I heard about, such punishments were not inflicted on grounds that could be called strictly academic, but for reasons related to discipline. Generally, Japanese schools enforce a strict dress code, which regulates the students' uniform, length of hair, and color of pants or skirts, and students are frequently hit because they have not respected one of the rules. For example, in 1985 an adolescent died after having been beaten by his teacher. He had broken a rule concerning school trips by bringing an electric blow-dryer with him! Beyond the apparently innocuous nature of the offenses and the disproportion between the wrongdoing and the punishment, what is striking is that the discipline in question does not aim to promote a certain type of interaction between agents, but a code of behavior. Its aim is not to ensure what we would spontaneously call class discipline, but to train children to respect general rules that apply to each child individually. What I mean is that such discipline is not intended to prevent adolescents from creating an uproar, from fighting or stealing, by teaching them to develop different forms of interactions with others, but aims to bring them to comply with an abstract code of conduct. It is not directed to forms of interaction, but to respect a set of rules concerning dress or behavior. This is why there is no contradiction between the rigidity and extent of the discipline that is exerted even outside school and the freedom and disorder that reigns in schools. The two go hand in hand. They are inseparable.

Two things result from all this. First, the relation between teachers and students is essentially conflictual. It is a relation of opposition characterized by a good measure of violence. Often the correct description of students and teachers is that they are enemies. Second, such violence is not related to the properly academic role of school, but to school as an institution for socialization. This is why I believe there is no reason to think that the greater number of cases of *ijime* reported in recent years is the result of recent changes in the Japanese educational system, such as increased competition or difficulty of university entrance examinations, because such changes belong mainly to the academic dimension. The socialization produced by Japanese schools is of a very special type, not only because it teaches children to respect general rules that apply to them individually, rather than to respect rules of interaction, but also because academic results are themselves the first general rule they learn to respect in this way. School teaches children that marks provide a scale that the rest of society must respect when careers and benefits are distributed. It shows children that general, abstract criteria have precedence over their interactions. At the same time, schools assign academic grades—in other words, they classify students according to academic criteria. It follows that adolescents are, rightly, very rapidly convinced that everything is at stake, that their whole future will be decided during those few years when they are at the mercy of their schoolmasters.

Under such conditions, it is easy to understand how the victims of *ijime* are scapegoats in the sense in which Girard uses the term. They are substitute victims, safety valves through which pass all the hatred, violence, and frustration that cannot be expressed or resolved otherwise. This is almost too clear. It is true that there are bullies, little brutes, ringleaders, torturers. Yet without exception, the notes left by those who commit suicide repeat the same thing: "They are all against me," "No one helps me," "They all reject me." The unanimity goes even further. In newspapers there are articles in which educators and other social workers propose that a solution to the problem would be to provide special psychological help for the victims of *ijime*, for according to such workers, it is the victims, not their torturers, who have difficulty behaving properly! Of course children sometimes go too far, and teachers must make sure such excesses do not occur, say such educators, but it is the persecuted, not the persecutors, who are at fault. Today such suggestions give rise to indignation, at least in some people, but until relatively recently they expressed the, if not official, at least unofficial doctrine of most schools. "If your child is victimized by his or her classmates," schools often said to parents, "it is because he or she acts in a certain way. It shows that he or she has not succeeded in adapting to others."

In consequence, I believe that the large number of cases of *ijime* now reported do not indicate a growth in the phenomenon, but the crumbling of (or at least a few cracks in) the wall of silence. It indicates that the mechanism is working less and less well. The unanimity often includes teachers, and the notes of suicide victims often identify a teacher as the worst of the victim's torturers, sometimes responsible for physical violence against the victim, as we have seen, but also for psychological violence. This should not surprise us. Given the conflictual relation opposing children and their teachers, the teacher is often a designated victim of collective violence. By choosing another victim, but one who is also a victim of the children, the teacher can deflect the amassed resentment and succeed in bringing the threatened discipline back into the classroom, by re-creating unanimity. This is not properly a strategy that teachers use consciously. To the contrary, everything leads us to believe that they are firmly convinced that the student they are punishing is at fault, and they do not consider it surprising that the same students who are victims of their classmates also often get into trouble. This shows that their peers do not reject them without reason.

All but one of the characteristic circumstances of the typical situation involving the scapegoat mechanism are present here. First, there is a social and cultural crisis marked by generalized undifferentiation. This is symbolized by the school uniform, which removes the marks of social differentiation that come from the children's families. It makes all students equals. From rivalry between these equals a new social differentiation emerges, one that, in Japan, mirrors the structure of society almost perfectly.[5] School also teaches children to respect this structure. Second, the victims commit crimes that threaten the social order. This is what the participation of teachers in this process means. Victims are students who have broken a rule, worn a skirt too short or brought a hair dryer on a school trip, an insignificant rule, an inoffensive transgression, but which, like Remus crossing over the line drawn by Romulus to mark the limits of the city yet to be built, threatens the whole social order. Third, the victims have marks that identify them as victims, differences that in themselves are often insignificant, but which isolate them from the group. Their classmates accuse them of smelling bad, being ugly, being animals, being foreigners, having hair too long, and so on. Fourth, the violence exerted against them is unanimous. Fifth, the violence is invisible. Clearly no one is persuaded of having done wrong. It is only through the notes of the suicide victims or because the brutality reached such a case that the police had to intervene that the wall of silence is beginning to crumble. To my knowledge there is only one thing missing: the metamorphosis of the victim into a beneficent being, the consecration of the victim, his or her salutary destiny.

However, when we think about it, that the victim does not undergo such a metamorphosis should not surprise us. Rather, it is what we should expect given the situation. In fact, it even constitutes a confirmation of the preceding analysis. The order that comes out of the victimization process in this case is by definition structured in a conflictual manner. The opposition between students and teachers as a result of the victimization process only disappear for a very short time. It is rapidly reasserted. Thus it is normal that conflicts, and the same conflicts, reemerge rapidly. However, the metamorphosis of the victim into a sacred being, unlike the rediscovered peace, is not an immediate consequence of the victimization mechanism. It occurs little by little, as peace lasts and becomes established. Then and only then does the evil being that was the victim become salutary.[6] Only then does the victim come to be seen as responsible for the new peace and harmony. However, in the cases we have been examining, everything leads us to believe that the period of harmony following the death of the victim is generally too short to lead to this transfiguration. Note in passing that in the Sudanese sacred kingships studied by Simon Simonse, among whom the king is at the same time the enemy and the victim of his people; collectively murdered scapegoat kings are never made sacred after their death. Only rulers who die of natural causes become sacred.[7]

A note of caution in conclusion: one of the interests of this example or illustration of the scapegoat mechanism at work is that it brings the phenomenon closer to home. Of course, one might be tempted to say: "these are strange people, living in a faraway land, the products of a very different culture, it is therefore not surprising if they should act in a bizarre way." It is true that we think of the Japanese as very different from us. But they are also very much like us and quite good at what we think we do best: modern science, modern technology, and modern economy. What I want to stress is not the distance, but the proximity. When we read René Girard's description of the scapegoat mechanism in *Violence and the Sacred*, we tend to represent to ourselves a definitively nonmodern environment, in which strangely dressed others are subject to a fit of wild violence and excitement.[8] *Ijime* suggests, I hope, that the violent mechanism that brings peace back into society may correspond to much more "normal" behaviors.

Another point of interest is that *ijime* constitutes what may be called a proto-institution, something that is in between an institution, like monarchy or a sacrificial ritual, and a simple regularity of behavior. In that way it is somewhat like "The Ancient Trail Trodden by the Wicked" as analyzed by Girard in *Job: The Victim of His People*.[9] Neither a real institution, nor a purely spontaneous outburst of violence, *ijime* bears witness to the social efficacy of the mechanism of scapegoating by showing us how victimization can be present within an institution like education and play there a fundamental role without seeming in any way to structure the institution itself. Simultaneously, it helps us understand why the mechanism of victimization can be so hard to see, though nothing hides it from us.

From Scapegoat to God

The Problem

How does the victim become god? According to Girard, it is through victimization, through the violence that is exerted against him or her that the victim is changed into a deity. That is the process through which violence is transmuted into the Sacred. It is the unanimous transfer of reciprocal enmity against a unique target that metamorphoses the scapegoat into an object of fear and veneration. Or at least so teaches *Violence and the Sacred*. But is this always the case? Is this epiphany of the victim a universal law of unanimous victimization? Does this extraordinary conversion of the cause of all evil into the source of life always take place? Or does it sometimes fail and the victim remain purely evil, nothing more than a justly condemned sinner and public enemy? According to Girard, the violent generation of the Sacred explains its ambivalence. It explains that what is sacred is simultaneously good and evil, beneficial and malefic, an awesome power whose wrath is to be avoided at all cost, while we must seek its benediction. In view of this our question can be reformulated more precisely: through what process does the victim gain its positive attributes? Is the last victim, the one that brings resolution to a sacrificial crisis, always so transmuted and metamorphosed that the target of universal hatred becomes a transcendent object not only of fear but also of veneration, a bringer of life?

The question arises because there are indications that the divine transubstantiation of the victim does not always occur. There are examples where the person on whom the entire responsibility of the sacrificial crisis has been transferred remains in death uniquely burdened with the attributed evil that was the cause of its demise. Simon Simonse[1] and I[2] have independently documented two categories of such cases where the targets of sacrificial victimage fail to partake in the ambivalence of the Sacred after their death, and I am sure that there must be many more. The problem then is: how should these phenomena be interpreted and what can they tell us about the mimetic crisis, and its resolution?

This question is important, central rather than marginal. What these examples challenge is one of the central theses of *Violence and the Sacred*. They question the efficacy of the mechanism that Girard postulates at the origin of religion and of human culture. If victims of collective violence are sometimes transformed into deities and sometimes not, then it seems that students of mimetic theory should be able to say why and when. Furthermore, as we will see, these counterexamples also call into question some aspects of Girard's interpretation of the historical influence of Christianity.

A Possible Solution

At first sight Girard's theory contains a very straightforward explanation of these apparently anomalous phenomena. It can be stated in one word, "Christianity." According to Girard, Christian Revelation renders the sacrificial mechanism of victimage inefficient. Because Christ's passion has revealed the innocence of the victim, Christianity prevents "generative scapegoating." Christianity does not eliminate collective or individual victimage, and it does not make such violence impossible or less likely, but it progressively reduces the ability of the mechanisms of violent victimization to transform scapegoats into gods. Unfortunately, in both of the cases mentioned above, and that will soon be described in detail, this solution is unavailable for both empirical and theoretical reasons.

The empirical reasons first: in both cases, the evidence comes from cultural areas where the influence of Christianity has been rather limited. In *Kings of Disaster* Simonse conducts a comparative study of regicide in southeastern Sudan. Even though some of the participants in the events he reports were raised in mission schools, there is little that suggests a Christian influence on the events he analyzes. The same can be said of *ijime*, the forms of violence and bullying in Japanese schools that I interpreted as a sacrificial crisis and its resolution. In both cases it seems unlikely that Christianity plays any role in explaining why these forms of persecution fail to sacralize their victims.

The theoretical reasons drive the point home. According to Girard, the reason why Christianity precludes the sacralization of the victim is because it reveals the victim as a victim, an arbitrary target on which has been transferred all the violence of the community. Christian revelation prevents the closure of (mis)representation that effects the sacred transformation. Because it lifts the veil of miscognition that allows the transfer of mutual resentment upon a unique victim, Christianity initiates a society in which there is always someone to side with the victims. As a consequence, it under-mines the cultural and religious creativity of collective victimage. According to Girard, the modern everyday use of the word "scapegoat" bears witness to the transformation of the way in which we perceive victims of collective victimage. We see them precisely as scapegoats, as innocents who are unjustly accused, and as neither gods nor evil demons, but as human beings who do not deserve the harm they suffer. In the evidence reported by Simonse and by me, this is precisely what does not happen. The victims are not seen as victims, but as evil, as deserving their condemnation, and as themselves ulti-mately responsible for what happened to them. The torturers believe that the victims deserve the harm they suffer. In other words, the misrepresentation of the scapegoat is complete, and at no point do the victimizers doubt the guilt of their hapless victim.

In view of the previous remarks, we can once again refine the formula-tion of our problem. What happens in certain African regicides (in *ijime* the process is somewhat different) is perhaps not so much that the victims do not become sacred, than that the two faces of the Sacred remain separated, and that the victims, which we foreign observers see as scapegoats, appear to the participants not as victims, but as malefactors or at least as not unjustly punished. It may seem at first that this makes the anomalous evidence easier to handle. Girard often says that as time goes by, as the distance from the original founding moments grows, the ambivalence of the Sacred becomes incomprehensible to religious thought, and the distribution of its two values, good and evil, upon different beings, gods and demons, is a normal evolution of religious thinking. If this is the case then both our examples should represent later stages in religious evolution and correspond to a moment when religious thought has begun to lose touch with the violent origin from which it sprang.

Neither Ritual nor Original Event

The difficulty is that in both these cases it is not clear that time has gone by and that we have in any way moved away from the "origin." One of the strengths of Girard's theory is that he distinguishes clearly between the "original event" and its reproduction in ritual, and consequently between two forms of substitution: sacrificial substitution and ritual substitution. The "original event" is the sacrificial crisis and the founding murder that puts an end to it. We should not think of the "original" event as the first sacrificial crisis. As Girard suggests in *Things Hidden*, there probably is not much sense in talking about a first crisis.[3] The original event is not "original" because it is first or because none came before, but because it gives birth to something, because it is the origin. The original event is the sacrificial crisis and its resolution inasmuch as it creates the Sacred, a culture, rules and prohibitions, rituals. The solution to the crisis rests on the sacrificial substitution, the founding murder, where the victim stands for every member of the community as the violent enmity of all is transferred upon only one. It is this hostile polarization against a unique victim that brings peace back. According to Girard, it is also from the universal hate and fascination focused upon a unique individual that the Sacred is born. The original event is a spontaneous mechanism for regulating violence that arises in a society when internal rivalry and conflict have reached a sufficiently high level of intensity. In the history of a community this mechanism can be activated many times.[4] No matter how many times it is repeated, it is always the "original event."

Yet it is a painful visitation: a violent crisis that must destroy before it can build anew. Rituals, according to Girard, are means of acquiring the benefits of the crisis's resolution without having to go through the destruction of a real mimetic crisis. They rest on a second form of substitution, namely, ritual substitution, where a ritual victim, be it human, animal, or even vegetable or symbolic, takes the place of the sacrificial victim of the original event. Rituals are to the original event as material objects are to Platonic forms: imperfect reproductions of lesser virtue. Thus, they necessarily institute time and establish a distance from the origin toward which they seek to bring us closer. There was a time in the past, the original time when the gods visited us, and it is that time that the ritual commemorates and tries to bring closer to the present in which the community lives. As the time and distance that separate them from the origin extends and as memory of the original event becomes clouded, the ambivalence of the Sacred gradually grows incomprehensible, and religious thought increasingly separates the two contradictory values that were once united in the sacrificial victim. According to Girard, the loss of contact with the original event explains the evolution of religious thought toward an ever greater separation of the beneficent sacred from the maleficent sacred.

The problem is that our two examples do not partake in the ritually instituted time that flows ever farther from the original event. Neither Japanese *ijime* nor Sudanese regicides are rituals. The kings of disasters analyzed by Simonse are executed for their failure as rainmakers, but not ritually. Their death comes at the end of a dynamic process of growing conflicts between and mutual accusations by the king and the *monyomiji*, the men of the ruling age group. The death of the king is not a preordained affair; it depends both on his luck as a rainmaker and on his ability to manage his conflictual relationship with the *monyomiji*. Even though many closely related societies—for example, the Dinka—practice ritual regicides, Simonse writes, in the cases he studied:[5] "Regicide as a deliberate act of the community is the tragic *denouement* of a protracted confrontation with its king. It is not a ritual and it is not a political assassination. It is the last resort in a process of increasing suspense. . . . It is rather, an inevitable, recurrent tragedy imposed on the society by its antagonistic, centralist structure."

Regicide then is the conclusion of a real opposition between members of the community. It puts an end to a series of increasing conflicts. It is not the terminal phase of a ritual. The king of disaster resembles more the sacrificial victim of the mimetic crisis than a ritual victim. His death unites the community through the unanimous opposition that motivates it.

Ijime, in the sense of school bullying, is not a ritual either. It has no blueprint or prescribed form, and no specific date or event requires it to be performed. It is a spontaneous mechanism that relieves tension through the transfer of the group's rivalry and frustration upon a defenseless victim. It, too, resembles more the original event than a ritual and reminds us more of the real thing than of a copy. Nonetheless, a suicide that puts an end to bullying is not, no more than is the violent death of Sudanese kings of disaster, the resolution of a real, full-blown mimetic crisis. This is a foregone conclusion. It is by definition that in neither case are we dealing with the original event, precisely because the deaths are not culturally and religiously productive.

Therefore the mystery remains. These phenomena are not rituals. They do not bear witness to the terrible efficacy of some distant event, or contain signs of it, obscured by time. They are more like the original event itself, a violent process through which the enmity that pervades the community is transferred upon a unique victim. They accomplish their work of appeasement through violence in the present. They gain efficacy through the mechanism that they are rather than through repetition of what once was. They are like aborted beginnings of the original event, crises that are resolved before violence has become too intense. How is such resolution possible? Is this why their victims are not transfigured?

A Spontaneous Mechanism

Before continuing we should note what difficulties the hypothesis that these events are crises that are spontaneously resolved before they reach a sufficiently high level of violent intensity could create for Girard's theory of religion and culture. The most important one is the following. Grant, for the sake of argument, that low-intensity mimetic crises take place and that they are resolved by forms of collective victimage that are relatively sterile religiously and culturally. Would they not preempt full-blown violent mimetic crises and prevent them from happening? If such crises are frequent and their resolution pacifies the community, why do we need the more extreme mimetic crisis that Girard postulates at the origin of the Sacred?

In *Kings of Disaster*, Simonse analyzes the events leading to regicide with the help of what he calls the "enemy scenario." In contrast to the all-against-one relationship characteristic of the original event and of the scapegoat scenario, in the enemy scenario two groups of relatively equivalent force oppose each other. As Simonse notes, one of the fundamental characteristics of this scenario is that it is reproduced at every level within a given community.[6] That is to say, at the lowest level of social division it is me against my brothers; at the next level it is me and my brothers against my cousins; at the next level it is me, my brothers, and my cousins against . . . , and so on. As one goes up levels of social organization, restrictions upon the use of violence in conflicts are progressively lifted, from fists to sticks and finally to spears. The repetition of the relation of opposition at every level ensures that the opposing groups are more or less of the same size and prevents the recurrence of the scapegoat scenario and the war of all against all that immediately precedes it. Therefore it is not surprising that many anthropologists have argued that segmentary social organization, which is similar to a crystallization of the enemy scenario, is a source of both social cohesion and division.[7] Simonse's fundamental contribution was to show, with the help of the examples he studied, that centralized social organizations such as kingships are not radically different from segmentary social organizations—for example, dualism. He argued that, to the contrary, they should be seen as a further expression of the enemy scenario.[8] In the Nilotic populations with which Simonse worked, the king is best described as an enemy of his people; in order to be great, a king should be not only admired but hated.[9] The king is the enemy of all his people, just as at each level social segments of potentially similar size are enemies. Through the relation of enmity the king brings to his people a unity that would not otherwise exist. What allows that single individual to face the whole community as an "equal" are his magical powers and his command over the rain, through which he can threaten the entire community with death, famine and disaster.

Kings are killed, publicly executed by the whole community, when they prove unable to make rain fall, or rather when they can no longer shift the blame onto the community and claim that its failings are what prevents the rain from falling. At that point they are accused of willfully holding back the rain. When they are killed and their belly is slit open, often a great quantity of water, namely the rain they were holding back, is said to flow from the king's corpse.[10] At other times, informants will report that abundant rain fell the day following their death. Furthermore, as Simonse argues, "In the process of tightening consensus around the victim, not only the differences between the sections and moieties recede: gender differences and diversity in age-grades become secondary as well."[11]

At the end of the process, the unanimity of the community with respect to killing the king or queen is complete, and no one will come to his or her defense: "By far the most frequently practiced method of putting the Rainmaker to death is burying him or her alive. The popularity of this mode of execution can be explained by its collective character. Every member of the community participates, and no one in particular can be blamed for the deed."[12]

Nonetheless, a communally executed king is not sacralized after his death. His body is abandoned in the bush, like that of an enemy. His grave does not later become a shrine. Members of the community fear revenge from the rainmaker they have killed and will take special means to protect themselves. They do not, however, expect any benefit from him. Furthermore, not only is the death of the rainmaker public, it is remembered as an action that was justified. Participants say that he would have destroyed the community and that he had to be killed in order to free the rain.

I argued earlier such regicides are clearly not rituals and do not occur after the whole community has collapsed into a fury of undifferentiated violence. On the contrary, as Simonse says, they are a normal result of the conflictual dynamic generated by the social structure of which seeing the king as the "enemy of his people" is an expression. Given this structure, regicide is a highly likely expedient in times of tension and impending danger. Moreover, the death of the king does not challenge the institution but, on the contrary, reinforces the very social organization in which he occupies the dominant position. All of this suggests that we are dealing with a spontaneous mechanism that restores unity and shores up the existing order by transferring all the tension and frustration found in the community to a single victim. Such regicides are akin to many rituals, but they are even more similar to the original event itself. Yet why is the victim not sacralized? Everything seems to be there in order for this transfiguration to take place: unanimity, belief in the scapegoat's extraordinary powers, even the beneficial results that immediately follow its death. Why is it that all these elements do not come together and give birth to a sacred being that is an object of fear and veneration? Why does the story end with a dead man or woman, his or her belly slit open, and left in the bush to be eaten by vultures?

Simonse proposes that it is the violence of his death that precludes the positive transfiguration of the victim.[13] He suggests that because murdered kings remain enemies of their people, a potential threat against which the community needs to protect itself through magic, it is difficult to approach them as all-powerful superior entities. This seems to me unlikely or rather it seems to me too high a price to pay in order to explain why rainmakers that are communally put to death do not become sacred. According to Girard, on the contrary, the unanimous violence exerted against the victim is the very process through which the victim becomes a god. Violence is the Sacred. Therefore, if Simonse's explanation is right, it entails not just a minor modification of Girard's theory. If the violence of their deaths prevents the positive transfiguration of victims of regicide, then one of the central tenets of the theory needs to be revised.[14]

Before coming to such an extreme solution, it may be useful to see whether Girard's theory has anything to tell us concerning this difficulty. The theory suggests that the violence of the regicide is not the reason why the victims are not sacralized. Rather, I will argue, it is because not enough violence surrounds their death.

Violence and Monstrous Doubles

There are many descriptions of the mimetic crisis and its resolution in Girard, but one is particularly relevant to the present discussion. It can be found in chapter 6 of *Violence and the Sacred*, "From Mimetic Desire to Monstrous Doubles." This description is less analytic and much more speculative than, for example, the one found at the beginning of *Things Hidden* for it is partially based on hypotheses concerning the mimetic psychology of participants in the crisis at the height of its violent frenzy. The description's importance stems from the fact that Girard addresses there a central problem that he never again discusses in such detail. The problem is that of sacrificial substitution: how does the victim come to represent each and every member of the community? Girard argues that in order for the violence of all to be transferred onto the victim, every participant must perceive the victim as identical with or equivalent to every member of the community. Otherwise the arbitrary character of the victim's designation would be too obvious. At the height of the crisis, says Girard, two different descriptions of what is happening must coincide. One description corresponds to the point of view of the participants; the other corresponds to the point of view of outside observers. For adversaries locked in conflict with one another, all that exists in their interrelations are differences, the immense differences that distinguish every individual from his or her enemies and that motivate his or her violent behavior toward them. External observers—namely, those who do not participate in the violence and conflicts—perceive only identity. All they see are doubles, identical violent twins similarly opposed to one another and desperately trying to assert what, in their eyes, is the absolute difference that separates them from their enemies. Girard argues that in order for the crisis to be resolved, these two descriptions of the situation must be made to coincide.

The coincidence requires two things. First, the crisis must involve the whole group; no external observers can remain. All must be engulfed by the violent fury. Second, the external description of the identity of the opponents must in some way impose itself on the violent rivals. The first condition ensures that once the crisis is resolved, peace will last, and no one will rise up and say "that victim was innocent." The second condition is necessary in order for the transfer to be efficient, in other words in order for each to recognize his or her own antagonist in the arbitrary victim. The experience of monstrous doubles, an experience of collective hallucination that occurs when violence reaches its highest intensity, is, according to Girard, what renders compatible these two contradictory descriptions of the situation. It provides the necessary midpoint between identity and difference that allows everyone to perceive his or her identity with every other, including the victim, and yet maintain the primary difference that urges them to violence. These two conditions together achieve the closure of misrepresentation. They guarantee that no one within the sacrificial system can perceive that the choice of victim is arbitrary.

For various reasons or perhaps for no reason in particular, Girard did not return to this problem. Since *Things Hidden* he has always preferred to explain the scapegoat mechanism as a result of the progression from mimesis of appropriation to mimesis of the antagonist. Perhaps is it because the latter explanation is more succinct and economical or perhaps because it accords less importance to the representations of agents. Mimetic theory generally gives priority to actions over representations, which are usually seen as providing rationalizations after the deed is done. However, the explanation in terms of monstrous doubles gives representations a fundamental role in the resolution of the crisis.[15]

Even if chapter 6 of *Violence and the Sacred* constitutes a more speculative and roundabout explanation, it has the advantage of showing clearly that two distinct operations are involved in the resolution of the crisis. One can be called affective transfer, namely, the process that burdens the scapegoat with all the violence, hatred, fear, resentment, and frustrations of the community. The other is identification, namely, the mechanism through which each comes to obscurely perceive every other member of the murderous group, and even himself or herself, in the victim. In that chapter Girard sometimes writes as if identification was the condition of (successful) affective transfer. It seems to me that this can hardly be the case. Early in *Violence and the Sacred* Girard states that the ability of sacrificial institutions to protect communities from violence rests on a fundamental characteristic of violence. Violence can be appeased by providing it with a substitute victim, an object that was not its original target, such as in the case of the man who vents his anger against his boss by kicking his car.[16] Yet even French academics living in the United States do not usually confuse their deans with motor vehicles. Affective transfer does not require identification, and if it did there would be no such thing as ritual substitution.[17] However, Girard is right: generative scapegoating does require identification and it is precisely identification that is lacking in both *ijime* and the regicides studied by Simonse. Furthermore, Girard is also right that the intensification of violence makes identification possible.

Losers and Winners

Victims of *ijime*—that is, school bullying in Japan—are usually not killed. They do not succumb to the violence that the whole community has exerted upon then. They kill themselves. They commit suicide in response and as a last attempt to escape from the constant harassment, petty insults and bad jokes, broken lockers and stolen books, angry teacher and laughing classmates, thefts, violence, and loneliness that every day is their lot. More than anything else, what pushes them to this desperate act is the unanimity of rejection—a unanimity that, interestingly enough, sometimes continues even after their death, since it is still frequent to hear in Japan that if a child is victim of *ijime*, it is because he or she is in some way unable to interact with his or her schoolmates. Even if what has happened is regrettable and even if the child's comrades have gone too far and gotten carried away, educators say that nonetheless they should not be blamed for what, ultimately, is another person's failings, the victim's inability to interact normally with other children. In consequence, some child psychologists specialize in teaching victims of *ijime* how to "fit in." Everybody agrees where the problem lies! Such educators, though they are unaware of it, share the victimizers' point of view. In cases like this the closure of misrepresentation is complete. Needless to say victims of *ijime* are not sacralized. They are mostly forgotten. This is not a topic one should talk about; school administrators and educators often either refuse to recognize that it happens or minimize the problem.

What certainly does not happen then is identification. Nobody wants to be confused with such complete losers! That is the very reason why the victims are universally rejected, even if, or perhaps precisely because, no one has any particular reason to reject them except that everybody else already rejects them. No one identifies with the victims because they are losers, because they fail to integrate into the group, and because there is nothing about them that is desirable. All of this of course simply reveals the tautological logic of mimesis, but it also indicates, negatively, what is required for identification: desire. It is those who bully who are imitated, and if one wants to be desired and imitated, one should imitate them.

The innocence of the victim of the founding murder is of a different kind. He or she is generally not a loser, but a winner, a victor at the game of violence until the very last and bitter end. Whatever else the gods of the Sacred may be, they are not whimpering weaklings, they are not losers, but objects of fear and desire. They may at times suffer injury and insults, but they exact in return a terrible revenge. To the contrary, the victims of *ijime* are characterized by their inability to succeed in the world of violence and rivalry, other than through the contradictory gesture of their own death, and that, I submit, is precisely the reason why they are not sacralized. Clearly, if the victims of *ijime* remain after their deaths what they were in life—namely, such misfits and losers—that sometimes even their parents are ashamed of them, it is because there is nothing that is to be desired or imitated in their unhappy lives. It is not the violence they suffered that prevents the positive transfiguration of these victims, but their incompetence in the world of violent rivalry.

A similar, though somewhat different, argument can be made about rainmakers. Unlike Japanese schoolchildren, Nilotic kings of disaster hold a position that is defined within a sacrificial system. Members of the rain clan, they are bearers of powerful magic and sacred beings who are ritually enthroned. The ambivalence of the Sacred suffuses them; while they are alive they are simultaneously hated and venerated. The question to be asked then is not: why is it that kings who are victims of regicide do not experience a positive transfiguration? Rather, it is why do the two values of the Sacred with which they were already endowed come apart at the moment of their violent death? An important point is that, in this case, it is not because the king is killed that he is sacred, nor is it because he is sacred that he is killed as in a ritual regicide. It seems more to the point to say that the king is killed in spite of the fact that he is sacred, because through his actions he has proven that he is essentially evil. A simple answer to our question therefore seems to lie at the surface of the murderers' representations: an executed rainmaker has already proven his evil intentions toward the community, and there is little sense in trying to appease him after he has been killed. This argument seems even more convincing to the participants, given that they believe the king was killed because of his stubborn refusal to mend his ways. On the contrary, a rainmaker that dies of natural causes has proven his utility and good intentions toward the community. Furthermore, now that the king is dead he no longer occupies the position of enemy of his people, which made him hated. He is therefore all the more likely to partake more of a benevolent deity.

This explanation remains superficial inasmuch as it is located at the level of the agents' representations. However, it is also possible to uphold it with an analysis of the conflictual dynamics that lead either to the collective victimage or to the survival of the king. The position of the king as enemy of his people is structural. It is not the effect of a personal choice, but inscribed within the social organization itself. Therefore, conflict with the *monyomiji* is not something that can be avoided, especially if one wants to be a great ruler, a famous rainmaker. It follows that victims of regicide do not only fail their community as providers of rain, they also fail in the brutal and dangerous rivalry that opposes them to the *monyomiji*. They show themselves inferior, losers, unable to succeed. Inversely, kings who pass away naturally are perhaps lucky with rain, but they also win a contest that others lose. Unlike kings who died of natural causes, but like sorcerers and witches who are caught, victims of regicide are losers. They are not masters of violence, their intention to do evil has been thwarted, and their power to do good must therefore be limited, precisely because they have been defeated.

Violence and the Sacred

Why are some victims sacralized and not others? Girard's answer in *Violence and the Sacred* is that victims that are sacralized become gods to their murderers because they have been violently executed. However, not all victims of violent death are sacralized. Girard's claim is that it is only those who were the targets of a unanimous process of collective victimization who are sacralized. In this essay I have argued that this condition though necessary is not sufficient. Some victims of collective unanimous violence are not sacralized. Why?

Sacrificial gods are not meek victims or impotent evildoers that can be easily defeated, but masters of violence and violent rulers of violence. At the beginning of the second chapter of *Things Hidden*, Girard argues that in the aftermath of the crisis, the victim appears retrospectively to have ruled and directed the whole series of events leading to its death; it is seen as having orchestrated the terrible visitation that shook the community to its very foundations. Neither kings of disasters nor victims of *ijime* fit that bill.

Later texts of Girard and many recent interpretations tend to emphasize the innocence of the victim, or, overly impressed by modern texts of persecution, they see in every sacrificial god a *figuratio Christi*. However, it is not because the agent or agents they refer to did not partake in violence that behind the names Oedipus or Dionysus stands victims, but because they were arbitrarily charged with the violence of all. After the Lebanese civil war had raged for about ten years, Béchir Gemayel, leader of one of the Christian militias, managed through force to reunite much of the country. On August 23, 1982, he was elected president of the republic. Even before power was officially transferred to him, government services started working again for the first time after many years, and a semblance of order returned. Three weeks later he was assassinated. During the three following days Christian militia men exacted vengeance for the death of their leader upon thousands of helpless refugees in the Palestinian camps of Sabra and Chatilla. Nonetheless, leaders of every ethnic and religious faction came to his funeral service, and that meeting was the occasion out of which grew the first government of national unity, led by his elder brother, and the first cabinet to include representatives of all the warring parties since the beginning of the hostilities. Around the same time, a rumor circulated in Beirut that Béchir would soon resuscitate and come back to rule all of Lebanon. However short lived and superficial was Béchir Gemayel's transfiguration from murderer of his political enemies, traitor, and ally of Israel, to mystical savior of the nation, it was the sacralization of a master of violence.

If we take seriously Girard's claim that violence *is* the Sacred, this conclusion should not surprise us. Many spontaneous phenomena of mimetic violence that lead to the expulsion of an arbitrary victim are religiously and culturally sterile because they are insufficiently violent. It is not because of Christianity's influence that they produce no idols, but because they are resolved long before violence seriously threatens existing norms and social differences. Do these phenomena not preempt full-blown sacrificial crises; do they not make them superfluous and prevent the recurrence of the original event? I believe that they certainly do prevent the recurrence of the original event, that they are part of the mechanisms that hold back sacrificial crisis, that delay the return of the sacred.

Violence and Indifference

The Contract of Mutual Indifference

In a recent book,[1] Norman Geras suggests that we are bound by a contract of mutual indifference, but neither in the sense that such a contract took place in the past between members of our society nor in the sense that a contract of indifference is a hypothesis that can explain our behavior or a rational fiction that founds our rights. Rather, the contract would be in the sense that, given our way of acting toward one another, it can be *morally imputed* to us. Geras's point of departure is a simple factual observation, namely, of our general indifference to the suffering of others. According to him, this indifference manifests itself in at least two ways. First, "in the shadow of catastrophe," such as during the Holocaust, the recent civil war in ex-Yugoslavia, and the genocides in Rwanda and Cambodia. By saying "in the shadow of catastrophe," Geras wants to insist on the fact that what strikes him is not only the real moral indifference of television viewers who feel sad about the suffering of others in faraway countries but who do nothing, invoking distance and urgent needs around them as excuses. It is also and above all, as is reported without exception in the narratives of these events, the too frequent indifference, the fact that people who are right there and able to help refuse to do so. Geras's examples include that of the merry-go-round located just outside the Warsaw ghetto, where mothers brought their children to play just a few meters from the wall on the other side of which civilians were being murdered and from where the children playing could hear screams and machine-gun fire.[2] Second, our indifference is shown in our attitude to poverty, those left behind by economic growth, social inequalities, the homeless, and "squeegee kids": discrimination and intolerance. On the one hand, we place responsibility for those in need in the hands of professional and state organizations, and believe that we have done our duty. On the other hand, at the same time, social aid becomes increasingly conditional on indigents demonstrating that they are, in some sense, "worthy." In consequence, a growing number of individuals slip through the holes in the social safety net and are left to their fates. What reveals our indifference is that the simple fact of being in need is no longer sufficient reason to have a right to support. According to Geras, these two forms of indifference are sufficiently widespread, sufficiently frequent, to be considered equivalent to demanding to be freed from the obligation to help people in distress or, more generally, other people in need.

Thus, the idea of a contract of indifference. Geras tells us that we cannot reasonably demand to be freed of the obligation to help others without in turn freeing them of their duty to help us. Imagining that we have the right to help from others when we are in need but that we have no obligation to come to their aid when they are in trouble would be not only unreasonable but irrational in the sense that it is a proposition that can never be the object of an agreement between free, rational individuals. Our behavior can gain moral, rational meaning only at the price of supposing that there is a contract of mutual indifference between us by which we each give up our right to help from others in order to be freed, consequently, from our obligation to help others. The contract is not what explains our behavior; it is what can be *morally imputed* to us in light of how we act. The consequence of this is that, in virtue of this contract, we have now renounced our right to receive aid when we are in need or, to put it another way, that right is now deprived of moral foundations.[3] Yet, and this is the paradox engendered by the contract of mutual indifference, there is clearly something unconditional,[4] or, to speak like Kant, categorical, in the obligation to help those in danger. Whatever the philosophical or religious foundation of the unconditional dimension of the duty to provide assistance, no matter what the origin of this "moral sentiment," if it really exists, no contract of mutual indifference can be binding. There can be no rational agreement that frees us of our obligation to help those in need.

We are thus confronted with two conflicting moral intuitions: on the one hand, that of a rational agreement that founds our rights, and, on the other hand, an unconditional duty that is independent of any agreement. A few years ago *Maclean's Magazine* published a survey that had found that, in 1998, 27 percent of men and 21 percent of women in Canada thought that the poor were themselves (morally?) responsible for their poverty and, consequently, that we had no duty to help them. In other words, 24 percent of the total adult population considered that the duty to help was not unconditional and that because their indigence was their own fault in a way, the underprivileged had proven themselves unworthy in a way that freed us from having to help them.[5] In contrast with this attitude, which requires that those who suffer should merit the help that we can offer them, there is another that considers that suffering in itself is sufficient justification for help. These are two irreconcilable and unreconciled intuitions that shed light on the hypothesis of a contract of mutual indifference.

Individualism

My goal is not to resolve or reduce the tension between the two moral intuitions brought to light by Geras, but to take it as a point of departure for reflection on violence. The opposition between the promise of indifference[6] and the unconditional obligation to help is, I think, revealing of an essential aspect of human violence and the institutions that we have established to try to solve the problems that it raises.

Indeed, if we look closely, we quickly realize that most of the examples Geras chooses to illustrate our indifference fall into the category of catastrophes caused by humans. I think that this decision, this conscious choice or unconscious selection, is important. By catastrophes of human origin, I do not mean simply catastrophes caused by humans, such as plane crashes and nuclear accidents, or even catastrophes in which the agents responsible are human, such as when a disaster flows from human error, but catastrophes that have their sources in human action and that have germinated in the fabric of social relations, such as the Holocaust, wars, genocides, race riots, poverty, and even the major famines in recent history.[7] All of Geras's examples[8] suggest that the indifference of which he speaks is connected to violence, at least in the sense in which, if this indifference is not expressed only on the occasion of disasters engendered by human violence, it is probably more shocking in these cases because they are precisely the ones that have caught his attention. This indifference is also in league with violence because in situations of suffering caused by human violence, it is difficult to escape the impression that indifference constitutes tacit support for the violent. Taking one's children to play on a merry-go-round from which one can hear gunfire and the screams of men, women, and children being killed on the other side of a wall seems to be a form of behavior that is possible only for those who accept the well-foundedness of the violence, who think that it is not human beings who are being killed, but social parasites or subhumans who are being exterminated.[9] Clearly, these two things are not independent, and if indifference to the victims of human violence seems to us to be morally more reprehensible, it is precisely because it seems to mean taking sides, more or less openly, against those who are being persecuted. In contrast, indifference to the victims of uncaring nature, as cruel as it may be, is easier to accomplish without raising suspicion of taking a position against the victims, and can more easily be justified using calculations of prudence according to which helping would be too dangerous, time consuming, or costly in terms of energy or money. In the case of natural misfortunes, our obligation to help seems to be counterbalanced by our other obligations and responsibilities. It does not impose itself in such an unconditional manner. Why not? If in the case of human violence the obligation to help is unconditional, is it not precisely because in such circumstances there is apparently no room for indifference—in other words, because in such situations being indifferent is always to take sides, to oppose the victims, and to be in league with the persecutors? Is it not because in such circumstances being indifferent is always a trick and a lie that one uses on oneself and others, but which is a poor attempt at hiding true hostility?

While almost all of Geras's examples are more or less directly related to violence, all of the moral commitments that he discusses are individualist. Both the contract of mutual indifference and the unconditional obligation to help those in danger address each of us individually, even though their ways of being individualist are not quite the same. In the former case, the contract is individual owing to the reciprocity that it involves. We each renounce our right to be helped, and each is in return freed of the obligation to help. Consequently, the contract is universal through individualism, so to speak, by summoning individuals one by one. In the latter case, in contrast, the unconditional obligation to help is individualist through universality. As a categorical obligation, it applies in all cases where individuals are in danger, independent of any consideration of age, race, sex, social origin, or religious beliefs. This time, the obligation is individualist because it is universalist. It is because it addresses us all that it addresses each individual. This time, the universal does not suppose and does not require reciprocity.

Yet there is tension between this individualism and universality, on the one hand, and, on the other hand, the suggestion that in situations of human violence, indifference is never real and is always equivalent to taking the side of and engaging in action to help those who exert violence against those who are victims. Thus, in the contract of mutual indifference, the contract, as its name indicates, supposes reciprocity between the agents, between one who renounces a right and one who is freed of a duty to help. This reciprocity is what is signified by the individualism of the contractual procedure by which each makes an individual commitment. However, when indifference is equivalent to the fact of being against, reciprocity does not exist. It is already broken. My inaction cannot be both assimilated to a tacit agreement of disengagement and to the fact of supporting those who persecute the victim. We again find related tension in the case of unconditional obligation. The categorical dimension of the obligation supposes universality, which is contradicted by the fact of having to take sides. The unconditional, categorical nature of the obligation means that every suffering being solicits me and has the right to my assistance. However, as soon as there is a conflict, as soon as there are aggressors and victims, there is no longer universality but division between those who suffer and those who inflict suffering. In such situations, we can quickly be led to resort to force in order to fulfill our duty to help, and, despite all the verbal precautions we may take, it is then clear that we can no longer universally meet the requirement to help persons in distress. As soon as there is conflict and side-taking, the obligation to help is no longer unconditional. It becomes subject to the condition dictated by the way the conflict is divided. It binds us more to those who are "for" than to those who

are "against," to those who are "us" than to those who are "them," to those
who are attacked than to those who are attacking.

It seems that the only way we can avoid this contradiction is through
"sainthood" or, if one prefers, a certain form of nonviolence. It means rejecting indifference and taking the victims' side by agreeing to share their fate,
but without exerting any force (aside from moral) against their attackers.
However, it is not certain that such a solution is consistent because if one
does not have strong faith in the final victory of the Good, Truth, and Justice,
it is not clear how such a sacrifice could help anything at all. This nonviolence
thus seems forever torn between effectiveness, which drags it toward force,
and "sainthood," which condemns it to impotence.[10]

Given this tension, indifference and individualism can appear to us in a
different light. Rather than a simple expression of insensitiveness, indifference would correspond to a refusal to take sides, an effort to break the spontaneous movement that pushes us to choose one camp over another. This
movement is visible both in our impression that indifference is equivalent
to taking part and in the apparent impossibility of universally fulfilling the
obligation to help. Indifference would thus be equivalent to the fact of not
choosing between victims and attackers. More precisely, our indifference,
that psychological disposition that Geras deplores, would result in an insti-
tutionalization of this refusal through the individualism established by the
rupture of traditional ties of solidarity.[11] Understood in this way, the contract
of mutual indifference consists in accepting that others do not take sides in
my conflicts, in recognizing that they have no special obligation to help me,
and in committing myself in return to not intervening in their clashes. This
is more or less what we do when we abandon the monopoly of legitimate
violence to the state—in other words, through the social contract that
establishes the sovereign as the unique arbitrator of disputes and as holding
sufficient force to carry out that task. We sign the contract of mutual indifference. Geras is right to think that our modern political regimes encourage,
or at least legitimize, this indifference.[12] However, he is wrong to insist on
what distinguishes the contract of mutual indifference from the social contract in the classical sense of the term.[13] While the differences between the
two contracts are real, they should not make us overlook the deep kinship
between them. It is also important not to view, as Geras occasionally seems
to do, the contract of mutual indifference as containing a moral failing or as

the expression of psychological weakness, which is fully revealed in certain especially tragic events in recent history. On the contrary, it is important to recognize in this institutionalized indifference a fundamental structural aspect of our form of social organization. It is equally important to see that this indifference plays a role, that it has a function.

Violence

If being sensitive to the suffering of others is a characteristic shared by all individual members of the human species, if it is universal, it is so in a very special way. Indeed, while we are *all* solicited by the suffering of some victims, no one is, I think, solicited by the suffering of *all victims*, at least when the suffering is caused by human violence. This helps to explain what was discussed above, namely, that it is impossible to satisfy in a noncontradictory manner the unconditional obligation to help victims of human violence when it is understood as a categorical, universal obligation applying to all persons indiscriminately. This is because helping victims of human violence requires taking sides by definition, at the risk of being in turn led to violence and forced to create new victims. We will say that those victims are not innocent. Perhaps, but asserting that the obligation is unconditional and categorical is simply to say that it makes no distinction between innocent victims and enemies, that the obligation to help applies equally in both cases. Yet this indifference is deeply foreign to us, deeply in contradiction with our spontaneous, natural reactions, which lead us to take sides and to help those who are victims, or at least those we recognize as victims.[14]

It is not easy to gauge the exact extent of this phenomenon and the difficulties raised by what we can call our essential partiality. René Girard is certainly one of those who has done the most to help us do this. His essential thesis concerns the mimetic nature of violence—in other words, the links between violence and imitation. According to him, violence is mimetic in three essential ways. First, violence is mimetic in the sense that it comes from imitation, but not so much imitation of appearance, which he sometimes calls "behaviors of representation" such as dress, manners, and ways of speaking, which are very visible forms of imitation and the driving forces behind social conformity. Girard focuses instead on imitation of desire. This form of imitation is more difficult to perceive, but it is very real. Two rivals who hate one another and think they have nothing in common share at least one thing: the same goal, the same hunt for success in business, pursuit of the same triumph in love, the same desire to win a sports competition, in short, the same objective that they are competing with each other to obtain. The fact that they seek the same goal is less visible to us because we are most sensitive to the actions by which the antagonists oppose each other and try to exclude each other. We think: "What could be more opposite to imitation than rivalry and enmity?" Yet, and this is at the heart of Girard's demonstration, what we desire is all the more desirable when another desires it, and our reciprocal opposition is all the more stronger when what we desire is more desirable, more important, more valuable. According to Girard, there is an inherent link between desire and opposition, an inextricable link because it remains hidden. This veiled convergence of desires onto the same objects is a child of imitation, an inexhaustible source of conflict, and the principle by which conflict grows.

Second, violence is mimetic in the sense that it makes those who are violent increasingly alike, in both the social and the psychological senses. The greater the violence grows, the more it forces rivals to resort to the same tactics, actions, and violence if they do not want to lose. Countless conflicts prove this: after a time, both guerrillas and armies murder peasants, burn their crops, destroy their villages.[15] It thus becomes impossible, except for those who have unwavering faith in the justice of their cause, to distinguish the "good" from the "bad," the oppressors from those defending the oppressed. This is not simply an unfortunate unintended consequence that can be explained by local circumstances. On the contrary, according to Girard, this lack of differentiation, this reduction in differences between antagonists, is the norm not the exception, the usual outcome of violent conflicts, and what requires special explanation is when, for some reason, this normal evolution of conflict does not take place. The identicalness of actions and methods gradually transforms into deep psychological identity. Behind the opposing ideological screens there hides the same escalation of violence, the same desire to win at any cost. However, lack of differentiation also has a social dimension. Violent conflicts gradually destroy social hierarchies, differences between persons that constitute the framework of the existing order. Riots make workers the equals of their bosses, and revolutionary tribunals make beggars the judges of judges—in other words, their equals. Once it has reached a certain threshold of intensity, violence makes us all alike: there are no longer any differences between men, women, children, the elderly, university professors, and homeless people. It levels the distinct positions that are produced by the social division of labor.

Third, violence is mimetic because it is contagious, because it tends to engulf ever more individuals in the conflict. For example, in westerns, a single punch very often suffices to unleash a free-for-all in the saloon. Despite their stereotypical, slapstick aspects, such scenes contain some truth. When there is a conflict, we are spontaneously inclined to join in, to take one side rather than the other. Of course, a sufficiently large imbalance between the sides may prevent us from acting. However, such deployment of strength generally only delays things. It changes our commitment in no way. Such contagion also occurs in another way that is less spontaneous but just as real. Once violence has reached a certain intensity, the main players refuse to allow anyone to escape the conflict. "If you're not with me, you're against me" becomes the adversaries' only rule, and odious devices are employed to ensure that no one escapes his or her violent "responsibility." For example, the militias in ex-Yugoslavia forced young people trying to avoid serving in the armed forces to kill "their" civilian from the other side in order to ensure their loyalty, they said—in other words, in order to enroll them definitively, with no possibility of escape, in the spiral of interethnic violence.[16] As Daniel Pécaut puts it so well concerning violence in Colombia, the result is that no third parties can resist the partisan polarization.[17]

These different dimensions of the development of violence are interdependent. They are in fact simply three aspects of the same phenomenon. Lack of differentiation fosters contagion, imitation accelerates lack of differentiation, and contagion condemns everyone to imitating those who are violent because there are no longer any other models available. Moreover, while violence erodes existing social differences, undermines their meaning, and wears away their prestige, it also becomes the principle of new hierarchies for which the only criterion is successful violence. Violence creates lords and masters. However, since those who are violent become more and more alike, and nothing concrete distinguishes between participants in violent rivalries, violence alone makes it possible to tell adversaries apart. Consequently, not only are these hierarchies fragile, shifting, and unstable, but maintaining them always requires more violence. Violence contains within itself the principle of its headlong rush into always more violence.

For Girard, the illusion par excellence of the modern world is the belief that we can always contain within acceptable limits the natural phenomenon of the escalation of violence, that we are at all times able to prevent violence from intensifying and escaping our control. The illusion is the belief that we are able to control violence and that we can use it for political, historical, social, and ethical purposes without succumbing to its fascination, without sacrificing the goal to the violent means employed to achieve it.[18] This illusion is deeply seated in us because it is rooted in our spontaneous reaction to take the victims' side and our feeling that our obligation to help them is unconditional. However, the substrate created by our primitive reactions produces different growths depending on the social organization that sows the seeds.

Indifference and the Obligation to Help

Not all forms of social organization are equal with respect to contagion by violence. Some make such contagion easier than others, in particular, those that transform solidarity obligations between members of the society's groups into duties that none can escape. In times of crisis and more particularly in times of violent conflict, this solidarity, which normally protects everyone from poverty or at least total abandonment, risks involving more and more people in the conflict. There are at least two reasons for this. The first is that in such societies it is difficult, if not impossible, to not take part. No one can shirk the duty to help, take vengeance, or engage in retaliation without being automatically considered an enemy, without in turn becoming an attacker in the eyes of members of his or her group.[19] As Marcel Hénaff notes in his paper on traditional societies,[20] in some cases it is as if there were an awareness of this danger, and those who are obliged to take revenge for victims are limited in number and specified in terms of status and kinship relations. However, these limits are flexible, as M. Xanthakou shows clearly, and the obligation to take vengeance takes precedence. If there is no brother, a nephew will be taken; if there is no man, a woman will be taken, even if she is the murderer's wife and therefore a member of the clan that is taking revenge.[21] The second reason is because in segmented societies where such obligations reign, they apply to all, but each individual has a duty only to the members of his or her segment. Consequently, every conflict threatens to polarize into two groups a large part of the society, and to involve from the start, at least potentially, all members of those groups. I am not minimizing traditional societies' mechanisms for preventing this kind of escalation, or confusing the ritualized vengeance of "vindicatory systems" with the untamed vengeance typical of the modern world.[22] The point is instead to show that in these societies, solidarity ties act as conductive lines along which pass the current of violence at the risk of contaminating all members of society, despite the relays and breakers deployed to control the flow.[23]

The contract of mutual indifference cuts these lines. By abandoning the monopoly of legitimate violence to the state, we free ourselves of the obligation to participate in the conflicts of others. Each person is thus individually responsible for his or her violence, both the violence he or she suffers and the violence he or she commits, and with respect to disputes involving others, we all become third parties, outside observers who are required by law not to intervene. It is easy to see the advantages of such atomization of conflicts. Rather than placing every antagonist in a network of support that takes his or her side, the modern world isolates adversaries and their conflicts. It limits each individual to using only his or her strength. This is what makes it possible for the state to always intervene with sufficient means to put an end to conflicts. In fact, in terms of reduction of internal violence, the historical success of this model is truly prodigious. Contrary to a widespread impression, the modern world has been marked by constant reduction in internecine violence, and our societies are by far those in which conflicts internal to the community create the fewest victims. How many less? According to the best statistics available, the homicide rate in traditional segmented societies is somewhere between 0.5 and 1 percent, whereas in our societies it is between 0.04 and 0.002 percent.[24] In other words, there is a reduction by a factor of ten or twenty, depending on the statistics used. Of course, this is in a sense misleading because the numbers do not take into account the much greater destruction caused by modern wars, in particular civil wars, as W. Palaver shows,[25] and because in traditional societies it is not always easy to distinguish murder from an act of war. However, the purpose of these remarks is not to assign points for good or bad results, or to determine which societies are, in the end, the most violent. It is to shed light on the link between forms of social organization and conditions for violence. It is quite certain that the abandonment of traditional ties of solidarity protects our societies from some forms of escalation of internal violence and that the prosperity we enjoy is probably not independent of the relatively low level of violence in the societies in which we live.

Yet as the reading of Geras reminds us, this abandonment of traditional solidarity ties and the accompanying protection against violence has a price: indifference. Some could be led to see in this indifference the realization of the evangelical precept that asks us to renounce violence and make no difference between the good and the bad, the just and the unjust, just as God causes the sun to rise and the rain to fall on both. However, this is not a realization of the precept so much as a caricature of it. As Geras shows, our indifference is not unrelated to violence, and sometimes engenders even greater violence than that from which we hope it is protecting us. This is because it secretly takes sides against victims. It always suggests that those who suffer deserve what they get. We should nonetheless not see it simply in the framework of a theory about moral sentiments, as a form of insensitivity that is especially widespread in the modern world and that urgently needs to be replaced by more humane sentiments. It is not that such insensitivity is unusual, but abandonment of some of the most spontaneous forms of the duty to help others in distress is a structural feature of our social organization. Goodwill does not suffice to put an end to such indifference, especially since this indifference is useful: it truly protects us from our own violence. The dilemma of modern societies is that we can neither be satisfied with this indifference nor give up the protection that it provides.

Mimetism and Genocides

The Problem

At first sight, detailed descriptions of modern collective violence, especially political violence, such as pogroms, race riots, ethnic cleansing, the Holocaust and genocides, make these phenomena look very different from the mimetic crisis described in Girard's theory. Indeed, almost all analyses of these forms of violence are consistent in that they acknowledge the importance of leaders, main political actors, specialists, and veritable agents of violence without whom the massacres would not have occurred and the events would have taken a completely different turn. Far from being spontaneous or the effect of contagion invading all of society, collective violence, according to some of the best examples that we have, seems to be planned, organized, thought out—if not rational, it at least seems to be the result of concerted, coordinated action. How can these descriptions be reconciled with the Girardian description of the crisis, the role it gives to mimetism, and the importance it places on contagion phenomena? If the major episodes of collective violence in the twentieth century are not the work of wild crowds but of organized, structured, disciplined groups, are we not required to explain their actions in terms of the reasons and beliefs that motivated the members of these groups and the institutions that they represented rather than in terms of an obscure imitative mechanism that would have carried them away against their will? As Jacques Sémelin notes in a recent work,

> Girard's work makes those who wish to remain close to social and histori-
> cal facts feel uneasy. His theory is constructed on a seductive hypothesis
> about the mimesis at the foundation of all human relations . . . on the basis
> of which he intends to explain both war and conflict in love. However,
> while he seems convincing when he performs psychological analysis of the
> heroes of Shakespeare or Dostoyevsky, he remains allusive or mute with
> respect to contemporary conflicts.[1]

Is it possible to explain this difference, to fill this gap, or do we have to, on the contrary, conclude that a number of phenomena of modern collective violence escape Girard's theory?

In fact, this difference raises two distinct types of problems that should be distinguished. First, there is what we could call the applicability problem. Can Girard's theory explain modern episodes of collective violence? Despite many observers' inability to see mimetism in modern political violence, can it be found at work and provide us with a mimetic explanation in relation to existing analyses? Moreover, supposing that we are able to give a positive answer to this first question, a new order of difficulties arises. This time, the problem is internal to mimetic theory: modern political violence is marked by the failure of the scapegoat mechanism. These are crises without resolution. The Armenian genocide, the Holocaust, and the Rwandan genocide are atypical in the Girardian universe in that they lack the scapegoat mechanism that resolves the crisis. The violence stops, if it stops, either because there are no more combatants, or no more victims, or because there is outside intervention. Scapegoats are not lacking; in fact, the problem is that there are too many: no one becomes the victim who is in the process of becoming sacred and putting an end to reciprocal violence.

While the failure of the scapegoat mechanism is an atypical phenomenon in the world of mythology as described by Girard, it appears, on the contrary, to be characteristic of examples of political violence with which we are all too familiar. This is why these two questions are closely linked, for even if mimetism really is present in political violence, does not the failure of the scapegoat resolution challenge one of the central tenants of the theory?

Mimetic theory postulates the existence of a self-regulating mechanism for violence, and uses this mechanism to explain, in the last analysis, all of human culture. However, if this mechanism is not involved in modern political violence, then is there not a fundamental problem, a difficulty that becomes all the more significant if we recognize that such violence results from a mimetic dynamic?

Girard has a general answer to this objection. It consists in saying that Christian Revelation has made it impossible for there to be the *unanimity less one* that puts an end to the crisis. It requires us to find reconciliation without victims. Thus, the failure of the scapegoat mechanism in modern political violence should not surprise us. It corresponds to what we should expect. Unfortunately, even supposing that this answer were right, we have to admit that it does not answer the question at all because it does not make it possible for us to understand how to differentiate between mimetic regimes that lead in one case to the successful expulsion of a single victim able to reconcile the community, and in the other case to an escalation into horror that seems stoppable only for contingent reasons external to the violent dynamic itself. We thus need to explain and understand in terms internal to the theory the incapacity of modern political violence to end spontaneously through reconciliation against a single victim.

Methodological Interlude

Part of the answer to the question of the gap between Girardian analysis and sociological descriptions of collective violence is methodological. Every observation is guided by a theory. The fact that many observers do not identify the kind of phenomena on which Girard bases his demonstration may be because they are not looking for them, or even because when they see them, they do not pay attention to them. For example, in *The Politics of Collective Violence*, Charles Tilly mentions, though only in passing as a phenomenon that is not very interesting, that in France in the eighteenth century, many episodes of collective violence began with an attack against pariahs or dishonored persons.[2] He never mentions it again, as if this "quirk" had nothing to do with the topic of his book. Perhaps the failure of many observers to recognize mimetic phenomena reflects less the absence of such phenomena than the blinders they wear. Such observers are often meticulous and attentive, but they have other theoretical prejudices. The phenomena that interest Girard seem to them to be more anecdotal than significant. However, this methodological remark will remain bankrupt so long as we have not used empirical examples to show that mimetism is at work in modern collective violence. This is what I am going to try to do, based mainly on Manus Midlarsky's comparative analyses of genocides in *The Killing Trap*.[3] I will try to show that the explanation of genocides that he proposes is essentially a scapegoat theory.

Massacre and Mimetism

Jacques Sémelin says, "There is something paradoxical about reasoning about the individual in himself, as if he were a molecular unit of the social. Because the individual does not really become a mass murderer except by being related to a community of which he is only a link."[4] Moreover, he adds, "the killers are in a *group*. Whether they advance masked or unmasked, in uniform or in civilian dress, they are assembled. . . . One thing is sure: it is the group that is the collective operator for mass murder. It is the group that metamorphoses individuals into killers."[5] Yet Sémelin does not see any mimetic dimension in this violence. He uses the notion of ideology to explain the murderous future of human groups. Certainly, incendiary speeches do play a role, and homicidal ideologies are often fundamental to the formation of aggressive assemblies, bloodthirsty militias, and paramilitary groups. However, Sémelin also provides us with another answer: he says it is the group that transforms the individual into a killer. While ideologies change, the group remains in all cases the universal operator of this transmutation. Whether we like it or not, we have to acknowledge that the Girardian hypothesis at least has the advantage of allowing us to understand why and how such a metamorphosis occurs. It accounts for the way that collective power replaces individual decisions and leads agents to perform actions that they would never do as individuals under normal circumstances.

As Girard points out in his analysis of the "miracle" of Apollonius of Tyana, in normal times, when people are not under the influence of the mimetic contagion that causes them to converge against designated victims, no one wants to be the first to attack defenseless innocents.[6] Whether it is structured and disciplined or an informal gathering, the group makes it possible for each individual to do no more than all the others. Mimetism, imitation is what facilitates action, what makes the unthinkable possible and converts ordinary people into killers. However, and as an *a contrario* proof of the hypothesis, Christ's behavior in the adulterous woman episode dissolves the group, sending each individual back to his or her personal responsibility: "He that is without sin among you, let him first cast a stone at her." It is thus not by chance that killers are always in groups; it is no accident that they come in bands rather than one by one. Sémelin simply acknowledges the importance of groups in the violence that he analyzes; he simply observes that killers come together, that they do not take action in isolation, but the mimetic theory makes it possible to understand why this is the case.

The central position of groups in genocidal violence leads us to the question of the preponderant role of political agents, organized groups, and specialists of violence. Collective violence is rarely spontaneous. Despite superficial appearances, the violent outbursts of crowds generally result from manipulation and concerted action by determined individuals. Such outbursts do not look like the results of imitation's gradual invasion of a community. On the contrary, they are organized. They occur because there are leaders, political agents who find them useful, who know how to exploit them, and who strive to excite the crowd. Without such agents, there would be no massacres, or many fewer. Is it thus not toward the interests that they represent that we should look to understand the eruption of violence rather than to imitation? Why appeal to a contagion mechanism when we are dealing with structured groups, disciplined troops able to resist being drawn into violence and to respond only to specific orders against set targets?

Yet can we not apply to the leaders and political agents the idea that an individual is not a "molecular unit of the social"? Can we not consider that they too are only "links" in the community? To put it differently, agitators, slogans, activists, political leaders do not prove the absence of mimetism.[7] On the contrary, leaders require followers, and they are leaders only if they are followed. As Jean-Pierre Dupuy has shown, between a panic and a structured crowd such as an army or church, there certainly are important differences, but the same imitation mechanism can explain both of them.[8] The presence of leading political actors does not falsify the role of mimetism: it verifies it.

There is no imitation without a model. In the mimetic crisis, models seem to disappear only when each has become the model for all. However, while it seems there are no longer any models, this is in fact because everyone has become a model. There is no longer a unique point on which all eyes converge. The focus of all desires will reappear at the resolution of the crisis, when the reconciling victim becomes the external mediator par excellence, the source of all authority.

In political violence, the situation is completely different. Such violence is kindled by the authorities in power or by political agents who challenge them—in other words, by leaders, models, people who hold up their hatred and resentment to be imitated. Whether what is in question is legitimate power or those who challenge it, violence does not take hold, does not transform from terrorism or political assassination into massacre or genocide unless leaders and the majority of society members agree upon the chosen victims. Victims are not chosen by chance. They belong to a group, to a minority (or several), to the category of "others" who are excluded from the community in which the leaders, like "ordinary people," are simply links. However, genocidal violence does not erupt unless there is an agreement against the victims. This agreement is a political condition for mass persecution. First, because the greater the persecution, the more collaboration required from more participants. Second, because such action is politically possible only if those who carry it out and the third parties who let them do so, whether they benefit or not, are assured that tomorrow it will not be their turn. This assurance will not be felt unless they are persuaded that the victims are guilty, that the punishment that falls down upon them is justified, owing to their crimes or to simple prudence.

The Killing Trap

The Killing Trap is a comparative analysis of three genocides: the Armenian massacre in Anatolia, the extermination of six million Jews in Europe, and the Rwandan genocide. Midlarsky compares these three events in order to identify their common features. Then, juxtaposing them with ethnic cleansing in Bosnia and Pol Pot's regime in Cambodia, he seeks to isolate the essential characteristics of genocides in relation to other types of collective violence. From this, he draws a general theory of genocides as a specific form of political violence.

His explanatory model has four fundamental components: first, continuity of killing; second, validation; third, loss; and fourth, altruistic punishment. These four components are the necessary conditions for genocides in the sense that a genocide can occur only if these conditions are satisfied. However, they are not sufficient; their simple presence is not enough to trigger a genocide. A political choice is also required, namely, recourse to imprudent realpolitik. The author of *The Killing Trap* does not make an explicit distinction between the first four conditions and the fifth as I have done. However, his way of seeing things suggests that there is an important difference because the first four conditions are constraints or refer to situations that are imposed on agents from the exterior, while the fifth is related to the actions of political decision makers, to their way of responding to events. Midlarsky's approach consists in showing that in all cases of genocide, these five conditions have been present, but in situations where any one of them has been absent, even in circumstances that we might think should have led to a genocide, genocidal policies have been avoided. This was, for example, the case of Bulgaria, which was allied with Nazi Germany during World War II but which managed to protect its Jewish population from deportation.

The two first conditions are closely linked. Continuity of killing means that genocides do not spring out of virgin ground that is free of violence and persecution. They occur in places and within populations that have already experienced or practiced on a lesser scale and in a less intense manner persecution behavior of the same type. The continuity is not a simple chronological series, but the fact that past and present violence is linked. As he says:

> What is required is that perpetrators be aware that massacres of elements of the victim population have occurred in the recent past and that they identify with the political goals and mindset of earlier perpetrators. Identification can provide a bridge between the recent past and present, and make subsequent mass murder more likely to occur. Vulnerability of the victim, a necessary condition for genocide, has been clearly established.[9]

The continuity of killing thus refers to two separate phenomena: identification of past and present agents with one another and victims' vulnerability. Identification, the fact that the killers are not the first, means that they are not simply crazy or senseless. There have already been others who have thought and acted like them. They can refer to models. The vulnerability of the victims, their defenselessness, makes them sacrificable victims. These two components, victim vulnerability and the well-foundedness of homicidal policies, their acceptability, are again confirmed by what Midlarsky calls "validation." What he means by this is impunity in the broad sense—in other words, the fact that past massacres had few or no unpleasant consequences for those who perpetrated them. Past massacres are also validated and genocidal intentions encouraged by the indifference and sometimes the enthusiasm of large segments of the local community, and finally by the international community's lack of interest. Understood in this way, validation of past massacres has at least two consequences for the dynamics of genocides. It confirms the sacrificable nature of the victims and vastly increases the identification effect. The persecutors have not only past models but now also support; they are surrounded by third parties who do not punish them. Validation means that there are others who approve the actions of those who commit homicide, or at least who understand them and are ready to close their eyes. It also means that the victims truly can be sacrificed, that no one will take their side.

Midlarsky calls "loss" the fact that states that have adopted a genocidal policy have suffered a "loss" in the past—for example, a dispossession of land, military defeat, or major political failure. Whatever the nature, genocides always occur in response to a loss that is real or felt to be so. According to him, it is significant that the genocide of the European Jews did not really begin until 1941, when the Germans were beginning to realize that they would lose the war. It was also not by chance that it grew ever larger as military defeats became more numerous.[10] Just before the beginning of the Armenian genocide, the Ottoman Empire had suffered significant military defeats that were all the more traumatic owing to the fact that in the preceding century the empire had lost all of its European territories. Its entry into the war was a risk taken to try to recover its past grandeur. In 1915, the decision to participate in the conflict alongside the central powers looked increasingly like a mistake. Finally, in Rwanda also the genocide was triggered in a situation of "loss." The preceding year, only French military intervention had saved the regime of President Habyarimana in extremis. Part of the territory was then under rebel control, and the July 1993 Arusha Accords, which established peace, imposed the end of a one-party regime and devolution of power to Tutsi rebels and Hutu moderates. In all three cases, the genocides occurred in situations where the government in charge had just suffered major losses, and, according to Midlarsky, the genocides were a form of compensation for or response to these failures.[11]

Midlarsky considers loss of territory as the paradigmatic form of loss because it often entails forced population migrations, flows of refugees. In effect, eastern Europe, Anatolia at the beginning of the twentieth century, and Rwanda in 1994 were, for various reasons, home to large numbers of refugees. According to him, refugees often play a twofold role in the dynamics of genocides. First, they comprise a population that has experienced loss more acutely than any other, that has been directly affected, uprooted, displaced. Refugees are people who have lost their homes, all or part of their possessions, their country, and sometimes family members. They are "loss incarnate," a living memory of failure. They make it difficult to forget, to let go of the past. Second, and this is related, it is often within such displaced populations that the principal agents of genocides are recruited.[12]

The fourth necessary condition is, according to Midlarsky, "altruistic punishment." He considers that it is related to "loss"; it is, according to him, a means of compensating for loss, a response to failure. What is "altruistic punishment"? Midlarsky defines it on page 110 as "a punishment inflicted on a defector from cooperation, which is costly to the punisher and without material gain."

It is punishment inflicted on someone who has refused to cooperate. It is costly to the people who impose it and brings them no material gain. According to Midlarsky, "altruistic punishment" is a notion that explains why so many people support genocidal policies that are very expensive to states and provide them with no material gain. Germany diverted significant resources from the front in order to continue its extermination policy. Moreover, we know that the genocide intensified when German military defeats increased, thus when Germany's resources could have been employed in a much more useful manner. Some authors consider that the Armenian genocide and subsequent expulsion of the Greeks from Anatolia delayed Turkey's economic growth by 100 years since the two groups constituted the majority of the merchant and craftsman classes.[13] In the case of Rwanda, we can consider that the resources spent on training genocidal militias and buying machetes could have been employed more usefully to fight the rebels, whose offensive had recommenced. According to Midlarsky, "altruistic punishment," the propensity to punish those who defect, even when doing so is costly, explains why entire populations adhere to monstrous policies that bring them no gains and are even self-harming. From Midlarsky's point of view, "altruistic punishment" is the fact that populations that have suffered losses agree to spend a lot on punishing those they think are responsible for those losses.

This is Midlarsky's perspective on the genocide mechanism. First, models, examples, a form of authorization that makes the murderous behavior acceptable; second, a group of people that can be sacrificed; third, a loss or failure, refugees, a wounded population that demands compensation for the loss it has suffered; and finally, fourth, "altruistic punishment," the compensation itself, the misfortune that is imposed on those who are held responsible for the loss. In short, Midlarsky describes the victims of genocides as scapegoats, neither more nor less, and he acknowledges that imitation of past examples, peer pressure, mimetism without naming it, has a fundamental role in the process. In order for genocide to occur, the victims also have to be sacrificable; they have to be good scapegoats in Girard's sense. In other words, they have to be defenseless and have no one to defend them. There has to be no one ready to help them. Finally, the motive, the driving force, behind the homicidal behavior is nothing but a shift of violence, compensation, vengeance against sacrificable third parties for a failure that was inflicted by others.

Mimetism and Politics

Yet according to Midlarsky, this is not sufficient. For a genocide to occur, it is also necessary for the state to adopt means of action of a certain type: realpolitik. He tells us that realpolitik is a political notion according to which success is the whole measure, and in which success is defined as the fact of maintaining and strengthening the state.[14] However, what really makes the difference is not so much a specific theory as a certain type of action. He adds that realpolitik as such rarely if ever leads to genocide.[15] Only "imprudent realpolitik" can lead to genocide. Imprudent realpolitik is a policy of brute force that reacts in a disproportionate manner to provocation, obstacles, reversals of fortune.[16] Imprudent realpolitik is thus not a conception of politics, but refers to a state reaction characterized by disproportionate violence and repression. Recourse to imprudent realpolitik so defined as an explanatory concept poses two problems. The first is that imprudent realpolitik conceived of as a series of actions rather than as a political theory cannot be used as a causal explanation for genocide because it is no longer distinguishable from the behavior, actions, and murderous policies that constitute genocide. Understood in this way, realpolitik amounts to saying that genocide causes itself! The second problem is that if this is the meaning we have to give to "imprudent realpolitik," then it is the exact opposite of realpolitik as it is generally conceived of as a political theory.

If realpolitik consists in thinking that success is the measure of all politics and protecting the state is the measure of success, then it seems that realpolitik is not imprudent *by definition*. Indeed, this is what its major proponents have always thought. A state may, and sometimes even must, take risks, but calculated risks. Those who accept crazy risks, who adopt policies that are clearly disastrous with the sole goal of punishing those they consider responsible for their past failures, have manifestly lost sight of the fact that success is the measure of all politics and the survival of the state is the measure of success. All that imprudent realpolitik has in common with realpolitik is the name. It is not a special type of politics—for example, realistic—but simply the fact that those who perpetrate genocides adopt the policies that they adopt. The two problems boil down to the same: imprudent realpolitik explains nothing, especially not why those who practice it elect such "imprudent" policies.

Mimetic theory makes it possible to answer this question. Those who choose imprudent realpolitik do so because the four other conditions are satisfied. In order to see this clearly, it suffices to reformulate Midlarsky's four conditions in terms of mimetic theory. The first condition, continuity of killing, is the existence of violent models, paradigms that determine the behavior to be adopted and that designate victims. The second condition, validation, means that there is a group of victims that can be sacrificed—in other words, victims who are defenseless and have no defenders, for whom no one will later take revenge. This is the meaning of impunity: the indifference of the local population and the international community. The third condition, loss, is the disaster that strikes the community, the crisis, the evil that has to be compensated for, exorcized. Finally, the fourth condition, which Milardsky calls "altruistic punishment," is the violence transfer mechanism, the process by which a victim who can be sacrificed is substituted for an inaccessible enemy or compensates for an evil that nothing can be done about. This is all. Nothing more is needed. Imprudent realpolitik adds nothing, explains nothing. It is nothing other than the genocide itself. The genocide is thus a scapegoat policy that is not self-aware, like all scapegoat policies.

Midlarsky's demonstration is useful in two ways. First, from an epistemological point of view, completely unaware of Girard's theory[17] and following as closely as possible the historical and sociological data on three genocides, he rediscovers without knowing it the fundamental features of the scapegoat mechanism. He lacks the mimetic hypothesis, but nonetheless the macrosociological variables that he identifies are the very ones that mimetic theory predicts. Midlarsky's work is thus a very significant test of the Girardian theory insofar as the inquiry in *The Killing Trap* was conducted with neither the intention to prove nor the intention to refute the scapegoat victim hypothesis. Midlarsky can be accused neither of excessive indulgence nor of special animosity. He has simply tried to understand a terrible phenomenon.

Second, his contribution from an anthropological point of view is, I think, even more significant. Midlarsky's research discovers the structure of sacrificial violence in a political context essentially void of any religious dimension. The genocides of the twentieth century have been secular massacres, political crimes in which the roles of religious ideologies, when present, were extremely small compared with political justifications. I see in this supplementary proof of the universality of the Girardian hypothesis. That we would find outside of any religious context the fundamental structure of the sacrificial mechanism supports the thesis that the scapegoat mechanism is at the origin of all of human culture and a central component of our collective life. This testifies to the fundamental role of mimetism in human societies and suggests that mimetic convergence against victims is a kind of fixed point in our social systems, an *extremum*, toward which they spontaneously evolve when they are abandoned to themselves.

Sacrificial Violence and Crisis

If the preceding analysis is correct, it is possible to understand why in the course of a genocidal episode a single victim does not emerge against whom all of the community finds reconciliation. Genocides should not be thought of as forms of the original crisis and founding murder, but rather as human sacrifices performed outside of a ritual framework. One of the essential characteristics of the sacrificial crisis is the rivals becoming doubles, the fact that the differences between the adversaries fade little by little to leave only violent indifferentiation, in which all become alike. This means that, in the course of the crisis, the difference between the victims and the executioners gradually disappears. Each adversary seeks to grasp hold of the difference and proclaims that the victims on his or her side are the real innocent victims, whereas his or her adversaries are bloodthirsty monsters who deserve the violence that strikes them, but through this very process the sameness of the violent parties is established. They become twins in violence. This dual future of the rivals is indispensable to the resolution of the crisis. It is the necessary condition for the universal substitution of violence that makes it possible for all hatreds to be slaked on the blood of the same victim.

In contrast, genocidal violence is marked by asymmetry between the victims and the executioners. This asymmetry is not temporary, destined to disappear as the violence changes. On the contrary, it remains from the beginning to the end of the genocide, and this is why the transfer of violence onto a single victim remains impossible. On one side, there are armed groups, militias, regular troops, or crowds encouraged by the forces of order and local authorities; on the other side, there is a defenseless people, women, children, the elderly, men who may or may not be armed, but who are in any case overwhelmed, unable to resist. This asymmetry is true of all genocides, and it defines the victims not as rivals of the executioners, not as their adversaries, but as prey, sacrificable victims. They are not those against whom we fight, but those upon whom falls a frustrated violence so that we can be freed if possible from an evil the cause of which escapes us. Genocides resemble sacrifices because they are performed by designated officiants who are most often specialists of violence and are approved and invested with moral sanction by those in charge. Genocides resemble rituals, staged scenes the purpose of which is to bring order back into society. Like sacrifices, they are organized by recognized authorities, and most often their performance is placed in the hands of specialist officiants.

However, these "sacrifices" occur outside of any ritual framework. This is also what explains why they never end. A ritual is not just specific actions, different roles, a division of labor; it also defines a separate time and space. It breaks with everyday continuity. A ritual is introduced by known actions that are repeated year after year, and which establish a sacred space and time. There is a beginning and an end, and they are repeated periodically. In contrast, genocide is in continuity with everyday life. It is part of the way things happen. It is not a separate interlude the purpose of which is to seek, on a level other than that of day-to-day life, solutions to problems that arise in our day-to-day lives. Genocide is a policy; it is not a sacrificial ritual. This is why it has no end, no natural term but total consummation.

Suicide Attacks

Military and Social Aspects

According to those who carry them out, suicide attacks result from a power imbalance. They are the weapons of the weak and the poor. Those who cannot afford the luxury of computer- and laser-guided smart bombs launched from high altitude instead send fighters ready to die carrying bombs to wherever they will have greatest impact.[1] From this point of view, suicide attacks are a second-best, a way of compensating for a technological and military disadvantage that is too great, a way of reestablishing a balance of power. In fact, this rebalancing supposes above all a shift in the location of the clash.

Smart weapons, bombs, and rockets, as well as electronic surveillance, are part of a special tactical approach, that of massive aerial bombing designed both to weaken the adversary by destroying the infrastructure needed for efficient fighting and to reduce the number of victims among one's own soldiers. The ideal scenario—the one that the North Atlantic Treaty Organization (NATO) attempted to implement in Kosovo—is to win the war before putting a single person into the field, to force the adversary to capitulate before any of one's soldiers are exposed to enemy fire. This kind of approach requires a major imbalance that can be exploited to a maximum. The air superiority of one transforms the other into powerless prey. Aerial weapons eliminate distance. They make it possible to strike anywhere in the adversary's territory without having to cross hostile terrain between key targets. In this context, smart weapons serve two purposes. First, they reveal and make possible the destruction of the most secret, well-hidden, and best-protected facilities. They pierce the thickest armor. Second, and this is nonnegligible, they make it possible to claim to reduce the adversary's civilian losses to a minimum. Smart bombs are supposed to spare noncombatants and to be able to destroy a military stockpile without harming the hospital located right next door.

In a conflict in which there is such an imbalance, such flagrantly unequal strength, smart bombs are also an excuse, a way of seeking forgiveness for the superiority and radical inequality that they imply. They are signs of the restraint that those who control the game impose on themselves, the proof of their moral care in the very midst of the struggle. This is a concern that, they believe, distinguishes them from their adversary. Smart weapons are thus also a moral argument, an argument that is designed to make us forget the reality of the war that it warps and hides. It leads us to believe that it is possible to take action with surgical precision so as to strike only military objectives and enemy soldiers, but spare innocent civilians. Smart weapons are portrayed as a technological solution to the problem of distinguishing between combatants and noncombatants.

Faced with them, suicide attacks can be viewed as a countertactic and as a moral counterargument. Indeed, suicide attacks are often used to strike targets that would otherwise be inaccessible and to inflict maximum damage on the adversary. Thus, in their conflict with the Sri Lankan government, the Tamil Tigers have used suicide attacks to target ministers, kill highly placed officials, destroy military facilities, and, most spectacularly, assassinate the prime minister of India, Rajiv Gandhi. The Kurdistan Workers' Party (PKK) has used this tactic to attack Turkish police stations, and in Lebanon two especially deadly suicide bombings carried out against American and French troops in 1983 led to the withdrawal of the contingents of those countries. Today, the same tactic is used by the Taliban in Afghanistan and by insurgents in Iraq against military convoys, the occupying forces' roadblocks, and recruitment centers for the new Iraqi army.

Like aerial weapons, though on a smaller scale, terrorist attacks eliminate distance. They make it possible to get rid of the difference between places that are close and those that are far from the theater of operations. They can strike anywhere, at any time. The aerial army does not see territory as an obstacle. The terrorist threat rejects the political concept of the territorial monopoly of legitimate violence. Like airborne attacks, terrorist action is designed to make it difficult or even impossible to create sanctuaries that shelter some people, either for military purposes or simply so that the majority of the population can continue existing in parallel with the combat and lead normal lives next to the reality of the fighting, as if the war did not exist. Like aerial threats, terrorist threats show that the state cannot protect its citizens. Used in this way, suicide attacks are to classical terrorist attacks what smart weapons are to the bombs of earlier generations, except that instead of being controlled from a distance, they are guided by hand in the true sense. Dissimulation, the fact of going unnoticed until the very last minute, makes it possible for kamikazes to get as close as possible to targets that are shielded and well protected. Human bombs, like smart weapons, can identify their targets, even track them if necessary. They can thus play roles quite similar to targeted attacks such as those, for example, of a state like Israel against Palestinian terrorist and political leaders. Suicide attacks replace assault helicopters and remote-controlled rockets by determined pedestrians.

Suicide attacks can be used in this way, and they have been sometimes, but they are not always, and the most spectacular, the ones that strike us most, seem to follow a logic of a different order. At least two reasons explain the evolution of this tactic toward a different use. First, terrorists' enemies learn. While it may be difficult to protect against suicide attacks, it is nonetheless possible to do so to a certain degree. Major potential targets, such as military installations, high-ranking officers, and political leaders, as well as crucial civilian facilities, can be made relatively safe from this kind of attack. It is impossible to make terrorist attacks impossible, but we can make them much more difficult and significantly reduce their chances of success, especially if we are ready to leave the land to the terrorists in order to keep control over the resources. Suicide attacks can compensate for power imbalances only for a short time, against imprudent, excessively ambitious adversaries with too much confidence in their superiority. Yet protecting against such attacks is costly, especially in terms of reputation and legitimacy, because doing so requires imposing major restrictions on the civilian population. Moreover, such protection very often requires taking the initiative and neutralizing attacks before they have been declared. This means stopping, before it is too late, individuals who are apparently innocent though they are committed to dying. Consequently, it is inevitable that mistakes will sometimes be made and blameless citizens will be taken for terrorists: Jean-Charles de Menezes was executed, and cars carrying women and children have been machine-gunned. What from one's point of view looks like a "regrettable mistake" in occupied territory inevitably smudges the distinction between combatants and noncombatants. Terrorists then have at least two reasons to shift toward soft, relatively unprotected targets—in other words, toward civilian targets and noncombatants. On the one hand, there is the relative facility of succeeding in such operations, and on the other hand there is vengeance. The very means employed to defend facilities and people considered indispensable create the atmosphere that makes it acceptable to carry out attacks against civilian targets and give terrorists the support they need.

The second reason why suicide attacks do not distinguish between military and civilian targets, as smart weapons are claimed to do but rather often tend to strike indiscriminately, flows from the fact that they are also moral arguments. In both cases—in other words, in the case of smart weapons as in the case of suicide attacks—the expression "moral argument" does not mean that the argument is accurate, legitimate, or well-founded. It means only that the action, the recourse to smart weapons or suicide attacks, claims to state what the world should be. The action is justified in "moral" terms. More specifically, the action itself is an attempt to change the world and make it more consistent with what should be. Smart weapons say that war should differentiate between civilians and military personnel. They assert that this difference is built into the deadly technology itself. Terrorist attacks that target noncombatants, such as buses, subways, and the World Trade Center, say on the contrary that the distinction between combatants and noncombatants does not exist, or has disappeared, or rather they say that the distinction does exist but that it does not reflect the power disparity, that it exists only for the others, for their adversaries, but not for those whose relative powerlessness forces them to employ suicide attacks. Those who claim the opposite, the rich, the well-armed, are lying. They are scandalized, but only selectively, by actions that do not respect this difference. They invoke the distinction between combatants and noncombatants to say that their adversaries are immoral, but do not hesitate to transgress it themselves. In order to counter the terrorist threat, they resort to private security companies that escape all legislation and all legal responsibility—in other words, that are outlaws in the true sense of the term.

From this point of view, the loss of difference that is characteristic of so many terrorist operations is in no way accidental. On the contrary, it is voluntary. It is not a form of confusion, but of undifferentiation. It contains de-differentiation first at the level of those who call themselves "martyrs," namely, those who commit suicide themselves. Their mission's success requires them to melt into the anonymous crowd and disappear, so that until the fatal moment there is nothing to distinguish them from the others. This loss of distinction between combatants and noncombatants is even greater when the kamikazes are women, who seem to be the category par excellence of noncombatants. While the fact of being female sometimes makes it easier for terrorists to meet the dissimulation and anonymity requirements of their mission, by turning themselves into means of destruction they themselves prove that there is no border separating uniformed enemies from innocent women and children. Difference also disappears at the level of victims, who are no longer soldiers or highly placed political officials, but each of us, nobody and anyone. Finally, it disappears in the weapon itself, which strikes in all directions at once, destroys people, and turns the torn arms and legs into anonymous parts that specialists later try to identify.

◆ ◆ ◆

It has always been the case that in every war the combatants accept at least the risk of dying to defend the cause for which they fight. This is part of the very definition of combat. When the danger becomes too great, some tend to want to turn tail and flee. Yet as John Keegan has shown, this is when they are at greatest risk of both perishing and dragging all their friends with them.[2] This is why it is important to try harder and convince some to accept the supreme sacrifice, not only the risk of death, but death itself. Only the death of some can save the others and make the undertaking a success. We can speak of sacrifice in this sense. These are sacrifices around which a whole military mythology has been built. The great feats of glory in military narratives are not only those of the victors but also those of the heroic sacrifices of a few who, thanks to their fierce resistance, saved others and made victory possible. The sacrifice of soldiers who die to save their close companions in arms or simply others whom they have never seen before and whom they do not know is not generally called suicide. This is because those who die in this way in combat to save their comrades are not seeking death, but life, that of others, and generally they do not kill themselves but are killed by the adversary in circumstances where death is difficult to avoid. They do not choose their death, but they accept it when they cannot do otherwise.

We might think that suicide attacks are part of the same system. In fact, this is often how they are described by the groups that are behind them and how they are viewed by the communities that support such practices. The authors of suicide attacks are celebrated as heroes, as "martyrs" who agreed to die to defend their cause, save their homeland, protect their religion, and expel the invaders. They are compared to soldiers on the battlefield, to those who give their lives for others. However, the comparison hides important differences. The authors of suicide attacks do not die so that others can live; they die so that others may die. One might say that the same could be said of soldiers on the battlefield. Is not their primary function to deliver death? Certainly, but soldiers' actions are given meaning through the military advantage that they provide rather than through the simple fact of producing victims. For example, their actions are given meaning if they manage to deprive the enemy of important information, rather than if they simply kill seven soldiers before being killed. From a strictly military point of view, useless sacrifices have the double disadvantage of both being pointless and undermining troop morale.

The driver of a tanker truck full of gas and explosives who detonates the vehicle in the middle of a crowded square does not die so that others can live, but in order to kill. The author of such a suicide attack accepts dying, but the very meaning of the action is not that others will be able to live, that his or her side will have time to escape or to regroup, but that he or she will not be the only one to disappear. Such attackers spread death and destruction, but the advantage produced by their actions seems to be on a completely other level than a simple tactical advantage on the chessboard of combat. The author of the suicide attack acquires a strange solidarity with the victims by dying himself or herself, by imitating them by dying himself or herself, and his or her death is just as indispensable and fundamental as the damage done to the adversary.

It is not only literally that the authors of suicide attacks do not die so that others may live but so that others may die; it is not only in relation to the immediate results of their actions, but also in relation to their intent, to the goal they pursue. This is because suicide attacks, like terrorist attacks in general, as soon as they abandon military targets for civilian targets, as soon as they shift their strategic objectives toward the average individual, no longer aim for victory and cannot achieve it. On the contrary, they target renewing the conflict and, in a sense, reestablishing the community. Attacks targeting the civilian population solicit retaliation that will be suffered by the group that those who order the attacks claim to represent. They strike so that the struggle can continue, so that it will start up again, to convince the adversary that it is not finished, and thus so that others will die again, others in the enemy group, of course, but also others in their own group. The authors of suicide attacks kill themselves so that the violence will not end. In this sense, it is difficult to speak of sacrifice, at least in the manner in which it is generally conceived of in the military tradition, which measures the value of a sacrifice in terms of its military utility. Yet we should not think that this difference can be explained simply by the fact that we are dealing with poor strategists and desperate fighters.

Attacks of this type often have the effect of making the situation worse, more unbearable, for those with whom the authors of the attacks identify themselves, and this can in a sense be seen as their goal. They aggravate the situation of those they are claiming to protect and whose rights they say they are defending. The reason for this is that the repression that follows these attacks increases the unity of those who are subject to it and makes terrorist violence more acceptable in their eyes. It is not necessary to imagine that this effect, this "goal," is conscious, that it is an objective that the terrorists seek in a cynical manner, though we also cannot exclude a priori that it is at least sometimes a conscious strategy. What is important is that its spontaneous emergence from the dynamics of the conflict provides an essential condition for its "reproduction," in a quasi-biological sense. The repression ensures that the terrorists lack neither support nor recruits for other similar attacks. This effect does not have to be sought in order for it to emerge, but once it does, it tends to become rooted and stable because it facilitates the survival of terrorism, ensures its "reproduction." Such situations can be all the more stable when the repression is, for some social bodies, the means of their control over political power. Repression ensures that terrorists have the support they need, and terrorist attacks strengthen the position of the authors of repression within the state. When this is the case, maintenance of the violent status quo becomes an independent objective that tends to enter into contradiction with the official goal of the struggle: victory. This dynamic partly explains the existence of what Anne Hironaka calls "neverending wars."[3]

I have argued elsewhere that terrorist actions are designed to establish the friend-enemy division where it did not previously exist. Violent actions draw a line between us and them, between the Popular Front and the fascist state, between the Sunnites and the Shiites, between the Russians and the Chechens, between the Turks and the Kurds, or whatever. It does not seek so much to conquer the adversary as to render open, manifest, explicit an opposition that may already have existed but remained unsaid, dissimulated, or to cobble one together when none was already available. Understood in this way, terrorism is not blind. Its attacks are not indiscriminate. On the contrary, terrorists strike to create discrimination, to make a distinction part of reality. Terrorist attacks are actions that distinguish, divide, and separate. The reason they seem to us to be indiscriminate is because the line separating friends from enemies that they are meant to create does not yet exist, and the targeted division is orthogonal to our established criteria. It does not distinguish between combatants and noncombatants, between men, on the one hand, and women and children, on the other. It seeks to separate us from one another, to make some into friends and some into enemies, to divide yesterday's neighbors, to tear apart married couples, to break friendships. The apparent lack of distinction is in fact the expression of a different distinction that is at right angles to those we are used to, and above all, that does not quite exist yet, that has not yet entirely taken form. Terrorist actions seek to bring it into existence, or to give it a meaning and solidity that it does not yet have.[4]

What crystallizes the new friend-enemy dichotomy, and finally makes it firm, is the reaction to which terrorist actions give rise. If they are followed by repression that strikes arbitrary members of the group with which the authors of the attack are associated, the reaction will draw the separating line for which the terrorist action was only the starting point. It is not that the violence of the attack will look to all members of that group as immediately justified or that it will seem to them that those who perpetrated it were right.

On the contrary, many will probably curse them. However, the repressive reaction of the forces of order will nonetheless teach them this: there is a difference between us and them; we are not the same. Initially, it will pencil in, more or less darkly, the friend-enemy division that the terrorists were seeking to establish. New terrorist acts will lead to increased repression, which will increase support for the terrorists, and so on. This phenomenon can find a form of stability when the repression ensures the reproduction of terrorist ranks and terrorist actions give rise to exactly the right amount of repression to ensure this and the population's indispensable support. The fact of reaching such a fixed point in the repression-terrorism circle does not exclude the victory of either party in the end, but above all favors continuation of the conflict, the establishment of never-ending war.

In these cases, violence maintains itself in a manner that seems to go on forever. However, it requires outside support in order to survive. This is because violence is costly. It consumes and destroys. It impoverishes. One of the reasons repression always gives rise to new terrorist recruits is because it withdraws other options from the members of the community who suffer it. It radically reduces their lifestyle choices. It prohibits young people from having access to a normal education. It reduces job options and economic possibilities. It condemns displaced persons to dependency and inactivity. Just as repression is a major weight on the state that engages in it, terrorism absorbs growing quantities of resources and slows growth. Never-ending conflicts gradually impoverish all those involved, and cannot continue without a constant influx of new resources. These can come, for example, from a more or less wealthy diaspora that is ready to support the struggle, from friendly countries, or from major powers that see self-interest in the success of one of the parties or simply in the weakening of the other. Never-ending wars are parasites attached to the body of the world economy, which they exploit for their own destructive purposes.[5] They produce nothing but death and destruction.

It is against the background of such inevitable, constant, repeated destruction, of this impoverishment of communities that are prisoners of never-ending confrontations, that we have to understand suicide attacks. If there is repression, then the internal solidarity of the group that suffers it grows. Yet while it leads individuals to come together and imposes on them a degree of solidarity that they did not necessarily have at first, pursuing the conflict beyond a certain threshold has the opposite effect. Violence breaks up and divides what it used to unify. As the conflict continues and victory is always pushed off until tomorrow, each becomes poorer and at the same time sees his or her possibilities and those of his or her children diminish. In such cases, some turn toward the most extremist groups, while others become ready to settle for less, and turn to the adversary to try to find an arrangement.

◆　◆　◆

A number of analysts have noted that suicide attacks take place not at the beginning of a conflict, but only once a dispute has entered into a second phase. They do not occur at the starting of the struggle, but after a certain period of fighting has gone by. This is the case, for example, in Palestine, where suicide attacks began only during the Second Intifada, just as in Sri Lanka it took years before the Tamil Tigers resorted to this kind of tactic. The same can be said about what is now happening in Iraq and Afghanistan. Recourse to suicide operations seems to mark aggravation of the struggle, and be signs of difficult periods that require combatants to make greater sacrifices. The only apparent counterexample, to which we will return, are Al-Qaeda's attacks against the United States, which seem to have begun with this type of operation.

In Palestine, suicide attacks have given rise to a culture of martyrdom that Maria Alvanou has recently analyzed.[6] "When news of a successful suicide strike is broadcasted, candy is distributed in the streets and women respond with traditional cries of joy."[7] Militants, friends, and acquaintances go to the home of the martyr's parents to congratulate and honor them. They give out sweets and speak of how extraordinary it must be to be able to become a martyr. The parents do not complain. They do not mourn. On the contrary, they display joy and pride. If the author of the suicide attack is a woman, her death is likened to a marriage "in heaven." Her parents are congratulated in the same way that a bride's parents are traditionally congratulated. A few days later, tracts and photos of the martyr are distributed, and a there is public celebration, procession, or display. In short, everything is done to honor the author of the attack, to glorify him or her. He or she becomes a hero, a model to be imitated, an exemplary person. The martyr's family is not simply covered with honor in the operation but also obtains major material rewards.

For example, Hamas offers the families of martyrs free education and medical care, as well as a monthly payment of $300 to $600. However, as Alvanou points out, all of the material advantages, both those provided by the organizations that order suicide operations and the various donations from private individuals and other organizations, have to be seen first as signs of the social importance and value of the attacks. There is no reason to think that purely economic reasons lead individuals to die so that others can die. The financial assistance to the families may certainly comfort some, who would otherwise wonder what will happen to their loved ones after their death, but above all they express the importance of the action that the martyr performs and the unanimous support of the community. Like the popular culture, which glorifies suicide attacks and sings the praises of those who commit them, the material support given to the families expresses the community's agreement and the social value of the terrorist act. Children collect and exchange cards with photos of martyrs, just as North American children do with baseball and hockey cards.

We may wonder why martyr operations are so important, what purpose do they serve? Are they really so strategically effective? Do they inflict losses that will lead the enemy to give up or withdraw? This seems unlikely. On the contrary, suicide attacks, especially those that have civilian targets, have a tendency to make worse and weaken the situation of the community that supports them, even though they often improve the relative position within that community of the groups behind them. It is thus tempting to see the rivalry between terrorist organizations as the cause or reason for this kind of attack. Each group would thus be perpetrating ever more radical, spectacular attacks in order to obtain the community's support. For example, we know that at the time of the Second Intifada, suicide attacks against civilian targets brought so much popular support to Hamas that Fatah believed it necessary to employ the same tactic, which it had until then abstained from using. This made some observers say that suicide attacks are rational and part of a rivalry strategy and power struggle between the groups that order them. However, this rational explanation faces two difficulties. The first is empirical: it is not always the case. While it is true that we can correlate suicide attack campaigns with the rivalry between Palestinian organizations, the Tamil Tigers had eliminated all of their competitors long before they began using suicide attacks. It is thus difficult to link suicide operations with radicalization due to rivalry between terrorist groups. The second difficulty is more theoretical. Supposing that this "rational" explanation were correct, why would such attacks obtain support in the community that is so universal and enthusiastic that it becomes rational to carry them out in order to benefit from such popularity? In short, what this explanation does not explain and simply takes as given is why popularity is increased by engaging in this kind of operation.

In fact, I think popularity is a side effect. What suicide attacks target and to a certain extent accomplish is the unanimity of the threatened community. What they bring to the eyes of all, to the adversary's eyes of course, but also to the eyes of the members of the community itself, is that the community is united in its struggle, that there are no divisions. Maria Alvanou's analysis reveals this clearly. She says that the attention with which the parents of martyrs are surrounded, the congratulations they receive as soon as the news about the attack arrives, expresses social pressure and constitutes a form of soft but strong coercion that is almost impossible to resist. The social pressure makes it impossible to mourn, to say that the event is not happy but tragic and that death is not a marriage, even "in heaven." Yet this pressure is nothing other than the unanimity of the group in which the parents are invited to participate. For obvious reasons, they are the most likely to rebel and oppose the faction that organized the death of their child, but they are also closest to the victim, and the ones whose agreement is indispensable. Without them, no unanimity is possible. The parents' agreement with, pride in, and consent to the death of their child express the community's unanimity. All the data indicate that suicide attacks unify the community over and above the rival factions that are behind them. Martyrs are the shared property of the whole community. Their value is universally recognized. The victim's voluntary death expresses the community's unanimity. From this point of view, suicide attacks are sacrificial rites designed to produce the community's unity.

However, it will be objected that even when support for this kind of operation was at its greatest, it never rose above 75 percent. While this is high, it is far from unanimous. However, despite its name, a public opinion survey does not measure a public phenomenon, but a private one. It aggregates individual opinions. Unanimity, the community's unity, is, on the contrary, a public, external phenomenon. It does not concern primarily the internal feelings of parents and others, and especially it does not mean that all approve of suicide attacks. The community's unity is the fact that all admire and praise the authors of the attacks. It is expressed in public ways, such as by distributing candies and shouting traditional cries of joy. The question is thus: why do these sacrifices require the deaths of others?

◆　◆　◆

In fact, there are a number of different kinds of suicide attacks. For example, often the assassins of politicians are killed by their victim's bodyguards. Such murders are suicide attacks, especially when those who commit them know that their own death is more or less certain, and in the nineteenth century this was a frequent form of terrorist action. Today, however, this is not generally the type of operation that springs to mind when we hear the term. For us, suicide attacks are inseparably linked with a special way of dying: blowing oneself up. The authors of suicide attacks destroy themselves in a radical manner: they die by the very means that they use to kill others. Living bombs, they explode and scatter themselves into a thousand pieces. They disappear entirely. They leave no corpse. While they may leave bodies behind, theirs is not among them, since they were at the center of the explosion. The missing body is not without religious meaning. For example, in Euripides's *Iphigenia at Aulis*, at the point when Clytemnestra and Agamemnon's daughter is about to be sacrificed, she disappears, removed directly by the goddess and replaced by the bleeding body of a deer "impressive . . . in its vastness and its beauty."[8] The proof that Iphigenia has been saved, of her direct ascension to heaven, is that she has disappeared and left no corpse. Not leaving a corpse is a feature of the elect, of those who die without dying, and will continue another life in another world. Nonetheless, this "proof" is not unambiguous, and like Clytemnestra we can ask:

> O my child, which of the gods has stolen you?
> By what name can I call you? How can I be sure
> that this story has not been made up to console me
> so that I can lay to rest
> my cruel grief over you[9]

Agamemnon tells her that rather than mourning, "My wife, we may be happy for our daughter's sake. For I tell you truly, she lives among the gods."[10] Yet for Iphigenia to be "saved," for her to be able to go to heaven and enjoy the company of the gods, it was nonetheless necessary for a deer "impressive . . . in its vastness and its beauty" to die. Why? The narrative tells us that it is the goddess herself who provided the victim, thus indicating that she preferred an animal victim to a human one. We could see in this the affirmation of what the gods require of victims, which we cannot entirely deprive them of, and recognize in it the traces of progress, the shift from human to animal sacrifice. While the two interpretations might be compatible, they are nonetheless inadmissible because they simply repeat what the text says, and the text lies. It lies because Iphigenia has disappeared. She is no longer among the living but "in heaven." She has indeed been sacrificed. The text lies because it transforms the violence of Iphigenia's sacrifice into a divine kidnapping and metamorphoses her death into happiness. Then why does there still have to be a sacrifice within the sacrifice? We can suppose that, like the candies that are distributed when the death of a "martyr" is announced, the deer is killed to provide a "story . . . made up to console" Clytemnestra. Agamemnon's assertion expresses the community's unanimity. It says that even those who for obvious reasons would have motives to oppose the sacrifice are in agreement, support it, and rejoice in it. Achilles, who had taken Iphigenia's side for most of the play and said he was determined to save her by force if necessary, becomes one of the officiants at the sacrifice in the end. Iphigenia's decision to voluntarily accept death motivates his transformation from opponent to assistant sacrificer. She says, "If Artemis has decided to take my body, am I, a mere mortal, to oppose the goddess. No, it is impossible. I give my body to Greece. Sacrifice me and sack Troy. This shall be my lasting monument, this shall be my children, my marriage, and my glory."[11] She gives her life so that the Greek army can finally set sail for Troy, where it will sow death and destruction. Iphigenia also dies so that others may die, and her glorious death is the substitute for what she will not have experienced: children and a spouse. Hers is a marriage "in heaven," so to speak. Between Iphigenia and the authors of suicide attacks, the essential difference is that the distance between the action and its deadly consequence, the purpose that motivates it, is shortened. It is not necessary to wait for the Greeks to cross the sea in order for carnage to rain on the enemies of the authors of suicide attacks: the result is immediate. It is through their very death at the instant when it occurs that the destruction and desolation are achieved. Moreover, the devastation has no intermediary. Under social pressure to die, which is as she herself says the will of gods and men, Iphigenia finally accepts her demise and wants to make it a glorious death. While she says that she will die so that the Greeks can go to war, she will not pillage Troy herself, and this is why it is easier to recognize her as a victim. Suicide attacks eliminate the space that separates the place of the sacrifice from the place of destruction. They merge into a single action the voluntary death and death imposed on others.

For Iphigenia, the people of Troy are nothing other than enemies, others to whom she owes nothing but death and destruction because they have insulted Greece. She has no obligations to them, and the distance, perhaps, is what makes her feel indifferent toward them. It prevents her from imagining exactly what the ruin of Troy, for which she accepts to die, means to the women and children as well as the fighters of that city. However, what about those who sit in the bus, rub elbows with those they are going to destroy, and are looking at them a second before deciding to explode the bomb? In the end, Iphigenia takes the side of the assembled Greeks, who are demanding her death so that they can go to war. Only this decision can give meaning to an inevitable death. By calling for the destruction of Troy, she revenges herself for her own death, which her people have imposed on her.

Maria Alvanou points out that the women who commit suicide attacks often have troubled pasts, or at least pasts in contradiction with the fundamental values of Palestinian society. Examples include a girl who was raped when she was fourteen, a wife who was repudiated because she was unable to have children, a woman who had committed adultery, and a woman in love with a married man. In these cases, we can see psychological reasons for the decision to die, but I think that we should see above all a category of sacrificable victims, individuals marked by what René Girard calls "victimary signs." These women are either outcasts because of the sexual violence they have suffered or the inability to reproduce with which they are marked, or they are in danger of being killed by members of their own family for having tarnished their honor. In these conditions, we may think that they find it easier to "die with honor than to live in humiliation," as an Arab proverb says.[12] Yet we have to remember that such a decision cannot be reduced to a simple question of individual psychology because honor and humiliation are in the eyes of others: they have the power to raise us up or put us down, to make us pay with our lives for the honor that they refuse to give us. Those others are the people close to us, our family, friends, neighbors. Strangers are nothing compared with this community of those close to us, which forces and convinces us to give our lives for it. We have no obligations to those who do not belong to our moral community. Their death provides revenge for the death that we have chosen freely, but which is nonetheless imposed upon us.

◆ ◆ ◆

Global terrorism, that which has struck in Yemen, Morocco, Indonesia, Kenya, Spain, England, and the United States, seems to be a counterexample to the preceding thesis according to which suicide attacks occur in the second stage of a conflict and are related to human sacrifices the purpose of which is to re-create the unity of the struggling community, which is threatened by the duration of the conflict and the adversary's efforts to divide it. As a number of observers have pointed out, the fact is that such global terrorists do not belong to an identifiable community that is already in conflict with a recognized adversary, as are, for example, the Palestinians in the Occupied Territories and the Tamils in Sri Lanka. On the contrary, they form a poorly defined set of individuals with diverse origins.[13] Many recruits come from the Muslim diaspora in Europe and North America, and the flagship organization Al-Qaeda began as a group of volunteers from everywhere in the Arab and Muslim world who were brought together to fight in Afghanistan. These terrorists belong to what Olivier Roy has called "globalized Islam." On average, its members are relatively well educated—they have often done part of their studies abroad—come from wealthy circles or are uprooted and living in the Arab world but outside of their country and original community. The only community they really belong to is composed of friends and relatives, and aside from that they identify themselves not as Palestinian, Saudi Arabian, Iraqi, or Syrian, but as members of the Ummah, the universal community of believers. The informal networks of relatives, friends, and companions in the local mosque or Muslim student association constitute the social foundations of such decentralized, nonterritorial terrorist groups. Links with organizations such as Al-Qaeda are often relatively weak and more likely symbolic of membership in a global community, in a political party that, like the Communism of yesterday, has a global target and mission. However, in its structure, this terrorism reflects the nonhierarchical, decentralized organization of religious practices in Islam rather than the rigid structure of a militant, quasi-military political party that claims to be the expression of the class struggle.

In these conditions, the community with which these terrorists identify, the friend-enemy division that they claim to express, does not yet exist. They have to make it concrete, shed light on a division that exists only in a hidden manner or in principle, normatively. However, most important, this friend-enemy dichotomy travels through two separate spaces at the same time. First, it crosses the international space, where all Islam lands are considered as a whole separated from the non-Muslim world. This is a physical space in which the targeted dividing line would be on the periphery of a political domain. Second, the dividing line crosses a social and religious space, where it separates "real Muslims" from those who claim to be Muslims but are not. The dividing line is drawn both outside of the community that the division is intended to bring into existence and inside the Muslim world as it exists today, where it is supposed to separate "the chaff from the wheat." The violence targets both the inside and the outside, as can be seen, for example, in its evolution in Iraq, where intercommunity attacks have gradually replaced in number and scope attacks against the American occupiers. At the international level, it targets one by the other: the inside by the outside.

The community's nonexistence raises two problems in the context of suicide attacks. First, there are no rules, no shared norms that can be used to impose social constraints: everything has to be invented from nothing. Similarly, there is no recognized category of sacrificable victims. Enthusiasm is required to find consenting victims. We have to wonder whether in this case there might be a redemption and conversion discourse at work here. Indeed, we know that up until very shortly before their sacrifice, many suicide attackers have lived relatively dissolute, not very "Muslim" lives. Second, the terrorists are unknown. They have no names. They have no faces. Since the community that they target is global and includes hundreds of millions of people, they are only anonymous individuals. There are no networks that will distribute their photos tomorrow, and even if there were, no one will say "I knew him," "he lived across from my sister," "he was a brilliant student and very religious from an early age," or "it seems she had run away for days with a boy from . . ." They are nothing and no one. They can count only on their action to give them a presence in the vast crowd. The first problem explains the "private enterprise" aspect that is characteristic of many of these terrorist operations. The second explains the spectacular dimension of the attacks, the fact that the goal is to produce as many victims as possible so as to make those who perform them visible and provoke a reaction that will finally galvanize the community.

However, this inflation changes nothing in the fact that in both cases the victims are the wrong ones. The terrorists are too unknown to make optimal violence transfer possible. They are too far from the community for everyone to be able to transfer their hatred and frustration onto them. The victims of the attacks for their part are, paradoxically, too close. It is not clear they are really "others," "enemies." These attacks fail to create the unanimity that could be the foundation of a community. Only the reaction, the irresponsible exploits of the war on terrorism, might be able to merge divided peoples into a community united against a single enemy.

Inside Out

Political Violence in the Age of Globalization

One characteristic of globalization that often goes unnoticed, perhaps because it is so evident, is that it has no outside. There is nowhere beyond, no place that can be viewed as an outer space, as a location that globalization has not reached. Globalization has no border that indicates that this is where it ends; rather, it closes upon itself like the globe whose shape it adopts. It is a house that you cannot leave. There is no other world that is further than, that is past globalization. There is no area where you can go that escapes its closure. Outside of globalization, there is no outside, no land that can be inhabited or even discovered and explored. This is not a problem of imagination. The difficulty to which I wish to point to is not that we cannot imagine a life different from life in the globalized world; in fact, that is relatively easy to do. What I want to argue is that the process we call globalization changes the shape and structure of our relations to each other, because it has no outside. Globalization (whatever else it may be) is a totalizing process in the sense that there is nowhere that is not part of the globalized world.

If it is not possible to go outside of globalization, to go beyond it, it is however possible to fall from globalization, it is possible to be left behind and overlooked by globalization. This "fall from grace" so to speak corresponds to a form of internal exile rather than to a departure for another country. This "exile" may be self-imposed, as was (and is) the case of cloistered monks. Men and women "abandon the world" for the service of God within monasteries, islands of peace that are both inside and outside the world. However, historically this voluntary internal exile was a departure where those who left did not entirely vanish from the society where they had previously lived. As history has shown, in Europe monasteries were important economic actors during the Middle Ages, and they played a fundamental role in the evolution of the social and political structure of Europe, as well as in the transformation of its natural environment. Similarly those who choose internal exile in today's globalized society also remain important actors in the process they denounce.

Internal exile can, however, also be externally imposed; individuals and even entire populations can be dropped out of globalization. Yet in no case does this falling out give access to a place that is not inside the global world. It does not lead anywhere that is not surrounded by it. To use a somewhat different image, globalization contains holes into which one can tumble and out of which it may be difficult to climb, but it has no outside. There is no outer space. That is precisely why it is called globalization! It encompasses the whole globe.

Why is the outside important? Essentially, because outside of where we live is where "others" live. It is a place that is inhabited by those who are not us. Who are they? It could be that the answer to that question is not very important, as long as they are not us. The word "outside" suggests first of all a separation in physical space. It is opposed to inside, and inside those who are not us do not live, or if they happen to live there, it is only by accident, with our permission and temporarily. This spatial separation is what globalization has transformed. "Others" are now among us. Through globalization the coincidence between political, social, and cultural separation, on the one hand, and distance in space, on the other, has come to an end. It is not true anymore that those who are not us, those who are different inhabit a different place, that they live somewhere else. We now share with them the same "global" world and integrated space. That which we call globalization corresponds, among other things, to the fact that difference in spatial location no longer coincides with important social, cultural, and political differences.

This aspect of globalization is usually understood to refer to the presence among us of foreigners. Migrants, foreign workers, refugees, the globalized world is a cosmopolitan world. Large cities of the Western world are inhabited by people of all origins and nationalities.[1] This demographic difference from what existed let us say fifty years ago, this diversity of origins that is clearly visible in the streets, on buses and subways, in stores, and in the range of products we find on the market, is certainly an important new phenomenon. The collapse of the difference between us and them, as simultaneously a difference between the inside and the outside, is most visible in this increase on the streets of large cities of foreigners, or of those whom, in North America, we call "visible minorities."

However, as is often the case, that which is "most visible" hides an even more fundamental transformation. The coincidence of spatial difference with social, political, and cultural differences is inseparable from the modern notion of "national territory" and from the international division of the world into exclusive territories. Globalization brings about the end of territories, to quote the title of a book by Bertrand Badie.[2] The "territory" is a form of political and social organization at both the domestic and international levels that has profoundly shaped the world in which we live, and which we take for granted as the normal order of things. We tend to think that territories always existed, and that they cannot not exist. Because the erosion of the territorial order is gradual and resembles more the slow ruin of a house than the sudden collapse of a building, we are mostly unaware that it is giving way to different forms of local and global political organization.

At first sight it may seem that the territory is nothing else than the physical space over which a political entity exercises its control. Given that any political organization has to exist in physical space, it seems that territories have always existed, that they are unavoidable. However, what is at stake, what is particular to territories as we understand them in relation to modern nation-states is a special type of political and social relation to physical space that did not always and everywhere exist. Moreover, even if it is true that every political organization exists in physical space, it does not follow that all need entertain a particular or privileged relation to any part of that space. For example, a club, a corporation, a guild, or any network of allegiance exists wherever and whenever two or more of its members meet.[3] Such political entities are not attached to any particular territory, to any particular region of physical space. Their operation is independent of "place"; it is constitutive of such political organizations, of the relations between their members, not the location where they happen to be. Though the position of its members relative to each other is fundamental to the functioning of such political entities, these relative positions are independent of any absolute location, contrary to what is conveyed by the idea of territory. It is therefore not true that all forms of political organization need to or even de facto do entertain a special relation to some portion of physical space.

Nomadic tribes usually recursively revisit the same regions or even the same specific places at regular times during the year. Often they do not claim exclusive use of these places with which they profess to entertain an important relation. Furthermore the intervening space that separates these "places" is often conceived of as free empty land that is nobody's in particular. It constitute a distance to be traveled, an open domain that may contain some other less important "places," but that belongs to none and to all.[4] This way of interacting with physical space, these repeated journeys through a limited range do not give rise to a territory in the modern sense of the term. Even though a special relationship with certain parts of physical space is involved, that way of interacting with the physical space a group "occupies" is completely different from what constitutes a territory. It is structured by what may be called the logic of place. The relation to space is organized around certain "places" or locations that have value and are sacred. Such "places" in a sense are not part of normal space; they are not continuous with it. They are qualitatively different. Sacred "places" are openings unto another world or witnesses to its irruption into this one. A space in which there are sacred places, a space that is structured by their presence, is, by definition, discontinuous and heterogeneous. Understood in this way, the course traveled by a nomadic tribe does not determine a territory so much as it describes a pilgrimage. It does not, that is, delimit a continuous space over which a group or political entity claims exclusive authority.

The territory of a modern nation-state, to the contrary, is isotropic and continuous. In many ways the territory exhibits the basic characteristics of Euclidian space. Apart from some rare historical examples that have usually proven unstable, the territory of a modern nation-state is continuous in the sense that each part of the territory is contiguous to another part of the territory.[5] Nothing separates one part of a state's territory from the next part. All portions or divisions of the territory touch each other, and going from one to the next does not entail any qualitative difference as far as being part of the territory is concerned. Territory is also exclusive. While the same place—for example, Jerusalem—can be sacred for more than one religion, Jerusalem cannot be part of the territory of both Israel and of the kingdom of Jordan. A choice must be made; a decision has to be reached. Political territories exclude each other just as do the parts of Euclidian space. Territorial space is also isotropic in the sense that no part of the territory is more or less part of the territory than any other. Alsace-Lorraine is just as much part of France as is either Touraine or Paris. There may be important qualitative differences between various regions of a country's territory concerning, for example, economic importance; climate; majority population; or linguistic, cultural, or culinary particularity; however, inasmuch as it is a part of national territory, every part of the national territory is as much a part of the territory as any other.

The political translation of these spatial aspects of territory is also typical of the state that occupies a particular territory. The monopoly of legitimate violence characteristic of modern states may be viewed as a form of political continuity. It indicates that political power exercises its rule without breaks or holes, without stops and new beginnings. The power of the modern state is not only supreme, in the sense that no other power within society can challenge it, but it is also sovereign. That is to say, in principle, at least, local powers can only exist as powers through the state's authority and permission. The formal equality of all citizens is the political equivalent of isotropy. Every citizen, just like every part of space, has an equal worth, every member of the state has the same value. Formal equality, it is often claimed, is not enough, which is certainly true. However, this criticism of formal equality, no matter how it is formulated, should not be understood as a form of rejection of formal equality. Rather, this criticism only makes sense against the background of an existing formal equality, of its promises and of what it implies. There is, however, a sense in which political equality can only be formal. While the parts of Euclidian space are really identical to each other, individual human beings and social agents are different from each other in many ways, along many dimensions. Formal equality is the political decision that for *certain* purposes, and in *certain* domains, *some* of these differences will not be taken into account. The criticism of formal equality reflects disagreements concerning the purposes for which significant differences between agents should be ignored and the domains in which equality will be taken for granted. That is to say, it is the expression of a debate concerning which differences are to be disregarded and in what domains. The modern state is the tool, the institution through which the "fiction" of equality is, in a sense and to some extent, made "real," but only within a certain territory and more so for those who entertain with that territory a particular relationship of "belonging."

This particular relationship of belonging is primarily legal in the form of citizenship. That is a political characteristic that is usually determined in relation to space, that is, by the place of birth. The particular relationship of belonging also has a cultural dimension that may enter into contradiction with and sometime even overrule the spatial determination of citizenship. Those who share the same culture are often understood to "belong" to the same territory. Citizenship will thus more easily be granted to "foreigners" who share the same language or belong to the same ethnic group as most nationals. Inversely, those who occupy the same territory are made to share the same culture, understood in a wide sense. This can be done through the expulsion or destruction of minority populations as Heather Rae documented in *State Identities and the Homogenisation of People*.[6] It can also be, and historically was most often, done through assimilation, education, and repression of minority languages. The populations of modern nation-states were not originally homogeneous but were "made homogeneous" through explicit state policies. Like equality, homogeneity is also a "fiction" in the sense that there are always many dimensions along which a population is heterogeneous, and as in the case of equality there is always a choice of the dimension(s) along which people are made to be homogeneous—for example, religious, linguistic, ethnic, or shared culture in a more specific sense. As in the case of formal equality, formal homogeneity overlooks many important differences between members of the population—for example, differences in income and education, which are taken not to be politically significant.

In spite of the fact that a territory corresponds to the domain where a state exercises an exclusive jurisdiction, territory also is, and perhaps primarily, an international institution. At the international level the territorial order is characterized by the existence of a plurality of mutually exclusive territories.

Territories determine a certain type of relation between states based on the existence of hard borders delimiting exclusive portions of political space. States claim exclusive jurisdiction over certain areas as if this were something that essentially proceeded from their own power and sovereignty, but borders are only real and meaningful to the extent that they are recognized by other states. One of the characteristics of the territorial order is that it implies the existence of a plurality of states that are formally equal in the sense that they recognize each other's exclusive sovereignty over a certain portion of space. Each state's territory, its monopoly of legitimate violence over that territory, only exists to the extent that other states recognize it, agree to it. Outside of one state's territory exist other territories, the territories of other states that have the same status and characteristics. This plurality is fundamental. Unlike the fluctuating boundaries of an empire surrounded by empty land and roaming barbarians that determine the limit of the state viewed as a sanctuary in a largely unknown and hostile world, borders separate from each other states that are formally equal and that constitute a community of spatially exclusive political entities.

This community of territories corresponds to a particular institution of the friend/foe dichotomy that Carl Schmitt posits as fundamental to politics. The central characteristic of the modern European state, according to Schmitt, is that the friend-enemy distinction coincides with the separation between the inside and the outside of the state. This allotment of enmity and friendship is realized through the equality and homogeneity of citizens, on the one hand, and the exclusive and continuous dimension of territory, on the other. Outside of the territorial state live not only "others" but also enemies. Not that all "others" are enemies, or that all those who live outside are enemies. Rather, it is that those who live inside are friends; among them, resorting to violence is illegitimate. Conflicts should be resolved by appealing to and by submitting to the arbitration of a third party. Enemies, says Schmitt, are others with whom it is possible to have conflicts that cannot be resolved by appealing to either shared rules or the decision of an agreed-upon arbitrator.[7] Schmitt has been mainly interested in the relation a state entertains with its enemies and with what that entails concerning the nature of sovereign power. However, the coincidence of the friend/foe distinction with the spatial limit of the state also implies a certain type of relation between "friends"—that is to say, between those who live together.

The state's monopoly of legitimate violence and the imposition of the rule of law are only one aspect of the expulsion of enemies outside the borders of the state. Social justice adds another dimension to the requirement of equality, one that is based on the solidarity of those who "belong together." Since the end of the Second World War the development of the welfare state has been the central means of preventing the reappearance of enemies within the state. It has been both the way in which citizens have been made friends and the symbol that they are. Social justice has been the custodian of a central aspect of the territorial order, the absence of enemies within the space over which the state exercises its jurisdiction. That has been fundamental to the state's capacity of maintaining its monopoly of legitimate violence.

Social justice as it has been implemented through the welfare state rests on indirect reciprocity. This reciprocity is indirect first of all because it is not realized directly in the relation of agents to each other, but arises through the operation of a center that redistributes resources. It is also indirect because it is deferred. "Reciprocity," properly named—that is to say, the other half of the reciprocal relation—is pushed back in time, either until it is needed, in the case of those who give, or until it can be done, in the case of those who receive. Indirect and deferred reciprocity is a kind of promise, and the modern state has been the guardian of that promise in the name of all its citizens.

◆　◆　◆

"Others," "enemies" are now among us. That is to say, we cannot anymore take it for granted that the space that we inhabit together is free from individuals or groups who feel they can legitimately resort to violence. We call them terrorists. The "war against terrorism" is a sign of the disappearance of the territorial order, of the disappearance of the state's monopoly of legitimate violence, and of the disappearance of wars as we used to know them. War as we have come to understand it is something that takes place between nations, sovereign states, or, in the form of civil war, it is a conflict that pitches against each other within a state, factions that vie for the monopoly of legitimate violence. War in that sense has a beginning and an end. There are winners and losers, and when the war is over peace returns. There are many signs that such wars are disappearing, that this type of violent confrontation is being replaced by what Frédéric Gros calls "*états de violence*," that is to say, "states of violence," where the word "state" is to be understood in the same way as it is in "state of affairs."[8] Ann Hironaka in *Neverending Wars* shows that since 1944, both the number and the duration of civil wars have grown dramatically; what has grown even more dramatically is the number of ongoing civil conflicts, indicating that hostilities tend to last longer and longer. In fact, these extremely long civil wars are not exactly "civil wars" anymore, they are not simply conflicts whose goal is the seizure of the state's power and that come to an end when that is done. Take, for example, the case of Afghanistan. The civil war started in 1978; the following year the country was invaded by the USSR. The Russian occupation lasted ten years, during which fighting never stopped; after the Russians departed the civil war continued. Even once the Taliban captured Kabul and gained recognition as the Afghan regime by the international community, fighting did not end, and in some parts of the country war raged on until 2001. Then once again Afghanistan was invaded, this time by the Americans in the hope of capturing Bin Laden and destroying Al-Qaeda. Today Germany, France, Canada, England, Italy, Poland, and the United States all have soldiers there, and the North Atlantic Treaty Organization (NATO) is asking its member states to make a long-term commitment of troops. Since 1978 more than thirty years have gone by; that is long enough for an individual to be born, to become an adult, to have children, and to die—all this within the duration of a war. There is a sense in which this is not war anymore, but a state of violence. That is to say, violence in such situations is not a means to a certain end, a means that will be discarded once that end has been reached. It does not correspond to a moment of decision but constitutes a permanent state of affairs.

There are many places in the world today that seem to have fallen into such states of violence—for example, Palestine, Iraq, Afghanistan, Somalia, Congo, and Colombia to name but a few. These states of violence are not wars, civil or otherwise; they are not war as we used to know it, but violence as a way of life, as a mode of existence, not only for certain individuals, like mercenaries or soldiers, but for entire regions. In fact, these states of violence often do not concern whole states or countries but are limited to particular areas, confined to parts only of a state's territory. Around them life continues more or less as usual. These enclaves of violence sometimes have an important economic role or strategic value, and many different types of agents can participate in the hostile relations that characterize them: government troops (and more or less official paramilitary units), rebel forces, private security companies, local warlords, tribal combatants, troops from neighboring countries, and members of international peacekeeping forces. This incomplete list brings out two important features of states of violence. First, their internationalization: very rarely are the participants, the parties to the conflict, limited to citizens of one state only; most of the time foreigners play an important role in the evolution and lengthening of the struggle.[9] Second is the presence of nonstate actors, rebel troops, of course, but also private security companies, the corporations that hire them, and organized crime. In fact, it is often difficult to distinguish between political conflict and large-scale criminal activities as insurgents turn to various forms of illegal activities to fund their operation. When that happens winning often stops being the goal anymore. The struggle itself becomes a form of economic enterprise. Violence is a means of monopolizing, for example, the profits of drug production, or diamond trade, or smuggling. The conflict thus gets integrated into the world economy. Simultaneously this localized fighting, as long as it does not get out of hand, can serve the purposes of certain groups within the state and help them maintain their hold on power. When such is the case the continuation of the conflict may be in the interest of all the parties involved.

States of violence are holes of lawlessness and violence in the tissue of international relations and in the territory of each state involved. These "holes" in the national territory and in the international territorial order may, however, be perfectly well integrated in the world economy. What this means is that there is a sense in which these conflicts are not accidents and anomalies. Rather, they represent the new face of the world order. The expression "war against terrorism" indicates that major powers have now accepted this transformation of the international scene. Declaring war against terrorism is not an official, legal international act. It does not create any particular legal liabilities or responsibilities. The Americans do not recognize terrorists as enemy combatants and do not extend to them the protection of the Geneva Convention. They refuse to be bound by the rules of international law with regard to them. They kidnap people in various countries, either friendly or hostile, and deliver them to other countries where torture is practiced. That is to say, they exploit to their advantage the existence elsewhere of different sets of rule, somewhat in the way multinational corporations take advantage of legal and economic opportunities in different countries. They violate the air space of independent states and bomb terrorist installations (or what they think are such) anywhere in the world. It would be false to think that only Americans do this. France, England, Israel, Russia—any country that has the power to intervene outside its borders and has reasons to believe it should, does so.

The war against terrorism does not recognize the structure of the international community as made up of independent nations separated by hard borders. The space in which this "war" takes place is not that of territories. It is not made up of parts that are exclusive of each other, and it is not homogeneous or isotropic. Rather, it is structured by something that resembles more the logic of place. The world is now divided into "hot spots" of violence and "cool spots" of relative peace and order. The primary goal of the international politics of major states is not to bring peace to these "hot spots," but to maintain certain particularly valuable areas as sanctuaries that are protected from violence.

The organization of space into sanctuaries and their exterior has a fractal quality. That is to say, the space in which we live now has the same type of structure or shape at different levels or scales that can be understood either in terms of physical distance or of social and cultural proximity. For example, at a smaller level or scale of resolution we find the green zone in Baghdad where a relative security is maintained compared to the rest of the city. At a much larger level, the American fortress is defended by biometric methods of identification, strict rules concerning immigration and entrance, and an ever-growing quantity of personal data on foreign nationals coming to the United States, or even simply flying over it.[10] At an intermediary level between these two extremes, we have the wall that Israel has built to defend itself from suicide bombers, or the thousands of kilometers of fence that run along the border between the United States and Mexico in the hope of keeping out illegal immigrants. At the microlevel we find walled-in housing complexes defended by private guards in the middle of supposedly policed cities, protected neighborhoods where one can only enter if he or she lives there or can state his or her business. This is not the territorial order anymore, this is not a space that is continuous, isotropic, and whose parts are exclusive of each other. Sanctuaries can be embedded in each other. The edges of these zones of relative peace and security are not marked by borders in the classical sense: imaginary lines that exist because and inasmuch as they are recognized by the community of nations. It is not an international agreement that determines where the boundaries of these safe spaces will be, but the relative strength of the adversaries. In fact, these protections, fortified walls, and security checks are there because borders do not function anymore. Enemies cannot be identified on the basis of their passport; borders are not an adequate tool to keep them out.

This disappearance of territory goes hand in hand with the disappearance of equality that was characteristic of the territorial order. "Others" are different from "us." They do not belong here, and the same rules and protections should not be extended to them. There is nothing particularly new about this. It has always been the case that foreigners were subjected to different regulations. The territorial order provided a rational for this distinction and simultaneously a procedure that was both simple and public to determine who is subjected to what rule. In consequence, it was possible to maintain the equality of "us," because it was clear who was "us" and who was "them," and even, in a sense and to some extent, to maintain the equality of "them." Enemies are now among us. They are hidden, anywhere and everywhere, and they can be anyone. This means that at any time, on the basis of a suspicion, the rule of law can be suspended in relation to some unknown individual, an individual who, until he or she was "discovered," was exactly like everyone else—that nothing evident distinguished from any one of "us." Enemies, unlike criminals, are not arrested after the fact or presumed innocent; they have to be stopped before they act. It is the hostile intentions that they harbor that make them enemies, rather than any action they may have yet committed. With the disappearance of the territory there is no simple and public procedure that allows us to make the distinction between friends and enemies. We are in consequence already beginning to get accustomed to the fact that we are not all treated equally, on the basis of suspicions, that appear at times justified and at others arbitrary. It should be remembered that suspicion is the very opposite of the rule of law according to which you can only be sentenced for a crime you have committed, against a law that is public, and where the penalty is proportioned to the offense. Enemies suspected of evil designs are not properly sentenced to anything or for anything they have done. They are rendered unable to harm anyone before they can act. The objective pursued is not justice, proportion between the offense and the punishment, but expediency, at the price of some unfortunate mistakes, as shows the death of Jean-Charles de Menezes.[11] Suspicion is to the rule of law what a preemptive strike is to a declaration of war.

In consequence, the war against terror cannot have any clear end in time. There is no official act that can restore peace, that can signify that this war is over and that we can from now on live in peace. Danger may be viewed to be more or less great at different times; acts of terrorism may become more or less frequent. That is to say, the safety of the sanctuary can be ensured with a greater or lesser success. There can be lulls in the struggle and long periods of calm. This, however, is not a "war" that can be won, but is a war that can be lost. The war against terror constitutes a "state of violence," and it is inseparable from the existence of other states of violence. It is, in other words, an expression of the way in which violent conflicts have become institutionalized in the globalized world. It cannot be won, but it can disappear if we succeed in reducing the number and the extent of states of violence, in institutionalizing in a different way violent conflicts. It can be lost because sanctuaries can become smaller, more unequal, and all spend ever more resources on defending themselves.[12]

Conclusion

Ethics, Economics, and the State

his book began with economics; it ends with politics. It opened with
an analysis of scarcity as a means of protection against violence, while
its last chapter is on political violence in the age of globalization. This
end, however, brings us back to the beginning. As I have tried to argue elsewhere, modern politics as we have understood it since the seventeenth century, the theory and practice of the modern state as holder of the monopoly
of legitimate violence, is rooted in the institution of scarcity,[1] which results
from a transformation of the sacred initiated by Christian Revelation. The
form that political violence takes in the modern world is inseparable from
the new ecology of moral relations characteristic of scarcity. This, however, is
not a static phenomenon, but a dynamic process. The ongoing globalization
of the economy is leading to a profound transformation of the modern state,
one that is often analyzed in terms of withdrawal or retreat on the part of
states that are seen as bowing to market forces.[2] Such analyses are not incorrect, but the phenomena we are witnessing go deeper: states are not simply
giving up, yielding to the forces of the market. They are not on the verge of
disappearing, but are engaged in a process of transformation that could lead
to the end of politics as we have hitherto understood it; this could lead to
new forms of the friend-foe relationship, but not to its disappearance.

At this juncture, ethics is often called upon to fill the gap opened by what is seen as the failure of politics to resist the dictates of the financial world. Ethics is viewed as a discipline that can constrain what politicians should be allowed to do and provide alternatives to economic answers crudely presented in terms of cost-benefit analysis. Beyond this image of it as a bulwark against the excesses of economic power, ethics sometimes appears as a kind of universal savior that allows us to find our way in a maze of issues as different as biomedical choices, relationships between men and women, technological risks, environmental protection, sexual orientation, international relations, and business transactions. It seems that there is no activity (assistance ethics), discipline (engineering ethics), object (robot ethics), issue (feminist ethics), or approach (Darwinian ethics) to which the word "ethics" cannot be added to create a new discipline. This recent universal claim to knowledge or, perhaps better, the service proposal of ethics in so many different domains is at first sight surprising.

Throughout the twentieth century, the dominant mood among professional philosophers was "skepticism in ethics." This was not only the suspicion but also the broadly trumpeted claim that ethics is not really knowledge, that it does not correspond to a coherent body of true, justified statements about existing objects. Good and bad, it was argued, are strange, "exotic" properties that do not belong to the natural furniture of the world. There are no natural characteristics of objects or events that make them either good or bad, and these terms also do not correspond to independent entities that exist as such. Rather, good and bad reflect the prejudices and preferences of agents, or perhaps they track some natural properties, such as pleasure and pain. In any case, it follows that statements about good and evil do not have any truth value.

So, what has happened? How did ethics, which was generally assumed not to be knowledge by those who claimed to be specialists of the discipline, gain prominence and authority in so many domains? One possible answer is that the epistemic impotence of ethics is a major factor in its recent success. For example, J. L. Mackie and B. Williams both argued, in different ways, that ethics is a form of critical evaluation that helps us decide what we want to do through a reflexive process of judgment based on information from the best sources of knowledge that we have about the issue at hand.[3] From this point of view, the epistemic limitations of ethics are not an obstacle, but precisely what make it such an excellent tool for approaching so many different domains. Because ethics has given up its claim to truth, its claim to constitute an independent unified body of knowledge, there is no area of human activity to which it may not pretend to contribute as a form of critical reflection. In consequence, rather than a repository of established truths, today's applied ethics should be understood as exercises in democratic discussion about issues as different as medical practice, scientific research, and policy decisions.

This said, the idea that ethics is essentially second-order reflection upon already existing forms of knowledge is perhaps not as recent a phenomenon as we may be tempted to think. Numerous authors have argued that classical moral philosophy had very little to say concerning what is usually called first-order ethics, that is, about what one should do in different situations and circumstances.[4] On the questions of whether I should repay a loan, keep my promises, or help those who are in danger, classical moral philosophy rarely innovated and generally took for granted whatever was the received opinion of the day. The central problem that moral philosophy sought to resolve was not: what should I do? The answer to that question was assumed to be known and to be provided either by religion or by conventional opinions concerning what is right and wrong. Classical moral philosophy focused its attention on the question of justification.[5] The question was not "what should I do?" but "why should I do it?" What are the source, nature, and origin of the moral obligation? In what sense is it binding?

In *The Invention of Autonomy*, Schneewind argues that in the seventeenth and eighteenth centuries there appeared a new form of moral philosophy that challenged the existing conception of morality as obedience. "The conception of morality as self-governance provides a conceptual framework for a social space in which we may each rightly claim to direct our own actions without interference from the state, the church, neighbors, or those claiming to be better than we. The older conception of morality as obedience did not have these implications."[6]

This freedom from interference is the main point of morality as self-governance, as its name indicates. What is essential is not its content, which may be the same as that of older forms of morality, but the way in which obligations relate to individual agents: directly rather than through the mediation of institutions or other individuals. Hence the central place that reflection upon the nature and source of the "internal ought," as Steven Darwall calls it,[7] occupied in classical moral philosophy. Like present-day applied ethics, classical moral philosophy was therefore already to a large extent a form of "metaknowledge," reflection upon a body of knowledge it had received from another source. From the beginning, modern moral philosophy and ethics have been second-order reflections on already existing social knowledge that is, as Schneewind and many others have recognized, closely related to the rise of the modern state and market economy. They suggest that it is the modern state that made the morality of self-governance possible.

On Moral Obligation

In his *Enquiry Concerning Political Justice* (1793), William Godwin claimed that if, for example, a fire broke out in the palace of the bishop of Cambray and one had the choice between saving either Fénélon or his chambermaid, because circumstances were such that only one could be saved, the rational and moral thing to do would be to save Fénélon given his greater contribution to human happiness through his writing, or, if you prefer, because of his greater social utility. Godwin added that this would still be the case even if the chambermaid happened to be one's wife or mother. In later editions, after his marriage to Mary Wollstonecraft, author of *A Vindication of the Rights of Woman* (1792), Godwin changed the example from a chambermaid to a valet, perhaps to drive home the point that the argument was strictly about social utility and to avoid any suggestion that he thought men were worth more than women. This is a rather (in)famous example that is usually considered as damning for utilitarians who consider that social utility constitutes the ultimate source of all moral values.

However, what kind of response might we get from one who argues that all moral obligations derive from agreement among free rational and equal agents? More precisely, if one claims that moral rules of behavior are only those that could be agreed to by a notional community of free and equal rational agents, could one argue that no rational agent would agree to such a rule? Why, asks the utilitarian, would rational agents object that in cases where all cannot be helped, priority should be given to those who contribute more to the general welfare? Is it not the only rational rule to adopt? The contractarian, they would argue, is in this instance not rejecting the rule; he or she is simply making an exception for his or her mother, an exception that he or she would perhaps not make in favor of a different chambermaid. In this case, the choice simply reflects a strong preference, an emotional attachment, but there is no properly moral reason that justifies this preference. The contractarian, or so argues the utilitarian, has no real moral argument to support his or her reticence and only shrinks from the, in this case, unfortunate consequences of a general rule that he or she has no particular reason to reject.

To this a contractarian may well respond that moral theory should be designed for real human beings. It is not a set of prescriptions that only abstract, purely rational agents can follow. Given their psychology and biology, humans will not agree to moral principles that lead to such "unnatural" consequences. Interestingly enough, present-day utilitarians more or less agree—in other words, they come to the same conclusion, as Godwin did later in life. They argue that, given the way we are made, transgressing the rule that demands that we show gratitude to those who have helped us in the past, especially to our parents, leads to greater disutility than whatever advantage may come from saving a "superior person."[8] Godwin's paradox has been happily resolved.

This strategic retreat from the more outrageous consequences of their ethical principles on the part of the two main currents of modern ethics is revealing. Usually when scientific knowledge concerning, say, heat or microbial infection or the movement of the earth clashes with everyday opinions, it ultimately displaces them. After a while we start using the more coherent scientific image of the world to guide our actions. Here, the opposite happens. Advocates of the two leading approaches in contemporary ethics seek accommodation. They eschew ascertaining the superiority of their knowledge of ethics over everyday beliefs. Both utilitarians and contractarians wish to retain their preferred scheme of justification and our common way of behaving. This attitude tends to confirm what was argued earlier, namely, that in classical ethics providing justification is more important than determining what is the right action. Why is justification so important?

Godwin's original formulation assumes that the individual faced with the dilemma is not bound by any particular duty to help either Fénélon or his chambermaid, as a valet would be to help his master or a husband to help his wife. Between the individuals involved, there are no reciprocal obligations of solidarity. The further precision concerning the identity of the valet/ chambermaid emphasizes that even if any such duty exists, either it is not properly moral or, if it is moral, it is overruled by the obligation to maximize utility. Yet if it is the case that I am not attached in any way to either one or the other, if I do not have any prior obligation to any of them, why should I bother? Why should I risk my life and enter the flaming palace? What is the origin of that obligation?

Godwin does not directly ask that question, but he does answer it. What obliges one to intervene is the duty to maximize utility. That is why, if one is forced to choose between two persons in danger, one must settle for whomever's survival brings the greatest utility. It is the only choice that is consistent with the reason that obliges one to provide help if one can. The contractarian also has an answer to that question. Given that anyone can (and will) need help at some time, rational individuals will reject a universal rule that dispenses them (and all others) from the duty to help those who are in need, for that would leave everyone helpless when need strikes. The only rule they can accept is one that obliges them to help to the extent that they can. However, because the universal agreement postulated by this conclusion presupposes the equal value of all human life, it entails nothing concerning whom to choose, should choice prove necessary. Furthermore, given that a universal agreement constitutes the basis of the moral obligation to help, it is hard for a contractarian to provide a truly moral justification for his or her preference for saving his or her mother. Kantian contractualism, just like utilitarianism, assumes that there are no prior obligations between the agents involved and suggests that if ever there are any, those obligations would not be properly moral. Remember that the contractarian's objection to Goodwin's recommendation rested on the issue of feasibility—human beings will simply not do that—rather than a question of morality. For both types of theory, if there are reciprocal obligations that attach particular individuals to one another, they are bothersome and obstacles to the exercise of true morality.

In a traditional society, all interactions among agents are constrained by reciprocal obligations of solidarity that shape each individual's behavior toward different individuals and groups. The question "how should I act toward those to whom I am not attached by reciprocal obligations?" rarely arises. When it does arise, it is usually not as a moral question. Toward those to whom I owe nothing, I owe nothing, precisely. That is to say, I can act toward them as I wish, or as I can. Rules of conduct do not apply to our relationships. I can exploit them, reduce them into slavery, destroy them, or befriend them. In consequence, relationships with strangers, that is, with those who are exterior to my network of reciprocal obligations, are dangerous because they can always veer to violence. The best way to prevent that, if it is what I wish, is to include them in my network of positive reciprocity, through the magic of the gift or of hospitality, and thus to bind them with reciprocal obligations. Otherwise, violence—negative reciprocity—threatens to put a rapid end to all uncertainty concerning the Other's future behavior. In a society structured by networks of reciprocal obligations, the question of how to act toward those to whom we owe nothing does not usually arise. When it does, it is not so much answered as the conditions that allow it to appear are removed. Encounters with strangers either lead to violence, or the Other is included in the network of reciprocal obligations. In either case, the question is neither properly raised nor answered: recurring complex interactions with those to whom we do not owe anything are ruled out.

To the contrary, modern ethics—the morality of self-governance that centers on the issue of obligation—seems entirely dedicated to answering that question. Modern moral philosophy seeks to provide rules of conduct for those who do not owe anything to one another. It answers the question: how should those who are unattached by reciprocal obligations act toward one another? Hence the importance of the question of justification: Why do we owe anything to those to whom we owe nothing? Why do we have any duties toward them? Such is the fundamental question that modern ethics needs to answer. What has happened to suddenly make central a problem that was previously nonexistent?

Scarcity and Obligation

In fact, the modern morality of self-governance does not simply seek to provide rules of conduct for those who owe nothing to one another, but to provide rules that apply equally to those who do and to those who do not owe anything to one another. That is to say, its goal is to determine universal rules of conduct, rules that apply to everyone, that are indifferent to the presence or absence of any prior obligations among the agents whose interaction they regulate. That is why, as we will presently see, they often clash with traditional obligations of solidarity. The origin of such conflicts is not so much that the content of the obligation is different but that its extension is greater.

In "The Ambivalence of Scarcity" I defined scarcity as the result of the progressive abandonment of traditional reciprocal rules of solidarity. Ethics in this context appears as filling the gap, as providing new rules to replace those that have been abandoned. However, as we have just seen, it does more than that. As Godwin's infamous Fénélon example indicates, the morality of self-governance sometimes directly contradicts the recommendations of traditional obligation. Yet the basis of that contradiction is not in the abstract content of the rule itself, "help those who are in danger," but in its extension and justification: who should help whom and why? Ethics is thus part of the process through which reciprocal rules of solidarity are discarded. It is characterized by the introduction of a new, different concept of obligation that makes possible a morality of self-governance about which arises the question of justification, which did not previously exist.

Reciprocal obligations of solidarity are inseparable from duties of hostility, not only because duties to help include obligations to defend and to protect but also because reciprocal obligations distinguish those to whom we owe something from those to whom we do not. Hostility and solidarity in this context are two sides of the same coin. Because of the close link between obligations of solidarity and violence, failure to fulfill one's obligation tends to be seen as an act of aggression toward those one should help. Reciprocal obligations of solidarity police themselves in consequence: transgressions are punished because they constitute a threat to the whole group, and they are generally punishable because traditional obligations clearly determine who owes what to whom—in other words, they clearly determine when a transgression has occurred, who has committed it, and who is the victim. In such a situation the question of justification does not arise. "Why should I honor my obligations?" is a question that receives a very straightforward answer in terms of social sanctions and punishments. The question of justification does not arise for another reason. Having this or that obligation is simply part of who I am as a member of this family, this clan, or this tribe. In order for traditional obligation to be abandoned and scarcity instituted, this close connection had to be severed; the link between solidarity and violence had to be, if not broken, at least transformed and relaxed. The modern concept of moral obligation sprang from this separation, and with it the relentless question of justification.

The fundamental characteristic of modern moral obligation that separates it from traditional obligations of solidarity is that it is free. At first sight this may seem surprising since if I have a moral obligation or duty—for example, to be truthful—then by definition I am not free but obliged. Moral obligation is nonetheless free, to begin with, in the sense of gratuitous, because it is not reciprocal. If we have a moral obligation to be benevolent or truthful toward others, then this duty does not depend on them being benevolent or truthful in return. Modern moral obligation is, as Kant said, categorical. It is a duty whose fulfillment neither requires nor brings forth a further obligation that unites the beneficiary to the benefactor. Otherwise, as Kant also argued, the action would not be truly moral because it would be done out of interest conditional on the other reciprocating. A benevolent person may well expect to be treated kindly in return, but that is not the reason why he or she is benevolent. This absence of reciprocity, freedom as gratuitousness, is the first characteristic that distinguishes modern moral obligation from traditional reciprocal solidarity obligation. This entails that modern moral obligations extend to everyone. While reciprocal obligations of solidarity are nominal, in the sense that they apply to identifiable persons who satisfy particular conditions, modern moral obligations, in consequence of their gratuity, fulfill the two classical requirements of universality and anonymity.

Modern moral obligations are free in yet another sense that marks them as profoundly different from traditional reciprocal obligations: they cannot be enforced. Not only is it the case, at least in liberal societies, that moral obligations are beyond the state's authority: in such societies morality cannot and should not be made law. There is also a sense that when moral rules are enforced by the state or by some other coercive authority, they no longer constitute strictly moral obligations. Moral obligations cannot be properly enforced. It is part of our conception of morality as self-governance that moral obligations are free in the sense that individuals are at liberty to not fulfill the obligations that they have the duty to fulfill. This is paradoxical inasmuch as it is also part of the concept of obligation that if you have an obligation to do something you are not free not to do it. Yet an obligation is strictly moral, rather than legal, if one has the freedom to not fulfill it. Hence the centrality of the question of justification; "why should I fulfil my obligations?" is a question that arises only when I am at liberty not to fulfill them. The modern morality of self-governance is characterized by the fact that I am not free from the obligation, in the sense that I have that obligation, but that I nonetheless retain the freedom to not fulfill it. What is the meaning of this paradoxical freedom that is characteristic of modern morality?

Of Economic Exchange and Scarcity

One of the defining characteristics of modern economic exchange, interestingly but not surprisingly given the above analysis of scarcity, is that it takes place between agents who are not attached by reciprocal obligations of solidarity.[9] When Adam Smith argues at the beginning of *The Wealth of Nations* that it is not from the benevolence of the butcher, the baker, or the brewer that we should expect to receive our dinner, but from the attention these merchants give to their own interest, he implicitly assumes that the reader is neither the son nor the wife nor aging mother of the butcher, baker, or brewer. He assumes in short that no obligation of solidarity binds the parties together. Such obligations, as anthropologists are well aware, constitute obstacles to the rise of a modern market economy.[10] Economic exchange involves free, independent agents, and the "laws of economics" will apply only if agents are free and independent. Furthermore, as Mark Anspach has argued, unlike ceremonial exchange, which we find in traditional societies, modern economic exchange does not create any new obligations to reciprocate. Once I have paid the baker for the bread or the brewer for the beer I have received, I do not owe him or her anything, and he or she does not owe me anything either.[11]

Economic exchange is an instance of interaction between agents who are not bound by reciprocal obligation. It also constitutes a rule of behavior between agents who do not owe anything to each other, not in the sense of an explicitly formulated rule but in the sense of a regularity of behavior, like in the expression "as a rule this is what people do." The particularity of economic exchange, in comparison with disciplines such as ethics, law, and even economic science, which propose explicit rules of behavior, is that exchange takes the rule of the interaction from the interaction itself. "Whoever," says Adam Smith, "offers to another a bargain of any kind proposes to do this. Give me that which I want, and you shall have this which you want, is the meaning of every such offer; and it is in this manner that we obtain from one another the far greater part of those good offices which we stand in need of."[12] According to Adam Smith, barter—in other words, exchange—regulates itself. It is not subject to any external rule. Its "rule" flows from each agent's regard for his or her own self-interest. Given that, if agents are free and independent, no one would voluntarily enter into such a transaction unless it satisfied the condition that what is to be received is worth at least what is to be given, the rule is by definition fair, in that once the deal is done none of the parties can have a legitimate claim against the other. In consequence, this regularity of behavior can also constitute a rule in the normative sense of the word. Economics teaches us that a deal is fair to the extent that it is self-regulating and that if it were not fair it could not be self-regulating. The two characteristics are inseparable. Economic exchanges are self-regulating only if they are fair, and they are fair only if they are self-regulating. They are fair only if they are exchanges in which free, independent agents would voluntarily engage. Further, this rule of fairness is the only one possible if the rule is to be taken from the relation itself.

Deception, force, and fraud cannot constitute rules that emerge from the relation itself because by definition they negate the relation that they pretend to regulate. None of these strategies can be applied recursively between agents who are free to enter or exit the relation—for example, agents who dare to not be attached by reciprocal obligations of solidarity. One may, for example, once again lend money to a member of one's family who regularly fails to reimburse, but one will not do this for a stranger, for someone to whom one is related only through the interaction that consists in lending money. Deception or fraud cannot become a rule in situations of independence and equality, but only exceptions that exclude all prospects of further relations.[13] If circumstances bind you to a unique supplier or if he or she enjoys a de facto monopoly, then unequal exchange, unfairness, can become a rule in the sense of the regular outcome of the interaction, but it is an exogenous rule, imposed from the outside on the exchange relation. The fairness of exchange will emerge spontaneously only if agents are free and independent. Traditional reciprocal obligations of solidarity and hostility are obstacles to this freedom and independence, but they are not the only obstacles possible, and any circumstances that limit the freedom and independence of agents will tend to lead to unequal exchanges.

On Benevolence

> But man has almost constant occasion for the help of his brethren, and it is in vain for him to expect it from their benevolence only. He will be more likely to prevail if he can interest their self-love in his favor, and show them that it is for their own advantage to do for him what he requires of them.[14]

The above quotation and the passage that immediately follows in Adam Smith's *Wealth of Nations*, according to which it is not from the benevolence of the butcher, baker, or brewer that we should expect our dinner, but from their regard to their self-interest, are usually taken to indicate his rejection of the importance of benevolence, and by extension of virtue and morality in general in economic affairs, and to indicate that the self-regulating rule of exchange is sufficient to order the economic world. This apparent rejection of morality has given rise to what has been called the "Adam Smith problem," which is to reconcile the older author of *The Wealth of Nations* with the younger author of *The Theory of Moral Sentiments*. Note, however, that Adam Smith writes that "it is in vain for him to expect it from their benevolence *only*." The implication of that little word, "only," is that benevolence does not constitute a *sufficient condition*; it may nonetheless be the case that it is a *necessary condition* if we are to receive from others the help that we need. When he adds that it is from the merchants' regard to their self-interest that we should expect our dinner, Adam Smith assumes that the butcher's, baker's, and brewer's self-interest will not incite them to rob us, kill us, or provide us with some inedible or dangerous product. Otherwise it would not be dinner we should expect from the merchant's self-interest but violence, fraud, and deception. Benevolence, understood as a minimal disposition toward the good of others, as the absence of enmity, may very well be necessary if we are to expect our dinner, rather than something else, from the merchants' regard for their own self-interest.

As Daniel Finn has powerfully argued, in order for the market to exist, agents must abstain from certain abusive forms of behavior in interactions with one another; otherwise market relations simply become impossible.[15] Interestingly enough, these forms of behavior—violence, fraud, and deception—which, according to Finn, are detrimental to the proper functioning of market relations and need to be eschewed in order for a modern economy to arise and flourish, are precisely those that, according to Marshal Sahlins, in traditional societies characterize exchanges that sometimes take place between agents who are not bound by reciprocal obligations.[16] It is not in all circumstances that exchange between agents who do not owe anything to each other will actually give rise to abundance and economic growth, that is to say, be beneficial to all parties, rather than lead to violence and fraud. Self-regulating as it may be, the rule of exchange can take root only in a social environment where certain conditions are satisfied. As suggested by Adam Smith, benevolence may be taken as a first approximation of what these conditions are.

Benevolence, as understood by Adam Smith, has the typical characteristics of modern moral obligations. Taken as an obligation it is, unlike reciprocal obligations, categorical, and its scope is potentially unlimited. Benevolence should be extended to all, rather than limited to those whom we have reason to believe will reciprocate, and of course it is free in the sense that, unlike the case with reciprocal obligations of solidarity, failing to be benevolent does not immediately constitute a punishable transgression. Alternatively, benevolence can be considered as a virtue. Like generosity, courage, or honesty, benevolence so understood is a disposition toward certain desirable, commendable forms of behavior, and though the behavior itself may well be obligatory, we are not obliged to have the disposition as such—even if there is a sense in which we all ought to be virtuous. However, whether it is a duty or virtue, benevolence is in any case unconditional and its scope unlimited. Though benevolence understood either as a virtue or as a duty is, according to Adam Smith, insufficient to provide the help we constantly need from one another, minimal benevolence is nonetheless indispensable to the transformation of self-interest into public benefit. Without it, or something like it, we would look in vain to the butcher's self-interest for our dinner and be back in the Hobbesian state of nature.

The Moral Authority of the State

If benevolence or the modern morality of self-governance is so important to the success of a society structured by scarcity, what makes it possible? What explains the rise of these paradoxically free obligations? The answer is the modern state, a state defined as the holder of the monopoly of legitimate violence over a given territory. We have come to consider the distinction between a properly moral and a merely political authority as fundamental, and that distinction is profoundly anchored in the modern conception of moral obligation as strictly unenforceable. A moral authority simply declares what is right and what is wrong. Morality is viewed as constituting its own authority. There is an "internal ought," a feeling of obligation that guides us toward certain actions and away from others. Failing to abide by the recommendations of morality may entail a sanction, but this sanction is either "not of this world" or takes the form of social pressure. Failure to fulfill one's moral obligation—for example, by lying, not honoring one's promise, or being ungrateful—does not as such constitute a legally punishable offense. Rather, as argued earlier, moral obligation is free, and the very morality of the obligation is understood to rest on that freedom.

In contrast, we consider that political authority can enforce its decisions, though it is perhaps unable to ground them by itself—in other words, though it may lack the properly moral authority to justify the decisions it enforces. This way of understanding the relation between moral and political authority is, however, misleading. Clearly the most important rule that a modern state needs to enforce in order to maintain itself is its own distinction between good and bad violence, the distinction between illegitimate violence and legitimate use of force. A state that fails to do this does not have the monopoly of legitimate use of force that we deem to be its defining characteristic. It is a failed state. Yet in order for a state to be able to impose by force the distinction between good and bad violence, its own use of force must generally be recognized as legitimate. The state's ability to enforce the distinction between legitimate and illegitimate violence presupposes that its authority to make that distinction is generally accepted; it presupposes, in other words, that the state has the properly moral authority to make that distinction. The state's monopoly therefore constitutes a fundamental moral authority, the authority to distinguish between good and bad violence.

Modern states have succeeded in monopolizing this moral authority, which was previously distributed among many instances: religion, family, clan, lineage, and the numerous different types of reciprocal obligations that structured social life.

In the moral ecology of the reciprocal obligation of solidarity, enmity and solidarity are two sides of the same coin: obligations to help are immediately duties to engage in violence. Morality as self-governance, the free obligation of modern morality, relaxes that bond. For example, because benevolence is categorical and universal, because it is not conditional on others being benevolent in return, failing to be benevolent does not entail violence as a response to transgressing the "duty of benevolence." Even though such failings may occasion violence for different reasons, what is broken is the connection that immediately associates violence with the obligation. Modern obligations, because they are not nominally reciprocal and do not require a specific response on the part of the beneficiary, can be separated from violence. It is not enough to say that the state's monopoly of legitimate violence made this separation possible: the state's monopoly of the legitimate use of force requires it. However, the state also reestablishes, but at a different level, the connection between solidarity and enmity. Interestingly enough, that level is also where reciprocity reappears in our understanding of moral obligations.

In modern societies and social theories, reciprocity plays an important role. However, it takes a very different form from that which it has in traditional societies. Modern individuals are not related to specific Others by reciprocal bonds that simultaneously exclude other Others. Instead, each is reciprocally related to all. Reciprocity is universal, but, as we will see, this universality is closed. The nature of modern reciprocity is particularly clear in social contract theory. The universal agreement, on which this moral contract rests, erases the identity of the agents. There is nonetheless reciprocity to the extent that each individual's agreement is conditional on the agreement of all others. This reciprocity does not entail any particular relations or bonds between specific individuals; it exists only as the conditional dependence of the agreement of each on the agreement of all others. This is a very abstract, virtual form of reciprocity in which agents are not bound to any particular Others, but in which each is reciprocally related to all and everyone. In fact, in recent social contract theories, such as Rawls's theory of

justice, since any one agent is deemed to decide as all others do, there is no
need or place for even an implicit agreement among agents. Convergence of
opinions is guaranteed by the rationality of the agents and the similitude of
the circumstances.[17] A form of reciprocity yet survives this ultimate rarefac-
tion of relationships in the fundamental interchangeability of all agents. It is
a fundamental aspect of the theory that anyone can occupy the social place
and role of any other, and vice versa.

The very abstract forms of reciprocity that we find in these theories
reflect central aspects of the societies in which we live, and we usually refer to
these aspects using the term "individualism." Individualism means first that
we are independent agents who are not bound to each other by nominally
reciprocal obligations of solidarity. Second, it means that we are free in the
sense implied by the modern morality of self-governance, that we can fail to
fulfill the moral obligations that are laid upon us without suffering any sanctions. Third, individualism means that we are equal, in the sense of having
transferred to the state the sole authority to decide between good and bad
violence. In consequence, we are equal in that we are free and independent
in the way that is assumed by economic theory. Individualism finally implies
that reciprocity reappears only at the level of the state, at the level where
what constitutes legitimate violence is determined. This is where the universality characteristic of individualism is closed. At the level of the state, where
reciprocity reappears as a fundamental dimension of rules of solidarity, rules
of solidarity become enforceable and are also exclusive and conditional. We
do not owe the same solidarity to nonnationals who do not belong to the
scheme of reciprocity that characterizes us as members of this or that state.[18]
Further, in international contexts, in our relations with foreigners, often
even moral obligations, such as truthfulness and promise keeping, tend to be
conditional on the beneficiary's response. They require reciprocity and lose
in consequence the freedom and unconditional character that made them
properly moral.

The state's monopoly of legitimate violence is the fountainhead from
which springs what we call morality; free obligations, transgression of which
does not immediately unleash sanctions, can exist only in its shadow. Ethics
is an offspring of the modern state and so are modern economic markets.
The recent move away from obligation as the central moral category may
be viewed as liberating, but it is also linked to naturalization of ethics, to

its transformation into science, that is to say, into an authority that stands outside the domain of democratic discussion. The profound transformation of the modern state that we are witnessing is not accidentally linked to the present failure of market mechanisms. Financial markets that escape the control of individual states have come to dominate the world economy, but as André Orléan has recently argued, financial markets do not satisfy the necessary conditions to be self-regulating.[19] Equality and freedom are two very fragile, imperfect achievements of the modern state that rests on the violent mechanism of transfer that grounds its monopoly of legitimate violence, its ability to distinguish between good and bad violence.[20] The present metamorphosis of the modern state threatens these achievements; it is also progressively but clearly changing our relationship to legitimate violence. Paragons of democratic virtue, exemplars of states where there is rule of law, like Canada and the United Kingdom, have recently decided that evidence obtained under torture can be received as legal in courts of law. There is little reason to believe that this constitutes progress.

Notes

Introduction

1. Simon Simonse, *Kings of Disaster: Dualism, Centralism and the Scapegoat King in Southeastern Sudan* (Leiden: E. J. Brill, 1992).

2. Norwood R. Hanson, *Patterns of Discovery* (Cambridge: Cambridge University Press, 1958).

3. Thomas S. Kuhn, *The Structure of Scientific Revolutions* (Chicago: University of Chicago Press, 1962).

The Ambivalence of Scarcity

"The Ambivalence of Scarcity" originally published in French as "L'ambivalence de la rareté" in P. Dumouchel and J.-P. Dupuy, *L'enfer des choses: René Girard et la logique de l'économie*, (Paris: Seuil, 1979), 137–254; translated by Mary Baker.

1. K. Marx and F. Engels, *The German Ideology*, ed. C. J. Arthur (New York: International Publishers, 1970), 56.

2. C. de Secondat, Baron de Montesquieu, *The Spirit of Laws*, trans. Thomas L. Nugent (London: Colonial Press, 1900), 316.

3. J. Austruy, *Marginalia* (Proceedings of the Congress of French-Speaking Economists) (Paris: Sirey, 1969); cf. D. Flouzat, *Économie contemporaine* (Paris: PUF, 1972), 1:7 [translator's note: our translation].

4. L. Dumont, *From Mandeville to Marx: The Genesis and Triumph of Economic Ideology* (Chicago: University of Chicago Press, 1977).

5. B. Mandeville, *The Fable of the Bees*, ed. F. B. Kaye (1752; repr., Oxford: Oxford University Press, 1966).

6. J. M. Keynes, *Essays in Persuasion: Economic Possibilities for Our Grand-Children* (1930; repr., New York: Macmillan, 1972), 381.

7. H. Lepage, *Demain le capitalisme* (Paris: Le Livre de poche, 1978), 47.

8. P. Samuelson and W. D. Nordhaus, *Economics*, 12th ed. (New York: McGraw-Hill, 1985), 26.

9. Durkheim, in *The Rules of Sociological Method* (1895), argues that the first and most fundamental rule concerning the observation of social facts is to consider social facts as things. E. Durkheim, *Les règles de la méthode sociologique* (1895; repr., Paris: PUF, 1981), 15.

10. L. Dumont, *Homo aequalis: genèse et épanouissement de l'idéologie économique* (Paris: Gallimard, 1977).

11. K. Polanyi, *The Great Transformation* (Boston: Beacon Press, 1944).

12. M. Sahlins, *Stone Age Economics* (Chicago: Aldine, 1972).

13. M. Sahlins, *Tribesmen* (Englewood Cliffs, N.J.: Prentice Hall, 1968), 74.

14. Sahlins, *Tribesmen*, 74.

15. The mode of production has to be considered to include technological and economic means of production as well as production relations—in other words, relations among producers.

16. In this sense, we can also say that there is no scarcity in primitive societies. Since their production is adequate, there is no gap between needs and available resources. Contrary to classical economists who think that the only way of reducing the gap between needs and goods is to increase the real quantity of goods available, Sahlins uses ethnological documents to remind us that most of humanity has always preferred a different solution, which consists in limiting needs. Even though Sahlins's attitude is by far superior with respect to scarcity because it eliminates the illusion of real quantity, we nonetheless have to reject it and go beyond it. This is because the ethnological solution—in other words, the Zen solution to the problem of scarcity—simply reverses the terms of the dilemma. The problem remains untouched. No more than Marx or Ricardo, Sahlins cannot explain the ambivalence or aporia of scarcity. He can only postulate that it does not exist, but this is also what classical economics does.

    Yet it is clear that to explain the aporia and ambivalence of scarcity, we have to abandon the concept of scarcity as a relationship linking people to things. We have to explain scarcity in terms of relationships among people. If the aporia and ambivalence of scarcity mean anything, it can only be this: scarcity cannot be a simple relationship between people and things. We thus have to distinguish the present hypothesis from that of Sahlins in that we reject what he accepts, namely, the classical definition of scarcity as the gap separating human needs from the quantity of goods and resources available.

17. Sahlins, *Stone Age Economics*, 205.

18. Polanyi, *Great Transformation*, 46–47.

19. Theoretically, Chayanov's Rule supposes a given relationship between the labor force (the number of workers) and the work (hours of work per member) done by a medium-sized family. In practice, this is never found, though the average does follow the rule. It seems that the variations in relation to the average are correlated with social position. Cf. Sahlins, *Stone Age Economics*, chapter 2.

20. Sahlins, *Tribesmen*, 4–13; Sahlins, *Stone Age Economics*, chapter 5.

21. R. Firth, *Social Change in Tikopia* (New York: Macmillan, 1959).

22. Strictly speaking, scarcity does not emerge in primitive societies because its emergence destroys the stage on which it is supposed to appear.

23. R. Girard, *Violence and the Sacred*, trans. P. Gregory (Baltimore: Johns Hopkins University Press, 1977).

24. R. Girard, "The Underground Critic," trans. P. N. Livingstone and T. Siebers, in *To Double Business Bound* (Baltimore: Johns Hopkins University Press, 1978), 39.

25. Girard, *Violence and the Sacred*, 67.

26. Girard, "Underground Critic," 40.

27. Girard, *Violence and the Sacred*, 79.

28. Girard, *Violence and the Sacred*, 79.

29. Girard, *Violence and the Sacred*, 79.

30. We have to say "their violence" and not "violence" because, as we will see, being outside is always relative. Moreover, the word "their" provides a clear indication of the structural limits of the demystification that can be achieved by objective knowledge.

31. Girard, *Violence and the Sacred*, 160.

32. Girard, *Violence and the Sacred*, 161.

33. Girard, *Violence and the Sacred*, 188.

34. R. Girard, *Things Hidden since the Foundation of the World*, trans. S. Bann and M. Metteer (Stanford, Calif.: Stanford University Press, 1987), 285.

35. Girard, *Violence and the Sacred*, 189.

36. Girard, *Violence and the Sacred*, 33.

37. Girard, *Things Hidden*, 147.

38. Girard, *Things Hidden*, 148.

39. Girard, *Things Hidden*, 164.

40. Here, we have to distinguish between two different frenzies: a frenzied implosion, which is that of the sacrificial crisis, and a frenzied explosion specific to scarcity, which is both the engine of growth and the mechanism that creates exchange value. The frenzied implosion is the gradual convergence on a single victim.

41. J.-P. Dupuy, "Le signe et l'envie," in P. Dumouchel and J.-P. Dupuy, *L'enfer des choses: René Girard et la logique de l'économie* (Paris: Seuil, 1979), 112.

42. Samuelson and Nordhaus, *Economics*, 26

43. Girard, *Things Hidden*, 9.

44. In *Pour une sociologie du roman* (Paris: Gallimard, 1964), Lucien Goldmann establishes a link between exchange values and mediation as we find it in Girard. Goldmann credits Girard with shedding light on the fact that, in novels, the hero's access to any value, no matter what, is always mediated. He suggests that this phenomenon can be explained by a structural homology between literary creation and everyday life in a market-based society, where access to everyday values is always mediated by the accumulation of sufficient exchange values.

However, two things have to be pointed out. First, in Girard's work, mediation is not a purely literary or novel-based phenomenon, but something very real: it is the fact that people mediate objects of desire—not values—for one another, and that this mediation establishes the value that is given to those objects. Second, Goldmann's explanation is in complete contradiction with our own. According to Goldmann, the existence of a market-based society explains what Girard calls mediation. We argue that mediation in Girard's sense explains the emergence of a market-based society.

45. Polanyi, *Great Transformation*.

46. C. Bruaire, *La Raison politique* (Paris: Fayard, 1974), 13 [translator's note: our translation].

47. Girard, *Violence and the Sacred*, 13.

48. Girard, *Violence and the Sacred*, 15.

49. C. Péguy, *De Jean Coste*, in *Oeuvres completes* (Geneva: Slatkine Reprint, 1974), 2:47 [translator's note: our translation].

50. The very last sentence of Camus's *The Myth of Sisyphus* is "We must imagine that Sisyphus is happy" and was intended by him as summarizing the philosophy of the absurd.

51. D. Hume, *An Inquiry Concerning the Principles of Morals* (Indianapolis: Bobbs-Merrill, 1957). This is a republication of the 1826 edition, which indicates the variations of the different editions of the *Inquiry* that were published during Hume's lifetime.

52. Hume, *Inquiry*, 15.

53. Hume, *Inquiry*, 16.

54. Hume, *Inquiry*, 17.

55. Hume, *Inquiry*, 18.

56. Hume, *Inquiry*, 19.

57. Hume, *Inquiry*, 20.

58. Hume, *Inquiry*, 25–26.

59. Hume, *Inquiry*, 13–14.

60. Hume, *Inquiry*, 13.

61. Hume, *Inquiry*, 120–21.

62. Hume, *Inquiry*, 122.

63. Moreover, the possibility that the result of a system of action can contradict the results of the actions that comprise it is both the logical structure of economic justice and also the social and epistemological condition of what we commonly call the social sciences. This is obvious.

   If sociology always supposes that actors do not have access to the meaning of their actions when they are in the midst of them, then the rupture between the immediate and the social consequences of actions is the condition sine qua non of all sociology. Cf. D. Vidal, *Essai sur l'idéologie* (Paris: Anthropos, 1971), 19, 62; Alain Touraine, *Pour la sociologie* (Paris: Ed du Seuil, 1974). Indeed, this disjunction is the social institution that prevents people from understanding the meaning of what they are doing when they are doing it. The fact that the system's outcome contradicts individual results ensures, socially, the validity of the fundamental sociological supposition.

   However, it is immediately clear why some societies in which this disjunction occurs produce social sciences in a desperate effort to make people aware of the truth of their actions. In contrast, in other societies where this disjunction does not occur, morals are invented that insist on the concurrence of immediate thought and action. In fact, the passage from the sacred *religiare* to the exteriority of members of society is the community's transformation into a society in accordance with Tönnies's categories of pure sociology. Sociology's attempts are desperate because the space where they take place is determined by the disjunction. It cannot show people the meaning of their acts because one of its axioms is that they cannot have access to such knowledge. It cannot grasp the social relativity of its epistemology.

64. Mandeville, *Fable of the Bees.*

65. Mandeville, *Fable of the Bees*, 1:354–55.

66. Hume, *Inquiry*, 121.

67. B. Mandeville, "A Search into the Nature of Society," in *Fable of the Bees*, 1:344.

68. Mandeville, "Search," 346.

69. B. Mandeville, "Essay on Charity and Charity Schools," in *Fable of the Bees*, 1:311.

70. Mandeville, "Essay on Charity," 286.

71. B. Mandeville, "Remark (Q)," in *Fable of the Bees*, 1:192.

72. Mandeville, "Essay on Charity," 1:287.

73. B. Mandeville, "The Fourth Dialogue," in *Fable of the Bees*, 2:180.

74. B. Mandeville, "Remark (R)," in *Fable of the Bees*, 1:206.

75. W. Townsend, *Dissertation on the Poor Laws*, Section VIII, 1786, http://socserv.mcmaster. ca/~econ/ugcm/3ll3/townsend/poorlaw.html.

76. Polanyi, *Great Transformation*, 125.

77. Hume, *Inquiry*, 122.

78. Polanyi, *Great Transformation*, 125.

79. Hume, *Inquiry*, 17.

80. Townsend, *Dissertation on the Poor Laws*, Sections III and IV.

81. Townsend, *Dissertation on the Poor Laws*, Section IV.

82. J. Bentham, *Principles of the Civil Code*, chapter 4 in *The Works of Jeremy Bentham,* published under the Superintendence of his Executor, J. Bowring (Edinburgh: William Tait, 1838–1843). 11 vols., vol. 1.

83. Townsend, *Dissertation on the Poor Laws*, Section III.

84. Hume, *Inquiry*, 34.

85. Hume, *Inquiry*, 34–35.

86. Hume, *Inquiry*, 124.

87. Hume, *Inquiry*, 35.

88. G. Lukács, *History and Class Consciousness*, trans. R. Livingstone (Cambridge, Mass.: MIT Press, 1971), 83–222.

89. Polanyi, *Great Transformation*.

90. In the following, the description of the way land was formerly occupied, the terms employed, and their exact definitions come essentially from P. Mantoux, *Le Révolution industrielle au XVIIIe siècle* (Paris: Génin, 1973), and G. Slater, *The English Peasantry and the Enclosures of Common Fields* (London: Archibald Constable, 1907).

91. This was more frequent than one might think, and above all easier to achieve because the poor helped one another. First, they gathered the necessary materials, then, on the chosen evening, carried them to the place where the house would be built. One night was longer than a group of skilled workers needed to build a rudimentary home. Once the right to stay was acquired, the peasant had as much time as needed to improve his or her home. Cf. Slater, *English Peasantry*.

92. Mantoux, *La révolution*.

93. Mantoux, *La révolution*, 163.

94. Mantoux, *La révolution*, 131.

Indifference and Envy: Girard and the Anthropological Analysis of Modern Economy

1. For example, R. Girard, *Mensonge romantique et vérité romanesque* (Paris: Grasset, 1961), 18–23; R. Girard, *Des choses cachées depuis la fondation du monde* (Paris: Grasset, 1978), 82–88.

2. M. Anspach, "Les fondements rituels de la transaction monétaire, ou comment remercier un bourreau," in *La monnaie souveraine*, ed. M. Aglietta and A. Orléan (Paris: Odile Jacob, 1998), 53–83; A. Feenberg, "Le désordre érotique et économique" in *Violence et vérité, autour de René Girard*, ed. P. Dumouchel (Paris: Grasset, 1985), 201–210; P. Lantz, "Monnaie archaïque, monnaie moderne" in *Violence et vérité, autour de René Girard*, ed. P. Dumouchel (Paris: Grasset, 1985), 159–181; A. Orléan, "Monnaie et spéculation mimétique" in *Violence et vérité, autour de René Girard*, ed. P. Dumouchel (Paris: Grasset, 1985), 147–158; A. Orléan, "Mimétisme et anticipations rationnelles: Une perspective keynésienne," *Recherche économique de Louvain* 52 (1986): 1; A. Orléan, "Mimetic Contagion and Speculative Bubbles," *Theory and Decision* 27 (1989): 1–2; A. Orléan, "Comportements mimétiques et diversité des opinions sur les marchés financiers" in *Théories économiques et crises sur les marché financier*, ed. P. Artus and H. Bourguinat (Paris: Economia, 1989); G.-H. de Radkowski, *Les jeux du désir* (Paris: PUF, 1980); L. Scubla, "Jamais deux sans trois? (Réflexions sur les structures élémentaires de la réciprocité)" in *Logiques de la réciprocité*, Cahier du Crea 6 (Paris: Ecole Polytechnique, 1985), 7–118.

3. Interestingly, twenty-four years later, in the second, vastly enlarged edition of that work, *Le capitalisme* (1995), the reference to Girard has disappeared though the text of the original work, which now constitutes the second part of the book, is otherwise reprinted in its entirety.

4. Actually Polanyi in *The Livelihood of Man* (1977) sees the origin of the debate in C. Menger's *Principles of Economics* (1871). Let us say then that it found its first modern formulation in the work of Polanyi.

5. Published posthumously in 1977.

6. For example: K. Polanyi, C. Arensberg, and H. Pearson, eds., *Trade and Markets in the Early Empires* (New York: Free Press, 1957), 382; and K. Polanyi, *Dahomey and the Slave Trade: An Analysis of an Archaic Economy* (Seattle: University of Washington Press, 1966), 204.

7. J. Baechler, "Mercato e Democrazia," *Mondo Operaio* 38.12 (1985): 64–73; J. Baechler, "I Primi

Esperimenti di Mercato e Democrazia," *Mondo Operaio* 39.1 (1989): 82–90; J. Baechler, "Mercato e Democrazia: Il Percorso della Modernita," *Mondo Operaio* 39.2 (1989): 86–94.

8. N. Geras, *The Contract of Mutual Indifference: Political Philosophy after the Holocaust* (London: Verso, 1998), 181.

A Mimetic Rereading of Helmut Schoeck's *Envy: A Theory of Social Behaviour*

1. H. Schoeck, *Envy: A Theory of Social Behaviour* (Indianapolis: Liberty Press, 1969).

2. Schoeck, *Envy*, 19.

3. Of course Schoeck is well aware that two envious persons could very well envy each other, but he argues that the empirical possibility does not change the conceptual point.

4. E. E. Evans-Pritchard, *Witchcraft, Oracles, and Magic Among the Azande* (1937; repr., Oxford: Clarendon Press, 1976).

5. Schoeck, *Envy*, 422.

6. A. R. Holmberg, *Nomads of the Long Bow: The Siriono of Eastern Bolivia*. Smithsonian Institution, Institute of Social Anthropology Publication No. 10. (Washington, D.C.: Smithsonian Institution, 1950).

7. Schoeck, *Envy*, 423.

8. Schoeck, *Envy*, 422

9. It should be noted that envy and the fear of envy could very well be completely absent from the eating habits of members of the Siriono tribe. Limited resources and a social rule prescribing sharing could also explain this behavior. The problem is that what Schoeck tells us does not allow us to decide between these contradictory explanations.

10. Schoeck, *Envy*, 414

11. H. G. Barnett, *Innovations: The Basis of Cultural Change* (New York: McGraw-Hill, 1953), 403–406.

12. The expression is from F. A. Hayek. *The Mirage of Social Justice* is the title of the second volume of his multivolume work *Law, Legislation and Liberty* (Chicago: University of Chicago Press, 1976).

13. Since the time when Schoeck was writing, many welfare economists have developed formal models in which the absence of envy constitutes the criteria of a just society. See P. Van Parijs, "La justice économique comme absence d'envie," *Recherches Économiques de Louvain* 60 (1994): 3–7.

14. J.-P. Dupuy, "Le signe et l'envie" in P. Dumouchel and J.-P. Dupuy, *L'enfer des choses: René Girard et la logique de l'économie* (Paris: Seuil, 1979), 57–97.

15. For example, R. Ogien, *Portrait moral et logique de la haine* (Paris: L'Éclat, 1993).

16. For example, R. Frank, *Passions within Reason* (New York: Norton, 1988).

17. R. Girard, *Deceit, Desire and the Novel,* 14.

18. "Desire is what happens to human relationships when there is no longer any resolution through the victim, and consequently no form of polarization that is genuinely unanimous and can trigger such a resolution." R. Girard, *Things Hidden since the Foundation of the World*, trans. S. Bann and M. Metteer (Stanford, Calif.: Stanford University Press, 1987), 288, see also 283–294.

19. See this volume, chapter 1, "The Ambivalence of Scarcity"

20. For example, *Violence and the Sacred*, 14–24, and *Things Hidden since the Foundation of the World*, 284–287.

21. For example, pages 8 and 19.

Homo mimeticus as an Economic Agent

1. P. Dumouchel and J.-P. Dupuy, *L'enfer des choses: René Girard et la logique de l'économie* (Paris: Seuil, 1979).

2. R. Girard, *Violence and the Sacred*, trans. P. Gregory (Baltimore: Johns Hopkins University Press, 1977).

3. The close relationship between modern economy and warfare, especially the exportation of warfare through colonialism, but also through technological development linked to warfare, brings further proof of the claim that there is an important relation between modern economic development and the mechanism that regulates violence. See P. Dumouchel, *Le sacrifice inutile: Essai sur la violence politique* (Paris: Flammarion, 2011), translation forthcoming from Michigan State University Press.

4. This is suggested, among other things, by the numerous claims that economic deprivation constitutes a legitimate claim to violence. See, for example, T. Honderich, *Terrorism for Humanity: Inquiries into Political Philosophy* (London: Pluto Press, 2003).

5. In fact, the self-organizing character of markets is inseparable from the self-organizing dimension of the mechanism of protection against violence. The phrase "the result of human actions, but not of human designs" originally comes from A. Ferguson, *An Essay on the History of Civil Society*, ed. F. Oz-Salzberger (Cambridge: Cambridge University Press, 1995), which was first published in 1767.

6. A. Smith, *The Wealth of Nations* (London: Everyman's Library, 1975), 13.

7. Smith, *Wealth of Nations*, 13.

8. Dumouchel, *Le Sacrifice*.

9. M. Sahlins, *Stone Age Economics* (Chicago: Aldine, 1972).

10. Of course, one of the reasons why none are willing to help is because all are convinced that those who fail do so because of some fault of their own, such as incompetence or immorality, and therefore that no one has any obligation toward them.

11. A. Sen, "Rational Fools: A Critique of the Behavioral Foundations of Economic Theory," *Philosophy and Public Affairs* 6.4 (1977): 317–344.

12. "True altruism" can be defined as an altruistic behavior that cannot ultimately be reduced to a form of direct or indirect self-interest and therefore is more than just "apparent altruism."

13. See J. Roughgarden, *The Genial Gene: Deconstructing Darwinian Selfishness* (Berkeley: University of California Press, 2009).

14. R. Girard, "Preface," in M. Anspach, *Oedipe mimétique* (Paris: l'Herne, 2010), 7 [my translation].

15. A. Sen, *Rationality and Freedom* (Cambridge, Mass.: Harvard University Press, 2002), 19–26.

Mimetism and Autonomy

"Mimetism and Autonomy" originally published in French as "Mimétisme et autonomie" in *L'auto-organisation de la physique au politique*, ed. P. Dumouchel and J.-P. Dupuy (Paris: Seuil, 1983); translated by Mary Baker.

1. This text was originally presented at the conference on self-organization held at Cerisy-la-Salle in 1981; the proceedings were published in Dumouchel and Dupuy, eds., *L'auto-organisation de la physique au politique*. This text followed a talk of René Girard that was on the episode of Salome's dance from Mark's gospel (see 336–352 in *L'auto-organisation* and R. Girard, "Scandal and the Dance: Salome in the Gospel of Mark," *New Literary History* 15.2 [Winter 1984]: 1–24); hence the opening reference to the head of John the Baptist.

2. K. Polanyi, *The Great Transformation* (Boston: Beacon Press, 1944); see P. Dumouchel and J.-P. Dupuy, *L'enfer des choses* (Paris: Seuil, 1979); and "The Ambivalence of Scarcity," reprinted in this volume.

3. See F. Varela, *Principles of Biological Autonomy* (New York: North Holland, 1979).

4. Since this essay was first written numerous observations have demonstrated the existence of frequent intraspecific murders among chimpanzees. For a reevaluation of Girard's hypothesis in view of this new evidence, see P. Dumouchel "A Covenant among Beasts: Human and Chimpanzee Violence in Evolutionary Perspective," in *Can We Survive Our Origins?* ed. P. Antonello and P. Gifford (East Lansing: Michigan State University Press, forthcoming).

5. R. Girard, *Things Hidden since the Foundation of the World*, trans. S. Bann and M. Metteer (Stanford, Calif.: Stanford University Press, 1987), 70.

Violence and Nonviolence

"Violence and Nonviolence" originally published in French as "Violence et Non-Violence" in *Esprit* 60 (1981): 153–165; translated by Mary Baker.

1. Christian Mellon, Jean-Marie Muller, Hervé Ott, and Jacques Sémelin. The initials between parentheses refer to these four names.

2. Those texts, with the exception of this essay, were published in *Alternatives non-violentes* 36 (January 1980): 49–72.

3. *Alternatives non-violentes*, 49.

4. *Alternatives non-violentes*, 68.

5. *Alternatives non-violentes*, 64.

6. J.-P. Dupuy, "Le signe et l'envie," in J. P. Dupuy and P. Dumouchel, *L'enfer des choses* (Paris: Seuil, 1979).

7. *Alternatives non-violentes*, 81.

8. *Alternatives non-violentes*, 49.

9. *Alternatives non-violentes*, 49.

10. *Alternatives non-violentes*, 145.

11. *Alternatives non-violentes*, 186.

12. *Alternatives non-violentes*, 195.

13. *Alternatives non-violentes*, 422.

14. *Alternatives non-violentes*, 303.

15. *Alternatives non-violentes*, 304.

16. *Alternatives non-violentes*, 94.

17. My emphasis.

18. *Alternatives non-violentes*, 203.

19. See R. Girard, *Violence and the Sacred*, trans. P. Gregory (Baltimore: Johns Hopkins University Press, 1977), 67.

20. *Alternatives non-violentes*, 445.

Differences and Paradoxes: Reflections on Love and Violence in Girard's Work

"Differences and Paradoxes: Reflections on Love and Violence in Girard's Work" originally published as "Différences et paradoxes: réflexions sur l'amour et la violence dans l'œuvre de Girard" in *René Girard et le problème du mal*, ed. M. Deguy and J.-P. Dupuy (Paris: Grasset, 1982), 215–223; translated by Mary Baker.

1. R. Girard, *Things Hidden since the Foundation of the World*, trans. S. Bann and M. Metteer (Stanford, Calif.: Stanford University Press, 1987), 270.

2. Girard, *Things Hidden*, 216.

3. Girard, *Things Hidden*, 338.

4. Girard, *Violence and the Sacred*, 161, my emphasis.

5. See F. Varela, *Principles of Biological Autonomy* (New York: North Holland, 1979).

Creation and Conversion in Girard

Translated by Mary Baker.

1. R. Girard, *Mimesis and Theory Essays on Literature and Criticism*, ed. R. Doran (Palo Alto, Calif.: Stanford University Press, 2008).

2. R. Girard, "Narcissism: The Freudian Myth Demythified by Proust," in *Mimesis and Theory*, 175–193.

3. R. Girard, *Critique dans un souterrain* (Geneva: L'Âge d'homme, 1976), 76 [translator's note: our translation]. See R. Girard, *Resurrection from the Underground*, trans. J. Williams (East Lansing: Michigan State University Press, 2012), 41.

4. R. Girard, *Deceit, Desire and the Novel*, 83.

5. Girard, *Deceit, Desire and the Novel*, 49–50.

6. L. Goldmann, *Pour une sociologie du roman* (Paris: Gallimard, 1973).

7. As Emanuele Antonelli has brilliantly shown, if the dead victim is the first sign, then that sign is indeed, as Derrida thought, the mark of a past that has never been present. This is because the person responsible for the crisis never existed in the present: he or she has to no longer exist, to be dead, in order to be responsible for the crisis. However, when dead, he or she is not responsible

for anything, and all that remains is his or her trace, the whole meaning of which is to be the trace of what never was. He or she was never responsible for the crisis and can become so retroactively only if he or she no longer exists. See E. Antonelli, *La Creativita degli eventi* (Turin: L'Harmattan Italia, 2011).

Mimetic Theory: Concepts and Models

"Mimetic Theory: Concepts and Models" originally written in French and first published in Italian as "La teoria mimetica: concetti e modelli" in *Studi Perugini* 10 (2000): 71–88; translated by Mary Baker from the original French language manuscript.

1. This is an impression that Girard has sometimes encouraged. For example, he more or less responded that "you have to take everything or leave it"(560 [translator's note: our translation]) when François Aubral asked him about the possibility of accepting some aspects of his conclusions during a discussion on *Violence and the Sacred* held by the journal *Esprit* in 1973. "Discussion avec René Girard," *Esprit* (November 1973): 528–564.

2. Before continuing, I should mention some of the important works that have guided my research: M. Anspach, ed., "Vengeance," *Stanford French Review* 16.1 (1992): 55–76; J.-P. Dupuy, "Le signe et l'envie," in P. Dumouchel and J.-P. Dupuy, *L'enfer des chose: René Girard et la logique de l'économie* (Paris: Seuil, 1979), 17–134; P. Livingston, *Models of Desire: René Girard and the Psychology of Mimesis* (Baltimore: Johns Hopkins University Press, 1992); A. Orléan, "Monnaie et spéculation mimétique," in *Violence et vérité, autour de René Girard*, ed. P. Dumouchel (Paris: Grasset, 1985), 147–158; L. Scubla, "Théorie du sacrifice et théorie du désir chez René Girard," in *Violence et vérité, autour de René Girard*, ed. P. Dumouchel (Paris: Grasset, 1985), 359–374; L. Scubla, *Lire Lévi-Strauss* (Paris: Odile Jacob, 1998).

3. S. Simonse, *Kings of Disaster: Dualism, Centralism and the Scapegoat King of Southeastern Sudan* (Leiden: E. J. Brill, 1992), 15–40.

4. Thus, Newton, in Section XI of *Principia*, wrote: "I have hitherto been treating of the attractions of bodies towards an immovable centre; though very probably there is no such thing existent in nature." See also N. Cartwright, *How the Laws of Physics Lie* (Oxford: Clarendon Press, 1983).

5. See C. Hempel, *Philosophy of Natural Science* (New York: Prentice Hall, 1966), 72–75.

6. R. Girard, *Things Hidden since the Foundation of the World*, trans. S. Bann and M. Metteer (Stanford, Calif.: Stanford University Press, 1987), 26.

7. K. R. Popper, *Objective Knowledge: An Evolutionary Approach* (Oxford: Clarendon Press, 1972); V. O. Quine, *Ontological Relativity and Other Essays* (New York: Columbia University Press, 1969), in particular, chapter 5, "Natural Kinds."

8. T. S. Kuhn, *The Structure of Scientific Revolutions* (Chicago: University of Chicago Press, 1962).

9. P. Dumouchel, "Ijime," *Contagion: Journal of Violence, Mimesis, and Culture* 6 (1999): 77–84, reprinted in this volume.

10. This is, for example, C. Lévi-Strauss's argument in *Totemism*, trans. R. Needham, (Boston: Beacon Press, 1963).

11. See, for example, J. P. Vernant and M. Detienne, eds., *La Cuisine du sacrifice en pays grec*, (Paris: Gallimard, 1979).

12. R. Needham, *Exemplars* (Berkeley: University of California Press, 1985).

13. Needham wrongly considers that since there is no science but of the universal, there is no science possible of objects that form polythetic classes. This is to forget that biology, for example, concerns precisely objects of this type and that there are many remarkable studies on classes of polythetic objects—for example, that by Berlin and Kay on color vocabulary: B. Berlin and P. Kay, *Basic Color Terms: Their Universality and Evolution* (1969; repr., Stanford, Calif.: CSLI Publications, 1999).

14. M. Hocart, *Social Origins* (London: Watts, 1954).

15. On this, see Scubla, *Lire Lévi-Strauss*, 275ff.

16. J.-P. Dupuy, "Totalization and Misrecognition," trans. M. Anspach, in *Violence and Truth*, ed. P. Dumouchel (Cambridge: Athlone Press, 1988), 75; see also Scubla, *Lire Lévi-Strauss*.

17. The theory of evolution by natural selection is morphogenetic. The evolutionary trajectory of a species depends on two types of variables, genetic mutations and environmental features, and it is constrained by the entire phylogenetic past. See J. Maynard-Smith et al., "Developmental Constraints and Evolution," *Quarterly Review of Biology* 60.3 (1985): 265–287, for the biological data; and P. Dumouchel "Good Tricks and Forced Moves," in *Dennett's Philosophy: A Comprehensive Assessment*, ed. D. Ross, A. Brook, and D. Thompson (Cambridge, Mass.: MIT Press, 2000), 41–54, for a conceptual analysis.

18. For a general analysis of this phenomenon with respect to physics, see the classic book by I. Prigogine and I. Stengers, *Order Out of Chaos: Man's New Dialogue with Nature* (London: Flamingo, 1984). For a discussion in the framework of Girardian theory, see P. Dumouchel, "Mimétisme et autonomie," in *L'auto-organisation de la physique au politique*, ed. P. Dumouchel and J.-P. Dupuy (Paris: Seuil, 1983), 353–364 ("Mimesis and Autonomy" in this volume); see also H. Atlan, C. Castoriadis and R. Girard, "Discussion sur le nouveau," in Dumouchel and Dupuy, *L'auto-organisation de la physique au politique*, 179–184.

19. I say the meaning of the shift and not the shift itself because it is in no way necessary to suppose that the agents are not aware of the fact that continuing the conflict is for everyone more important than obtaining the object that was the cause of the conflict. Moreover, it would very often be mistaken to do so. What the agents are unaware of is what motivates the shift, the process by which it occurs, and its consequences for the rest of the conflict. On the unconscious aspect of mimetism, see in particular Girard, *Things Hidden*, 283–392.

20. F. A. Hayek, *The Counter-Revolution of Science: Studies on the Abuse of Reason* (Glencoe, Ill.: Free Press, 1952).

21. In other words, it is not necessary to conceive of it as meaning that agents think it is advantageous to repeat behavior that was successful for them in the past.

22. See M. Donald, *Origins of the Modern Mind: Three Stages in the Evolution of Culture and Cognition* (Cambridge Mass: Harvard University Press, 1991); E. Webb, "Mimesis, Evolution and the Differentiation of Consciousness," *Paragrana* 4.2 (1995): 151–165.

23. Concerning intraspecific conflicts among primates, see G. B. Stanford, *Chimpanzee and Red Colobus: The Ecology of Predator and Prey* (Cambridge, Mass.: Harvard University Press, 1998). Concerning the relationship between group size and number of conflicts, see J. Bok "Un modèle d'auto-organisation: Le principe de moindre difficulté," in Dumouchel and Dupuy, *L'auto-organisation de la physique au politique*, 75–85.

24. S. A. Frank, *Foundations of Social Evolution* (Princeton, N.J.: Princeton University Press, 1998); E. Sober and D. S. Wilson, *Unto Others: The Evolution and Psychology of Unselfish Behavior* (Cambridge, Mass.: Harvard University Press, 1998).

25. For an example of influential work in evolutionary psychology, see J. Barkow, L. Cosmides, and J. Tooby, *The Adapted Mind: Evolutionary Psychology and the Generation of Culture* (Oxford: Oxford University Press, 1992).

"De la *méconnaissance*"

1. K. R. Popper, *Objective Knowledge: An Evolutionary Approach* (Oxford: Clarendon Press, 1972).

2. Up to a certain point, this is beginning to change in epistemology; see, for example, S. C. Goldberg, *Relying on Others: An Essay in Epistemology* (Oxford: Oxford University Press, 2010); and M. Kusch, *Knowledge by Agreement: The Programme of Communitarian Epistemology* (Oxford: Clarendon Press, 2002).

3. There may be other ways of lying to oneself than the one described below.

4. Again, there may be other ways of lying to others.

5. For this same reason: that it aims at changing the world, there also is a close relationship between lying to oneself and normative statements that would need to be analyzed in greater detail.

6. P. Dumouchel, *Le sacrifice inutile: Essai sur la violence politique* (Paris: Flammarion, 2011), see especially chapter 5.

7. E. De Martino, *La terra del rimorso Il Sud tra religione e magia* (Milano: il Saggiatore, 1961).

8. See the entry "tarantism" in Wikipedia.

9. J. Rawls, *A Theory of Justice* (Cambridge, Mass.: Belknap Press of Harvard University Press, 1971).

Hobbes: The Sovereignty Race

"Hobbes: The Sovereignty Race" originally published as "Hobbes: La course à la Souveraineté" in *Stanford French Review* 10 (1986): 153–176; translated by Mary Baker.

1. T. Hobbes, *Leviathan*, ed. J. C. A. Gaskin (Oxford: Oxford University Press, 1996), Chapter 20, 138.

2. Hobbes defines the Sovereign as a single entity, the assembly of all the people, the assembly of part of the people. We know that his sympathies lay with monarchy and that he regretted not really having demonstrated its superiority over other forms of government. In what follows, only monarchy will be in question.

3. K. Popper, *The Open Society and Its Enemies* (London: Routledge, 1995), 1:128–129.

4. R. Derathé, *Jean-Jacques Rousseau et la science politique de son temps* (Paris: PUF, 1950), 218 [translator's note: our translation].

5. Hobbes, *Leviathan*, Chapter 29, 212–221.

6. On irrational, rational, and reasonable orders, see P. Dumouchel, "Systèmes sociaux et cognition," in *Introduction aux sciences cognitives*, ed. D. Andler (Paris: Gallimard, 1992).

7. Hobbes, *Leviathan*, Chapter 13, 82.

8. Hobbes, *Leviathan*, 82.

9. Hobbes, *Leviathan*, 82.

10. Hobbes, *Leviathan*, 82.

11. Hobbes, *Leviathan*, 83.

12. Hobbes, *Leviathan*, 83.

13. Hobbes, *Leviathan*, 83.

14. Hobbes, *Leviathan*, 83.

15. Hobbes, *Leviathan*, 83.

16. Hobbes, *Leviathan*, 83–84.

17. This is a principle of rationality that is relatively closely related to what J. Watkins calls "imperfect rationality." See J. Watkins, "Imperfect Rationality," in *Explanation in the Behavioural Sciences*, ed. T. Brager and F. Cioffi (Cambridge: Cambridge University Press, 1970), 167–230.

18. For example, if one morning I am awoken by the noise of footsteps in the cave where I sleep, and I see ten armed men who are blocking the only way out, it is rational for me to try to negotiate with them, rather than to attack them, despite what my "territorial instinct" might suggest.

19. Hobbes, *Leviathan*, Chapter 17, 114.

20. Hobbes, *Leviathan*, Chapter 17, 115.

21. This interpretation would liken Hobbes to those who hold a dual contract theory: one contract of association and a second contract of government.

22. Hobbes, *Leviathan*, Chapter 17, 117.

23. Hobbes, *Leviathan*, Chapter 13, 84.

24. Hobbes, *Leviathan*, Chapter 3, 18.

25. See note 1.

Ijime

1. The important information, which I do not have, would be to compare the number of *ijime*-related suicides to the total number of suicides in Japanese high schools.

2. See, for instance, R. Benedict, *The Chrysanthemum and the Sword* (Tokyo: Charles Tuttle, 1954), 253–316.

3. If *ijime*, as I believe, is closely related to the Girardian mechanism of victimage, the fact that torturers do not see their tortures as such, but to the contrary as justified, explains why we should not expect them to view their activity as one of victimization, hence as *ijime*, but as legitimate punishment.

4. These comments should be nuanced by taking into account the differences between the way small boys and small girls are treated—especially the fact that tantrums are not dealt with in the same way and parents expect very different behavior from them in this regard.

5. The social hierarchy matches, or perfectly reproduces, the academic hierarchy, in that students who graduate from the best schools with the best marks hold the best positions in the economic and political hierarchy. For example, since the end of World War II and until at least 1995 all prime ministers of Japan have been graduates of the Department of Economics of the University of Tokyo.

6. That at least is the implication of Girard's analysis of the difference in the character of Oedipus in *Oedipus King* and *Oedipus at Colonus*. See R. Girard, *Violence and the Sacred*, trans. P. Gregory (Baltimore: Johns Hopkins University Press, 1977), 68–88.

7. S. Simonse, *Kings of Disaster: Dualism, Centralism and the Scapegoat King in Southeastern Sudan* (Leiden: E. J. Brill, 1992).

8. Girard, *Violence and the Sacred*.

9. R. Girard, *Job: The Victim of His People,* trans. Y. Freccero (Palo Alto, Calif.: Stanford University Press, 1987).

From Scapegoat to God

1. S. Simonse, *Kings of Disaster: Dualism, Centralism and the Scapegoat King in Southeastern Sudan* (Leiden: E. J. Brill, 1992)

2. P. Dumouchel, "Ijime," *Contagion: Journal of Violence, Mimesis, and Culture* 6 (1999): 77–84, reprinted in this volume.

3. "We can conceive hominization as a series of levels that allow the domestication of ever greater levels of mimesis divided from each other by catastrophic but fecund crisis" (my translation). In R. Girard, *Des choses cachées depuis la fondation du monde* (Paris: Grasset, 1978), 105.

4. Concerning the "original event as a spontaneous mechanism regulating internal violence," see P. Dumouchel, "Mimétisme et autonomie," in *L'auto-organisation de la physique au politique,* ed. P. Dumouchel and J.-P. Dupuy (Paris: Seuil, 1983), 353–364 (reprinted in this volume); and L. Scubla "Rois sacré, victime sacrificielle et victime émissaire," *Qu'est-ce que le religieux? Religion et politique, Revue du Mauss* 22 (2003): 197–221.

5. Simonse, *Kings of Disaster*, 372, 373.

6. Simonse, *Kings of Disaster*, 26–28.

7. J. Black-Michaud, *Feuding Societies* (Oxford: Basil Blackwell, 1975).

8. The importance of that contribution cannot be overstated. Since the inception of their discipline, anthropologists have argued that the two forms of social organizations are radically different and unrelated. Simonse's discovery therefore challenges one of the fundamental axioms of modern anthropology.

9. Simonse, *Kings of Disaster*, 195.

10. In that sense, of course, the king's death is beneficial to the community. However, it is not the dead king himself who is credited for this good fortune and happy rain, but the violent actions of the group.

11. Simonse, *Kings of Disaster*, 373.

12. Simonse, *Kings of Disaster*, 365.

13. Simonse, *Kings of Disaster*, 25, 366, 422.

14. It seems that Simonse came to his conclusion that violence is what prevents the positive transfiguration of the victims because rainmakers who pass away in a nonviolent way are sacralized and become objects of veneration. It is to them, he argues, that is attributed the positive effects of the scapegoat mechanism (Simonse, *Kings of Disaster*, 422). Therefore, a satisfactory explanation of why victims of regicide are not sacralized should have something to say about this difference.

15. Note that these representations are not individual representations, but elements in a collective process through which all agents involved end up with similar representations.

16. R. Girard, *Violence and the Sacred*, trans. P. Gregory (Baltimore: Johns Hopkins University Press, 1977), 14–15.

17. Concerning the distinction between sacrificial substitution and ritual substitution see the above section "Neither Ritual nor Original Event" as well as Scubla, "Rois sacré."

Violence and Indifference

"Violence and Indifference" originally published as "Violence et indifference" in *Comprendre pour agir: violences, victimes et vengeances*, ed. P. Dumouchel (Québec: Presses de l'Université Laval, 2000), 207–225; translated by Mary Baker.

1. N. Geras, *The Contract of Mutual Indifference: Political Philosophy after the Holocaust* (London: Verso, 1998), 181.

2. Geras, *Contract of Mutual Indifference*, 3–4; 24.

3. At least in the framework of contractualist morals.

4. Geras, *Contract of Mutual Indifference*, 49.

5. *Maclean's* 111.52 (December 28, 1998): 33–34.

6. Despite everything paradoxical in this formulation.

7. The major famines of the twentieth century have all, without exception, been caused by or taken on disastrous dimensions thanks to negligence, indifference, military undertakings, and government repression in the areas where they have occurred. See, among others, S. Courtois et al., *Le livre noir du communisme* (Paris: Robert Laffont, 1997), 122–147, 530–541, 748–757; A. Sen, *Poverty and Famines: An Essay on Entitlement and Deprivation* (New York: Oxford University Press, 1981).

8. Even though he himself says nothing about this.

9. On this, see also C. Vidal, "Le génocide des Rwandais tutsi: cruauté délibéré et logiques de la haine" in *De la violence*, ed. F. Héritier (Paris: Odile Jacob, 1996), 325–366.

10. Cf. P. Dumouchel, "Violence et Non-Violence," *Esprit* 60 (1981): 153–160, reprinted in this volume.

11. P. Dumouchel and J.-P. Dupuy, *L'enfer des choses: René Girard et la logique de l'économie* (Paris: Seuil, 1979), 265.

12. Geras, *Contract of Mutual Indifference*, 59.

13. Geras, *Contract of Mutual Indifference*, 27–30.

14. This is why political regimes that are based on this indifference, such as liberal democracy, have always appeared artificial to analysts. Cf. P. Dumouchel, "Communautés, droits et justice sociale" in *Mondialisation, citoyenneté et multiculturalisme*, ed. M. Elbaz and D. Helly (Québec: Presses de l'Université Laval, 2000), 79–86.

15. Cf. D. Pécaut, "Réflexions sur la violence en Colombie," in Héritier, *De la violence*, 223–272.

16. The incident is reported by R. Hardin in *One for All: The Logic of Group Conflict* (Princeton, N.J.: Princeton University Press, 1995), 288. Other examples of similar forms of behavior by

main players in conflicts can be found in D. Pécaut, "Réflexions sur la violence en Colombie," in Héritier, *De la violence*; Vidal "Le génocide des Rwandais tutsi"; and N. Werth "Un État contre son peuple," in *Le livre noir du communisme*, ed. S. Courtois et al. (Paris: Robert Laffont, 1997), 49–122. There is also an interesting analysis of the phenomenon in Dostoyevsky in chapter 6 of Part III of *The Devils*, trans. D. Magarshack (London: Penguin, 1953).

17. Vidal, "Le génocide des Rwandais tutsi," 237.

18. G. Sorel, *Réflexions sur la violence* (1907; repr., Paris: Slatkine, 1981), 394, presents a remarkable example of this illusion.

19. J. Black-Michaud, *Feuding Societies* (Oxford: Basil Blackwell, 1975), 270.

20. M. Hénaff, "La dette de sang et l'exigence de justice," in *Violences, Victimes et Vengeances*, ed. P. Dumouchel (Québec: Presses de l'Université Laval, 2000), 31–64.

21. M. Xanthakou, "Violence en trois temps: vendetta, guerre civile et désordre nouveau dans une région grecque," in *De la violence II*, ed. F. Héritier (Paris: Odile Jacob, 1999), 171–191.

22. R. Verdier *La vengeance*, 4 vols. (Paris: Cujas, 1980–1986).

23. For a more complete analysis of this phenomenon, see P. Dumouchel "L'ambivalence de la rareté," in Dumouchel and Dupuy, *L'enfer des choses*, 153–165, 179–195 (also reprinted in this volume).

24. M. Daly and M. Wilson, *Homicide* (New York: A. de Gruyter, 1988), 275–291; see also P. Bonnemère "Suicide et homicide: deux modalités vindicatoires en Nouvelle-Guinée," *Stanford French Review* 16.1 (1992): 19–43. This confirms the statistics reported by R. Collette of 0.002 percent for Canada in "Réintégrer pour mieux protéger," in Dumouchel, *Violences, Victimes et Vengeances*, 165–182.

25. W. Palaver, "De la violence: une approche mimétique," in Dumouchel, *Violences, Victimes et Vengeances*, 89–110.

Mimetism and Genocides

"Mimetism and Genocides" originally published as "Mimétisme et génocides" in *Cahier de L'Herne René Girard*, ed. M. Anspach (Paris: L'Herne, 2008), 247–254; translated by Mary Baker.

1. J. Sémelin, *Purifier et détruire: usages politiques des massacres et genocides* (Paris: Seuil, 2005), 117 [translator's note: our translation].

2. C. Tilly, *The Politics of Collective Violence* (Cambridge: Cambridge University Press, 2003), 159

3. M. I. Midlarsky, *The Killing Trap: Genocide in the Twentieth Century* (Cambridge: Cambridge University Press, 2005).

4. Sémelin, *Purifier et détruir*, 287 [translator's note: our translation].

5. Sémelin, *Purifier et détruire*, 288 [translator's note: our translation]. The significance of groups is also recognized in L. May, *Crimes against Humanity: A Normative Account* (New York: Cambridge University Press, 2005), who even makes it a feature that defines crimes against humanity; see 80–90.

6. R. Girard, *I See Satan Fall Like Lightning*, trans. J. G. Williams (Maryknoll, N.Y.: Orbis Books, 2001), 49–61.

7. In the course of his analysis of fused groups based on the example of collective violence in *Critique of Dialectical Reason*, trans. A. Sheridan-Smith (London: NLB, 1976), Jean-Paul Sartre shows

clearly the identity of the group and its leader, and makes this equivalence the keystone of his theory of political freedom.

8. J.-P. Dupuy, *La Panique* (Paris: Les empêcheurs de penser en rond, 2003).

9. Midlarsky, *Killing Trap*, 43.

10. Midlardsky, *Killing Trap*, 147.

11. Midlardsky, *Killing Trap*, 86–90.

12. Midlardsky, *Killing Trap*, 164.

13. Midlardsky, *Killing Trap*, 70.

14. Midlardsky, *Killing Trap*, 92.

15. Midlardsky, *Killing Trap*, 113.

16. Midlardsky, *Killing Trap*, 83.

17. At least, this seems to be the case, though I have not put the question to him directly. He never mentions the mimetic hypothesis, and none of Girard's books appear in his bibliography.

Suicide Attacks: Military and Social Aspects

Translated by Mary Baker.

1. On the effectiveness of suicide attacks, see S. Atran, "The Moral Logic and Growth of Suicide Terrorism," *Washington Quarterly* 29.2 (Spring 2006): 127–147. According to Atran, even though suicide attacks account for a minority of terrorist attacks, they are responsible for the majority of terrorist-related deaths (127).

2. J. Keegan, *The Face of Battle: A Study of Agincourt, Waterloo and the Somme* (London: Jonathan Cape, 1976).

3. A. Hironaka, *Neverending Wars* (Cambridge, Mass.: Harvard University Press, 2005).

4. P. Dumouchel, "Le terrorisme à l'âge impérial," *Esprit* (August–September 2002).

5. L. Napoleoni, *Terror Incorporated* (New York: Seven Stories Press, 2005).

6. M. Alvanou, "Palestinian Women Suicide Bombers: The Interplaying Effects of Islam, Nationalism and Honour Culture," Strategic Research and Policy Center, National Defense College, IDF, Working Paper Series, Paper No. 3, May 2007, 111.

7. Alvanou, "Palestinian Women Suicide Bombers" 47.

8. Euripides, *Iphigenia at Aulis*, in *Euripides Bacchae and Other Plays*, trans. J. Morwood (Oxford: Oxford University Press, 2000), 131 (ll. 1587–1590).

9. Euripedes, *Iphigenia at Aulis*, 132 (ll. 1614–1618).

10. Euripides, *Iphigenia at Aulis*, 132 (ll. 1621–1622).

11. Euripides, *Iphigenia at Aulis*, 126 (ll. 1395–1400).

12. Quoted in Alvanou, "Palestinian Women Suicide Bombers," 80. Mia Bloom suggests that the same applies to Tamil Tiger women who are authors of suicide attacks. See M. Bloom, *Dying to Kill: The Allure of Suicide Terror* (New York: Columbia University Press, 2005).

13. O. Roy, *L'Islam mondialisé* (Paris: Seuil, 2004); Atran, "The Moral Logic and Growth of Suicide Terrorism," 127–147.

Inside Out: Political Violence in the Age of Globalization

1. Actually, migrants tend to settle in and around large cities.

2. B. Badie, *La fin des territoire* (Paris: Fayard, 1995).

3. They do not even need to meet in physical space; communication through the Internet is often enough.

4. In Australia, the program to restitute land ownership to aborigines has faced precisely this difficulty. How can you translate in modern terms of land ownership such a different form of relation to the spatial environment? See E. A. Povinelli, *The Cunning of Recognition* (Durham, N.C.: Duke University Press, 2002).

5. Among the rare and unstable counterexamples to this rule are Pakistan before the separation of Bangladesh and Germany between the First and Second World Wars, during which period Prussia was divided by the Dantzig corridor.

6. H. Rae, *State Identities and the Homogenisation of Peoples* (Cambridge: Cambridge University Press, 2002).

7. C. Schmitt, *La notion de politique* (Paris: Calmann-Lévy, 1972).

8. F. Gros, *États de violence: Essai sur la fin de la guerre* (Paris: Gallimard, 2006).

9. A. Hironaka, *Neverending Wars* (Cambridge, Mass.: Harvard University Press, 2005): "On average, civil wars with interstate intervention, broadly defined, are 300 percent longer than wars without intervention" (51).

10. I. Traynor, "Bush Orders Clampdown on Flights to US," http://www.guardian.co.uk/world/2008/feb/11/usa.theairlineindustry.

11. Jean-Charles de Menezes was shot and killed by officers of the London Metropolitan Police who mistook him for a terrorist. See http://en.wikipedia.org/wiki/Jean_Charles_de_Menezes#Biography.

12. According to the Stockholm International Peace Research Institute (Sirpi), world military spending has gone up by 45 percent in the last ten years. See http://www.lemonde.fr/economie/article/2008/06/09/les-depenses-militaires-mondiales-ont-bondi-de-45-en-dix-ans_1055614_3234.html.

Conclusion: Ethics, Economics, and the State

1. P. Dumouchel, *Le sacrifice inutile: Essai sur la violence politique* (Paris: Flammarion, 2011), translation forthcoming from Michigan State University Press.

2. For an analysis of the recent financial crisis in those terms, see J.-P. Dupuy, *L'avenir de l'économie* (Paris: Flammarion, 2012), translation forthcoming from Michigan State University Press.

3. J. L. Mackie, *Ethics: Inventing Right and Wrong* (London: Penguin Books, 1977); B. Williams, *Ethics and the Limits of Philosophy* (Cambridge, Mass.: Harvard University Press, 1985).

4. S. Darwall, *The British Moralists and the Internal "Ought" 1640–1740* (Cambridge: Cambridge

University Press, 1995); J. Rawls, *Lectures on the History of Moral Philosophy*, ed. B. Herman (Cambridge, Mass.: Harvard University Press, 2000); J. B. Schneewind, *The Invention of Autonomy: A History of Modern Moral Philosophy* (Cambridge: Cambridge University Press, 1998); Williams, *Ethics and the Limits of Philosophy*.

5. It is interesting and revealing that contemporary attempts at naturalizing ethics do exactly the same thing: most of them essentially try to find a biological or an evolutionary justification for current moral tenets rather than develop a natural science that aims to discover new ethical "truths." See, for example, L. Arnhart, *Darwinian Natural Right: The Biological Ethics of Human Nature* (New York: State University of New York Press, 1998); W. B. Casebeer, *Natural Ethical Facts: Evolution, Connectionism and Moral Cognition* (Cambridge, Mass.: MIT Press, 2003); R. Joyce, *The Evolution of Morality* (Cambridge, Mass.: MIT Press, 2006); and for a criticism of this approach, see P. Dumouchel "Naturalizing Ethics, a Girardian Perspective," *Contagion* 20 (2013).

6. Schneewind, *Invention of Autonomy*, 4.

7. Darwall, *British Moralists*.

8. P. Singer, L. Cannold, and H. Kushe, "William Godwin and the Defense of Impartialist Ethics," *Utilitas* 7 (1995): 67–86.

9. This and the following sections closely follow part 2 of P. Dumouchel, "Ethics and Economics— Of Value and Values," *Zfwu Journal for Business, Economics and Ethics* 9.1 (2008): 28–40.

10. D. Akin and J. Robbins, eds., *Money and Modernity: States and Local Currencies in Melanesia* (Pittsburgh: University of Pittsburgh Press, 1999).

11. M. Anspach, *A charge de revanche: figures élémentaires de la réciprocité* (Paris: Seuil, 2002).

12. A. Smith, *The Wealth of Nations* (1776; repr., London: Everyman's Library, 1975), 13.

13. See P. Dumouchel, "Rational Deception," in *Deception in Markets: An Economic Analysis*, ed. C. Gerschlager (New York: Palgrave Macmillan, 2005), 51–73.

14. Smith, *Wealth of Nations*, 13.

15. D. K. Finn, *The Moral Ecology of Markets* (Cambridge: Cambridge University Press, 2006).

16. This is to say exchanges that do not belong to the category of ceremonial exchanges and which, to the extent that they do not create obligations to reciprocate in the future, resemble modern economic exchanges. See M. Sahlins, "On the Sociology of Primitive Exchange," in *Stone Age Economics* (Chicago: Aldine, 1972), 185–230.

17. See J. Rawls, *A Theory of Justice* (Cambridge, Mass.: Belknap Press of Harvard University Press, 1971); and D. Boucher and P. Kelly, eds., *The Social Contract from Hobbes to Rawls* (London: Routledge, 1994), 276.

18. On this issue, see P. Dumouchel "Partial Commitments and Universal Obligations," in *Social Bonds as Freedom*, ed. P. Dumouchel and R. Gotoh (forthcoming).

19. A. Orléan, *L'empire de la valeur, refonder l'économie* (Paris: Seuil, 2011).

20. Dumouchel, *Le sacrifice inutile*.

Bibliography

Akin, D., and J. Robbins, eds. *Money and Modernity, States and Local Currencies in Melanesia*. Pittsburgh: University of Pittsburgh Press, 1999.

Alvanou, M. "Palestinian Women Suicide Bombers: The Interplaying Effects of Islam, Nationalism and Honour Culture." Strategic Research and Policy Center, National Defense College, IDF, Working Paper Series, Paper No. 3, May 2007.

Anspach, M. *A charge de revanche: figures élémentaires de la réciprocité*. Paris: Seuil, 2002.

———. *Cahier de L'Herne René Girard*. Paris: L'Herne, 2008.

———. "Les fondements rituels de la transaction monétaire, ou comment remercier un bourreau." In *La monnaie souveraine*, ed. M. Aglietta and A. Orléan. Paris: Odile Jacob, 1998.

———, ed. "Vengeance." *Stanford French Review* 16.1 (1992): 55–76.

Antonelli, E. *La Creativita degli eventi*. Turin: L'Harmattan Italia, 2011.

Arnhart, L. *Darwinian Natural Right: The Biological Ethics of Human Nature*. New York: State University of New York Press, 1998.

Atran, S. "The Moral Logic and Growth of Suicide Terrorism." *Washington Quarterly* 29.2 (Spring 2006): 127–147.

Austruy, J. *Marginalia*. Proceedings of the Congress of French-Speaking Economists. Paris: Sirey, 1969.

Badie, B. *La fin des territoire*. Paris: Fayard, 1995.

Baechler, J. "I Primi Esperimenti di Mercato e Democrazia." *Mondo Operaio* 39.1 (1989): 82–90.

———. *Le capitalisme*. Paris: Gallimard, 1995.

———. *Les origines du capitalisme*. Paris: Gallimard, 1971.

———. "Mercato e Democrazia." *Mondo Operaio* 38.12 (1985): 64–73.

———. "Mercato e Democrazia: Il Percorso della Modernita." *Mondo Operaio* 39.2 (1989): 86–94.

Barkow, J., L. Cosmides, and J. Tooby. *The Adapted Mind: Evolutionary Psychology and the Generation of Culture*. Oxford: Oxford University Press, 1992.

Barnett, H. G. *Innovations: The Basis of Cultural Change*. New York: McGraw-Hill, 1953.

Benedict, R. *The Chrysanthemum and the Sword*. Tokyo: Charles Tuttle, 1954.

Bentham, J. *Principles of the Civil Code*. In *The Works of Jeremy Bentham*. Published under the Superintendence of his Executor, John Bowring. Edinburgh: William Tait, 1838–1843.

Berlin, B., and P. Kay. *Basic Color Terms: Their Universality and Evolution*. 1969. Repr., Stanford, Calif.: CSLI Publications, 1999.

Black-Michaud, J. *Feuding Societies*. Oxford: Basil Blackwell, 1975.

Bloom, M. *Dying to Kill: The Allure of Suicide Terror*. New York: Columbia University Press, 2005.

Bonnemère, P. "Suicide et homicide: deux modalités vindicatoires en Nouvelle-Guinée." *Stanford French Review* 16.1 (1992): 19–43.

Boucher, D., and P. Kelly, eds. *The Social Contract from Hobbes to Rawls*. London: Routledge, 1994.

Bowle, J. *Hobbes and His Critics*. London: F. Cas, 1969.

Bruaire, C. *La Raison politique*. Paris: Fayard, 1974.

Cartwright, N. *How the Laws of Physics Lie*. Oxford: Clarendon Press, 1983.

Casebeer, W. B. *Natural Ethical Facts: Evolution, Connectionism and Moral Cognition*. Cambridge, Mass.: MIT Press, 2003.

Courtois, S., et al. *Le livre noir du communisme*. Paris: Robert Laffont, 1997.

Daly, M., and M. Wilson. *Homicide*. New York: A. de Gruyter, 1988.

Darwall, S. *The British Moralists and the Internal "Ought" 1640–1740*. Cambridge: Cambridge University Press, 1995.

Deguy, M., and J.-P. Dupuy, eds. *René Girard et le problème du mal*. Paris: Grasset, 1982.

Derathé, R. *Jean-Jacques Rousseau et la science politique de son temps*. Paris: PUF, 1950.

"Discussion avec René Girard." *Esprit* (November 1973): 528–564.

Donald, M. *Origins of the Modern Mind: Three Stages in the Evolution of Culture and Cognition*. Cambridge, Mass: Harvard University Press, 1991.

Dumont, L. *From Mandeville to Marx: The Genesis and Triumph of Economic Ideology*. Chicago: University of Chicago Press, 1977.

———. *Homo aequalis: genèse et épanouissement de l'idéologie économique*. Paris: Gallimard, 1977.

Dumouchel, P. "Communautés, droits et justice sociale." In *Mondialisation, citoyenneté et multiculturalisme*, ed. M. Elbaz and D. Helly. Québec: Presses de l'Université Laval, 2000.

———. "A Covenant among Beasts: Human and Chimpanzee Violence in Evolutionary Perspective." In *Can We Survive Our Origins?*, ed. Pierpaolo Antonello and Paul Gifford. East Lansing: Michigan State University Press, forthcoming.

——. "Ethics and Economics—Of Value and Values." *Zfwu Journal for Business, Economics and Ethics* 9.1 (2008): 28–40.

——. "Good Tricks and Forced Moves." In *Dennett's Philosophy: A Comprehensive Assessment*, ed. D. Ross, A. Brook, and D. Thompson. Cambridge, Mass.: MIT Press, 2000.

——. "Ijime." *Contagion: Journal of Violence, Mimesis, and Culture* 6 (1999): 77–84.

——. *Le sacrifice inutile: Essai sur la violence politique*. Paris: Flammarion, 2011.

——. "Le terrorisme à l'age impérial." *Esprit* (August–September 2002).

——. "Mimétisme et autonomie." In *L'auto-organisation de la physique au politique*, ed. P. Dumouchel and J.-P. Dupuy. Paris: Seuil, 1983.

——. "Naturalizing Ethics, a Girardian Perspective," *Contagion* 20 (2013).

——. "Partial Commitments and Universal Obligations." In *Social Bonds as Freedom*, ed. P. Dumouchel and R. Gotoh. Forthcoming.

——. "Rational Deception." In *Deception in Markets: An Economic Analysis*, ed. C. Gerschlager. New York: Palgrave Macmillan, 2005.

——. "Systèmes sociaux et cognition." In *Introduction aux sciences cognitives*, ed. D. Andler. Paris: Gallimard, 1992.

——. "Violence et Non-Violence." *Esprit* 60 (1981): 153–165.

Dumouchel, P., and J.-P. Dupuy. *L'enfer des choses: René Girard et la logique de l'économie*. Paris: Seuil, 1979.

Dumouchel, P., and J.-P. Dupuy, eds. *L'auto-organisation de la physique au politique*. Paris: Seuil, 1983.

Dupuy, J.-P. *La Panique*. Paris: Les empêcheurs de penser en rond, 2003.

——. *L'avenir de l'économie*. Paris: Flammarion, 2012.

——. "Le signe et l'envie." In P. Dumouchel and J.-P. Dupuy, *L'enfer des choses: René Girard et la logique de l'économie*. Paris: Seuil, 1979.

——. "Totalization and Misrecognition." Trans. Mark R. Anspach. In *Violence and Truth*, ed. P. Dumouchel. Cambridge: Athlone Press, 1988.

Durkheim, E. *Les règles de la méthode sociologique*. 1895. Repr., Paris: PUF, 1981.

Euripides. *Iphigenia at Aulis*. In *Euripides Bacchae and Other Plays*. Trans. James Morwood. Oxford: Oxford University Press, 2000.

Evans-Pritchard, E. E. *Witchcraft, Oracles, and Magic Among the Azande*. 1937. Repr., Oxford: Clarendon Press, 1976.

Feenberg, A. "Le désordre érotique et économique." In *Violence et vérité, autour de René Girard*, ed. P. Dumouchel. Paris: Grasset, 1985.

Ferguson, A. *An Essay on the History of Civil Society*. Ed. F. Oz-Salzberger. Cambridge: Cambridge University Press, 1995.

Finn, D. K. *The Moral Ecology of Markets*. Cambridge: Cambridge University Press, 2006.

Firth, R. *Social Change in Tikopia*. New York: Macmillan, 1959.

Flouzat, D. *Économie contemporaine*. Paris: PUF, 1972.

Frank, R. *Passions within Reason*. New York: Norton, 1988.

Frank, S. A. *Foundations of Social Evolution*. Princeton, N.J.: Princeton University Press, 1998.

Geras, N. *The Contract of Mutual Indifference: Political Philosophy after the Holocaust*. London: Verso, 1998.

Girard, R. *Critique dans un souterrain*. Geneva: L'Âge d'homme, 1976.

———. *Des choses cachées depuis la fondation du monde*. Paris: Grasset, 1978.

———. *I See Satan Fall Like Lightning*. Trans. James G. Williams. Maryknoll, N.Y.: Orbis Books, 2001.

———. *Job: The Victim of His People*. Trans. Y. Freccero. Palo Alto, Calif.: Stanford University Press, 1987.

———. *Mensonge romantique et vérité romanesque*. Paris: Grasset, 1961.

———. *Mimesis and Theory Essays on Literature and Criticism*. Ed. Robert Doran. Palo Alto, Calif.: Stanford University Press, 2008.

———. "Preface." In Mark Anspach, *Oedipe mimétique*. Paris: l'Herne, 2010.

———. *Resurrection from the Underground*. Trans. James Williams. East Lansing: Michigan State University Press, 2012.

———. "Scandal and the Dance: Salome in the Gospel of Mark." *New Literary History* 15.2 (Winter 1984): 1–24.

———. "The Underground Critic." Trans. Paisley N. Livingstone and Tobin Siebers. In *To Double Business Bound*. Baltimore: Johns Hopkins University Press, 1978.

———. *Things Hidden since the Foundation of the World*. Trans. S. Bann and M. Metteer. Stanford, Calif.: Stanford University Press, 1987.

———. *Violence and the Sacred*. Trans. Patrick Gregory. Baltimore: Johns Hopkins University Press, 1977.

Goldberg, S. C. *Relying on Others: An Essay in Epistemology*. Oxford: Oxford University Press, 2010.

Goldmann, L. *Pour une sociologie du roman*. Paris: Gallimard, 1973.

Gros, F. *États de violence Essai sur la fin de la guerre*. Paris: Gallimard, 2006.

Hanson, N. R. *Patterns of Discovery*. Cambridge: Cambridge University Press, 1958.

Hardin, R. *One for All: The Logic of Group Conflict*. Princeton, N.J.: Princeton University Press, 1995.

Hayek, F. A. *The Counter-Revolution of Science: Studies on the Abuse of Reason*. Glencoe, Ill.: Free Press, 1952.

———. *Law, Legislation and Liberty*. 3 vols. Chicago: University of Chicago Press, 1976.

Hempel, C. *Philosophy of Natural Science*. New York: Prentice Hall, 1966.

Hénaff, M. "La dette de sang et l'exigence de justice." In *Violences, Victimes et Vengeances*, ed. P. Dumouchel. Québec: Presses de l'Université Laval, 2000.

Hironaka, A. *Neverending Wars*. Cambridge, Mass.: Harvard University Press, 2005.

Hobbes, T. *Leviathan*. Ed. J. C. A. Gaskin. Oxford: Oxford University Press, 1996.

Hocart, M. *Social Origins*. London: Watts, 1954.

Holmberg, A. R. *Nomads of the Long Bow: The Siriono of Eastern Bolivia*. Smithsonian Institution, Institute of Social Anthropology Publication No. 10. Washington, D.C.: Smithsonian Institution, 1950.

Honderich, T. *Terrorism for Humanity: Inquiries into Political Philosophy*. London: Pluto Press, 2003.

Hume, D. *An Inquiry Concerning the Principles of Morals*. Indianapolis: Bobbs-Merrill, 1957.

Joyce, R. *The Evolution of Morality*. Cambridge, Mass.: MIT Press, 2006.

Keegan, J. *The Face of Battle: A Study of Agincourt, Waterloo and the Somme*. London: Jonathan Cape, 1976.

Keynes, J. M. *Essays in Persuasion: Economic Possibilities for Our Grand-Children*. 1930. Repr., New York: Macmillan, 1972.

Kuhn, T. S. *The Structure of Scientific Revolutions*. Chicago: University of Chicago Press, 1962.

Kusch, M. *Knowledge by Agreement: The Programme of Communitarian Epistemology*. Oxford: Clarendon Press, 2002.

Lantz, P. "Monnaie archaïque, monnaie moderne." In *Violence et vérité, autour de René Girard*, ed. P. Dumouchel. Paris: Grasset, 1985.

Lepage, H. *Demain le capitalisme*. Paris: Le Livre de poche, 1978.

Lévi-Strauss, C. *Totemism*. Trans. Rodney Needham. Boston: Beacon Press, 1963.

Livingston, P. *Models of Desire: René Girard and the Psychology of Mimesis*. Baltimore: Johns Hopkins University Press, 1992.

Lukács, G. *History and Class Consciousness*. Trans. Rodney Livingstone. Cambridge, Mass.: MIT Press, 1971.

Mackie, J. L. *Ethics: Inventing Right and Wrong*. London: Penguin Books, 1977.

Mandeville, B. *The Fable of the Bees*. Ed. F. B. Kaye. 1752. Repr., Oxford: Oxford University Press, 1966.

Mantoux, P. *Le Révolution industrielle au XVIIIe siècle*. Paris: Génin, 1973.

Martino, E. De. *La terra del rimorso Il Sud tra religione e magia*. Milano: il Saggiatore, 1961.

Marx, K., and F. Engels. *The German Ideology*. Ed. C. J. Arthur. New York: International Publishers, 1970.

May, L. *Crimes against Humanity: A Normative Account*. New York: Cambridge University Press, 2005.

Maynard-Smith, J., et al., "Developmental Constraints and Evolution." *Quarterly Review of Biology* 60.3 (1985): 265–287.

Midlarsky, M. I. *The Killing Trap: Genocide in the Twentieth Century*. Cambridge: Cambridge University Press, 2005.

Napoleoni, L. *Terror Incorporated*. New York: Seven Stories Press, 2005.

Needham, R. *Exemplars*. Berkeley: University of California Press, 1985.

Ogien, R. *Portrait moral et logique de la haine*. Paris: L'Éclat, 1993.

Orléan, A. "Comportements mimétiques et diversité des opinions sur les marchés financiers." In *Théories économiques et crises sur les marché financier*, eds. P. Artus and H. Bourguinat. Paris: Economia, 1989.

———. *L'Empire de la valeur, refonder l'économie*. Paris: Seuil, 2011.

———. "Mimetic Contagion and Speculative Bubbles." *Theory and Decision* 27 (1989):1–2.

———. Mimétisme et anticipations rationnelles: Une perspective keynésienne." *Recherche économique de Louvain* 52 (1986):1.

———. "Monnaie et spéculation mimétique." In *Violence et vérité, autour de René Girard*, ed. P. Dumouchel. Paris: Grasset, 1985.

Palaver, W. "De la violence: une approche mimétique." In *Violences, Victimes et Vengeances*, ed. P. Dumouchel. Québec: Presses de l'Université Laval, 2000.

Pécaut, D. "Réflexions sur la violence en Colombie." In *De la violence*, ed. F. Héritier. Paris: Odile Jacob, 1999.

Péguy, C. *De Jean Coste*. In *Oeuvres completes*. Vol. 2. Geneva: Slatkine Reprint, 1974.

Polanyi, K. *Dahomey and the Slave Trade: An Analysis of an Archaic Economy*. Seattle: University of Washington Press, 1966.

———. *The Great Transformation*. Boston: Beacon Press, 1944.

Polanyi, K., C. Arensberg, and H. Pearson, eds. *Trade and Markets in the Early Empires*. New York: Free Press, 1957.

Popper, K. R. *Objective Knowledge: An Evolutionary Approach*. Oxford: Clarendon Press, 1972.

———. *The Open Society and Its Enemies*. London: Routledge, 1995.

Povinelli, E. A. *The Cunning of Recognition*. Durham, N.C.: Duke University Press, 2002.

Prigogine, I., and I. Stengers. *Order Out of Chaos: Man's New Dialogue with Nature*. London: Flamingo, 1985.

Quine, V. O. *Ontological Relativity and Other Essays*. New York: Columbia University Press, 1969.

Radkowski, G.-H. de. *Les jeux du désir*. Paris: PUF, 1980.

Rae, H. *States Identities and the Homogenisation of Peoples*. Cambridge: Cambridge University Press, 2002.

Rawls, J. *Lectures on the History of Moral Philosophy*. Ed. B. Herman. Cambridge, Mass.: Harvard University Press, 2000.

———. *A Theory of Justice*. Cambridge, Mass.: Belknap Press of Harvard University Press, 1971.

Roughgarden, J. *The Genial Gene: Deconstructing Darwinian Selfishness*. Berkeley: University of California Press, 2009.

Roy, O. *L'Islam mondialisé*. Paris: Seuil, 2004.

Sahlins, M. *Stone Age Economics*. Chicago: Aldine, 1972.

———. *Tribesmen*. Englewood Cliffs, N.J.: Prentice Hall, 1968.

Samuelson, P., and W. D. Nordhaus. *Economics*. 12th ed. Repr., New York: McGraw-Hill, 1985.

Sartre, J.-P. *Critique of Dialectical Reason*. Trans. Alan Sheridan-Smith. London: NLB, 1976.

Schmitt, C. *La notion de politique*. Paris: Calmann-Lévy, 1972.

Schneewind, J. B. *The Invention of Autonomy: A History of Modern Moral Philosophy*. Cambridge: Cambridge University Press, 1998.

Schoeck, H. *Envy: A Theory of Social Behaviour*. Indianapolis: Liberty Press, 1969.

Scubla, L. "Jamais deux sans trois? Réflexions sur les structures élémentaires de la réciprocité." In *Logiques de la réciprocité*. Cahier du Crea 6. Paris: Ecole Polytechnique, 1985, 7–118.

————. *Lire Lévi-Strauss*. Paris: Odile Jacob, 1998.

————. "Rois sacré, victime sacrificielle et victime émissaire." *Qu'est-ce que le religieux? Religion et politique, Revue du Mauss* 22 (2003): 197–221.

————. "Théorie du sacrifice et théorie du désir chez René Girard." In *Violence et vérité, autour de René Girard*, ed. P. Dumouchel. Paris: Grasset, 1985.

Secondat, C. de, Baron de Montesquieu. *The Spirit of Laws*. Trans. Thomas L. Nugent. London: Colonial Press, 1900.

Sémelin, J. *Purifier et détruire: usages politiques des massacres et genocides*. Paris: Seuil, 2005.

Sen, A. *Poverty and Famines: An Essay on Entitlement and Deprivation*. New York: Oxford University Press, 1981.

————. "Rational Fools: A Critique of the Behavioral Foundations of Economic Theory." *Philosophy and Public Affairs* 6.4 (1977): 317–344.

————. *Rationality and Freedom*. Cambridge, Mass.: Harvard University Press, 2002.

Simonse, S. *Kings of Disaster: Dualism, Centralism and the Scapegoat King in Southeastern Sudan*. Leiden: E. J. Brill, 1992.

Singer, P., L. Cannold, and H. Kushe. "William Godwin and the Defense of Impartialist Ethics." *Utilitas* 7 (1995): 67–86.

Slater, G. *The English Peasantry and the Enclosures of Common Fields*. London: Archibald Constable, 1907.

Smith, A. *The Wealth of Nations*. 1776. Repr., London: Everyman's Library, 1975.

Sober, E., and D. S. Wilson. *Unto Others: The Evolution and Psychology of Unselfish Behavior*. Cambridge, Mass.: Harvard University Press, 1998.

Sorel, G. *Réflexions sur la violence*. 1907. Repr., Paris: Slatkine, 1981.

Stanford, G. B. *Chimpanzee and Red Colobus: The Ecology of Predator and Prey*. Cambridge, Mass.: Harvard University Press, 1998.

Tilly, C. *The Politics of Collective Violence*. Cambridge: Cambridge University Press, 2003.

Touraine, A. *Pour la sociologie*. Paris: Editions du Seuil, 1974.

Townsend, J. *Dissertation on the Poor Laws*. Section VIII. 1786. http://socserv.mcmaster.ca/~econ/ugcm/3ll3/townsend/poorlaw.html.

Van Parijs, P. "La justice économique comme absence d'envie," *Recherches Économiques de Louvain* 60 (1994): 3–7.

Varela, F. *Principles of Biological Autonomy*. New York: North Holland, 1979.

Verdier, R. *La vengeance*. 4 vols. Paris: Cujas, 1980–1986.

Vernant, J.-P., and M. Detienne, eds. *La Cuisine du sacrifice en pays grec*. Paris: Gallimard, 1979.

Vidal, C. "Le génocide des Rwandais tutsi: cruauté délibéré et logiques de la haine." In *De la violence*, ed. F. Héritier. Paris: Odile Jacob, 1996.

Vidal, D. *Essai sur l'idéologie*. Paris: Anthropos, 1971.

Watkins, J. "Imperfect Rationality." In *Explanation in the Behavioural Sciences*, ed. T. Brager and F. Cioffi. Cambridge: Cambridge University Press, 1970.

Webb, E. "Mimesis, Evolution and the Differentiation of Consciousness." *Paragrana* 4.2 (1995): 151–165.

Williams, B. *Ethics and the Limits of Philosophy*. Cambridge, Mass.: Harvard University Press, 1985.

Xanthakou, M. "Violence en trois temps: vendetta, guerre civile et désordre nouveau dans une région grecque." In *De la violence II*, ed. F. Héritier. Paris: Odile Jacob, 1999.

Index